KEEPING THE FAITH

Keeping the Faith

American Catholicism
Past and Present

Philip Gleason

UNIVERSITY OF NOTRE DAME PRESS
NOTRE DAME, INDIANA

The author and publisher gratefully acknowledge permission to reprint, in revised form, articles which originally appeared in the following journals:

The Catholic Historical Review for chapter 1, originally entitled "Mass and Maypole Revisited: American Catholics and the Middle Ages" in the July 1971 issue, and for chapter 7, entitled "In Search of Unity: American Catholic Thought, 1920–1960" in the April 1979 issue.

Social Thought for chapter 2, originally entitled "Ethnicity, Immigration, and American Catholic History" in the Summer 1978 issue.

Communio for chapter 5, originally entitled "The Bicentennial and Other Milestones: Anniversary Assessments of American Catholicism" in the Summer 1976 issue.

U.S. Catholic Historian for chapter 6, originally entitled "Baltimore III and Education" in nos. 3–4, 1985.

Theology Today for chapter 9, originally entitled "A Browser's Guide to American Catholicism, 1950–1980" in the October 1981 issue.

Library of Congress Cataloging-in-Publication Data

Gleason, Philip.
   Keeping the faith.

   Bibliography: p.
   Includes index.
   1. Catholic Church—United States—History.
2. United States—Church history. I. Title.
BX1406.2.G58 1987   282'.73   86-40579
ISBN 0-268-01227-X

The study of history is said to enlarge and enlighten the mind. Why? Because, as I conceive, it gives it a power of judging of passing events, and of all events, and a conscious superiority over them, which before it did not possess.

John Henry Newman

CONTENTS

INTRODUCTION:
PAST AND PRESENT
IN AN ERA OF CHANGE

THE AUTHORS OF THE MOST RECENT general histories of American Catholicism use strikingly similar language to characterize the period since 1960. James Hennesey calls it "A Revolutionary Moment"; Jay P. Dolan speaks of "The Catholic Reformation, 1960–84," and describes the emergence of "A New Catholicism."[1] I agree with my esteemed colleagues in seeing the most recent epoch as one in which the Catholic Church in the United States was shaken by profound changes, and I believe, as they do, that these changes pose a significant challenge to historical understanding.

The essays brought together in this volume were written in the midst of Hennesey's "revolutionary moment," Dolan's "Catholic reformation." The earliest was originally published in 1969; the most recent—hitherto unpublished—were written in the early and middle 1980s. Unlike the relevant chapters in Hennesey's and Dolan's histories, none undertakes to provide a comprehensive survey of developments in the era of change. Nor do all of them taken together add up to a systematic interpretation of the epoch of upheaval. Yet, taken individually as well as collectively, these essays do constitute a response to the historical challenge presented by the crisis of change.

The kind of response they represent varies from one essay to another. In certain cases—for instance, the essay on the "crisis of Americanization" —I focus directly upon the contemporary scene and try to draw upon knowledge of the past to shed light on movements currently under way. In others, a commemorative occasion such as the bicentennial of the nation provides the stimulus for a historical juxtaposition of past and present. In still a third kind of investigation—exemplified by the discussion

1

of American Catholic medievalism—contemporary shifts in point of view prompt a new look at some aspect of the past. Hence even when they deal with topics remote in time, the essays collected here bear the impress of the times in which they were written and reflect a conscious concern with the problem of past and present. I will say more about them and the order of their presentation at the end of this Introduction, but first let us consider the more general theme of the relation of past and present, which constitutes the unifying principle that runs through the whole collection.

In saying that these essays reflect a conscious concern with the problem of past and present, I am not laying claim to extraordinary historical sensitivity. On the contrary, I do not see how anyone who was both a Catholic and a historian interested in the Catholic Church in the United States could have avoided being drawn to the problem of past and present by the shifts taking place as these essays were written. For, paradoxical as it may seem, changes in the present made the past a more timely and intriguing subject than it is when tradition reigns supreme.

The reason is that in periods of stability people don't give much thought to their history, and when they do, they are apt to assume that, except for being "earlier" and simpler, the past was pretty much the same as the present. They may know in a general way—as, in the case at hand, American Catholics did know—that their ancestors endured much suffering and struggled against heavy odds. This kind of traditional folk history can reinforce pride in one's heritage or sustain resentment against remembered foes, but it doesn't raise many intellectual problems or do much to stimulate historical curiosity. For, so long as we think of ourselves as operating within the same basic framework of beliefs and values as our ancestors did, there is little about their thought or behavior that seems puzzling on the face of it, that needs to be *explained*. The past, in other words, is unproblematic to the degree that traditional attitudes, beliefs, and institutions persist without change. While this condition prevails, past and present generations remain linked by a continuity that is experienced without being reflected upon in a self-conscious way.

But what happens to this linkage in an era of drastic change? Then even the unreflective sense, however obscurely, that the continuity between past and present has received a shock, has become a problem in a way that it was not before. Laypersons would not use these terms, to be sure, but the condition to which they refer can hardly be missed. Change by definition involves a departure from accustomed ways; by its very nature it calls the heritage of the past into question. Proponents of change urge us to revise our views, reform our attitudes, restructure our institutions. And whether we agree that these things should be done or not, we cannot avoid reviewing the past in a new light as we confront these challenges.

To the degree that change actually takes place, with or without our approval, we find as a result that we are set in a new relationship to the past because we can no longer take for granted what had earlier seemed "natural," simply the way things are. The past, in these circumstances, is no longer what it used to be.

By making the past problematic, change makes history more timely and interesting—and also more controversial. For change always arouses conflicting reactions and, since it implies a new relationship to the past, attitudes toward change simultaneously imply attitudes toward history. However much they may be stereotypes, the stock figures of the conservative and the liberal illustrate the point. No individual embodies the type perfectly, but we conventionally think of the conservative as disposed by nature to hold fast to the old ways. He—or, of course, she—is usually willing to grant that change is inevitable and that it may on occasion even be desirable. But these are grudging concessions. Being strongly committed to tradition, the conservative feels a natural piety toward the past and entertains a positive attitude toward history—or at least toward the traditionally accepted version of history. Upon reform, however, the conservative casts a skeptical eye; for reformers he feels a suspicion that turns easily into outright hostility. The Catholic traditionalist movement offers the most extreme example of this mentality, and James Hitchcock has given more moderate and sophisticated expression to the conservative's attachment to tradition, respect for history, and sensitivity to the dangers arising from loss of contact with the past.[2]

Ranged against the conservative is the liberal—better designated in this context as the "progressive." As a class, progressives are favorable to change; those furthest left on the spectrum are prepared to call themselves revolutionaries. Just shy of this extreme are the radical progressives for whom change cannot come too fast, nor reform go too far. For these two varieties of progressive, the past is a negative quantity and history a nightmare from which we must arouse ourselves. This puts it too strongly for many more moderate liberals, but as a type the progressive feels no spontaneous sympathy for history. The characteristic attitude was stated in lapidary fashion by a participant in a mid-sixties symposium on the changing Church: "the past is irrelevant and the future will be essentially different."[3]

While most apt to dismiss the past with impatience or reject it with indignation, progressives are not opposed to history in an unqualified way. On the contrary, they look favorably on "revisionist" history and many of them would endorse the statement that "historical consciousness," or an awareness of "historicity," is a fundamental element of the progressive mentality. Both of these positions, which are ostensibly oriented toward history and the past, often reflect a one-sided present-mindedness.

Revisionist history may appeal to progressives in either its negative or its positive form. By negative revisionism I mean the kind of history that presents in an unfavorable light earlier manifestations of Catholic belief or behavior that progressives deplore in the here and now. In its crudest form, negative revisionism makes a history a grab bag of horrible examples, the exhibition of which serves to drive home a polemical point in current controversy. Dorothy Dohen's *Nationalism and American Catholicism* (1967), a critique of the hyper-patriotic language of American bishops from John Carroll to Francis Spellman, although a serious and responsible work, veers dangerously in the grab-bag direction because of its unrelenting present-mindedness and its abject failure to do justice to the historical context of the passages being analyzed.[4]

The positive form of historical revisionism is sometimes spoken of as an attempt to recover a "usable past." The expression, introduced by Van Wyck Brooks in 1918 and revived in the 1960s, principally by New Left scholars, points toward the goal of this kind of revisionism: the elaboration of an understanding of the past more in keeping with the new outlook of the progressives than the traditional interpretations that held sway before the forces of change built up momentum. This is a perfectly legitimate aspiration, and it has been a factor in — although it does not wholly account for — some of the best work done by American Catholic historians in the past two decades. But the present-mindedness that animates this kind of revisionism also encourages abuses, the nature of which is suggested by the title of an article (not on Catholic history) that appeared in the late seventies: "The Radical Left Expects the Past to Do Its Duty."[5]

Concerning "historical consciousness" as a feature of the progressive mentality, it is difficult to generalize because of the vagueness of the terminology and the fleeting nature of most allusions to the subject. My personal impression is that the terms "historical consciousness" and "historical-mindedness," as they are usually used by progressives, imply a highly relativistic understanding of history. According to this understanding, change is such a sovereign universal that nothing perdures from one epoch to another; every age, including our own, is uniquely itself, unaffected by anything that went before, and is therefore to be understood strictly on its own terms. Applied to the present situation, the surprising upshot of this kind of historical consciousness is the conclusion that history is perfectly irrelevant to contemporary concerns because our problems are those of our own times and knowledge of other times helps us not at all in grasping or in solving them. Here radical presentism usurps the name of history itself!

As these brief remarks indicate, attitudes toward history quickly become complicated, even if we confine our attention to the stock figures of the conservative and the progressive. But these two types do not exhaust the possibilities so far as approaches to the past-and-present issue are concerned. There is another stance that is more characteristically historical in quality. Although it probably occurs more frequently among conservatives than progressives, it is not so much an intermediate position on the ideological spectrum as it is a distinctive response to change. There is no convenient label for this mentality, but we can think of it as a reaction aroused by unanticipated changes that bring about a sudden displacement of the perspective from which the past had hitherto been viewed and its relation to the present understood. Acting upon minds of a certain sensibility, this displacement of perspective can make a person marginal to his or her own past—marginal in the sense of having been pushed involuntarily to a position of semi-detachment from the tradition in which one is a participant.

Here I am adapting the term "marginal" from its use in the study of intergroup relations, where it was introduced by Robert E. Park to refer to the situation of second-generation immigrants, persons of mixed racial background, and others who find themselves uneasily straddling the frontier where two cultures meet and overlap.[6] Belonging to two cultural worlds, yet being distanced from each by attachment to the other, the marginal person may experience a good deal of psychological stress, but he or she is uniquely qualified to observe both cultures with a combination of the insider's sympathy and the outsider's detachment. By analogy, those made marginal to their own history by a sudden displacement of perspective see both past and present in a new and different light.

Consider, for example, the marginalizing effects of recent changes in Catholic ecclesiological thinking. In the past, American Catholics had something quite definite in mind when they spoke of the Church. They were working, as a contemporary ecclesiologist might put it, with a clear-cut model of the Church.[7] But Catholics of yesteryear would have rejected that kind of language because they regarded their understanding of the Church as corresponding to what it actually is in itself, not simply as one among several possible ways of conceiving the Church. And so long as more recent generations shared that same understanding, the Church was not a problem historiographically speaking—that is, the historian did not have to explain how Catholics of an earlier time conceived of the Church or inquire how their views on that subject were linked up with other aspects of their religious and social outlook. To be a Catholic was to hold a certain view of the Church, and that was all there was to it. But when ideas about the Church began to change, and especially after theologians popularized the expression "models of the Church," the older, naive view was no longer available to the historian. The traditional assumption that

the Church simply *was* thus and so had been discredited, and the historically attuned Catholic had thereby been made marginal to an important
dimension of the religious past.

The most drastic result of this kind of marginalization—and what
makes it psychologically distressing—is that it threatens religious faith by
seeming to relativize religious truth. For, to continue with the example of
ecclesiology, if Catholics in the past were mistaken about something as
basic as what the Church is, how do we know that the new views advanced
today are any more reliable, any truer? And if we cannot be sure what is
really true—what the Church really is—then the suspicion suggests itself
that there is no real truth to be arrived at in this matter, that the Church
is simply what Catholics at different times and places say it is. This line
of reasoning may be theologically crude, but it follows with a kind of psychological inevitability when traditional beliefs are discredited and new
teachings vie for acceptance. Most pertinently for our purposes, this relativizing process cannot help but detach the believer to some degree from
the religious tradition in which he or she stands.

Besides having an impact on the historian's interior state as a believer
(assuming a historian susceptible to this kind of reaction), being marginalized as a result of being set between an old and a new interpretation of
the nature of the Church poses practical questions for the writing of Catholic history. How, for example, should the historian apply the new People-
of-God ecclesiology to the American Catholic past? It differs significantly
from the older view by stressing that the Church is a community of persons bound together in faith rather than being a self-existent spiritual entity characterized in its "visible" form by clear-cut institutions arranged
in a firmly defined hierarchical structure. Does this mean that the Catholic
immigrants of the last century are to be portrayed as the People of God
in action, even though they did not think of themselves, or of the Church,
in those terms? In what ways can this approach be used to enrich and deepen
our understanding of the past? What risks do we run if we apply categories
of interpretation unknown to the people whose lives we are studying and
perhaps uncongenial to their accustomed modes of thinking? Is there still
a place for the older "institutional" history, with its emphasis on the development of ecclesiastical structures and the doings of the bishops?

All these questions, and many others, arise as we look back from
the present into the past and seek to understand it in the light of recent
shifts in Catholic thinking. Still other questions arise if we make a
180-degree turn and inquire how these recent shifts themselves grew out
of, and were shaped by, the past. The marginalized sensibility can come
into play here too. For a person who has undergone a psychic disloca-
tion as a result of change is not very likely to regard the new views as un-

problematically correct and true, simply the long-overdue rectification of earlier errors. On the contrary, such a person will surely feel that the new views likewise stand in need of explanation. And one way of explaining them is to show how they emerged from the past, or at least to identify the historically conditioned features of American Catholic life that contributed to their acceptance and popularization. It would not be difficult, for example, to relate the acceptance of People-of-God ecclesiology to the themes of equalitarianism and anti-institutionalism in American society at large, and to a contemporary preoccupation with social history and the lives of ordinary people on the part of scholars.

Although ecclesiology is of fundamental importance, it is by no means the only area where change has had a marginalizing impact. Changes in how the Mass and sacraments are understood, massive resignations from the priesthood and religious life, the erosion of traditional norms of sexual conduct, increasing numbers of divorces among Catholics, challenges to ecclesiastical authority on the part of dissident theologians and feminist-oriented nuns and lay women—these dramatic shifts and many others jarred Catholics loose from accustomed ways of thinking and opened new perspectives on both past and present. Nor was change in the Church the only force impinging on Catholics over the past two decades. Along with other Americans, they were shaken by the violent upheavals set off by the racial crisis of the sixties, the Vietnam War, the campus disruptions, the emergence of the counterculture and women's liberation, the Watergate scandal, and the skyrocketing inflation and other economic dislocations of the seventies and early eighties. The atmosphere of cultural crisis in the nation at large, which reached its climax in the late 1960s, coincided with the high point of postconciliar excitement among Catholics. This coincidence reinforced tendencies toward extremism among Catholics, while at the same time the spectacle of the Roman Church in eruption added to the general sense that the social fabric was about to give way.

Given this background, it is hardly remarkable that the perspective on past and present reflected in these essays was affected by the changes taking place at the time they were written. If I know my own mind, they proceed from something like the marginalized sensibility outlined above. The essays were, of course, composed independently of each other over a considerable span of years. They are naturally not linked together as integrated parts of a comprehensive whole. I have, however, revised them for this collection and provided each one with a headnote. I trust that the reader will be able to discern a thematic continuity deriving from the fact that they all address the American Catholic experience with a special concern for the interaction of past and present.

The sequence in which the essays are presented combines chronological order with thematic linkages. The first deals with a topic remote in time, but it features past and present quite explicitly in tracing how Catholic attitudes toward the Middle Ages developed in the nineteenth century and have been reshaped in the past few years. The second takes up an issue—ethnicity—that is part of the more recent history of American Catholics and assesses recent developments in the light of the immigrant past. The connection between the second and third essays is thematic, since the latter makes use of an interpretive model derived from the study of Catholic immigration in analyzing the postconciliar situation. The fourth essay likewise focuses on the postconciliar scene, but it also suggests a historical parallel between the late 1960s and the Romantic era of the early nineteenth century.

The two essays presented in chapters 5 and 6 were written for anniversary occasions, the national bicentennial in the former case, the centenary of the Third Plenary Council of Baltimore in the latter. The exploration of the "search for unity," which constitutes chapter 7, analyzes the mentality of the preconciliar generation in an effort to explain why persons (like myself) who matured in that era often found the changes of the sixties deeply unsettling to their faith. The next essay sets the challenge of "keeping the faith" in the perspective of American Catholic history since Independence. Part II takes up matters bibliographical and theoretical. Chapter 9 provides an informal review of the major literary sources for American Catholicism in the era of change; chapter 10 deals critically with the loose way in which others have spoken of "historical consciousness" and concludes with a statement of my own views on the nature and value of historical work.

I would like to think that all of these essays combine a historically legitimate form of present-mindedness with due regard for the complex actualities of the past. Whether the results justify that aspiration is for the reader to decide.

PART I

1

AMERICAN CATHOLICS AND THE
MYTHIC MIDDLE AGES

The image of the Middle Ages held by American Catholics has shifted dramatically in my lifetime. When I was young, the medieval epoch was looked upon as a religious and cultural golden age, the high point of Christian civilization. Growing up in that atmosphere, I assumed that such a view had always prevailed and that it would continue to do so in the future. The first thing I can recall that complicated my naive impressions on the subject was reading Walter Ong's brilliant essay, "The Renaissance Myth and the American Catholic Mind."* Here Ong showed that the men who first popularized the belief that an idealized past could be revitalized —a belief Catholics applied to the Middle Ages—were the humanists of the Renaissance who actually regarded the Middle Ages with contempt. Moreover, Ong made clear, a number of the educational and cultural values that American Catholics prized most dearly were in fact derived from Renaissance humanism and not from the Middle Ages.

Not long after my encounter with Ong's essay, I stumbled upon the role played by the romantic movement in awakening enthusiasm for the Middle Ages in nineteenth-century Europe. I say "stumbled upon" because the context of this discovery was research on my doctoral dissertation, which dealt with the social-reform interests of German-American Catholics in the twentieth century. Much to my surprise, I learned that the tradition of Catholic corporative thought, of which my subjects' social-reform theories were a part, took its origin in German romanticism, which portrayed the Middle Ages as the exemplar of an organically unified social order in contrast to the chaotic individualism of modern industrial civilization.

Thanks to these discoveries, I was quite prepared to acquiesce in the

---

*Walter J. Ong, *Frontiers of American Catholicism* (New York, 1957), 52–85.

opinion—commonplace among educated Catholics as the decade of the sixties opened—that the Middle Ages had been grossly overidealized in the past. Indeed, I was beginning to realize that Catholic overidealization of the Middle Ages was in itself a historical phenomenon—a collective mental artifact, so to speak, produced by the religio-cultural needs and impulses of earlier generations. But despite my dawning recognition of the historicity of this particular vision of the historical past, I was not at all prepared for the suddenness (and in some cases the vehemence) with which American Catholics repudiated the golden vision of the Middle Ages after Vatican II. Something that made rejection of the medieval vision even more surprising—and ironic—was the romantic quality of the radicalism that suffused the American Catholic scene just as it was taking place. I called attention to this "new age of romanticism" in an article published in 1967,* and the paradoxical rejection of romantic medievalism in an era of new romanticism was one of the things that prompted me to look into the historical origins and development of Catholic medievalism.

The results of that investigation were first presented to the annual convention of the American Historical Association in 1969 and were published in the Catholic Historical Review *in 1971. The version presented here has been enlarged by the addition of the section headed "The Meaning of American Catholic Medievalism."*

Ours is not the first generation to be impressed by the profound changes of our own times. Almost 900 years ago, a chronicler of the First Crusade exclaimed in the prologue to his history of that great event: "The more studiously anyone directs his attention to this subject, the more fully will the convolutions of his brain expand and the greater will be his stupefaction."[1] The subject to which we turn in this essay is less spectacular than the First Crusade, and I hope it will not produce stupefaction. The story of American Catholic enthusiasm for the Middle Ages does, however, offer possibilities for expanding the convolutions of the brain. It is a story especially pertinent for us because it illustrates so vividly how the image of the past can help to form the mentality of the present, while at the same time being itself shaped by that very mentality.

E. R. Curtius, the great authority on medieval Latin literature, regarded American interest in the Middle Ages as a phenomenon of "deep spiritual meaning," which he likened to "that deep sentimental urge which

---

*Philip Gleason, "Our New Age of Romanticism," *America* 117 (October 7, 1967), 372–75.

we might expect in the man who should set out to find his lost mother."[2] His words are doubly applicable to American Catholics, for they were conscious of standing in a peculiar relation to the Middle Ages. They were much influenced by currents of medievalism affecting Americans generally, but the revival of interest in the Ages of Faith had a "spiritual meaning" for them that it did not have for any other group in American society. Living in a land without a medieval past, they accepted perhaps even more uncritically than their coreligionists in Europe an idealized vision of the Middle Ages. But, here as in so many other areas, American Catholics drew inspiration from Europe. Relatively little Catholic medievalism originated in the United States; we must therefore look back to Europe to trace our subject to its beginnings and to follow many of its turnings.

That a special relation exists between the Catholic Church and the Middle Ages is a truism—a truism accepted admiringly by some, scornfully by others, but accepted by all. In the 1930s, an ultraprogressive educator who wanted his young charges to "get the feel of the Middle Ages" arranged for them to spend a week in a Catholic retreat house.[3] In those days Catholic pride in the medieval connection was near its climax, and it seemed perfectly natural that Jacques Maritain should find in medieval Christendom the inspiration and paradigm for his "true humanism."[4] Another widely read work of the same era—E. I. Watkin's *Catholic Art and Culture*—portrayed the development of Western culture as passing through a metaphoric cycle of the seasons. The Middle Ages were of course the summer; the baroque era, autumn; and the modern period, winter. A respected Catholic historian could argue in 1936 that "we ought to look upon our medieval researches as a high and necessary form of missionary activity. . . ."[5] Scholarly Catholic interest in the Middle Ages resulted in the creation of special institutes of medieval studies at Toronto and Notre Dame. The same enthusiasm prompted graduate students at Notre Dame to write master's theses on such subjects as "The Medieval Spirit in the Drama of Paul Claudel" and "Some Aspects of Medieval Culture in Sigrid Undset's *Kristin Lavransdatter*."[6]

In the heady postconciliar days of the late 1960s, it made even moderately progressive Catholics cringe to be reminded that such things had ever been said or done. For what would have seemed unthinkable a generation before had come to pass: American Catholics had rejected their golden age. No longer did they look back with longing to the time when, in the words of Hilaire Belloc, men built "new white walls around the cities, new white Gothic Churches in the towns, new castles on the hills."[7] Indeed they did not. Quite the reverse. "Medieval" had become a shorthand term for all that ailed the Church. According to the author of a piece entitled "Resistance in the Church," it was the "feudal-medieval model" that had to be overthrown. He repeated the hateful epithet six times in the course of a brief article. The publisher of the *National Catholic Reporter* noted with satisfaction that the Middle Ages had "apparently been discarded once and for all," a change that he characterized as "so dramatic as to be palpable."[8] Eugene McCarthy, one of the Catholic heroes of the day, had matured in the era when the Middle Ages rated high; but when he ventured to say a good word for medieval universities before a late-sixties college audience, he was described by a student journalist as "relish[ing] in decay." So outraged by McCarthy's archaic views was the youthful reporter that he stooped to orthographic slander of the Middle Ages, spelling medieval "mid-evil."[9]

To a contemporary observer, it was as though the Daughters of the American Revolution had begun to treat George Washington as an embarrassment and to make the Founding Fathers a byword for ignorance and misguided zealotry. And just as such action on the DAR's part would signal a profound shift in thought and feeling, so was it in the case of American Catholics and the Middle Ages. The whole Catholic world was shaken by a spiritual earthquake, and the Middle Ages—among other things—were turned upside down. As the term *aggiornamento* itself began to seem faintly outdated, medievalism had become, if not a sin against the Holy Ghost, at least a sin against the *Zeitgeist*.

The Nineteenth-Century Medieval Revival

There was nothing new about the fact that current thinking influenced attitudes toward the medieval past. As Norman F. Cantor has pointed out, "the image of the Middle Ages which obtained at any given period in early modern Europe tells us more about the . . . intellectual commitments of the men of the period than it does about the medieval world itself."[10] Catholic antimedievalists of the 1960s would probably have conceded Cantor's point, but they would have been surprised, no doubt, to learn that Catholics were not the ones who originally sparked the enthusiasm for the Middle Ages in modern times. Rather they absorbed it as part of an earlier *Zeitgeist* which had its origin in non-Catholic sources. Not only was it once fashionable and modern to admire the Middle Ages; even more surprisingly, the Middle Ages were admired because they were associated with modernity itself. For according to the German romantics, the Middle Ages embodied the new cultural characteristics inspired by the Christian religion which made European civilization distinctively modern as compared to the civilization of classical antiquity.[11]

Romanticism was principally responsible for the awakening of enthusiasm for the Middle Ages. There was some medieval interest in the centuries that intervened between the Renaissance and the romantic era; it is true that there was a "Gothic Survival" as well as a "Gothic Revival."[12] But the classical taste predominated, and Greco-Roman antiquity was regarded as a cultural model far superior to anything the Middle Ages could show. With the romantics, however, curiosity about, sympathy for, and in some cases infatuation with, the Middle Ages came with a rush—and made the nineteenth century a medievalizing century. Lord Acton considered this "discovery of a [medieval] palimpsest, this renewal of an interrupted continuity" to be "the great work of the nineteenth century."[13] Heinrich Heine defined German romanticism as "nothing else but the reawakening of the poetry of the Middle Age,"[14] and the evidences of romantic medievalism are to be found everywhere in nineteenth-century European cultural history. In London, the Houses of Parliament were rebuilt in the Gothic style; in Cologne, work on the great cathedral was resumed in 1823 after a lapse of three hundred years; in France, Eugene Viollet-le-Duc restored the walled city of Carcassonne; and in Prussia, Joseph von Eichendorff was deeply engaged in the restoration of Marienburg castle, the medieval headquarters of the Teutonic Knights.[15] The names of Walter Scott, Alfred Tennyson, and Victor Hugo suggest the range of medievalism in literature; and it is worth recalling that the *Chanson de Roland* appeared in its first published version in 1837.[16] Romantic interest in the Middle Ages was one of the primary springs of modern historical studies. The great source collections—the *Monumenta Germaniae Historica* and the Rolls Series—brought together medieval materials, making it possible for the nineteenth century to carry out what Herbert Butterfield called "the greatest achievement of historical understanding—the recovery and exposition of the medieval world."[17]

This great medieval awakening was not the handiwork of Catholics. It originated among Protestants and persons unattached to any religion and, as Acton noted, Catholics were for a time "inactive and indifferent" to it.[18] But the Church could not fail to be positively affected by this reversal of feeling toward the period in which she had been the dominant spiritual and cultural force in Europe. The relative stability and continuity with the past that the Church represented also appealed to an age that saw the collapse of ancient institutions under the tidal waves of revolutionary upheaval and Napoleonic imperialism. Joseph de Maistre's work on the papacy illustrated the contemporary appreciation of the Church's stability. Friendly biographies of Gregory VII and Innocent III by the German historians Johannes Voigt and Friedrich von Hurter projected this favorable image of the papacy back into the Middle Ages. Hurter's admiration for the Church eventually led to his conversion, but political considerations were as deeply involved as religious. His three-volume work on

Innocent III has been described as the most graphic and effective presentation of antirevolutionary romantic medievalism.[19]

Hurter's was only one of a large number of conversions that dramatized the improving cultural status of Catholicism. In Germany, especially, these conversions were linked to the romantic enthusiasm for the Middle Ages. That of the poet Friedrich von Stolberg created a minor sensation in 1800;[20] other notable converts included Friedrich Schlegel, one of the founders of romanticism in Germany; Friedrich Overbeck, the leader of the "Nazarenes," a school of painters whose medievalism anticipated the Pre-Raphaelites; and Adam Müller, a writer on political-economy.

There were also important conversions to Catholicism in England. The Oxford Movement springs immediately to mind. But while the element of medievalism was present among the Oxford men, Newman, as someone has said, always seemed more at home in the fourth century than the thirteenth.[21] And by 1850, the earlier medievalism of the Oxford converts had been largely displaced by their newly acquired Italianate leanings and taste for the baroque. This development — or fall from grace — gave infinite pain to the real medieval enthusiasts among English converts, notably Augustus Welby Pugin and Ambrose Phillipps de Lisle.[22] These two close friends had rejoiced over the Oxford Movement and seen in it the beginnings of the return of the Anglican Church to the one true fold. Their own conversions were intimately connected with their medieval interests, and for both Pugin and Phillipps the true religion meant Catholicism as it had developed in the Middle Ages, complete with Gothic vestments, rood screens, and Gregorian "chaunt." Pugin, who collaborated on the rebuilding of the Houses of Parliament, was the first major theorist and practitioner of the Gothic Revival in architecture; his writings and his designs were well known in the United States, both among Catholics and non-Catholics. (One of his drawings, in fact, seems to have served as Richard Upjohn's model in designing Trinity Church in New York, perhaps the most important structure in the Gothic Revival in the United States.)[23] Phillipps lived a retired life, but maintained an extensive correspondence and worked quietly to further the Catholic movement. He also brought one of the major French contributions to medievalism to English and American readers by translating Count de Montalembert's *Life of St. Elizabeth of Hungary*.

There was a third English convert-medievalist whose impact on American Catholics was even greater than that of Pugin. This was the now forgotten Kenelm Henry Digby, the author of two lengthy panegyrics on the Middle Ages.[24] The first, his four-volume *Broad Stone of Honour*, dealt with chivalry and was little noted by Catholics in the United States. But his *Mores Catholici, or Ages of Faith*, which appeared in eleven volumes between 1831 and 1841, found a receptive audience here. It was often referred to by Catholic writers, portions of it were reprinted in the religious press, and a Catholic publication society brought out an American edition in 1842.[25] Another American edition was published at the turn of the century, and as late as 1942 the *Catholic Digest* undertook the heroic feat of condensing into eight pages Digby's interminable and formless monument to nostalgia.[26]

Before the romantic influences from Europe began to make themselves felt, American Catholics had shown no special interest in, or partiality for, things medieval. Indeed, Bishop John Carroll was advised by an English priest that American Catholics should shut their eyes to everything since the fourth century because all that was "essential" was to be found in "the Apostolic ages," while "the rest is abuse and usurpation." A listing of Catholic works published in the United States before 1830 yields only four items out of more than a thousand that can be associated by title or description with the Middle Ages.[27] In the 1820s Bishop John England of Charleston still regarded feudalism as "essentially despotic";[28] and the Reverend Charles Constantine Pise's *History of the Church*, published in the same decade, was quite restrained on the Middle Ages. "I will not attempt to dispel the gloom which has been thrown . . . over this period," Pise wrote, "nor will I deny that the torch of human science was very dim in some parts, and almost totally obliterated in others . . . during these obscure ages. . . ." Just how "succinct" he was may be inferred from the fact that he disposed of "S. Thomas of Aquin" in fewer than three hundred words, reserving for a footnote the intelligence that Thomas' "Sum" was the work for which he was best known.[29]

By the 1840s the Gothic tide was beginning to run strongly, but Bishop Francis P. Kenrick of Philadelphia still maintained his classical taste. "The Roman or Greek is the style we want," was his instruction concerning a new cathedral; and he added, "For the Gothic we do not care at all."[30] Orestes Brownson felt the same way in 1849. He was disgusted by Pugin's "exclusive and excessive praise" of Gothic; and in reviewing Digby's work, Brownson denied that the Church should be identified with medieval civilization. "The Middle Ages," he declared, are "a load which we have no disposition to carry."[31]

Brownson's objections were founded on apologetical considerations. Digby's portrayal of the Middle Ages was vulnerable on a number of points, and Brownson thought it would be a mistake to accept uncritically his romantic vision of the Ages of Faith—and an even greater mistake to acquiesce in the identification of the Catholic faith with that bygone age. For while Catholics had earlier been required to make excuses for the Middle Ages, now the situation had changed entirely and the task of the Catholic publicist was not "to defend or to apologize for the middle ages, but to moderate the excessive admiration of them."[32] Catholic truth and the interests of the Church took precedence for Brownson over dedication to any historical period considered in itself, or over any commitment to the cultural forms inspired by Christian beliefs in the past.

Motifs in Catholic Medievalism

The primacy of the apologetical consideration with Brownson highlights the importance of this factor in shaping Catholic thinking on the Middle Ages. Indeed, the apologetical theme is probably the most important and enduring among the several motifs that can be distinguished in Catholic medievalism in the past century and a half. Because the Church was so integral a feature of medieval life, it was difficult to say anything at all about the Middle Ages without its having some bearing on the Church in that era, and by extension on the Church in the contemporary era. Few Catholics could be unaware of this dimension of medievalism, and it surely colored the approach they followed in dealing with the Middle Ages, if only in suggesting uses to which their objective knowledge might be put, or in leading them to make applications which might not have occurred to a person who had no interest in the Church. For many others, apologetical considerations were more directly operative. The enemies of Catholicism used the Middle Ages against the Church. "Very well," said her defenders, "we will refute those attacks." Fortunately for the Catholic apologist, it grew easier, as the nineteenth century wore on, not merely to defend the medieval record, but to go over to the offensive and use the Middle Ages as positive evidence *for* Catholicism.

In the 1820s the tone of defiant defensiveness was strong on such matters as the Inquisition, papal power in the Middle Ages, and the supposed intellectual "darkness" of the era.[33] Twenty-five years later, a robustly combative temperament was still good equipment for the Catholic apologist, but a much more confident note is discernible in the work of a man like Bishop Martin J. Spalding. His task, according to his nephew and biographer, John Lancaster Spalding, "was to clear away the *débris* and rubbish" of "false history and ignorant prejudice." The elder Spalding undertook this work energetically, drawing on the researches of men like Henry Hallam, Samuel Maitland, and François Guizot—as well as those of Montalembert and Digby—to correct the "absurd and preposterous views concerning the history of the Church in the Middle Ages" which had earlier passed for fact.[34] It was also noteworthy that Spalding stressed those aspects of medieval Catholicism that were calculated to have a special appeal for Americans. Thus he dwelt upon the contributions of the monasteries, schools, and universities to education and culture. He argued that in defying the ambitions of secular princes, the medieval popes were pioneering in the separation of political from religious power. And he drew attention to the scientific advances and mechanical inventions of the Middle Ages.[35]

In the 1860s, the "darkness" of the Middle Ages became an issue in an ill-tempered debate between Archbishop John B. Purcell of Cincinnati and the Reverend Thomas Vickers, a liberal Protestant. Purcell touched on many of the points made by Spalding while giving Vickers a review of the newer historiography of the Middle Ages. Confident he was on strong ground here, Purcell snorted: "The gentleman proves by what he says of the so-called 'Dark Ages,' [that] he is in the dark concerning them."[36] Catholic apologists continued to stress medieval contributions to learning and the development of political liberty in succeeding decades.[37] But in the last quarter of the nineteenth century, the overwhelming prestige of natural science and the accompanying "warfare of science and theology" tended once again to link the theologically minded Middle Ages with obscurantism and superstition.[38] In these circumstances, the point that the medieval period had been one of scientific ferment and technological innovation assumed new apologetical importance. Considered from this angle, the emergence of James J. Walsh was nothing short of providential. Best known (some would say most notorious) for his widely circulated book *The Thirteenth, Greatest of Centuries* (1907), Walsh was a medical doctor who had been trained under Rudolph Virchow in Germany. He was thoroughly at home in the world of the natural sciences and laid great stress on the educational and scientific accomplishments of the Middle Ages. His apologetical work thus reflected one of the newest trends in medieval scholarship, and he was among the first to popularize the finding that the Middle Ages were more productive scientifically than the Renaissance.[39]

"Doctor Walsh," as he was known to lecture-goers of the day, was the outstanding American Catholic contributor to the tradition of popular medievalism and he did much to bring that tradition to a climax in the twentieth century. But more than apologetics was involved in the full flowering of the movement and it would be unfair to suggest that Walsh was animated by nothing else besides apologetical motives. There were other prominent motifs in American Catholic admiration for the Middle Ages. In practice these conceptually distinguishable themes interpenetrated each other, and the apologetical possibilities were rarely overlooked. But the picture would be quite distorted without a few brief words on four other recurring emphases which can be discerned in Catholic medievalism.

The apologetical motif was a perennial, but the second important theme—which I will call the romantic-aesthetic—followed a temporal sequence. Coming in strongly by the 1830s, it seems to ebb as a distinct and separate motif after midcentury but lingers on as a poetic resonance, a quietly evocative glow suffusing the whole medieval vision. The poet Novalis gave classic expression to this yearning for the dreamy peace and beauty of a bygone Catholic world in his fragment, "Die Christenheit oder Europa."[40] And Matthew Arnold caught its spirit perfectly when he spoke of Oxford as "steeped in sentiment . . . spreading her gardens to the moonlight, and whispering from her towers the last enchantments of the Middle Ages."[41] How could Catholics resist all this? The wonder is that they were not swept away to a man in the rush of enthusiasm for the age of pilgrimage and quest, for dim Gothic interiors, and for storied windows richly dight.[42] Delight in the atmosphere of medieval beauty inspired Pugin's heroic labors to revive the "pointed" style, or, as he preferred to call it, "Christian architecture," and it inspired Digby's unwearying report on his burrowings among the literary remains of the Middle Ages. For a man of aristocratic lineage, like Montalembert, there was a special attractiveness about the age of chivalrous nobility and saintly rulers.

The romantic spirit also inspired the appearance in popular Catholic magazines of many a poem with some such title as "The Ruined Castle" or "The Baptism of Clovis."[43] In the 1840s a serialized novel called *Treuga Dei, or the Truce of God* combined the following elements: a nostalgic picture of the eleventh century, a romantic tale of love and combat, an illustration of the civilizing influence of the Church, a defense of the medieval papacy, and a history of the quarrel between Pope Gregory VII and the Emperor Henry IV.[44] Of course artists of real stature also worked with medieval themes, and the great Dante revival of the nineteenth century likewise associated medievalism with the heights of literary achievement. Romanticism itself was long since spent, but George N. Shuster's *The Catholic Spirit in English Literature,* published in 1922, suggested a close connection between the Catholic spirit and the medieval spirit.[45] For reasons we will examine shortly, the medieval spirit meant something quite different then from what it had meant a century earlier, but for many Catholic readers the romantic afterglow still threw a softening nimbus around the realism of *Kristin Lavransdatter* or the spareness of *Murder in the Cathedral.*

The third important theme in Catholic medievalism is the social critique motif. Although often found in apologetical contexts, it is even more closely entwined with the aesthetic motif, for the social critique theme also originated in the romantic period. The term refers to the use of an idealized vision of the Middle Ages as alternative social model against which the defects of the modern world could be contrasted. As a variant of this theme, some particular characteristic or institution of the medieval scene

—such as the guild—might be singled out as providing the needed corrective for contemporary social ills. The development of this theme is highly ramified and what follows is only a sketch of the general pattern.

There were two relatively independent traditions of medievalist social criticism. American Catholics were most directly affected by the "nineteenth-century tradition" of English social criticism discussed by Raymond Williams in his *Culture and Society*.[46] Edmund Burke stands at the beginning of it, although the medieval alternative is largely implicit in his thought. In Robert Southey's *Colloquies* the medievalist element is more clearly defined, but still not given great emphasis. It was William Cobbett's slashing *History of the Protestant Reformation* that first drew a systematic contrast between the medieval days of roast beef and Catholicism, and the 1820s when men were reduced to eating seaweed in Ireland and robbing pig-troughs in Yorkshire.[47] Extreme though it was, Cobbett's version of the "Merrie England" myth was widely read and "its generalizations became the commonplaces of later medievalist propaganda." It was recommended with particular warmth by Catholics, and Cobbett himself claimed that it was "notorious that my work has softened all those asperities against Catholics that hitherto existed in the breasts of numerous Protestants."[48]

The only important nineteenth-century contribution to the English social-critique tradition made by a Catholic was Pugin's book, *Contrasts: or a Parallel between the Noble Edifices of the Middle Ages, and Corresponding Buildings of the Present Day, Shewing the Present Decay of Taste*. Pugin blazed a new trail in this book by using the art of a period to evaluate the quality of the society that produced it.[49] Particularly effective were his juxtaposed drawings of "a Catholic town in 1440" and "the same town in 1840," which showed not only the decay of taste, but the debasement of human life.[50] Almost as striking were his "Contrasted Residences of the Poor": on the modern side, a Benthamite panopticon; on the medieval, a monastery.

Monasticism enjoyed quite a comeback as a result of the medieval revival, in which the civilizing and socializing role of monks in the Dark Ages was prominently featured. Cobbett devoted the second volume of his *History* to a survey of all the religious houses in the British Isles despoiled by the Reformation; and one of the characters in D'Israeli's *Sybil* complains that since the dissolution of monasteries there has been "no community in England," only "aggregation."[51] But Carlyle's *Past and Present* is most relevant to our interest here, for it was his vivid portrayal of Abbot Samson of Bury St. Edmunds that established the monastery of the Middle Ages as the antithesis of the industrial city and its callous masters. Carlyle's work was well known to American Catholics, and it reinforced a vision of the Middle Ages in which "happy rustics gathered on the village green to wield the quarter staff, to leap, to run, to strike the bounding ball, to wrestle, and to draw the stout yew bow, while the joyous laugh and song went up from the group of dancing maidens, and the . . . sober elders . . . looked on approvingly. . . ."[52]

Pugin's linking of the splendors of Gothic architecture to the healthy medieval social order was carried much further by John Ruskin and William Morris. Both were in love with the Middle Ages; both preached that only a fundamentally just and organically unified social order, such as the medieval, could produce great art. The aesthetic, moral, and social realms were inextricably tied together in their thinking, and the nineteenth century was insupportable on all counts. Morris stated his feeling in the starkest terms: "Apart from the desire to produce beautiful things, the leading passion of my life has been and is hatred of modern civilization."[53] His commitment to a better arrangement of things in life and work and art made a downright socialist of him before his death; Ruskin, too, traveled far along the same path.

Medievalism had by now become thoroughly mixed up with the critique of individualism and industrial capitalism, with efforts to restore the sense of community, with anti-urbanism, with the "arts and crafts" approach, and with various philosophies of the dignity of work and the importance of good workmanship. It is impossible to attempt disentangling all this, but the continuity joining the nineteenth-century tradition with Guild Socialism and with the "Distributism" of Chesterton and Belloc seems clear. For American Catholics, Eric Gill—another English convert and a sort of Catholic William Morris—was an important link between the nineteenth-century tradition and a variegated assemblage of movements that ranged all the way from the Catholic Art Association through the rural life movement to the Catholic Worker people and other groups whose commitment to social reform was shot through with elements of medievalism.[54]

Besides the English tradition of medievalist social criticism, there was another current that began to affect American Catholics in the twentieth century. This was the tradition of Catholic corporative thought, which, though strong in Germany and France, had little impact on American Catholics until it was embodied in the social encyclicals, especially *Quadragesimo Anno* in 1931.[55] German Catholic corporative thinking was rooted in romanticism and called for the restoration of a *Ständeordnung* strongly redolent of the Middle Ages—that is, it called for a hierarchically structured and functionally differentiated, but organically unified society, that was to be based on "social estates" rather than on atomized individuals or economic classes. The explicitly medievalist elements were not uniformly pressed, but were seldom discarded completely in the many nuances of corporatism that developed in the nineteenth and early twentieth centuries. After 1900, an organization of German-American Catholics actively promoted a medievalist variant of corporative reform which they called "Solidarism."[56] It made little headway, but Pope Pius XI's call for the formation of "corporations" based on vocational groups stimulated much interest in what was often called the "guild" social order.

But even papal corporatism was handicapped in America, not merely because of the inherent vagueness of such schemes, but because it was so exotic, so foreign to the experience of Catholics in this country, that they found it difficult to comprehend and impossible to act upon. Its chief significance, I believe, was that it reinforced in American Catholics a theoretical antipathy to modern liberal, capitalist society, and deepened their sensitivity to the absence of *Gemeinschaft* values in the contemporary industrial world.

By the time *Quadragesimo Anno* appeared, however, a fourth motif of medievalism had developed of which it is hardly too much to say that it revolutionized the whole Catholic vision of the Middle Ages. This was Neoscholasticism or NeoThomism. Undoubtedly the most substantial result of the reawakening of Catholic interest in the Middle Ages, the Scholastic Revival was pioneered by several Italian and German priests in the mid-nineteenth century. In 1879 Leo XIII's encyclical *Aeterni Patris* enjoined on the Church universal the study of St. Thomas Aquinas. The later-Cardinal Désiré Mercier made Louvain an important center of the revival, and Mercier's student, historian of medieval philosophy Maurice de Wulf, held a faculty appointment at Harvard as well as Louvain in the 1920s, thus helping to bring Neoscholasticism into the American academic world.[57]

There were no notable American Catholic Thomists at that time, but the decade of the twenties did see the organization of the American Catholic Philosophical Association, which soon began to publish its journal, *The New Scholasticism* (1927). Another journal, *The Modern Schoolman* (1925), had already begun to appear at St. Louis University, and *Thought* (1926), the new quarterly of the Jesuits of Fordham, also carried many articles on philosophy by Neoscholastics. The great figures of Jacques Maritain and Etienne Gilson assumed commanding importance in the 1930s, and Neoscholasticism reigned supreme in the philosophy departments of Catholic colleges and seminaries through the 1950s.

The Scholastic Revival brought Catholic enthusiasm for the Middle Ages to a climax, but it was a very different kind of medievalism from that of the romantics. Indeed, it is difficult to conceive of two mentalities more unlike than the romantic and the Scholastic. Romantic medievalism was

poetic, vaguely idealistic, intuitive, impressionistic, undisciplined, and subjective. Scholastic medievalism was just the opposite—technical, bluntly
realistic, discursive, precise, systematic, and objective. This kind of listing
perhaps puts too fine a point on the contrast, and there were doubtless
Neoscholastics who delighted in medieval picturesqueness, just as some
of the romantics had appreciated St. Thomas's writings. Nevertheless, the
overall temper of the Scholastic Revival was definitely classical rather than
romantic, and its antiromanticism spilled over from philosophy into most
other spheres of Catholic thought in the second quarter of the twentieth
century.[58]

Calvert Alexander's *The Catholic Literary Revival,* published in 1936,
illustrated the fallout effect. Alexander not only dismissed romanticism
itself as vaporously subjective, he also scorned the medievalism of the
romantics—they admired the Middle Ages for the wrong reasons![59]
Liturgists also showed signs of coming full circle. The nineteenth-century
liturgical movement began with Dom Prosper Gueranger, a thoroughgoing
romantic medievalist who made Solemnes Abbey into a miniature Middle
Ages. By 1939, however, a German writer denied that the liturgical movement owed its origin to romanticism. On the contrary, he claimed that
"Benedictine liturgical piety is characterized by clarity, propriety, moderation
—by a classical temper." Fifteen years later, an outstanding liturgist, Louis
Bouyer, treated Gueranger as a sort of case study of what liturgical renewal should avoid, warning specifically against the temptation to roman-
ticize the medieval Church.[60] In somewhat the same manner, the Neoscholastic emphasis on systematically applied reason and on the natural
law tradition profoundly reshaped the organic-society theories of the romantic corporatists. The result was that the medievalist critique stemming
from continental romanticism was brought within an elaborate Scholastic
framework of social thought dealing with the common good, subsidiarity,
distributive and commutative justice, and so on.[61]

In addition to discrediting the romantic-aesthetic motif in Catholic
medievalism and reshaping the social-critique motif, Neoscholasticism simply absorbed the apologetical theme. After the time of Pope Leo XIII, medieval Christendom was defended and praised by reference to St. Thomas
and the perennial wisdom of which he was the supreme master. There remains one other theme of Catholic medievalism to be touched upon—the
motif of scholarship—and it too is well exhibited by the Scholastic Revival. By the scholarship motif I mean the absorption in the Middle Ages
that arose out of intellectual curiosity, out of a desire to know the truth
about them, quite apart from any concern about the polemical or apologetical uses the truth thus gained might serve. In any individual, the drive
for understanding might be interwoven with more distinctively religious

concerns and, taken as a whole, Catholic medievalism is richer in people who used their knowledge to serve some religious or social purpose than it is in persons for whom the scholarly concern was uppermost. But the scholarship motif is as much a reality as any of the others listed. It was present among the Neoscholastics—who could point to scholars whose dedication to the search for truth is as pure as could be found anywhere[62] —and among men identified in a more general way with Catholic research on the Middle Ages. Christopher Dawson was perhaps the most distinguished figure in the latter group, but many younger men were also attracted to medieval studies as the field grew in importance in twentieth-century historical scholarship in the United States.[63]

The Meaning of American Catholic Medievalism

This historical sketch of the development of American Catholic medievalism affords some basis for understanding its prominence in the second quarter of the twentieth century. After a few brief retrospective comments on the historical review, we can therefore turn to inquiries of a more broadly interpretive sort.

In looking back on the history of its development, the first point to be underscored about Catholic medievalism is precisely that it is a historical phenomenon. It is not, in other words, an attitude or outlook that perdured intact and unchanged from the medieval epoch itself. On the contrary, it came into being at a certain historical moment—the romantic era —in response to then-contemporary currents of feeling, and it has been molded by a variety of historical influences ever since, with different motifs assuming prominence at different times and places. Thus the image of the Middle Ages that prevails at any given time must thus be understood both as reflecting the thinking of that period and, at the same time, as reinforcing certain aspects of that thinking. Seen against this background, the shifts we have witnessed in American Catholic attitudes toward medievalism in the past half-century are not essentially different from what has happened in earlier times, although they are unusually dramatic and striking.

Secondly, we ought to note that although American Catholics kept themselves fairly well abreast of the currents of medievalism, they remained quite dependent on Europe for leadership in this area. Dr. Walsh—whose Thirteenth, Greatest of Centuries was still required reading in freshman history at Fordham in 1951—was the only American Catholic to make an important original contribution to the tradition of medievalism.[64]

Finally, it is worth reemphasizing that medievalism was not restricted to Catholics. As we have seen, enthusiasm for the Middle Ages originated among non-Catholics, and the best-known American medievalizers—Henry Adams and Ralph Adams Cram—were not members of the Roman Catholic Church (although Cram, a high church Episcopalian, was very much a Catholic fellow-traveler in the 1920s and 1930s). Like Adams and Cram, the leading American contributors to the nineteenth-century Dante revival —Henry Wadsworth Longfellow, James Russell Lowell, and Charles Eliot Norton—were not only *not* Catholics, they were of purest Puritan descent. And as Neoscholasticism neared its climax, the names of Robert M. Hutchins and Mortimer J. Adler, highly visible non-Catholics, were prominently associated with it. The appeal of the Middle Ages thus extended beyond the boundaries of the Catholic group, and historians have quite recently begun to inquire what it was that made medievalism attractive to such persons.[65]

And what, we must ask at this point, made medievalism so attractive to Catholics for such a long time? The question carries us well into the broadly interpretive realm and any answer to it will necessarily have a somewhat speculative quality. Acknowledging that fact, I would suggest that the short answer to the question—the obvious answer perhaps—is that Catholic medievalism is the obverse of Catholic antimodernism and its intensity reflects the degree of uneasiness felt by Catholics about the dominant tendencies of the modern world. Like all short answers, however, this one needs a good deal of unpacking, especially since the terms "modernism," "modernity," and "the modern world" are at least as multivalent as the terms "medieval" or "Middle Ages." The best way to sort out the complexities is to look first at the interwar years, when medievalism reached its climax, and then to examine the 1960s, when "medieval" became a byword and a hissing.

Neoscholasticism, which was the dominant form of American Catholic medievalism in the second quarter of this century, was profoundly antimodernist, but not in the sense that its promoters wished to "go back to the Middle Ages." That charge was often brought against them, and understandably so; but the champions of St. Thomas indignantly denied being animated by anything resembling historical nostalgia, a sentiment for which they felt nothing but scorn. The purpose of their endeavor, rather, was to recover from the past a system of thought that embodied *timeless* truths in order to bring its *perennially* valid principles to bear on the moral and philosophical dilemmas of the present day. The fact that this system had been most fully worked out in the Middle Ages was, in the Aristotelean terminology favored by the Neoscholastics, a purely "accidental" matter, which had no bearing, either positive or negative, on the validity of the system as such. In this sense, Neoscholasticism was, as many critics have pointed out, quite ahistorical; indeed, some of its more rigorous exponents denied that the results of historical study deserved the name of knowledge at all, since those results lacked the qualities of universality and necessity that marked true *scientia*.[66]

Not all Neoscholastics dismissed history quite so cavalierly, but the system itself was intrinsically antihistoricist in that it ruled out altogether the possibility that the passage of time and changing circumstances might require any *essential* modification of St. Thomas's synthesis of natural knowledge and supernatural revelation. Truth was truth and remained the same, despite changing outward circumstances. This powerful antihistoricist bent was related to Catholic opposition to modernity in two ways. On the more general level, the revival of Scholastic philosophy constituted a quite self-conscious response to, and rejection of, intellectual tendencies of the day (such as immanentism, skepticism, and subjectivism) that were intimately related to the broadly historicist way of looking at things that became so pronounced (and novel) a feature of modern thought in the nineteenth century. For this reason, James Hennesey is fully justified in describing Neoscholasticism as the central feature of a papal policy aimed at "intellectualizing the combat with modernity."[67] But the movement became even more polemically antimodernist in the early decades of the twentieth century because it was prescribed, and rigidly imposed, as the specific antidote to the drift of thinking that led to the heresy of "Modernism," which was condemned in 1907.[68] Historicist elements were, in fact, quite prominent in the thinking of Modernists like Alfred Loisy and George Tyrrell, which naturally reinforced the bias against history that was built into the Neoscholastic approach.

Much more would have to be said about the problem of history if we were to enter more deeply into the clash between Neoscholasticism and Modernism. But such a discussion would be out of place here, not only because I am unprepared to deal with the kind of philosophical issues involved, but also because it would distract from what is for us the main point. That point is that the Neoscholastics did not object to the modern age simply because it was "modern" instead of "medieval" (i.e., stood at this point, not that point, in a sequence of historical epochs); they objected, rather, to the erroneous views and attitudes held by "modern thinkers." It was a matter, in other words, of who was right (correct) and who was wrong (in error) about a number of basic questions involving God and man, nature and society. And because the Neoscholastics were convinced that they were right and the "modern thinkers" were wrong, their aim was not just to vindicate the soundness of their views, but also to *redeem the modern world by converting it from error to truth.*

This evangelical dimension of the Scholastic Revival, as we might call it, was fundamental to the hopes of Leo XIII, who, shortly before he became Pope, devoted two notable sets of Lenten discourses to a positive treatment of modern civilization and to what was required to bring about the full realization of its glorious possibilities.[69] Ecclesiastical policy took a sharply defensive, inward-looking turn under Pius X; but he also reinforced adherence to Thomism in the most stringent way, and the program of "Catholic Action" promoted in the 1920s and 1930s by Pope Pius XI restored a more positive, outward-looking thrust. In this country, the evangelically oriented mobilization set off by papally sponsored Catholic Action coincided with the heyday of Neoscholasticism as the generally accepted ideology of educated Catholics.[70]

The vast majority of these educated Catholics had little or no technical competence in philosophy or theology; but they knew that there was such a thing as "the Thomistic synthesis," had some generalized notions of what it encompassed, knew that it was the official Catholic position in philosophy and theology, and had been given to understand that its implications governed Catholic thinking in other areas, from political theory and economics all the way to aesthetics and literary criticism. In other words, the Neoscholastic synthesis was looked upon as providing the normative core of ideas that could give form to an integrally Catholic culture which it was the aim of the Catholic Action program to bring to realization, first among Catholics themselves and ultimately in society at large. Catholics, in short, had their own vision of modern civilization against which they could measure the defects of the prevailing forms of "modernity" and to which they hoped to convert their misguided contemporaries.

Two aspects of the drive to create a distinctively Catholic culture in the era of what was called the Catholic literary and intellectual revival demand special attention because of their connection with medievalism. The first has to do with the role of the Middle Ages as an analogue to what Catholics had in mind, an earlier examplar of a society molded by a Catholic worldview and suffused by a Catholic spirit. The intention behind analogical references to the Middle Ages was not to call for the medieval world's being reproduced in the present, but to encourage modern Catholics to do in their own day the same kind of thing that their medieval forebears had done in meeting the very different challenges of that earlier day. It was in this spirit, for example, that one of the pioneers of the Young Christian Workers movement, which is considered a quite progressive form of Catholic Action, spoke of the need for committed Christians to work for "a new world, a new Christianity, a second Middle Age, more glorious— more Christianlike than all."[71]

But the medieval analogy would not have had much point if there were not thought to be a substantial similarity, or even an underlying identity, between the kind of Catholic culture achieved in the Middle Ages and that which the promoters of a Catholic civilization had in mind in the 1930s. That point of similarity—the second aspect of the subject requiring elaboration—is the stress on synthesis, or unity. Unity was regarded as perhaps the chief distinguishing characteristic of medieval civilization, which had been memorably contrasted to modern civilization in precisely that respect by Henry Adams. And for Catholics of the 1930s, it was the capacity of their vision to integrate, to unify all the spheres of life, that made it so appealing and convinced them it offered a remedy for the social atomization and spiritual emptiness of a civilization torn by clashing ideologies and unchecked social and economic forces.[72]

The Catholic drive for unity will occupy us at greater length in chapter 7; here it will suffice to take note of a couple of instances that illustrate how the Middle Ages functioned as a model of the harmoniously integrated society. In one such case, a prominent Jesuit educator argued in 1933 that Catholicism constituted a culture whose "totality of view" set it at odds with the disintegrative spirit of modern civilization. He linked this "habit of looking at life as a whole, and not as a series of departments," with the Middle Ages and then added: "if that [medieval] unity and totality have passed from the civilization in which we now live, it has not passed from Catholic thinking on the fundamentals of existence." Three years later, a Catholic committed to social reform conceded that the unity of the Middle Ages was absent from the modern world. But, he went on: "Medievalism supplies us with the outlines of a Society which . . . was found throughout Christendom. It has yet to be shown that . . . the essential features of the mediaeval system [are] inapplicable to our own age. . . . Thomism today challenges the world to show reason why it should not be made the foundation of a world wide order capable of eclipsing the Soviet experiment."[73]

The allusion to Thomism was almost obligatory in those days, and it reflected the preeminent place of philosophy in the Catholic vision of unity. But the vision itself had an appeal that reached far beyond the ranks of technical philosophers, whose understanding of unity had a remote, hyper-intellectualized quality. The holistic yearning for a more integrated life, a more organically unified community, was central to the program of corporative social reconstruction, around which something of the romance of the old guild system still lingered, and to various "back to the land" prescriptions, some of which were more than faintly redolent of romantic medievalism. The same was true of the liturgical movement, the most active promoters of which were the Benedictine monks of rural St. John's Abbey in Minnesota. A growing interest in the theology of the Mystical body of Christ likewise testified to the desire for organic unity among the faithful; but this and other forms of religious thought were much less rationalistic in quality than the Thomistic synthesis of faith and reason. While the drive for unity thus reached its most comprehensive articulation in Neoscholastic terms, it suffused the whole of Catholic life in warmer, more emotionally satisfying forms as well.

There was a pronounced antimodernist quality to the Catholic drive for unity because it implied a sharp rejection of modern Western civilization as it actually existed. But Catholics were not the only ones who felt this way. They may have been unique in the degree to which they looked back to the Middle Ages for their model of a harmoniously integrated culture, but the very idea of *culture* itself carried strongly antimodern overtones as it was elaborated by contemporary anthropologists. Ruth Benedict, who was the leading popularizer of the anthropological concept of culture, found the competitive individualism of American life repugnant, and Edward Sapir contrasted the "inherently harmonious, balanced, [and] self-satisfactory" cultures of primitive peoples with the "spurious" American culture, which seemed to him a "hybrid of contradictory patches" that gave rise to a thousand "spiritual maladjustments."[74] The reference to the "Soviet experiment" in the passage quoted earlier should also remind us that the tradition of Marxian socialism, which exerted so strong an attraction on American intellectuals in the 1930s, embodied a passionate rejection of Western civilization as it actually existed and held up the vision of a world organically unified by a spirit of comradeship and social solidarity. Indeed, Peter Berger has argued that Marxism owes its special appeal to the fact that it manages to combine a vision of preindustrial harmony with a "scientific"—and therefore modern and progressive—prescription for how that condition is to be attained in the future.[75]

The inference I draw from these considerations is that the kind of antimodernism that animated Catholic medievalism in the 1930s was, in certain respects, less out of the mainstream than might at first appear to be the case. Despite the profound differences that put Catholic campaigners for unity at odds with the more up-to-date and "modern" critics of contemporary society, there was, nonetheless, an underlying spiritual kinship between these diverse groups. That kinship grew out of a shared alienation from the culture of their own day and expressed itself in a distaste for modern industrial society that in some cases approached detestation.

Alienation from American industrial society did not seem unreasonable in the depression era. The system, after all, had broken down. Many people were convinced that it would take more than New Deal tinkering to set it to rights, and demands for basic social reconstruction found a more sympathetic hearing than they would have received in more prosperous times. The coming of World War II, however, changed the situation dramatically. Not only did it bring about a rapid economic recovery and improved living standards for most Americans, it also enormously enhanced the moral status of the nation as the bastion of civilized values being crushed elsewhere in the world. Set against the monstrous contrast of Naziism, with its heavy overtones of romantic antimodernism, the American version of modernity—which was, of course, nothing other than the American way of life—looked very good indeed. In these circumstances, identification with American modernity, not alienation from it, became the order of the day.[76]

The wartime shift of feeling set the stage for what has been called the "American celebration." It also, in my opinion, marked the opening of a transitional period during which American Catholics effected a gradual rapprochement with modernity. For this rapprochement, Catholic Americanism served as the mediating ground. There was no sudden abandonment of the critique of modernity; on the matter of "secularism" it became more stringent than ever in the late 1940s. Nor was there any explicit disavowal of the Catholic-Action goal of redeeming American society by apostolically oriented programs. But this approach waned in attractiveness after the war, and by the early 1950s a definite countercurrent had set in against mobilization programs that had the practical effect of cutting Catholics off from others in American society. Accompanying the campaign against "Catholic separatism" was an increasingly warm espousal of the liberal American (and therefore modernist) values of pluralism and tolerance. It was time, Catholics were told by spokesmen for their own progressive elite, to end their self-imposed isolation, to break out of their ghetto, and to enter into the mainstream of modern life.[77]

Neoscholasticism still seemed firmly in place. Indeed, thinkers like Maritain and John Courtney Murray made creative use of its resources in developing a Catholic rationale for pluralism, democracy, separation of church and state, and religious freedom. As the rapprochement with modernity gained momentum, however, tensions began to build up that strained the Thomistic synthesis. Murray's work, for example, aroused strong opposition because it departed too openly from traditional teaching, had historicist tendencies, and made too accommodating an adjustment to the "secular" social order that had replaced the "sacral" society of the Middle Ages. Murray was forbidden to write on church and state for several years; other scholars sympathetic to new approaches in philosophy, theology, and biblical studies chafed under tacit restrictions imposed by the need to conform their work to the existing synthesis, restrictions reinforced on occasion by official admonitions. In the social sciences, Catholics were also becoming impatient with the idea that their findings were to be fitted into a preexisting Neoscholastic worldview.

Rising dissatisfaction with what was beginning to look like an out-moded worldview found release in the spectacular eruption of cultural self-criticism set off by John Tracy Ellis's 1955 article on the failures of American Catholic intellectual life. Implicit in the torrent of self-criticism was acceptance of modern secular standards in the realm of ideas and culture. This more positive stance toward modernity was powerfully reinforced when Pope John XXIII called an ecumenical council which had for its purpose *aggiornamento,* that is, bringing the Church up to date. The Council itself effected a drastic reorientation of Catholic thinking about modernity, particularly through the Pastoral Constitution on the Church in the Modern World, which took a far more positive approach than earlier teachings had in urging Catholics to identify themselves with forces for good already at work in the modern world. At the same time, the election of John F. Kennedy as president marked both the culmination of Catholic assimilation into American life and a climactic moment in the Catholic rapprochement with modernity.

Among certain elements of the American Catholic intelligentsia, enthusiasm for what was modern and secular reached near-euphoric levels in the early sixties. Though soon to be qualified, it lasted long enough to sweep Neoscholasticism from the scene—and with Neoscholasticism went any lingering vestiges of the belief that Catholics had their own distinctive vision of an alternative culture to which the modern world should be converted. Indeed, this older view became an embarrassment, a measure of the degree to which Catholics had in the past been benighted; for that reason it had to be rejected—in the view of some, rejected vehemently. This explains why the Middle Ages, formerly idealized, now became a butt of scorn, the "feudal-medieval" symbol of everything that was wrong with the Church.

But "the times," as we know, were "a-changing," and a-changing with stunning speed. For American Catholics, what happened next was surely one of history's most ironic twists—before they had had time to get used to being partisans of modernity, the modern world in its most advanced American embodiment became an object of loathing. This overstates the case as a description of public opinion in general, but it does not exaggerate the feeling that underlay the most impassioned attacks on the actually existing society, polity, and culture as those attacks were mounted by spokesmen for Blacks, students, opponents of the war in Vietnam, hippies, women, American Indians, and white ethnics. Criticism took its origin, in most cases, from outrage over specific defects in the existing order; but it quickly "escalated" (to use a sixties word) to a level of generality that bespoke throughgoing alienation from modern existence as such. Thus Theodore Roszak, the theorist of the counterculture, intimated a preference for witch doctors over modern medical science; and Susan Sontag drew the conclusion implicit in the outpouring of disaffection from American life: despite its achievements in art and literature and science, Western civilization was a mistake.[78]

There was in the neoprimitivism, the utopianism, and the longing for community that characterized much of the cultural criticism of the late sixties a deep streak of romanticism.[79] And that, as anyone who has read this far will realize, should have meant greater sympathy for the Middle Ages or even the emergence of new forms of medievalism. The former we unquestionably find, although not, perhaps, in sufficient strength to justify calling it the latter. Harvey Cox's writings provide the most striking evidence of the shifts in feeling as they bear on medievalism. His *Secular City* (1965), which enjoyed sensational success when it appeared, was a paean to modernity.[80] Only four years later Cox spoke from a very different "flower-child" perspective in calling for "festivity and fantasy." This message was conveyed in his *Feast of Fools* (1969), the opening sentence of which explained the book's title and, in doing so, testified to a new appreciation of the Middle Ages: "During the medieval era there flourished in parts of Europe a holiday known as the Feast of Fools." The religiously serious playfulness that Cox prescribed might well have reminded older Catholic readers of the "Mass and maypole" medievalism of G. K. Chesterton and Hilaire Belloc; indeed, Cox drew upon Chesterton and other Catholic writers and noted the way in which they had romanticized the Middle Ages.[81]

The newspaper report of his activities does not say what tradition of medievalism the Reverend Nick Weber was inspired by, but his approach was quite in keeping with Cox's festivity and fantasy. "Dressed in medieval tights and leather doublet, his bearded face painted like a clown," the young San Francisco priest strolled about the city employing a fire-eating act to attract the audiences for his one-man shows that aimed to inculcate "simple things like human kindness, love . . . generosity." The air of self-consciously serious frivolity that marked this kind of sixties romanticism is even more pronounced in the case of the Society for Creative Anachronism, Inc., which stages authentically outfitted medieval tourneys, jousts, and "revels." Organized at the birthplace of the counterculture (Berkeley, California) in 1966, the society claimed a national membership of 10,000 by the mid-1980s.[82] The spectacular development of academic programs of medieval studies existed on quite a different level, but it too reflected a kind of turning away from the modern world. As the *New York Times* reported in 1972, some academic medievalists regarded themselves as being "in the vanguard of an intellectual revolution against what one scholar termed anarchy and chaos in contemporary society."[83]

All of this could hardly take place without awakening an interest in medievalism itself as an intellectual movement or a dimension of modern thought. Such a development of reflexive self-consciousness had indeed taken place: there have been several recent studies of medievalism and a scholarly journal devoted specifically to that subject is presently struggling to get itself established on a firm footing.[84] A variety of intellectual or ideological positions are represented among those engaged in the work, but it is striking that certain scholars of a Marxist or New Left orientation have shown a decided sympathy for the medievalist ruminations of nineteenth-century figures like Ruskin, Morris, and Henry Adams, and have even spoken kindly of what appear to be hopelessly bourgeois developments such as the arts and crafts movement.[85] The reason for their sympathetic treatment of such seemingly reactionary tendencies is that these radical scholars recognize the medievalism of their subjects for what it is, a symptom of profound alienation from modern industrial society. Since they share the same distaste for modernity as it actually exists, they naturally feel a kind of fellowship for the romantic social-critique medievalists, even though they regard as inadequate the "solutions" put forward by the nineteenth-century admirers of the Middle Ages.

These various manifestations of sympathetic interest in the Middle Ages—countercultural, academic, and radical—do not seem to have affected American Catholics to any discernible degree, and there certainly has not been a general shift away from the antimedieval reaction that accompanied *aggiornamento*. In view of the recent date of that reaction, and its intensity, it would be premature to look for any such general shift in the direction of medievalism in the 1980s. Yet one may assume that Catholics are participating in the academic revival of medieval studies as fully as other segments of the population of university students and professors. And since many American Catholic radicals abhor the privatized consumerism of capitalist society as deeply as their Marxist brethren, I would be surprised if the positive reassessment of social-critique medievalism by leftist scholars did not eventually find a resonant echo among Catholic radicals too. Even if that should take place, however, the Middle Ages that Catholics might look to more sympathetically would not be the same Middle Ages they venerated in the interwar era. The image of the medieval past that prevailed in those days was the product of circumstances distinctive to that particular "present." Our present is different, and our image of the Middle Ages will differ accordingly. But of course our present continues to change, and both the Middle Ages as such and the tradition of popular medievalism will remain significant elements of the past with which the present is always in interaction.

2

IMMIGRANT PAST,
ETHNIC PRESENT

Another broad historical issue on which Catholic thinking has shifted over the past three decades concerns the place of immigration and ethnicity in American Catholic life. When I was in graduate school in the 1950s, educated Catholics were convinced that the great need of the day was for the Church to break out of the ghetto of its immigrant past and enter more actively into the mainstream of American society. Immigration and ethnicity were, in other words, matters that were to be put behind us. Catholic historians, it is true, spoke occasionally of the need for deeper study of immigration, but they shared fully in the prevailing assumption that what was needed was greater involvement by Catholics in the ongoing life of the nation. Indeed, their historical studies reinforced this point since the works that attracted the most attention in the fifties centered on the late nineteenth-century controversies over "Americanism" and generally sided with the liberal "Americanizers."

Historians gave increasing attention to immigration in the sixties, but the strongly assimilationist belief that Americanization was a good thing was not vigorously challenged until around 1970. The relative suddenness with which the change took place—and the sharpness of the reversal it represented—are well illustrated in the work of Andrew M. Greeley. His studies of the effects of Catholic schooling in the early and middle sixties alerted him to the importance of ethnicity as a significant variable in sociological analysis. Yet his Catholic Experience *(1967) maintained that acculturation was the main theme in American Catholic history, and he fully endorsed the consensus view that the Americanizers were correct in calling for the integration of Catholics into the dominant national culture. Shortly after this book appeared, however, Greeley's views began to change as a result of his absorption with the "new ethnicity." By 1972 he had ex-*

plicitly disavowed his earlier acceptance of what he called the "official" assimilationist version of American Catholic history; four years later he elaborated a "pluralistic" interpretation sharply critical of the Americanizing viewpoint he had previously championed.* Greeley's revised view was quite representative of the dominant opinion expressed by Catholic commentators on ethnic matters in the mid-1970s. The new conventional wisdom on immigration and ethnicity was thus diametrically opposed to what it had been twenty years earlier, but in both cases the prevailing vision of the past was intimately linked to the way the current cultural situation was understood.

My own involvement with the study of immigration and ethnicity goes back to the late 1950s when I was first getting into research on the German-American Catholics. Since then I have maintained a sporadically consistent professional interest in the subject. Despite my longstanding interest, however, I was as much taken by surprise as anyone by the great upsurge of scholarly and popular attention to ethnicity in the late sixties and seventies. The long-term results of this ethnic revival can hardly be other than positive, but many of the more popular discussions that appeared at the height of the revival were notably one-sided — they replaced an old oversimplification with a new one even more simplistic.

Since that was my view at the time, I was pleased to be asked by the editor of Social Thought *to prepare a short overview of immigration and American Catholic history as a background piece for other articles dealing with current ethnic issues. My intention in writing it was to show that a historical perspective can deepen our understanding of contemporary issues, and also to show that in order to achieve such an understanding we must forget about labels and try to do justice to the complexity of both past and present. The article originally appeared in 1978, with David Salvaterra of Loras College as coauthor. I have revised it somewhat for publication here and brought the bibliographical citations up to date.*

W<small>HILE THE</small> M<small>IDDLE</small> A<small>GES</small> belong to the remote past, and have taken on a mythic quality, the phenomenon of immigration is a live recollection in the collective memory of American Catholics. For great numbers of them it is part of their lived experience; for the Church as a whole, ethnicity

---

*See Andrew M. Greeley, *The Catholic Experience: An Interpretation of The History of American Catholicism* (Garden City, N.Y., 1967); "New Ethnicity & Blue Collars," *Dissent* 19 (Winter 1972), 277; "Catholicism in America: Two Hundred Years and Counting," *The Critic* 34 (Summer 1976), 14–47, 54–70.

is very much a present reality. Hence it is understandable that Catholics figured prominently in the "revival of ethnicity" that flourished in the 1970s, and that Catholic leaders in the 1980s are still keenly concerned about immigration and refugee policy. Accompanying the ethnic revival there was a notable awakening of scholarly interest in ethnic history, much of it having a revisionist character. Here I propose to look briefly at the role played by Catholics as spokesmen for the "new pluralism" and at the historical viewpoint their work embodied, and then to outline what I believe is a more satisfactory framework for understanding immigration and ethnicity as dimensions of the American Catholic story, past and present.

Catholics and the Revival of Ethnicity

The awakening of interest in ethnicity drew the attention of Catholics for several reasons. In the first place, most of the groups that came to be called "white ethnics" were heavily Catholic, since the term was applied principally to persons of southern and eastern European background whose ancestors had come from Italy, Poland, or the lands of the old Austro-Hungarian empire. In addition, Chicanos and other Hispanic Americans are overwhelmingly Catholic in religion, and they constitute a very important segment of the ethnic population whose visibility and influence were growing rapidly when the revival of ethnicity took place and whose situation presents problems still unsolved, most notably that of illegal immigration. In view of these facts, it is not surprising that several Catholics soon emerged as spokesmen for the new ethnic consciousness, even though the American Jewish Committee was the primary catalyst of the organized movement to promote the new pluralism.[1]

Four persons stand out among Catholics identified with the movement. Michael Novak, a leading lay intellectual of Slovak background, became the best-known publicist and prophet of the ethnic revival. His *Rise of the Unmeltable Ethnics* (1972) served as the semiofficial manifesto of the movement, and he continued to campaign actively in the ethnic cause through the decade of the seventies. In recent years Novak has turned from ethnic-cultural to more specifically religious and political-policy concerns, but he has not revised his views concerning the importance of ethnicity.[2]

Three priests—Andrew M. Greeley, Geno Baroni, and Silvano Tomasi —also played important roles in the areas, respectively, of social-scientific research, organizational activity, and attention to national policy on immigration and refugee matters. Greeley, a prolific writer and vigorous controversialist as well as an established authority in the area of national survey research, contributed immensely to putting the discussion of ethnicity on firmer ground, both empirically and conceptually. His *Why Can't They Be Like Us?* (1971) was an influential early statement, and his *Ethnicity in the United States* (1974), an authoritative "reconnaissance" of the whole field. Greeley also insured by his combustible presence and his 1972 volume *That Most Distressful Nation* that the Irish would not be overlooked among America's ethnic groups.[3]

Geno Baroni, the son of an Italian immigrant miner in Pennsylvania, served as Assistant Secretary for Neighborhoods, Voluntary Associations, and Consumer Protection in the administration of President Jimmy Carter. He won this high post by a record of unmatched effectiveness as an organizer of community development programs in ethnic neighborhoods in a number of cities. He also founded the National Center for Urban Ethnic Affairs, which carries on the publicist, lobbying, and organizational work in which Baroni excelled.[4]

Silvano Tomasi, an Italian-born member of the religious community founded by Bishop Giovanni Battista Scalabrini to work with Italian immigrants, continues to play an active role in ethnic affairs as director of the Center for Migration Studies in New York and as editor of its journal, *International Migration Review.* The Center has also published a number of useful monographs, among which Tomasi's *Piety and Power* (1975), an important historical study of Italian Catholic life in the New York area between 1880 and 1930, is particularly noteworthy.[5] Tomasi's book makes clear that he is by no means uninterested in the ethnic-religious past, but the Center and its *Review* give special attention to the current migration scene—in other countries as well as the United States—and to policy issues such as immigration law reform.

Although qualifications would have to be introduced to do justice to the four persons just named—to say nothing of other writers on the subject—it is, nevertheless, a fair generalization that spokesmen for the new ethnicity tended to be highly critical of the way America treats its ethnics. They also inevitably presented an unfavorable picture of immigration and ethnic affairs in the past—after all, the present situation is an outgrowth of the past; if it is deplorable, the past had to have been bad too. This kind of informal logic naturally carried over from the general area of national history into the field of Catholic history for those who were interested in that aspect of the ethnic past. Even without special animus on their part, champions of the new pluralism were predisposed to reach negative conclusions about how things were in the past, although they might not have been conscious of approaching their inquiries with such an intention. Since those predisposed to find negative evidence in the past are rarely disappointed, the impression gained acceptance that the historical record of the Catholic Church in respect to ethnicity was somewhere between embarrassing and disgraceful. Although held most strongly by ethnic activists, this opinion also made itself felt among educated Catholics, ecclesiastical policy-makers, and academic historians.

It goes without saying that a brief essay cannot pretend to give an adequate history of Catholic immigration. That is not what I am trying to do. Neither am I setting out to "answer" the new ethnic critics of the Catholic historical record, although I freely grant that my overall assessment of that record is more positive than theirs. My purpose, rather, is to *identify and discuss some of the more important features that recur in the history of Catholic immigration and ethnicity in the United States.* In doing so, I will begin with some observations about the Catholic Church's situation as an "institutional immigrant" existing in an environment initially quite hostile to Catholicism. Then the focus shifts to an examination of certain recurring features in the experience of Catholic ethnic groups. Incidentally, I speak mainly of immigrants rather than ethnics, for that was the term used by Catholics until the 1960s. Blacks and American Indians do not fall within the scope of the discussion because their situation vis-à-vis the Catholic Church was so different from that of immigrant groups as conventionally understood.

The Catholic Church as an Institutional Immigrant

All churches except the few (such as the Mormon) that originated in the United States are institutional immigrants in the sense that they were transplanted from abroad and had to adjust to a novel environment in this country. But as H. Richard Niebuhr pointed out almost sixty years ago in his *Social Sources of Denominationalism* (1929), these problems of adjustment were aggravated for what he called the "Churches of the Immigrants."[6] Among such, the difficulties of the Catholic Church were easily the most extreme, since it had to adjust itself to a society whose most influential founders had defined themselves "over against" Catholicism. For what was it that the Puritans wished to purify out of the Church of England but the vestiges of Catholicism? Throughout the colonial period and into the nineteenth century, innumerable earnest and well-meaning American Protestants believed the Pope was literally the Antichrist spoken of in the Book of Revelation. The organization over which the Pope presided was in no sense to be thought of as a branch of the Christian Church. His followers could never become good Americans because, in the minds of these Protestants, one of the things that defined Americanism was rejection of the Pope of Rome.

This apocalyptic view of Catholicism blended, in the era of the War for Independence, with the millennial republicanism of the revolutionary generation. The papacy and Catholicism were identified with the depraved political order of Europe upon which America had decisively turned her back. Thus John Adams (who is not usually classed among the more enthusiastic visionaries of the age) attacked the politico-religious system of Europe in his *Dissertation on the Canon and Feudal Law* (1765)—a work which the modern scholar, Ernest Tuveson, identified a few years ago as an important document in the tradition of American millennialism.[7] Thomas Jefferson differed with his New England friend on many matters, but he was in full accord with Adams's negative view of the Catholic Middle Ages, and he regarded all ecclesiastical institutions as hindrances to true religion. He and other representatives of the enlightened intelligentsia looked upon Catholicism as part of a benighted and vicious system, wholly at odds with republicanism, tolerable only because it was rapidly passing off the scene in Europe and because it could never prosper in the free air of America.

The virulence of these views ebbed with the passing of revolutionary and revivalistic millennialism, but the conviction remained among many Americans—liberals as well as evangelical Protestants—that Catholicism was intrinsically irreconcilable with Americanism on the level of principle. This conviction constituted a special problem for those responsible for the Catholic Church in America, notably the bishops, and it helps explain why they were always so sensitive to the need to vindicate the compatibility of Catholicism and Americanism. It likewise makes more understandable the desire of some churchmen to eliminate whatever stood in the way of appropriate Americanization of the Catholic religion.

Some forms of Americanization were bound to occur anyhow, because the Church had to adjust itself to the new environment just as an individual immigrant did. One such adjustment was the development of the Catholic school system. Other factors were also involved, but the basic reason a system extending from kindergarten through graduate school developed here and not elsewhere in the Catholic world was that here the Church found itself in a society that placed a higher value on universal education than any other in human history and that established free public educational institutions on an unprecedented scale. If they did not want to see their young people absorbed by a system that was definitely hostile to Catholicism in its formative years and that consistently regarded the "proper" socialization of children as a primary responsibility, Catholic churchmen felt that there was little they could do but encourage the establishment of schools where Catholic children could be socialized in their own tradition and where they would not be subject to overt or covert proselytization.

Considered as a positive accommodation to the needs and challenges of the American social environment, Catholic schools clearly illustrate a kind of Americanization. Moreover, they continued to be Americanized in the sense that their development was molded by the evolving forces of the American educational environment. The requirements for certification worked out by state departments of education and by independent accrediting agencies, for example, were highly concrete manifestations of the Americanizing influence of the surrounding social milieu. But if the Catholic schools cooperated with this kind of Americanization, they did not always do so with much enthusiasm, and, viewed in another light, the whole Catholic educational enterprise was animated by a desire to resist Americanization. This was, of course, most obvious at the beginning when Americanization was virtually indistinguishable from Protestantization in the minds of many public school educators.[8] But even in the mid-twentieth century there were those who argued that Catholic schools were un-American because they were "divisive," and Catholics have continued to resist Americanization if it is understood to require their giving up their schools.

Americanization, with all its ambiguities and contradictory meanings, extended far beyond the question of educational relations between Catholics and the larger society. *It was also an intra-Catholic problem.* Here, too, the schools were involved, but so was a whole range of other issues over which Catholics disagreed with one another—matters extending from the question of ethnic representation in the hierarchy to temperance, which some Catholics supported as a way of making the Church more acceptable to Americans but which others scorned as an offshoot of Puritan nativism. In all such controversies about Americanization, the fundamental difference of opinion among Catholics arose over the *right kind* of adjustment to make to American society. There was obviously no single, universally applicable, "correct" answer to this question. On the contrary, there was wide leeway for legitimate difference of opinion.

Controversy over these matters was most intense in the 1880s and 1890s.[9] Those who became known as Americanists, or Americanizers—notably Archbishop John Ireland of St. Paul, Bishop John J. Keane of the Catholic University of America, Denis O'Connell of the North American College in Rome, and, in a less partisan way, Cardinal James Gibbons of Baltimore—took what was thought of at the time and later as the liberal position. They admired the open, equalitarian American system; they thought the Church would flourish better here in a free republican society than she had in the tradition-bound states of Europe, and they therefore favored as much accommodation to the prevailing American ways as was compatible with essential Catholic doctrine. Their conservative opponents, led by Archbishop Michael A. Corrigan of New York, were unpersuaded on these points. They were convinced that maintenance of the traditional forms of Catholic life and thought was the surest way to preserve the faith of the immigrants and their children. They were skeptical of the rosy future painted by the liberals; they feared that flexibility might become laxity and that adjustment to a new environment could lead to capitulation to the enemy.

Ethnicity was involved in these controversies in ways too tangled to unravel here. It was most explicit in the battle over the role of German Catholics in the Church, a controversy often labeled "Cahenslyism" after Peter Paul Cahensly, a German Catholic layman who played a prominent role in the dispute. It was also referred to as the "nationality question," and that term gets to the heart of the matter but is misleading in suggesting that this was the *only* nationality question—in fact, there were similar, but less publicized, battles over Irish, French-Canadian, Polish, and other nationalities at various times.

The fundamental issue in all these nationality disputes was whether Catholic immigrants and their descendants should be encouraged to adapt to American ways, or should be encouraged to resist adaptation and to preserve as long as possible their inherited patterns of culture and conduct. In keeping with their generally positive attitude toward the American future, the liberals pushed adaptation and were adamantly opposed to any systematic efforts to perpetuate "foreign" languages and cultural forms beyond the not very long period which they thought of as appropriate for the transition to Americanism. For this reason, they looked askance at Catholic schools where foreign-language instruction functioned to preserve a transplanted language and culture beyond the span of time in which it would otherwise tend to disappear. They also opposed efforts to bind the American-born offspring of immigrants to national parishes if these young people were of age, could understand English, and wished to transfer out of the national parish.

The leaders of the German Catholics, on the other hand, insisted that systematic efforts to preserve language and culture were absolutely essential. Their arguments—which were, *mutatis mutandis,* the same as those of other Catholic ethnic groups—stressed the point that language saves faith, that if the children of the immigrants gave up their mother tongue they would also very likely give up their religion. One may doubt, however, that they valued language *solely* as a means of preserving faith. Rather, language, religion, and culture interpenetrated each other so thoroughly that it was impossible to think of them separately.[10] They made up an undifferentiated unity, and it was hard to conceive of this unity's being sundered, with language and culture withering away while religion adapted itself to a different cultural matrix in the alien soil of American society.

Being thus passionately committed to a radically conservative position in the nationality question, the German Catholics were naturally disposed to a conservative stance on other disputed issues of the 1880s and 1890s, such as whether Catholics could join secret societies like the Odd Fellows, whether they could take part in interfaith gatherings, and so on. In the heat of battle, both sides were driven to extreme positions and could be found uttering sentiments which, if taken out of context, appear rigid, doctrinaire, or even abhorrent. Yet enough has surely been said to make clear that both sides had legitimate arguments and that to treat "Americanization" as an ugly term associated with nothing but narrow chauvinism distorts the historical situation beyond recognition. For Americanization was also a strategy for adapting the Church to certain features of American life that we take for granted today but which were not part of the nineteenth-century European Catholic tradition—such things as the acceptance of republican government, social equalitarianism, separation of church and state, religious freedom, and willingness to cooperate with other religionists in social and civic undertakings. The Americanists were sometimes insensitive to the values of immigrants, but their conservative antagonists were slow to appreciate the positive American values that the liberals espoused.

Since Irish Americans played such a conspicuous role as Americanizers, it is perhaps worth noting that the religious state of affairs in their homeland was such as to make the American system particularly attractive. There the (Protestant) Church of Ireland was the established church, while Roman Catholicism depended for its flourishing, indeed its survival, upon the voluntary support of the faithful. This led the Irish to value religious freedom and church/state separation, and accustomed them to the system of voluntaryism that was the normal pattern in the United States. The Irish were thus predisposed to react favorably to American arrangements, and their first great episcopal spokesman, Bishop John England of Charleston, developed a body of theory justifying those arrangements. England was too "republican" for most of his ecclesiastical contemporaries, but he pointed in the direction of the later Americanists and, ultimately, of the Second Vatican Council.[11]

Recurring Patterns in Catholic Immigrant Experience

While it is useful for analytical purposes to distinguish between the Church considered as an institutional immigrant and the immigrant peoples who comprised the Catholic population, the two dimensions merge together in practical life. Having considered the matter first on the rather abstract level of institutional policy let us look now at the experience of the actual immigrants who made up the great mass of the Catholic faithful. Because of the great number and variety of Catholic immigrant groups, all I can do here is touch lightly on certain patterns that recur with most of them.

UPROOTEDNESS AND INSTABILITY

First, all the immigrants experienced to a greater or lesser extent what Oscar Handlin taught us to call "uprootedness."[12] Moving to a strange land and often continuing to move about during their first few years in America, the immigrants were jarred loose from their social and psychic moorings. A common result was disorientation for the individual and instability for the group. A German priest working in Wisconsin touched on the heart of the matter in an 1855 letter to a mission-support society headquartered in Vienna. "All the resolutions made in Europe dissolve as soon as one feels the breezes of the American coastline," he wrote, and "every tie, including the one with God, must be retied here and must undergo the American 'probatum est' before it can be said that it is secure."[13]

The adaptation of old habits and institutions and the creation of stable new relationships that this astute observer had in mind were not easily achieved for most Catholic immigrant groups. In religious behavior, the symptoms of unsettledness might be either apathy or chronic intragroup bickering. It was not unheard-of for such quarrels to reach the stage of physical violence. In rural northern Ohio, for example, Catholic immigrants from different parts of Germany fell out over whose traditional hymns would be sung at Mass, and the quarrel grew so embittered that one faction burned down the church.[14]

An important factor in such instability was the characteristic shortage of priests in the earlier phases of the immigration of nearly all groups —which continued as a more or less permanent shortage with the Italians. Without priests of their own, the religious situation of Catholic immigrants was inherently unstable. In cases where there was no other Catholic church near enough to attend, the immigrants were left without the Mass and the sacraments, which were essential to Catholic worship and around which the religious and social life of the group could form itself. Even where there was an existing church nearby, it was never fully satisfactory if dominated by another group, for that usually meant differences in language and in devotional practices. Immigrants could not feel at home, religiously, in such circumstances; and if they were numerous enough to draw much attention to themselves, they were apt to be treated as intruders by the original Catholic congregation.

Hence it is understandable that Poles, for example, who often started out in German parishes, or Lithuanians, who started out in Polish parishes, hived off as soon as they could to establish their own churches. The characteristic method was to form a church-building society to collect funds, acquire real estate, and purchase or build a structure to serve as a house of worship.[15] Once possessed of a building, Catholic immigrants were all the more determined to get their own priest, if they did not already have one. They importuned bishops and were resentful when no priest was assigned, even though the bishop who failed to comply ordinarily did so simply because he had no priest. The immigrants might also try to attract a priest from the homeland, or from elsewhere in the United States where their countrymen were settled. Unfortunately, not all priests who made themselves available to serve immigrant congregations were of the best quality, and bishops as far back as John Carroll complained bitterly of the problems created by the kind of vagrant clergymen whom Carroll once characterized as "missionary adventurers."[16] The fault, of course, was not always on the side of the priests; and from their point of view the real problem was episcopal despotism. But however one distributes the blame, dissensions were chronic in the formative years of many, perhaps most, immigrant congregations, as pastors came and went with dizzying rapidity. One student of Lithuanian immigration, for example, tells of a parish in Mount Carmel, Pennsylvania, that had seventeen pastors in twenty years.[17] Religious communities made up primarily or exclusively of members of the same ethnic group were sometimes given special responsibility for the pastoral care of their countrymen. But this arrangement was not without its own hazards. In Chicago, for example, serious rivalry developed between the Resurrectionist Fathers, who had a privileged position, and other members of the Polish-American clergy.[18]

TRUSTEEISM IN IMMIGRANT CONGREGATIONS

In the early nineteenth century, the term "trusteeism" was associated with troubles of the sort described above.[19] The term was derived from the legal arrangement widely prevailing in those days whereby ownership of local church property was vested in the hands of congregational trustees, nearly all of whom were laymen. Since they controlled the church property and the revenues accruing to it, the trustees were in a strong position to defy the bishop if he told them to accept as pastor a priest whom they disliked, or to dismiss one they did like, or if some other grievance arose between bishop and congregation. When such troubles developed, the congregation often split internally, so that trusteeism usually involved a struggle within the local group as well as between the local group and the bishop.

Disputes of this sort continued throughout the period of immigration.[20] Irish and German congregations were affected earliest because they were first on the scene; later in the nineteenth century, the French-Canadians, the Poles, the Italians, and other Catholic immigrant groups all went through the same thing. Trusteeism was a more serious matter in the early days, simply because the organizational structure of the Church was so fragile at the time and because the groups involved came closer to including the whole of the Catholic population then. But the phenomenon itself recurred as each new group passed through the period of instability characteristic of its formative years.

Trustee controversies usually healed with time, but in some cases permanent or long-standing schisms occurred. In the case of Eastern rite groups like the Ruthenians (also known as Rusins or Ukrainians), disaffected congregations often switched over to the Orthodox Church.[21] Three examples among Roman Catholic groups illustrate the continuity of the issues. The Hogan Schism (named after the rebellious Irish priest, William Hogan) grew out of trustee problems in Philadelphia in the 1820s and lasted a number of years.[22] Similar difficulties among Polish immigrants in Scranton in the 1890s ultimately led to the creation of the schismatic Polish National Catholic Church. The leader here was the Reverend Francis Hodur, a Polish immigrant priest who was consecrated a bishop by an Old Catholic prelate in Europe in 1907.[23] And in the 1970s, a congregation of Vietnamese refugees in Port Arthur, Texas, went into schism after a quarrel with their bishop that had all the classic elements of trusteeism. The bishop refused to appoint as pastor of the refugees the priest who came with them until the group turned over to him the deed to the building they had purchased as a place of worship. This the congregation was unwilling to do. They gave the bishop a deadline to meet their demands, and when he did not, they linked up with Archbishop Marcel Lefebvre's traditionalist Society of St. Pius X, where their desire to keep the Latin Mass (which is their mother tongue in religious matters) would not be the problem it might have been had they remained in the Roman Catholic Church.[24]

The determination of the Vietnamese in Texas to remain together and to reconstruct as much as possible of the religious life of their homeland is also a classic pattern among immigrants. This brings us to the "national parish," a characteristic feature of the Catholic immigrant scene and the device that made it possible for many groups to achieve what the Vietnamese had in mind.

THE NATIONAL PARISH

According to the provisions of the Council of Trent, all Catholics residing in a given area were supposed to belong to the territorial parish established for that locality. But in America, immigrants using different languages were settled heterogeneously in the same area, and it was obviously desirable for them to attend churches where they could hear the word of God preached in a language they understood. Hence, the national parish was one in which membership was defined according to language or nationality rather than by place of residence. One or more national parishes might be established in a locality already served by a territorial parish, with each of the former serving its own specific ethnic clientele.

Theoretically, or officially, language rather than nationality itself furnished the pastoral justification for departure from the norm set up by Trent. But for the immigrants, there was more to it than language. Since language, culture, and religion were all bound up in an undifferentiated unity, the desire of immigrants to have "their own" churches went deeper than the mere question of being able to understand the sermon or go to confession conveniently in the mother tongue. For that reason, it was not enough to have one sermon a week in the mother tongue, or even to use the basement of the territorial church on a regular basis. Rather, as Silvano Tomasi has shown for the Italians of New York, these were but the stages that preceded a successful group's establishment of its own autonomous parish.[25]

Not all ethnic parishes were national parishes. For if a certain nationality was first on the scene, and dominant in the area, they simply set up a church which became the territorial church of the locality. Thus, in some rural areas of the Midwest, the local church was "German" even though it was not a national parish. Similarly, a "Polish church" might become the territorial church for a neighborhood in Chicago. Indeed, Jay Dolan goes so far as to say that in New York City before the Civil War the coincidence of ethnic settlement and neighborhood made the distinction between national and territorial parishes "more fiction than fact."[26]

Topping off these complications, there were the Irish. They were certainly an ethnic group like other immigrant Catholics; yet they spoke English, and therefore their parishes were normally territorial rather than national parishes. Their situation was ambiguous and their feelings were correspondingly ambivalent.[27] They wanted "their own" churches just as the others did. And while they could accommodate the presence of a small number of outsiders in their midst, they were put off when the Germans, or Franco-Americans, or Italians, or whoever it might be, became numerous enough to be visible as a corporate body and assertive enough to demand special attention to their needs. But although they were as possessive as other groups about their parishes, the Irish also felt that, since they spoke the language of the country, they constituted the American Catholic norm and that it was up to the others to assimilate themselves to the language, mentality, and outlook of the Irish.

Given all these complications, plus the fact that the same parish might change its ethnic composition entirely as a result of continuing immigration and population shifts, it is entirely understandable that controversy often swirled around the national parish. It was so from the beginning. The first national parish was Holy Trinity in Philadelphia, formed in the 1780s by a group of Germans who split off from St. Mary's, which had previously served all of the Catholics of the city, both English and German-speaking. In its first decade of existence, Holy Trinity went through the pattern that became all too familiar—a dispute with the bishop over who was to be the first pastor, subsequent disenchantment on the part of the trustees with their first choice, his dismissal and replacement, the appearance of still another attractive candidate for pastor, internal divisions in the congregation, a more serious dispute with the bishop, and then into schism for several years.[28]

Since national parishes and trustee-type upheavals so often went together, bishops had good reason to regard them warily. But the arrangement was so obviously necessary to meet the overwhelming pressure for pastoral care of the immigrants that the bishops had no real choice but to employ it. Hence, the national parish appeared everywhere that non-English-speaking immigrants were present in any numbers in the nineteenth century. Contrary to the impression sometimes given, the national parish did not have to be forced down the throats of the Americanizing bishops in the 1880s and 1890s.[29] Cardinal Gibbons and his episcopal allies recognized as well as anyone else that the national parish performed an indispensable function. The point on which they would differ from the spokesmen for the Germans at the time of the nationality controversy was *how long* the national parish would be needed to perform this function.

If there was active opposition to the formation of national parishes, it was more apt to come from the pastors of territorial parishes who were reluctant to see a portion of "their" congregations spin off to establish churches that would compete with the territorial churches for support from the surrounding Catholic population. Pastors of national parishes, for their part, often leveled a charge against the territorial churches that amounted to poaching—that is, they claimed that territorial pastors received into their churches persons who really belonged to the national church, even though they might live within the geographic confines of the territorial parish.[30]

The poaching charge obviously raised the question of how permanently people were bound to the national parish. Must an immigrant always belong to a national parish even if he understood English and found it more convenient to attend the regular territorial church? And what about the American-born children of the national parish, who were ordinarily more adept in English than in the ancestral tongue, except in cases where the ethnic group was unusually isolated? Were they still obligated to attend and support the national church they grew up in?

Here we are back at a question already identified as one of the real issues dividing the Americanizers from those whom we can call ethnic loyalists. And while the desire of the latter to bind the second generation firmly to the national parish is perfectly understandable, it seems to me that the Americanizers were correct in insisting that it should be a matter of free choice with the second generation whether they stayed in the national parish or joined the English-speaking territorial parish. Archbishop George Mundelein of Chicago was the first Americanizing prelate who has been shown to have followed a deliberate policy of holding back on the erection of new national parishes, and even he had to bend on this matter, especially with the Poles.[31] He pushed this policy most vigorously in the 1920s, which was a particularly sensitive time with respect to the Catholic un-Americanism charge; by that date, Mundelein could also argue that the increasing numbers of the second generation made the need for new national parishes less pressing.

GENERATIONAL TRANSITION, THE LANGUAGE QUESTION,
AND IMMIGRANT INSTITUTIONS

Generational transition—perhaps the most profound and poignant theme in immigration history—affected other immigrant institutions besides the national parish.[32] We shall look briefly at how it interacted with three very important ones, namely, the schools, the press, and the network of associations created by each ethnic group.

But first another word about the Irish. Their situation was anomalous among Catholic immigrant groups because they spoke English.[33] Like all the others, the Irish established schools, newspapers, and various kinds of associations. But the fact that they used English affected the development of these institutions in two significant and interrelated ways. First, it meant that they were spared the "language question," the anguishing conflict over the dropping of the mother tongue and the shift to English that normally marked the transition of generations in non-English-speaking groups. Without the language shift, which was a conspicuous barometer of the overall change in foreign-language groups, generational transition among Irish Catholics was both less traumatic and less visible.

Secondly, the fact that Irish Catholic schools, newspapers, and societies used the language of the country made them more generically American and less particularistically Irish. This served to make the transition from Irish Catholicism to American Catholicism both easier and more elusive—elusive in the sense that it is difficult to get a fix on the process and trace its evolution. The linguistic situation of the Irish was thus a significant factor—together with their vast numbers, their early arrival, their unusually high production of priestly vocations, and their experience in voluntaryism in the religious sphere—in making the Irish the dominant group in shaping the Catholic Church in the United States and in predisposing their leaders toward an Americanizing position.

Conversely, the need to resist linguistic assimilation predisposed the leaders of non-English-speaking groups toward an anti-Americanizing position. For although the meaning of Americanization might be ambiguous in some respects, language was not one of them. Here it was brutally clear: Americanization meant loss of the mother tongue with all its precious associations. Hence the language question looms large in the story of the schools, press, and societies of foreign-speaking groups, and the transition of generations was tangled with the inflammatory issue of language transition.

In the case of the schools, preservation of the mother tongue was one of the primary goals of the institution itself. Bound up as it was with religion and culture, language was an integral part of the heritage which German, Franco-American, Polish, and other Catholic immigrants wished to hand on to their children through education. The Italians were a notable exception in failing to exhibit enthusiasm for the establishment of their own Catholic schools.[34] More typical were the Germans who claimed special credit for being more sensitive to the need for parochial schools than the Irish were. Since the aim was to socialize young children into the religio-linguistic culture of the ethnic group, the main effort was characteristically centered on elementary-level schools, but various groups also set up their own colleges and seminaries. It was more difficult to maintain foreign-language institutions of higher education, however, simply because the potential clientele was much smaller than in the case of primary schools.[35]

But besides wanting the schools to bind the young to their inherited culture, the immigrants also wanted them to prepare their children to advance in the new society in which they had been born. That these two goals were in tension with each other became unmistakable at the secondary and collegiate levels. On the one hand, it was clearly desirable from the viewpoint of ethnic-group interests that promising young people receive higher education in order to prepare a leadership elite. But on the other hand it was even clearer that higher education often had the effect of moving the young people who received it "up and out" of the ethnic group. Here generational transition was coupled with upward social mobility and both were keyed to higher education.[36]

The dilemma worsened in the twentieth century as educational opportunities were extended to wider segments of the population, first on the secondary level and then on the collegiate. Although different groups responded in somewhat different ways, the overwhelming trend in the last half-century has been for second- and third-generation immigrant Catholics to pursue the available educational opportunities as far as they can.[37] In doing so, they have become very much de-ethnicized in comparison with the immigrant generation. This came about, not because of any systematic program of Americanization carried out by the schools, but simply because these generations were born and lived in a different world from that of their parents and grandparents—a world made different to some extent by the widened horizons produced by increased educational opportunities.

Unlike the schools, which were developed with the needs of the second generation in mind, the other major immigrant institutions (the press and societies) evolved to meet the needs of the first generation. Among foreign-language groups, newspapers in the mother tongue were an obvious necessity for persons who immigrated as adults knowing no English. Hardly any group was too small to support its own newspapers and magazines, and the larger Catholic groups boasted scores of such publications. The German Catholics, for example, founded some sixty-four daily, weekly, and monthly publications between 1837 and 1937.[38]

The real problems of the foreign-language press came with the maturing of the second generation, for the American-born did not depend on materials published in the ancestral language as their parents did. The second-generation problem was masked, however, so long as immigration continued in heavy volume, since losses among American-born readers were made good by newcomers from abroad. But when immigration from the old country dropped off, a steady decline soon set in. Again, the Germans furnish an apt illustration. Immigration fell off sharply in the 1890s and the next decade saw the beginnings of an irreversible deterioration. The oldest German Catholic paper in the country, the *Wahrheits-Freund* of Cincinnati, founded in 1837, complained in 1900 that the young people would have nothing to do with the "Dutch language," and seven years later it gave up the struggle and closed its doors forever.[39]

The linguistic-generational transition is likewise observable among immigrant societies. As in the case of the press, here also it produced a good deal of bitterness and recrimination on the part of the older generation who regarded their American-born offspring as betraying their heritage. Although understandable, this reaction was somewhat unfair, since the second generation included many who wished to remain loyal to their heritage. The more perceptive of these younger ethnic loyalists were aware, however, that modifications would have to be made in order to retain a hold on those for whom America was the mother country. Thus they could argue with good justification that, far from being a betrayal, the shift to English was the only thing that could preserve the cultural identity of the group and prevent the institutions from dying out with the passing of the first generation. The bilingual phase—the use of both English and the mother tongue in the meetings and publications of an ethnic association—was a sure sign that the linguistic-generational transition was well advanced.[40]

THE ROLE OF IMMIGRANT SOCIETIES AND ASSOCIATIONS

Besides the generational problem, another thing that the associational life of Catholic immigrant groups had in common was the basic role played by benevolent, or mutual-aid, societies. Generally rooted in the ethnic parish, either territorial or national, the mutual-aid society provided a rudimentary form of economic protection from loss of income due to illness or injury. More comprehensive insurance schemes developed when the local societies joined together to form large national associations such as the German Catholic Central Verein (1855), the Irish Catholic Benevolence Union (1869), the Polish Roman Catholic Union (1874), or the First Catholic Slovak Union (1890).

More important than their insurance function, however, was the role played by the national federation as the representative organization of the ethnic group. All matters of interest to the group—such as immigrant-aid work, the situation of the homeland, school matters, etc.—were discussed in the annual conventions, which were sometimes associated with open mass meetings featuring special speakers, musical presentations, and so on. In this manner, the national ethnic federation became a focus of the immigrant Catholic's loyalties and a kind of symbol of the group itself. For the German Catholic to belong to the Central Verein, let us say, or even to read about its doings in the paper, gave him a better sense of who he was and what it meant to be a German-American Catholic. Indeed, Victor Greene, who has done important work on the subject, argues that the origins of Polish ethnic consciousness in America are to be sought in the competing claims put forward by the two leading Polish societies, the Polish National Alliance (PNA) and the Polish Roman Catholic Union (PRCU). Confronted by the two versions of Polishness represented by the PNA and the PRCU, the Polish immigrant had to decide for himself what it meant to be a Pole.[41]

The split between the PNA and the PRCU was between "nationalists" and "clericalists." For the former the political dimension of ethnicity was uppermost and the true Pole was one who threw himself into the cause of the oppressed fatherland (which had ceased to exist politically in the

1790s after being dismembered by Russia, Prussia, and Austria). The leaders of the PNA recognized a close connection between Catholicity and Polishness, but they did not regard religion as an indispensable element in their national identity. They welcomed all Poles to their ranks, including liberals or nonbelievers, and although some priests were active members, the leaders refused to be bound by clerical direction in their struggle for Polish liberation. The PRCU, on the other hand, held that one who was not a Catholic could not be a true Pole. It was founded by a priest and tightly controlled by clerics who were deeply suspicious of the irreligious tendencies of the lay-oriented PNA. But the appeal of Poland's national cause for the immigrant rank and file eventually led the PRCU to a closer approximation of the nationalism of the competing organization.

The nationalist/clericalist split played a more prominent role among the Poles than with most other groups, but it was present in one form or another with a number of others. Clerical leaders were alert to prevent their people from being led astray by secular nationalists, and the First Catholic Slovak Union is not the only example of a national federation that was organized primarily to head off such a threat.[42] But this did not mean that clerical leaders were not nationalists themselves. A great many of them were strongly nationalistic. Where they differed from the secular political nationalists was in their understanding of nationality. From their viewpoint, nationality could not be divorced from religion, and neither could movements mobilizing the spiritual allegiance of a people be safely entrusted to any but religious authorities.

Since the clergy assumed so great a leadership role among Catholic immigrants, it is not surprising that another kind of ethnic society found among many groups was the priests' society. And since the priests were quite self-conscious about their leadership function, it was likewise natural that such clerical associations often took a highly militant line in championing the cause of whatever group was involved, asserting its rights, and so on. Thanks to the research of Colman J. Barry and William Galush, we know more about the German and Polish groups than about other priests' societies, but similar associations existed among the Belgians, Dutch, and Slovaks.[43] Even the Irish formed such a society in Wisconsin, one of the few places they felt themselves to be the wronged minority. And a Lithuanian priests' society that was formed early in the twentieth century is still actively engaged in championing the ethnic cause: its vice president demanded at the 1975 "Ethnicity and Race" hearing sponsored by the National Conference of Catholic Bishops that "the American ethnic cultural parish be considered as being of permanent status because of its contributions religiously and culturally."[44] PADRES, organized by Mexican-American priests in 1969–70, is merely the most recent of such ethnic clerical associations which are dedicated to furthering the "religious, educational, and social rights" of the groups they represent. The very name PADRES declares this purpose, for it is an acronym for "Padres Asociada para Derechos Religiosos, Educativos y Sociales."[45]

The Ethnic Present

Mention of PADRES brings us back to the present. Although a full review of the contemporary situation is out of the question, the foregoing sketch of recurring patterns in the immigrant past suggests a few observations pertinent to the current scene.

In the first place, the fact that PADRES was founded less than two decades ago highlights the point that the American Catholic population is not only diverse in origin, but also that its constituent parts stand at quite different stages in their historical evolution. The case of the Spanish-speaking is particularly complex in this regard.[46] For despite the fact that Mexican Americans have deep roots in the southwestern states — being, indeed, the "charter group" in the area — they are, in another sense, among the most recent of large Catholic ethnic groups, since the overwhelming preponderance of the Mexican-American population derives from persons who entered the United States after 1910 and since heavy in-migration is still occurring, mostly in the form of so-called "undocumented workers." Other Hispanics (Puerto Ricans, Cubans, and persons from Central and South America) are even newer immigrants, most of them coming to the United States only after World War II. The relatively late date of large-scale immigration, along with strong reinforcement by continuing in-migration and other factors contributing to their social isolation (of which prejudice and discrimination were not the least important), combined to keep the Spanish-speaking population at the first-generation stage of development until the very recent past.[47] In terms of immigration and ethnicity, one might say that Hispanics are to the American Church in the 1980s what the Irish and Germans were a hundred years ago and what the Italians and Poles were in the early decades of this century.

Considering the relative salience of the mother tongue in the present ethnic consciousness of Hispanics as compared to Italians and Poles, to say nothing of Germans or Irish, drives home the point that *the content of a group's ethnicity does not remain the same over time.* On the contrary, the historical experience of the group — what happens to it over the years — is intrinsic to the quality of its ethnic identity at different points in its development. The history of the group is subject to unforeseeable contingencies which may affect its development significantly, as the First

World War did in the case of German Americans. But despite the limitation arising from the likelihood that unpredictable events will occur, we can gain a modicum of conceptual control over the multitude of factors that affect an ethnic group's development by classifying them into two broad categories: those that are internal to the group and those that impinge upon it from the surrounding culture. In the historical evolution of the group these internal and external factors interact with each other and with the biological constant of generational transition.

The language spoken by the group is an example of an internal factor that affects its development; others are the size of the group, its social composition (skilled, unskilled, etc.), whether its pattern of settlement was scattered or compact, whether its immigration took place within a short period or was stretched over a long span, and so on. For Catholic immigrant groups it also makes a difference whether they tend to produce many or few religious vocations, and whether loyalty to the Church is closely linked to their group consciousness (as in the case of the Irish, Franco-Americans, and Poles) or is relatively less central (as in the case of the Italians). Perhaps the most important external factor affecting group development is the structure of economic and educational opportunity in American society when an immigrant group arrives in significant numbers and when its second generation reaches maturity. It was, for example, very fortunate for the Irish that, having few skills, they arrived at a time when there was a great demand for unskilled workers in a rapidly expanding economy and that the coming-of-age of many second-generation Irish coincided with the opening up of new opportunities for white-collar employment around the turn of the century.[48]

Another important external factor is the overall attitude toward immigration and ethnicity that prevails in American society at any given time. Closely related is the question of whether a particular group is generally regarded in a positive way, is looked upon as less desirable, or is the object of special dislike and discrimination. Societal attitudes on these matters can and do change, and such shifts can influence a group's development significantly, especially if they are translated into changes in national policy on immigration or intergroup relations. Given the diversity of American ethnic groups and the complex interaction of internal and external variables in each case, it is hazardous to generalize about the overall situation. One can always safely say, of course, that things are in transition. In the mid-1980s, however, I think one can go further and assert that things are particularly unstable and that the national state of mind is more than usually unsettled in respect to race, religion, immigration policy, and ethnocultural affairs in general.

A fairly high degree of volatility is a natural, if not inevitable, result of the tremendous social and cultural upheaval we have experienced in the past two decades. Even the most economical listing would have to include the Black revolution, which was followed not only by sharp disagreements over what racial equality requires, but also by new militancy on the part of Chicanos, American Indians, women, and white ethnics; the revamping of immigration policy in 1965, which was followed by an influx of immigrants more massive than we have seen since the era of World War I; and on-going challenges to traditional values in the moral and religious sphere, which were made more traumatic for American Catholics by the changes set in motion by Vatican II. Change on this scale is difficult to accommodate and tends to produce cultural zigzags, or pendulum swings of the national temper.

In the 1970s, American Catholic understanding of ethnicity past and present followed (or perhaps led) the national pendulum swing of feeling in the direction of "cultural pluralism," a verbal talisman that was invoked in ritualistic fashion.[49] This meant that the goal of "assimilation" was rejected with passion; that the "melting pot" was reviled as a hateful symbol for a reprehensible policy; and that "Americanization" became a term of abuse. All claims advanced by ethnics, historical or contemporary, were automatically assumed to be grounded in justice, and liberal Americanists like Gibbons and Ireland, heroes to the historians of the 1950s, were scolded for being cultural bigots or, at best, treated patronizingly for their lack of "pluralistic" understanding. Even during the revival of ethnicity, few except propagandists for the movement itself accepted the extreme "pluralistic" position, but it exerted a profound influence on educated Catholic opinion. Insofar as it affected popular Catholic views on history, it tended, in my opinion, to create new stereotypes at least as misleading as any it displaced. For if it was simplistic to assume that the nationalistic Americanizers were always right in their controversies with Cahenslyites and other ethnic militants, it is equally simplistic to assume that these immigrant nationalists (for that is what they usually were) always had justice on their side.[50]

By the mid-1980s, the revival of ethnicity was over as a surge of popular sentiment and as a self-conscious "movement." Scholarly interest in ethnic history continues, however, and so do the realities of ethnic interaction in contemporary society and politics, with the Hispanics gaining greater visibility on the political, social, and religious scene and with Asians becoming a more significant element. It would be unfortunate if the pendulum swing in the direction of exaggerated "pluralism" were to be followed by an undue reaction in the opposite direction, although the unbalanced interpretations advanced by spokesmen for the ethnic revival require correction. With respect to American Catholic understanding of past and present, what we must try to do is free ourselves from stereotypes both old and new.

As I have tried to show here, recurring patterns can be discerned in the historic experience of the American Church with immigration and ethnicity. But the concrete situation at any point in history is qualified by the number and nature of the groups involved, the internal factors that give them distinctiveness, and the external factors relating to the larger socio-cultural environment within which the action takes place. But the most important point is that real differences of viewpoint and policy preference existed between the different groups in the past, and the same is true of the present. To do justice to these complexities intellectually—to say nothing of devising practical policies to deal with them—we must take seriously the claims of all the groups involved. No one's position should be dismissed out of hand merely by giving it an invidious label—calling it "ethnocentric," let us say, or dubbing it "a product of melting-pot thinking." We must, in other words, pass beyond the shibboleths not just of Americanism, but also of pluralism.

3

IMMIGRANT ASSIMILATION AND THE
CRISIS OF AMERICANIZATION

The essay that follows also grew out of my interest in immigration as a dimension of American Catholic history, but it differs from the preceding one in several respects. For one thing, it was written before the ethnic revival emerged as a distinct movement, and it therefore uses the term "Americanization" more freely than would have been likely a few years later when that concept had become more controversial. Secondly, my purpose in this essay is not to identify recurring patterns in Catholic immigration history, but to apply an analytical model drawn from close study of one group to the overall situation of the American Church in the late 1960s. A word or two about its background will perhaps make clearer what I mean.

This paper was originally written as the opening chapter of a book containing essays by scholars in various fields, each of whom dealt with some aspect of American Catholicism in transition.* The book came out when the postconciliar turmoil was at its height (in 1969), and my aim in the first chapter was to provide a general interpretation of the situation based on what I had learned about American Catholicism from studying its history and from observing the current scene. Just before undertaking this project, I had revised for publication my dissertation on the German-American Catholics, a task that plunged me once again into the intricacies of that group's historical development in the opening decades of the twentieth century. As I worked my way through those materials in the mid-sixties, it dawned on me that the struggles of the German Catholics to maintain their group identity against the forces of assimilation constituted what we had by that time learned to call an "identity crisis." Having reached

---

*Philip Gleason, ed., *Contemporary Catholicism in the United States* (Notre Dame, Ind., 1969).

that point, I was led naturally to the corollary hypothesis that an analogy might be worked out between the historical identity crisis of the German Catholics and the larger identity crisis of the American Church in the late 1960s. That idea, hinted at in the closing lines of the book on the Germans,* suggested the analytical approach followed in the essay reproduced here, which also incorporates the results of other work I had done on the history of Catholic higher education.

In preparing the essay for publication in this collection, I have made only minor revisions, dropping one paragraph, changing the tenses throughout, and adding a couple of citations. It was written almost two decades ago, and any serious effort to incorporate more recent material would extend its length unduly. As it is, however, I believe the essay provides a good example of the way historical insights may be used to illuminate contemporary issues, even in the midst of dizzying change. I remain convinced that the analytical model employed here is a useful one that could profitably be extended and refined. For the reason just given, I prefer to leave the essay basically unchanged from the form it had in 1969.

TRANSITION IS TOO MILD A WORD for what happened to the Catholic Church in the 1960s. Every day one heard of new crises—the crisis in vocations, the crisis of authority, the crisis of faith, and of course the identity crisis. So great was the turbulence of change that hints of uneasiness escaped even from those in the forefront of reform. Thus the editor of a journal with the bold title *Front Line* remarked on the danger that the baby might be sent flying out with the bath water, and Michael Novak pondered the question of whether Christianity was being renewed or being abandoned. Those of less sanguine temperament were understandably put in mind of Oliver Wendell Holmes's "wonderful one-hoss shay"; for in describing the vehicle that ran perfectly for a hundred years and then fell apart without warning, Holmes was commenting on the collapse of New England Calvinism.[1]

The dramatic shifts in American Catholicism could be analyzed from any number of perspectives, each yielding its own insights. To one who has learned something of the way immigrant institutions adjusted themselves to the American environment, it seems worthwhile to approach the subject in terms of assimilation or Americanization. This approach does not exhaust the possibilities and it may seem to slight the importance of

---

*Philip Gleason, *The Conservative Reformers: German-American Catholics and the Social Order* (Notre Dame, Ind., 1968).

influences from abroad. But if *aggiornamento* refers to bringing the Church into meaningful contact with the modern world, then for Catholics living in the United States it is surely the modern world in its American form that is of primary importance, and understanding the relationship between Catholicism and American culture is a pressing need.

The expression "crisis of Americanization" is new, but it is common knowledge that the Church in the United States has been profoundly molded by the processes of immigration and acculturation. In 1955 Will Herberg's *Protestant-Catholic-Jew* stressed the importance of immigration in understanding religious phenomena and underscored the complexity of their mutual interrelationships. A decade later, Andrew M. Greeley organized his sociological investigation of American Catholic history around the theme of Americanization.[2] The very familiarity of the cliché "emergence from the ghetto" bespoke widespread popular recognition that some sort of assimilation played a major role in reshaping American Catholicism. But it is not really very clear what it means to emerge from a ghetto. Our first task, therefore, is to try to put some substance into this expression by examining just how the processes of assimilation operated with immigrant groups. Having done this we can apply the findings to an analysis of the transitions of American Catholicism.

The Americanization Model

The terms are often used rather loosely, but in general "assimilation" and "Americanization" are understood as designating the processes by which individuals and identifiable social groups shed the characteristics that mark them as foreign, adopt the cultural norms of American society, become fully integrated into American life, and come to think of themselves simply as Americans.[3] "Assimilation," in other words, is a collective name for all the innumerable changes immigrants must make in order to get along in American society—changes in the way they act, talk, and think; changes in the pattern of their interaction with others; changes in the conceptions they have of themselves. These changes take place over a long period of time and relatively few persons who immigrate as adults become "fully Americanized." However, it is axiomatic with students of immigration that the American-born children and grandchildren of immigrants—the second and third generations—absorb American ways more completely and are therefore more fully assimilated.

The typical immigrant is not a solitary individual but a member of one or another ethnic, or nationality, group. These groups, made up of persons from the same homeland and sharing the same language and traditions, are held together by a common consciousness of kinship and are given formal structure by a network of institutions such as churches, schools, newspapers, and various kinds of voluntary associations. Assimilation may be thought of as operating on this group level as well as on the individual level. That is, the changes in habits, attitudes, and values among the individual immigrants—especially in the second and later generations—necessarily affect the group of which they constitute the membership and require corresponding adjustments in the institutions which hold the group together and give it form. Assimilation on the level of the organized group takes place more slowly than, and in response to, assimilation on the individual level, but once it has taken place it sets a sort of official seal on the degree of adjustment that has been made.

The "language question," a perennial issue among non-English-speaking groups, provides a good illustration of the relationship between assimilation on these two levels. As more individual immigrants adopt the English language, institutions of the group such as its press and organizations must gradually make room for English or they will eventually wither and die. The linguistic transition often arouses passionate resistance and bitter disagreement, especially between spokesmen for older and younger generations, but when it has been completed, the language shift constitutes an important reformulation of the modality of ethnic loyalty. If an organization of German immigrants, for example, adopts English in its meetings and printed records, the shift amounts to a kind of official group recognition of the legitimacy of a new way of "being German." What had formerly been thought of as essential to the identity and maintenance of the group—use of the mother tongue—is now designated as accidental. Spokesmen for the group then argue that the "German character" endures in spite of the language change and that those of German descent have an obligation to preserve it and to support the institutions created by earlier generations of immigrants.

Such an adjustment is absolutely indispensable because the institutions of the group are doomed to extinction if they do not keep pace with the Americanization of their clientele. But the need to keep pace with Americanization presents enormous difficulties both for discovering what adjustments are needed and for successfully effecting those deemed appropriate. For one thing, it becomes increasingly perplexing to identify the essence of the group's heritage as language and other concrete attributes of its traditional culture disappear. If assimilation on the individual level proceeds to the point where persons of a certain national descent abandon all their distinctive cultural characteristics, mix indiscriminately with Americans of other backgrounds, and lose all their ethnic consciousness, they are obviously no longer set apart from others in American society by reason of their ethnic heritage. In other words, they are no longer a group of their own. And when the group had been dissipated in this fashion, the institutions which served it can no longer continue on the old basis. They must either go out of business or justify themselves on the basis of some entirely different rationale, making no claims for support in the name of the heritage they formerly embodied and symbolized.

This hypothetically ultimate stage of assimilation is seldom or perhaps never reached, for a lingering sense of ethnic identity is a very persistent phenomenon. A few ethnic organizations may be able to keep going long after the group seems to have disappeared if there remains a remnant of ethnically conscious persons to support them. But let us take the case of a group at an earlier stage in the process of Americanization—a group still clearly recognizable as such, but one whose membership is rapidly becoming assimilated. The institutions serving such a group confront a dilemma: They must accommodate to the changes in their clientele; yet in doing so they must avoid betraying their heritage, for the preservation of that heritage is the fundamental purpose of their existence and the surest ground of their appeal.

A group in these circumstances must tread a narrow and precarious path between the opposing perils of self-isolation and total absorption. Through its institutions, it must find a way of preserving an inherited distinctiveness in American society without clinging rigidly to the past, cutting itself off from society, and becoming irrelevant to the concerns of its more assimilated constituency. On the other hand, the effort to appeal to its more Americanized members by becoming more actively involved in the "mainstream" of society will be self-defeating unless the peculiar heritage and identity of the group is preserved in some new formulation.

The group cannot afford to remain in a ghetto, to use the popular metaphor, but it cannot afford to come out either if emergence from the ghetto will lead to its dispersal, absorption, and disappearance as a group. There is another popular expression which could also be legitimately applied to a group caught in this predicament. It is undergoing an "identity crisis"—a climactic turning point in its development that requires it to resolve the contradiction of being different from what it was in the past, and yet the same. The fact that both of these expressions were widely used in discussing American Catholicism in the sixties suggests that there is a fundamental analogy between what happened to the Church and the general processes of immigrant assimilation. There are, of course, important differences between the Church and what we usually think of as an ethnic group. It is also true that the foregoing sketch is quite schematic and overlooks a multitude of factors that have conditioned the development of the various ethnic groups in the United States. But treating assimilation in this abstract fashion highlights some of the crucial features of the process and throws the central dilemma it posed for immigrant groups into sharp relief. This brief review, therefore, furnishes a "model" of the process of Americanization which can be fruitfully applied to an analysis of the postconciliar ferment in American Catholicism.

Assimilation on the Individual Level

In applying the model, let us begin by surveying developments within the American Catholic population. Our interest here is in assimilation on the individual level. What changes occurred in the life patterns of Catholics that tended to make them less distinctive as Catholics and more like other Americans, in the same way that analogous changes among the members of an immigrant group tended to assimilate them more fully into the national life?

One such change, directly related to immigrant assimilation, was that the Catholic population in the 1960s could no longer be thought of as a foreign population. It would be easy to overestimate the degree of change in this sphere; there are more Catholics than most people suppose who continue to think of themselves as Irish, Italian, Polish, German, and so on. In the case of Spanish-speaking Catholics, ethnicity is still a major constitutive element in their individual and group identity. But despite the persistence of ethnic consciousness in diluted form, the Catholic population considered as a whole was no longer made up of national "hyphenates"— people whose perception of themselves as Americans was qualified by the awareness that they belong to distinctive national minorities.

The relationship between ethnicity and religion is complex. Will Herberg argued that religion had become a sort of residuary legatee of ethnic feeling, with third- and fourth-generation immigrants identifying themselves more actively with Catholicism or Judaism as a means of retaining a link with their ethnic past. Herberg also emphasized, however, that Catholicism and Judaism now stand alongside Protestantism as equally legitimate forms of American religion.[4] And since their Church is considered one of the "three great faiths" of a society in which religion functions as a chief mode of social identification, Catholics are not set apart by their religion as "outsiders" in the same degree they were in the past.

As their fellow citizens grew more disposed to regard Catholicism as an acceptably American form of religious expression, many Catholics —especially the best educated and most forward-looking—became increasingly critical of the strictly ethnic loyalties still cherished in some sectors of the Catholic population. Ethnic cohesiveness and group feeling among

Catholics were associated with resistance to racial integration in cities like Chicago and Milwaukee and were prominently featured in the press, which reinforced the conviction on the part of liberal Catholics that the Church must cut itself free from these vestiges of the immigrant past. In the mid-sixties, Catholics of East-European origin received unfavorable publicity as opponents of open housing, but there were many earlier episodes of conflict between Irish and Negroes, and Irish Catholics were sometimes spoken of as particularly susceptible to racial prejudice.

Before the issue of racial integration drew attention to the unappealing forms that group loyalty could assume among Catholics of other derivations, the Irish were the chief targets for criticism by liberal spokesmen.[5] As Catholic self-criticism mounted in the 1950s, they were blamed for the things critics found most objectionable in the American Church — sexual puritanism, separatist tendencies, authoritarianism, anti-intellectualism, liturgical backwardness, and general conservatism. Since they were historically the most numerous and influential element, the Irish bear a heavy responsibility for the weaknesses as well as the strengths of American Catholicism, and there can be little doubt that much of the criticism was justified. But it is hardly probable that the negative effects of Irish influence were greater in the mid-twentieth century than at any earlier time. Why then did the critique gain momentum only in the 1950s and 1960s, and why did it sometimes assume a stridency that threatened to make anti-Irishism the anti-Semitism of liberal American Catholics? The explanation would seem to be twofold. First, the criticism underscored the inadequacies of immigrant Catholicism and the need to bring the Church up to date in American society. Second, by singling out the immigrant group with which the Church is most closely identified in the popular mind, the critics — particularly those with Irish names — dramatized their own liberation from the immigrant past and implicitly proclaimed their own Americanization.

Another aspect of the assimilation process closely related to the waning of ethnic loyalties among Catholics is their attainment of social and economic parity with American Protestants. From the onset of mass immigration before the Civil War, until the middle of the present century, Catholics were predominantly a low-status, working-class population. Immigrants from Catholic lands in Europe were mostly of peasant background; having little money and lacking the skills suitable to an urbanized industrial society, they came in at the bottom and moved up the status ladder relatively slowly. By 1900 Irish and German Catholics of the "old immigration" were beginning to move into higher-status occupations, but the continuation of peasant immigration from southern and eastern Europe through the middle 1920s brought in heavy reinforcements for the working-class

Catholic population. The Depression hampered upward mobility in the next decade, but the post–World War II era of prosperity coincided with the maturation of American-born generations even among the more recent Italian and Slavic immigrant groups, and these developments brought about a remarkable improvement in the socioeconomic status of American Catholics.

This notable upgrading of the social status of Catholics came about so rapidly after World War II that social scientists only became aware of its extent in the sixties. As late as 1955, John J. Kane, a respected Catholic sociologist, concluded on the basis of data published in the late forties and early fifties that "Catholics creep forward rather than stride forward in American society, and the position of American Catholics in the mid-twentieth century is better, but not so much better than it was a century ago."[6] Twelve years later, however, the authors of an article reviewing eighteen national surveys taken between 1943 and 1965 arrived at strikingly different conclusions. Their research corroborated the popular impression that in 1945 "Protestants in the United States ranked well above Catholics in income, occupation and education." But since then, "Catholics have gained dramatically and have surpassed Protestants [but not Jews] in most aspects of status. A lingering critical difference is in the percentages who have been to college. However, this may be only a residue of lower parental status, and even this difference seems to have disappeared among the youngest adults."[7] Greeley and Rossi's *Education of Catholic Americans* confirmed these findings and showed that the status edge of Catholics over Protestants held even when controls were introduced to prevent the Protestant sample from being skewed by including disproportionate numbers of Negroes or country dwellers.[8]

Just as in the case of immigrant groups, the processes operating to make Catholics more like other Americans — more assimilated — are keyed to generational transition as well as to shifts in the economic and educational structures of society. Hence, Catholics born after 1930 tended to be the most Americanized in their outlook. Those born shortly before that date went through the great common experience of World War II alongside Americans of other religious backgrounds, and took their places in middle-class occupations more or less indiscriminately with their fellow citizens. The postwar boom of higher education also provided a common experience in which younger Catholics shared much more fully than earlier generations. The influence of the automobile and the mass media in bringing all segments of the population together and furnishing a common fund of experience likewise tended to make younger Catholics more like other Americans. The generation entering society as young adults in the 1960s hardly remembered the period of "Protestant-Catholic tensions" in the early 1950s[9] — to say nothing of the Ku Klux Klan of Al Smith days — but they did know that John F. Kennedy was a Catholic who became President of the United States. Those young people had little reason to think of themselves as a minority threatened by the society around them, and they had good reason to believe that they were pretty much the same kind of Americans as everyone else. It was therefore not surprising that they wondered why older Catholics thought otherwise, that they questioned the need for separate Catholic schools or societies, or that they asked why Catholics should take different views from other persons of good will on such matters as divorce or abortion.

Assimilation on the Group Level

Changes in the attitudes and beliefs of the more assimilated younger Catholics brought about changes in Catholic institutions, just as immigrant organizations had to modify their original structures and programs to keep pace with the Americanization of their clientele. Developments among Catholic professional associations provide perhaps the clearest illustration of this sort of Americanization at the group level.

Catholic professional associations historically performed a function closely analogous to that of ethnic societies. Voluntary associations of immigrants came into being because people sharing a common background and common values saw that they could not fit comfortably into organizations already existing in American society. These ethnic organizations not only served as congenial settings for sociability and as agencies of mutual support; they also made it possible for those who had a sense of their "peoplehood" (to use Milton M. Gordon's term)[10] to take part as an organized group in the life of the local and national community. Ethnic associations therefore functioned both as institutional symbols of the immigrants' consciousness of their peculiar heritage and character and as organizational vehicles for their participation in American life. But as assimilation eroded the distinctive consciousness of the immigrants and permitted them to mix more freely in the larger society, ethnic organizations were hard put to keep going, because the needs that brought them into being were no longer felt in the same degree.

The case with Catholic professional associations is very similar. They are a relatively new form of Catholic organizational activity. The oldest one of any importance, the National Catholic Educational Association, dates back only to 1904, and an offshoot in the same general area, the National Catholic Guidance Conference, was organized in 1962, on the eve of the Catholic identity crisis.[11] Catholic professional associations are clearly a result of the professionalization of nearly all spheres of activity in a highly complex urban-industrial society. Those who set up these organizations were no doubt the first generation of Catholics to be involved in these various spheres of activity after they became professionalized in American society at large. Metaphorically, the founders were the first Catholic "immigrants" to these professional worlds. The organizations they created correspond to ethnic societies in at least three aspects. First, they were designed to improve the performance of activities carried on by, and in the service of, a specific social group. Second, this social group was set apart from other Americans by reason of its heritage, which was regarded as affecting the mode of the group's thinking, the position it should take, and the approach it should follow in whatever professional field was involved. Finally, the associations themselves served as vehicles for Catholics to participate in professional activities and communicate with others in the field on an organized basis, especially through the publication of a professional journal.

If Catholic professional associations performed functions analogous to those of immigrant societies, the question arose: Would they face the same problems as their membership became more Americanized? The answer is yes. There had been criticism for some time of such Catholic "ghetto" societies. The remark of a Fordham graduate that he remembered "laughing and crying at the same time" when he first heard of "an outfit called the Catholic Poetry Society of America" was typical of the attitude of Catholic liberals.[12] But it was even more significant that members of these professional organizations began asking in the mid-sixties if there was any justification for their perpetuation. Thus the *Linacre Quarterly* carried an article entitled, "The Catholic Physician's Guide—Do We Really Need One?" A writer in the *Catholic Library World* for April 1967 felt constrained to offer a vigorous defense for the existence of the Catholic Library Association. And only five years after the American Catholic Psychological Association began to publish a professional journal it printed an article calling upon the society to go out of business because it "represents a divisive, sectarian, ghetto mentality on the American scene."[13]

Skepticism about the desirability of such societies was heightened by the postconciliar winds of change, but the example of the identity crisis among Catholic sociologists indicates that the roots of the phenomenon are to be sought in processes indigenous to the American scene. It also furnishes some particularly apt comparisons with the experience of ethnic societies:

The study of sociology in Catholic institutions emerged from a matrix of concern over social problems and reform, and the earliest ventures into the field were by persons primarily interested in social work, social ethics, or moral theology.[14] The prehistory of sociology in non-Catholic universities was generally similar, but it established itself as an autonomous discipline around the turn of the century. Those who founded the American Catholic Sociological Society in 1938 belonged to the first generation of Catholic workers in the field who understood sociology as a subject distinct in inself, separate from philosophy or theology, which had its own proper object and methodology.

But while the first generation of professional Catholic sociologists regarded their discipline as a science, they held that it was "not in the full sense of the word an exact science"[15] because the values espoused by the investigator—his ideological stance or philosophy of life—inevitably colored his approach and the inferences he drew from his data. Sociology as carried on by non-Catholics was not fully acceptable because, although it claimed to be clinically neutral and to exclude considerations of value, it was really based on naturalistic assumptions that were viewed as being an integral part of the scientific method itself. In these circumstances Catholic sociologists felt that their position was denied a hearing in the existing professional organizations. They believed that by establishing their own society they could not only work more effectively to improve the teaching of sociology in Catholic schools, but could also provide a forum in which sociological investigations carried on within the framework of Catholic beliefs and values might be brought before the public.

The American Catholic Sociological Society thus began its career in the late thirties with the explicit determination to erect a "Catholic sociology" combining scientific methodology with the value system derived from religion. By the 1950s, however, there was growing dissatisfaction with this approach among the society's members. There was demand for greater scholarly competence—in keeping with the prevailing self-criticism of Catholic intellectual life in those years—and there was also some complaint about the unprofessional management and familial type of control exercised by the group's leaders. Two other factors are of special interest because they illustrate the trends of assimilation and social acceptance at work generally by midcentury. First, more young Catholics entered the society who had been trained in the leading secular graduate schools or in Catholic universities where sociology had become a fairly autonomous discipline, pursued in up-to-date fashion. These people had absorbed the viewpoint and approach characteristic of their speciality, and they chafed at what they considered the narrow and self-isolating stance of the organization. Second, the younger Catholics could point out that sociology was no longer dominated by the uncritical acceptance of naturalistic assumptions. There was increasingly wide recognition of the important role played by values in sociological investigation; hence Catholics were not automatically barred from gaining recognition in the profession simply because they operated within a religiously derived value system. Moreover, it was sometimes asserted, the values of Catholics did not differ importantly from those of other scholars in their implications for sociological study. For these reasons, the dissidents felt that a Catholic sociological society on the old basis was no longer justified, and they rejected the notion that there could be such a thing as "Catholic sociology." Rather, sociology had to be pursued as a fully autonomous discipline, with each scholar applying normative criteria worked out from a personal synthesis of his or her own fundamental philosophical or religious beliefs and professional knowledge.

By 1961, discontent arising from these sources led to the replacement of Executive Secretary Ralph Gallagher, S.J., who had been the principal founder of the organization and a leading exponent of "Catholic sociology." Those who championed a more autonomous professional approach were then free to reshape the Catholic Sociological Society in keeping with their views. Although some felt it should disband, what actually occurred was a reorientation of its activity and goals. At a meeting in 1963, the members voted to change the name of their organ from *American Catholic Sociological Review* to *Sociological Analysis* and to make it a journal specializing in the sociology of religion. An introductory statement in the first issue of the rechristened journal indicated that the change was the evolutionary result of two developments. First, the realization that Catholic sociologists found their proper professional lodgment in organizations differentiated according to their specialized interests rather than in a society organized on the basis of religion alone. Second, the recognition that the sociology of religion was an area of common concern to many members of the society and thus offered the most satisfactory rationale for its existence as a scholarly association. The name *Sociological Analysis* was chosen to avoid giving the impression that it was "a parochial journal" or one whose pages would present "a distinctly 'Catholic sociology.'"[16]

Catholic sociologists naturally had a sophisticated awareness of the identity crisis through which their organization was passing. Many quite possibly foresaw that the forces unleashed by the Council would carry the transformation of the society even further. But the main point is that the identity crisis itself took place earlier than, and independent of, Vatican II. The society weathered the crisis of the immediate postconciliar years fairly well. By making the study of the sociology of religion its *raison d'être,* it had formulated a new identity which incorporated meaningful links with the past while at the same time justifying its existence on strictly professional grounds. This evolution in the American Catholic Sociological Society is strikingly similar to the experience of certain ethnic societies. It was brought on by the assimilation of the society's individual members in the surrounding American milieu (in this case, the milieu of academic sociology in the United States), and by their gradual loss of the conviction that their heritage entailed an intellectual standpoint different from that of those outside the group. These internal changes, combined with declining external hostility, required the society to find a new rationale—one that maintained some continuity with the organization's distinctive heritage, but at the same time appealed to the interests of its more assimilated members.

This thumbnail history reveals that Americanization involves a basic intellectual reorientation as well as social and institutional shifts. The same fact is demonstrated even more clearly in the case of the American Catholic Philosophical Association. The identity crisis of the philosophers was not as far advanced as that of the sociologists at the time of the Council, and it was more strongly influenced by the general reorientation of Catholic thinking brought on by that great event. Moreover, the teaching of philosophy in Catholic institutions had always been more intimately related to European currents of thought than was the case with other academic disciplines. (Twenty-five percent of the Ph.D.'s teaching philosophy in Catholic colleges in the mid-sixties earned their degrees in Europe, as compared to less than 10 percent of those teaching in other American schools.) Yet the Catholic philosophers were moving appreciably closer to their counterparts in secular universities, and the existence of an identity crisis was confirmed by the title of the presidential address delivered before their society in 1967: "Who Are We?"[17]

In this address, a gem of sympathetic yet incisive criticism, Ernan McMullin pointed out that the founders of the American Catholic Philosophical Association in the 1920s had unbounded confidence that Thomism, the "official philosophy" of the Catholic Church, furnished a solution to problems in every sphere of thought and provided "a corrective to the anarchy and confusion prevailing in the modern intellectual world." That audacious optimism had been shattered, resulting in what McMullin called a "massive failure of confidence" on the part of many Catholic philosophers. Although it was a tragic mistake to impose a "philosophy by decree," McMullin argued that because of the special place of the subject in their colleges Catholics still had "a unique opportunity to make philosophy a living and important part of a college curriculum, an opportunity which scarcely exists in any other part of the academic world today."

In looking toward a new rationale for the American Catholic Philosophical Association, McMullin made two observations that pointed in what might legitimately be called an Americanizing direction. First, he noted that in formulating new goals and strategies, Catholic philosophers must keep in mind the characteristics of their "constituency"—the American undergraduate, whose resistance to having a ready-made philosophical system forced upon him was one of the main elements in "the rapid change now going on in the philosophy curriculum of Catholic colleges." Second, McMullin suggested that the goals of the organization might better be attained if Catholics were "to seek allies . . . among other philosophers who are concerned with the implications and demands that Christian faith lays upon the reflective believer in every age." In the future, the American Catholic Philosophical Association might well designate itself by the "perhaps philosophically more relevant title, 'Christian.'"

Ideological shifts and redefinitions in self-conception like those traced in these two professional associations could be discerned almost everywhere on the American Catholic scene. Just as the American-born descendants of immigrants tended to depart from traditional patterns and take their ideas and values from their social milieu, Catholics in the 1960s were orienting themselves to new reference groups and taking their values from new sources. This sort of Americanization could take puzzling or paradoxical turns — as when Catholics adopted the then-prevailing anti-Americanism of the Left — but basically it reflected the acceptance by Catholics of the norms of whatever segment of American society they felt closest to by reason of social and educational background, status aspiration, political preference, or ideological persuasion. The editors of *Commonweal,* for example, were disturbed that non-Catholics whom they respected criticized the magazine's stand on abortion.[18] One of them, Daniel Callahan, had earlier made the point, in connection with the theme of honesty, that as soon as an idea gained currency among Protestants it was very shortly taken up by Catholics. The hidden spring of new currents of thought among both Protestants and Catholics, according to Callahan, was "the contemporary world," which was reshaping the consciousness of modern man.[19]

Although the influence of the world upon the Church was anything but new, the effects of that influence were perhaps more far-reaching and deeper than at any earlier moment in the history of American Catholicism. Institutions that seemed immune to change — such as religious communities — felt the shock waves, and a general crisis of identity left Catholics wondering who they were and where they were headed. An examination of the controversy over Catholic intellectual life offers one way of approaching that crisis of confidence.

The Course of the Catholic Intellectualism Debate

It is quite obvious that the Catholic-intellectualism discussion ran parallel to, and was no doubt influenced by, the same sort of discussion in American society at large. The evils of anti-intellectualism and "mass culture" were staples of highbrow journalism in the 1950s when the Catholic controversy got under way in earnest. When the center of interest shifted to issues of higher education, a close correlation remained between the special Catholic concern and the general American preoccupation with the problems of the multiversity, student unrest, the dissenting academy, and so on. But while it was only a subspecies of the larger phenomenon, the intellectualism controversy had a special significance for Catholics and may be thought of as the first major phase of the transformation of American Catholicism.

The beginning of the great debate may be dated from the fall of 1955, when John Tracy Ellis's "American Catholics and the Intellectual Life" was published in *Thought*.[20] This thirty-seven page essay, which was reprinted in book form the following year, provoked a greater reaction than any other piece of comparable length in the history of American Catholicism. A collection of readings—*American Catholicism and the Intellectual Ideal,* compiled by Frank L. Christ and Gerard E. Sherry[21]—contains excerpts from forty-six books and articles appearing between 1955 and 1958. But while Ellis's article provided the spark for the explosion of critical writing, Catholics were far from unconcerned before 1955. Christ and Sherry's collection contains treatments of the subject that go back a century; more than two-thirds of their selections appeared before the publication of Ellis's essay. It was only in the 1950s, however, that assimilation had brought the Catholic community to the point where its intellectual status and prestige was a matter of sufficiently general interest to become the central issue in American Catholic life. A problem that previously seemed pressing to only a minority now occupied the attention of all thinking Catholics.

The controversy eventually took a turn that really was new, but it also included several themes that had already become standard. Three of these—the leadership theme, the prestige theme, and the missionary theme (to give them names)—share the basically apologetical orientation that had dominated earlier discussions. Although writers who stressed these themes no doubt appreciated the intrinsic value of intellectual activity, they focused principally on the role of intellectual work and achievement in advancing the mission and standing of the Church. In emphasizing the instrumental values of education, scholarship, and intellectual accomplishments, these Catholic writers were adopting the same position taken by spokesmen for immigrant groups. For these groups also realized they needed an elite who could provide leadership, and they developed schools, colleges, and various types of scholarship programs to help produce such an elite.[22]

One early example of the leadership theme was quoted by Monsignor Ellis: the plea of Archbishop John Ireland that Catholics strive to become leaders in intellectual circles.[23] Carlton Hayes agreed that "a large and vigorous intellectual class" was needed before Catholics could "influence profoundly the life and thought of America"; the statement of the American hierarchy in 1948 confirmed the point that "our institutions of higher learning are the natural training grounds for Christian leadership"; John J. Cavanaugh's widely quoted question of 1957 — "Where are the Catholic Salks, Oppenheimers, Einsteins?"—was taken from an address entitled "American Catholics and Leadership" and illustrates the persistence of the theme in the post-Ellis controversy.[24]

The absence of Catholic leaders was often associated with the question of Catholic prestige — or rather, the lack of it. Ellis opened the main body of his essay with Denis Brogan's remark that "in no Western society is the intellectual prestige of Catholicism lower" than in the United States. The remainder of the essay was devoted to explaining how this situation had come about. Earlier writers had also linked the need for scholars with the fact that the Church was "sadly lacking her share of top-ranking names in literature, the arts, and especially in science." A *Commonweal* author said in 1945, "Scientific research on the part of Catholics is the *sine qua non* for the attainment of Catholic status in this highly significant field of human endeavor." And one of the contributions to John A. O'Brien's 1938 volume *Catholics and Scholarship* was unabashedly entitled, "Enhancing Catholic Prestige."[25] Nowhere was the apologetical intent more frankly avowed than in Archbishop John T. McNicholas's preface to this volume. He wrote:

> Catholic Apologetics in our country at the present moment has two aims: first, to show that there is no conflict between science and religion, that Truth is one, and that the Church . . . welcomes truth in whatever field of research; second, to correct the false judgment which reputed scholars and their prejudiced followers have passed upon Catholicism because of their failure to view culture, philosophy, and science in true perspective.[26]

Implicit in the second aim listed by McNicholas is the belief that there is a Catholic perspective on "culture, philosophy, and science" which secular scholars lack, but which is necessary for the fullness of knowledge and the integrity of truth. This assumption coincides with what I have called the missionary theme. Treatments stressing this theme are usually without the pragmatically apologetical tone of those emphasizing leadership and prestige, but they relate learning to the Church's redemptive mission. Christopher Dawson, for example, whose ideas were discussed with some excitement in the 1950s and made the basis for curricular experiments, argued that the study of Christian culture is not something that benefits only Catholics but something that could serve to unify intellectual discourse in the Western world.[27] Other writers, such as Leo R. Ward, C.S.C., and Justus George Lawler, stressed that, while learning is worthwhile in itself and must be sought for its own sake, possession of the Catholic faith provides an added dimension without which the scholar is unable to encompass the full depth and breadth of reality.[28] According to this view, Christian learning or Catholic scholarship is needed to bring adequacy of understanding to the community of intellect. John Courtney Murray, S.J., one of the most eminent spokesmen for this position, put it rather strongly in saying that the role of the Catholic university is "to be the point of departure for a missionary effort out into the thickening secularist intellectual and spiritual milieu."[29] There is a suggestion of the same theme in the closing exhortation of Ellis's article, which takes note of the reawakened national interest in religious and moral values and calls upon Catholics to seize the "unique opportunity" to bring before the intellectual community the riches of "the oldest, wisest, and most sublime tradition of learning that the world has ever known."[30]

The traditional leadership, prestige, and missionary themes persisted in the 1950s, but the discussion soon moved beyond them. The effort to uncover the reasons for the lamentable intellectual record of Catholics and their failure to exert influence on American culture proportionate to their numbers led to a much more searching critique. When "the real culprit," in Daniel Callahan's words, was identified as "the American Catholic mentality,"[31] it followed that improvements in the intellectual sphere could be achieved only by basic changes in the patterns of Catholic life and thought.

But while the controversy broadened out to include practically all facets of Catholic life, the state of intellectual endeavor and the quality of Catholic schools remained important focal points. It was in the context of debate on these matters that a number of general weaknesses were first subjected to heavy criticism. Thus, in calling attention to the unfortunate effects of formalism, authoritarianism, clericalism, moralism, and defensiveness, Thomas F. O'Dea described these attitudes as "the basic characteristics of the American Catholic milieu which inhibit the development of mature intellectual activity. . . ."[32] On this account, those who committed themselves to a radical reordering of Catholic attitudes and values acquired a vested polemical interest in the finding that Catholics were anti-intellectual and that their schools were inferior. Since the woeful condition of Catholic intellectualism confirmed the need for drastic change, improvements in the intellectual sphere could hardly be admitted before drastic change was accomplished. This consideration makes more understandable the otherwise puzzling fact that some "self-critics" were quite reluctant to accept research that indicated a noticeable amelioration of Catholic intellectual life. Likewise, the sociological explanation of Catholic inferiority did not commend itself to some, because if immigrant background and lower-class status were primarily responsible, the situation could be expected to correct itself in time and the need for a purposefully executed reconstruction of Catholic life would be lessened.

The reaction to Andrew M. Greeley's investigation of the career plans of Catholic college graduates is very suggestive in this connection.[33] Although the failure of proportionate numbers to enter upon graduate studies had previously been offered as evidence of Catholic intellectual backwardness, Greeley's finding that Catholics were adequately represented in graduate schools in the 1960s was dismissed by some as irrelevant to the question of Catholic anti-intellectualism. Thus, John D. Donovan argued that the subjects of Greeley's study probably lacked the "free-wheeling, critical, creative, and speculative bent of mind that marks the intellectual," being instead merely "'intelligent' graduates of collegiate population." And James W. Trent implied that these young people would be "authoritarian, intellectually docile graduate student[s]" who would "contribute little more to the flow of intellectuality and creativity than the ordinary high-school graduate."[34]

These objections highlight a fundamental ambiguity that ran through the discussion. The nub of the difficulty was: What do terms like "intellectual," "intellectualism," and "anti-intellectualism" really mean? Not only was there no universal agreement on definitions, but the vagueness of the terminology was such that it was frequently impossible even to specify the points of disagreement. Donovan and Trent seemed to think that the term "intellectual" should be reserved to persons who engage more or less habitually in a certain restricted variety of mental operations. According to this view, the Catholic-intellectualism problem could not be overcome until there were considerably more Catholics who engaged in this sort of mental activity. Greeley, on the other hand, accepted the fact that more Catholics were pursuing postgraduate degrees and planning careers in scholarship as evidence of improvement in Catholic intellectual life. His position assumed that graduate work and professorial careers necessarily involve intellectualism, without any need to establish the freewheeling, critical, creative, and speculative qualities of mind that Donovan and Trent would insist on.

While concepts like intellectualism and anti-intellectualism remained nebulous, a significant development took place between the mid-1950s and the mid-1960s. At first, most writers accepted the premise that although Catholics had made a poor showing as scholars and scientists they could do better simply by trying harder; no inherent incompatibility was posited between being Catholic and being an intellectual. As the controversy waxed, however, more and more Catholic attitudes and patterns of life and thought were listed as obstacles to intellectualism. In order to make a real intellectual breakthrough, it appeared that many things traditionally associated with Catholicism would have to be eliminated. This trend culminated in the affirmation that prior commitment to a dogmatic religious position could not be reconciled with "love of intellectuality for its own sake." In other words, true intellectualism was defined in such a way as to exclude religious commitment. To operate as an intellectual, the Catholic would have to set aside doctrinal beliefs. The notion that a person might legitimately employ his intellect — as an intellectual — to explicate or defend the Church's position was rejected by Edward Wakin and Joseph F. Scheuer in their book dealing with the "de-Romanization" of American Catholicism. The expression "intellectual apostolate," they wrote, is "a contradiction in terms"; the exhortation to Catholics to take it up "threatens to subvert the intellectual and turn him into a holy panderer for the Catholic Church."[35]

What happened, in short, was that a campaign which was intended to increase the number of Catholic intellectuals had reached the point of denying that there could be such a thing as a Catholic intellectual. Not everyone who wrote on the subject accepted this conclusion; indeed, it was not even spelled out in its fullest rigor, although it was logically entailed in the line of reasoning adopted by Wakin and Scheuer. It also corresponded to the progression we have already traced in connection with "Catholic sociology" and to the analogous conclusion that there could be no such thing as a Catholic university.

The performance of the Catholic university had always occupied an important place in the intellectualism controversy. The question of scholarship is intrinsic to the university, and most of the other matters touched on in the debate — the role of the layman, clericalism, paternalism, social divisiveness, and so on — had a bearing on the functioning of Catholic colleges and universities. Moreover, the faculty and students in Catholic institutions of higher education constituted an increasingly large and articulate group with a personal interest in the outcome of the controversy. For all these reasons, which were dramatized by several spectacular eruptions over academic freedom, the discussion of Catholic intellectual life tended in the sixties to become a discussion of Catholic higher education.

As the debate evolved along these lines, Catholic higher education itself was reshaped by a number of changes. Enrollments more than doubled after World War II; the social and educational background of students was much higher than in previous generations; lay faculties grew and had better professional preparation; graduate schools dedicated to research set the tone in the better institutions; new patterns of administration and policy-making were introduced looking to the reduction, or elimination, of control by nonacademic religious authorities. These changes brought about a marked improvement in the academic quality of Catholic higher education, but they also had the effect of making Catholic colleges, and especially universities, more like other American institutions of higher learning. These improvements in quality, along with closer approximation to secular norms, inevitably raised the question: What is it that is specifically Catholic about Catholic colleges and universities?[36] Bernard Shaw's dictum that a Catholic university is a contradiction in terms was widely invoked; John Cogley, to whom the Catholic university was as outmoded as the Papal States, paraphrased Gertrude Stein in insisting that a university is a university is a university.[37] Contrary to the expectation of many who called for improvements, upgrading the Catholic university had not solved the problem; rather it uncovered the deeper problem of whether there was any justification for a Catholic university, regardless of how good it might be.

If this was an identity crisis, it was equally a crisis of assimilation. In the case of immigrants, it was precisely the identity of the group that was at stake in the process of assimilation. Like the spokesmen for immigrant nationalities, the early writers on Catholic intellectual life took it as a given fact that Catholics were a distinctive group with a distinctive outlook on the world. As such, they needed to train leaders who could expound their position and win recognition for it. Leaders were also needed to explain to the members of the group just what their position was, how it might be applied to the problems of life, and where it should be modified in keeping with changing circumstances. Catholic colleges and universities seemed so obviously the appropriate institutions to perform these functions that no one ever thought of challenging them to justify their existence. Earlier generations of Catholics were critical of the weaknesses of their colleges, but they never really doubted that such institutions had a vitally important role to play.

In the mid-sixties, however, assimilation had brought the Catholic population to the point where it differed only marginally from American society at large. Catholic scholars in various disciplines were discarding the belief that their faith dictated an approach different from that of non-Catholic workers in the same fields. Leading Catholic universities accepted the model of outstanding secular institutions, pledging their readiness to "pay any price, break any mold" in their pursuit of academic excellence."[38] Only a small minority demanded the outright secularization of Catholic higher education,[39] but the general trend was clearly in that direction. Those still convinced of the value of Catholic higher education and the need for Catholic universities found themselves increasingly perplexed at the rising clamor of demands that they explain the grounds of their conviction.[40] In the past, the need for Catholic universities had been an *assumption* — an assumption that arose from the consciousness on the part of Catholics that they were "different," a distinctive group whose needs could be met only by institutions that corresponded to their own unique character. Now the assimilation of the Catholic population and the acceptance of secular American norms by Catholic scholars and institutions of higher learning had eroded the social reality which made that assumption seem inevitable and right. Those who still believed that Catholic higher education was necessary and valuable could no longer regard their belief as a premise of action whose validity was beyond question. Rather, they were called upon to bring their assumptions up to the level of conscious analysis, explicate them, and demonstrate their validity to the world.[41]

This sort of task is never easy, for what is at issue is a people's basic understanding of who they are and what it is that makes them what they are. But when the experience of a people forces upon them the consciousness that they no longer are what they once were, yet leaves them uncertain as to their present identity, the task can hardly be avoided. Whether American Catholic intellectuals and educators could accomplish the task successfully was an open question.

The Ambiguities of Americanization

The developments reviewed here correspond closely to the Americanization model sketched earlier. Assimilation on the individual level not only brought Catholics abreast of their fellow citizens in respect to social and economic status, it also resulted in a new self-conception for those who increasingly adopted the attitudes and beliefs prevailing in secular society. These changes in the social composition and outlook of the group required a reshaping of Catholic institutions to bring them into line with the shifting configuration of the clientele whose needs they serve and whose values they symbolize and embody. A number of these institutional and ideological changes were already under way before Vatican II, but the loosening of traditional patterns set in motion by the Council vastly accelerated the general tendency. All the old beliefs and patterns of action were called into question; all the old institutions were challenged to justify themselves afresh and demonstrate their relevance to the new situation.

When an immigrant group reached an analogous stage in the process of assimilation, the challenge faced by its institutions — and by the group as a whole—was to find some middle way between the opposing perils of self-isolation and total absorption. Rigid adherence to traditional attitudes and structures condemned the group and its institutions to slow extinction. But unreservedly embracing the norms and values of the dominant culture was tantamount to admitting that the group stood for no values of its own worth preserving, that it had nothing distinctive to bring to the larger culture, that it was prepared to confess its spiritual destitution and submerge itself in the "mainstream" of society.

This was the kind of Americanization crisis that confronted the Catholic Church in the United States. Far-reaching changes were needed to bring the Church into line with modern society and culture and to accommodate to the new mentality gaining ground among Catholics. But it is cruelly difficult to make such changes while at the same time preserving an underlying continuity with the past, preventing the loss of identity, and maintaining minimal cohesiveness within the Catholic community. One of the principal problems of the day was to form an adequate idea of what was happening, and especially to grasp clearly the dialectical relationship of the demands and dangers of a situation in which the Church must maintain identity without isolation and achieve relevance without absorption. To judge from the contemporary literature, the ambiguities of this situation were not very well understood; indeed, the terms in which the discussion was usually carried on tended to conceal the problem rather than to clarify it.

Consider for example, the metaphor of "the mainstream." Lionel Trilling pointed out many years earlier that the expression "main currents in American thought" was misleading because it tended toward monism and obscured the fact that culture is a dialectical process involving confrontation and interchange between differing or opposed ideas and values.[42] In the sixties, the Church was regularly admonished to plunge into "the mainstream" and make itself "relevant." Presumably it would not have become particularly relevant if it did nothing more than float with the tide. Yet spokesmen for the mainstream policy had little to say about the distinctive additions the Church might make to the mainstream. Nothing that characterized the Church in its "ghetto" days was acceptable; rather the implicit message seemed to be that the Church should "get with it" by conforming itself completely to the prevailing currents of American society. It was equally unclear what "openness" required, but it might be interpreted to mean that a Church that was "completely open" had no character of its own and must take its substantive content from sources outside itself. And did it not imply something quite similar to say that the only way for the Church to be Catholic with a capital C is to be catholic with a small c?

A theologian writing at the time stated flatly that "There is in fact *no* opposition between what is temporal and what is spiritual and eternal."[43] Were Catholics then to conclude that the world in which they found themselves was sufficient unto itself and that the Church had no unique message to bring to it, no standpoint of its own from which the world could be brought under judgment? If this conclusion were to be accepted, one would have to say that Catholicism emerged from its ghetto with nothing specifically its own to contribute to American society. According to that view, the Catholic identity would be nothing but the natural accretion of the history of certain social groups, built up by their common past and sustained by purely temporal institutions that came into being in the ordinary course of human affairs. This sort of Catholic identity would not differ essentially from the Germanness of German immigrants, or the ethnic identity of any other nationality group. It would amount to nothing more than another kind of tribalism. How ironic it would be if American Catholic reformers, who began with the determination to eradicate the vestiges of ethnic tribalism from their Church, found themselves at the end with nothing to cling to but a new kind of tribalism! Yet Rosemary Ruether suggested this line of reasoning when she wrote that "the terms 'Protestant' and 'Roman Catholic' should be regarded as statements of our tribal affinity . . . and not statements of our faith."[44]

Few Catholics would have been willing to concede that their Church was a tribal affair. On the contrary, the vast majority of American Catholics, as well as the officially constituted authorities of the Church, would have insisted that it was precisely at this point that the Americanization model derived from the experience of ethnic groups broke down. The classic teaching, as understood at the time, affirms that the identity of Catholics *as Catholics* is of an entirely different order from the culturally generated inheritances that define various ethnic groups. It is of a wholly different order because of something at the core of Catholicism that is *not* purely natural, *not* merely the accretion of the human past. That which specifically defines Catholicism comes to the Church from outside history: It is the transcendant element of divinity which entered decisively into human history through the person of Jesus Christ and has remained present to the world in and through the Church. And precisely because this essential element in the Church is transhistorical and transcultural, Catholicism—and hence the Catholic identity—*can* adapt and maintain itself through manifold historical and cultural changes.

But while the essential dimension of Catholicity is transhistorical and transcultural, the Church must embody itself in time through changing human structures and engage itself in the concerns of persons who live in a variety of shifting social and historical situations, persons whose identity as Catholics becomes closely interwoven with historically conditioned ways of acting and ways of conceiving of themselves. So there inevitably arises a tension—which has always been present in the history of the Church—between what the Church is in its fullest ontological reality and what it becomes in the contingencies of historical existence. Both elements in this polarity are necessary; the dialectical tension between them will remain for as long as the Church and the world exist. What postconciliar American Catholics found themselves grappling with was their own particular form of the classic problem of Christ and culture or the relationship of the Church to the world.[45] Small wonder then that the crisis of Americanization has not yet been fully resolved.

4

CATHOLICISM AND
CULTURAL CHANGE IN THE 1960s

This essay was published only three years after the preceding one, but the national temper was quite different in 1972 from what it had been in 1969. Racial, ethnic, and political passions still ran high; the "long national agony" of Watergate was about to begin, and there was ample evidence of what President Carter later characterized as "malaise." Even so, one had the sense that the crisis point had been safely passed, that the worst of an epoch of turmoil was over. Such was my own personal feeing, and it was shared by colleagues at Notre Dame who participated in a symposium convened to consider the question whether the nation was passing through a period of fundamental cultural change. "In 1972," the organizer of the symposium observed, "the mood of the country was one of relative calm after the dislocations of the preceding years."*

The following discussion was my contribution to the symposium. It reflects my conviction that the nation and the Church had definitely been shaken by a profound cultural upheaval and also my belief that the upheaval had by then abated and that one could therefore begin to sort out what had happened and why. Unlike the preceding essay, which was written while change was in full flood and which tried to analyze the challenges it presented, this one looks back on a process that had, in a sense, run its course and tries in general terms to make a preliminary assessment of that process. It was, of course, written at a moment very close in time to the developments under consideration; because it was so distinctly an essay in contemporary history, I have made only minor stylistic revisions in the version published here.

---

*Ronald Weber, ed., *America in Change: Reflections on the 60s and 70s* (Notre Dame, Ind., 1972), 8.

Brief as it is, this piece of contemporary history illustrates more than one facet of the historian's sensibility, more than one way of using historical knowledge to illuminate the present. The first three sections require no commentary: they constitute a straightforward effort to bring to bear on current issues the perspective of one who has studied the American Catholic past with particular attention to the interaction of the Church and the national culture. The final section—"Romanticism and Crisis"— tries to do something different, and it may be worthwhile to say a word about the historical analogy proposed there.

Whereas the first three sections undertake to identify the forces directly involved in the American Catholic upheaval of the sixties, the aim of the last is to highlight the spirit that pervaded the whole epoch of change. That spirit seemed to me unmistakably romantic. As noted in the headnote to chapter 1, this perception played a role in arousing my interest in shifting Catholic attitudes toward the Middle Ages, and in 1967 I published the article cited there, which argued that romanticism was a powerful force on the contemporary cultural scene. Given this background, it seemed appropriate to add to the up-close historical review presented in this essay a more speculative glance at the broad parallels that existed between the 1960s and early nineteenth-century romanticism. Historical analogies of this sort do not, of course, prove anything. Nor can they be proven valid themselves in any very strict sense. Rather, their value depends on the degree to which they sensitize us to features of one or both of the periods in question that we might otherwise overlook. Whether this particular analogy has that kind of value I leave to readers to decide.

A REAL CULTURAL SHIFT DOESN'T HAPPEN very often. Skepticism about whether one took place in the 1960s is quite natural, especially in view of the rapidity with which cultural fashions came and went in that decade and the one preceding it. The New Conservatism had hardly crested before it was succeeded by the End of Ideology, which was displaced with equal speed by the New Left. In the religious sphere, the revival of the early fifties gave way to the Death of God a few years later. This proved even more ephemeral. With its companion, the Secular City, it was left behind in a welter of new movements—occultism, mysticism, and various forms of millenarian religious revolutionism. Paradoxically, the dizzying pace of change itself seemed to argue that nothing very profound was going on.

Yet American Catholics should be more open-minded than others on this question of a radical cultural shift. They know such things can happen, for their Church went through a seismic upheaval in the 1960s. The most traumatic shocks seem to be over, but there are lingering tremors and the whole Catholic landscape has been transformed. This religious earthquake coincided with the social and political storms of the sixties. Although it had its own distinctive sources and character, the Catholic revolution both influenced the general American cultural crisis and was influenced by it.

The spectacle of the Catholic Church in eruption probably had the most pervasive impact on the general cultural picture. What permanence was left if the Catholic Church could blow up? It was surprising, as Garry Wills pointed out, how many people outside the Church were disconcerted and angered by the crack-up of Catholicism. The importance of the Roman Church as a symbol of permanence and stability was not appreciated until it began to crumble. In doing so it aggravated what Walter Laqueur called "the feeling of confusion, decadence, and disintegration which manifested itself in culture and politics alike" in the 1960s.[1]

The revolution in the Church did more than occupy a segment of the chaotic background of the sixties. It also released the energies of individuals and groups who attached themselves to other movements.[2] Priests and nuns became familiar figures in the civil rights movement. Father James Groppi's open-housing marches in Milwaukee made him, for a time, the most publicized white leader in the Black revolution. Catholic radicals, led by the redoubtable Fathers Berrigan, stole the whole show in the peace movement. Three men who gave a new shape to American politics were Catholics—John F. Kennedy, Robert Kennedy, and Eugene McCarthy. Their relation to the Catholic revolution defies easy summation, but one can hardly doubt that the relation existed. All were in some sense men of the "new politics"; they were also representatives of a novel kind of American Catholicism.

The high visibility of Catholics in public life accounts in part for the unprecedented attention Catholicism won from the media in the 1960s. But it was what was happening to the Church internally that really intrigued Americans. They watched in fascination as the Barque of Peter, now increased to ponderous tonnage, swung around to take new bearings, bustled into the work of trimming ship and dropping ballast, and then was swept by mutiny, fire, and explosion. Well might the *National Review* ask, "What, in the name of God, is going on in the Catholic Church?"[3]

It was a good question in 1965, and is not an easy one to answer, even now. This essay offers some interpretation of what happened to the Church. It stresses the interaction of Catholicism with the American environment; but we must begin with a review of the European background.

Influences from Abroad

As part of what used to be called the Church universal, American Catholicism has closer ties with Europe than any other religious tradition in the United States. The lines of jurisdictional authority lead directly to Rome. American Catholics have been famous for their devotion to the pope, and thousands of priests were trained in Rome. Missionary priests and sisters from Europe were essential to the growth of American Catholicism, and in some parts of the country are still numerous and important. The mass of the faithful are of immigrant stock; many of them cherish familial or emotional ties with various European homelands.

American Catholics have always leaned heavily on Europe for ideas. Philosophy and theology were imported from France in the 1940s and 50s and from German-speaking areas in the 1960s. The tone changed notably between the days of G. K. Chesterton and the era of Hans Küng, but European intellectual luminaries always filled the house on lecture tours in the United States. And back in the days of the post–World War II religious revival, bright Catholic undergraduates read the works of English converts like Evelyn Waugh and Graham Greene, or of French Catholics like Leon Bloy, François Mauriac, and Georges Bernanos.

Practically all the self-consciously reformist movements that grew up among American Catholics in the thirties and forties drew upon European models for inspiration. Catechetical reform, the liturgical renewal, the ecumenical movement, Catholic Action groups like the Young Christian Workers and the Young Christian Students, all had links with Europe. The postwar French "worker priests" were widely admired by Catholic intellectuals in this country. Contact with them strongly affected Daniel Berrigan, even to the point of inspiring his costume of turtleneck sweater, ski jacket, and beret.[4]

Against this background, it is quite understandable that American Catholics were predisposed to respond positively to the *aggiornamento* set in motion by Pope John XXIII. The personality of Pope John, his simplicity and transparent goodness, touched the great mass of American Catholics who had no direct contact with any of the new currents of thought among European Catholics. The American Catholic intelligentsia, who did know something about the ferment of ideas in Europe, were even more enthusiastic about the prospect of updating the Church, bringing it into closer touch with the modern world, opening the windows and letting in some fresh air, as Pope John had said.

No one could have foreseen the forces that Pope John's Council was to unleash. The Second Vatican Council went on a long time. Preliminary work lasted more than two years, and the sessions of the Council spanned three more years. People's ideas and expectations changed. It was a great educational experience for the bishops and their advisers who were present and for the multitudes who followed events from afar, saw the great spectacles on television, and heard or read innumerable explanations—or sometimes exposés—of what was happening.

The Council undertook an immense task—to bring the Church to a new understanding of itself, of its forms of worship and discipline, and of its relation to, and responsibilities toward, other Christian Churches, non-Christian believers, and the whole modern secular world. The various solemn statements of the Council embodying the position of the Catholic Church on these issues are documents of fundamental importance. They mark a historic new departure for Catholicism, the long-range effects of which are still not wholly clear.

But even more important, for the contemporary scene at least, was what came to be called "the postconciliar spirit." The Council shook everything loose. The splits that developed in the ranks of the Council fathers revealed deep disagreements about what the Catholic faith was, and what its implications were, among those who were thought of as authoritative teachers on such matters. The journalistic treatment of progressive *versus* conservative battling demystified the whole proceeding and hastened the polarization of Catholic attitudes. By the middle 1960s some American Catholics felt that the Council had changed everything and looked forward to a rapid actualization of all the new departures it implied. Other Catholics were already visibly uneasy about just how much "everything" included, and fearful lest the deposit of faith be departed from. The great mass of Catholics distributed itself between these extremes, most not knowing what was afoot but prepared to move with the Church.

The impact of the Council was felt throughout the Church, but quite unevenly. In a work published in 1969, for example, a French writer could say that the Church in his country was "calm," while in nearby Holland all was in ferment.[5] By then the American Church was in a state approaching uproar. We must look to the American context to understand why the conciliar spark set off such a detonation.

The American Context

Both internal and external factors were at work in the American context. Developments indigenous to the Catholic group itself constitute the internal factors. The external factors impinged upon Catholicism from the larger arena of national life in the 1960s.

In the quarter-century following the end of World War II Catholics definitely "made it" as members of the American middle class. That sums up the most important internal factors. In 1945 Catholics were distinctly below Protestants and Jews on all the main indicators of socioeconomic status. Two decades later, they had overtaken Protestants, but not Jews, in terms of wealth and occupational status, although still slightly behind in percentages that attended college.[6] Among younger Catholics the differences in educational attainment tended to disappear as well. Special efforts had been made for a long time to upgrade Catholic schools and encourage promising students to go as far as they could. By 1961, Catholics were represented proportionately in the ranks of graduate students.[7]

As Catholics came up in the world so rapidly, they lost their sense of being outsiders. They saw the world in much the same light as other Americans. In short, they became thoroughly assimilated and Americanized.[8] The better-educated progressives were uncomfortable about the vestiges of ethnic loyalty still felt by laggard elements in the Catholic population and for a time the Irish Catholic tradition was made a kind of public whipping boy. At the same time, intellectuals and the liberal Catholic press mounted a sustained critique of "the ghetto mentality" and "separatist tendencies." Acceptance of prevailing American norms was also reflected in embarrassment over the deficiencies of Catholic intellectual life and in the pursuit of "excellence" on the part of Catholic colleges and universities. By the middle 1960s, Catholic professors were asking for full academic freedom, and the institutions in which they taught resembled more and more the standard secular model of the American university.

Assimilation to the norms of modern secular society led naturally to a series of identity crises among various groups of Catholics and the institutions they had founded in an earlier day when their faith had seemed to set them definitely apart from others. What was the point of having an organization of Catholic sociologists, for example, if Catholic sociologists did not differ from other sociologists in the way they studied their subject, taught it, or did research in it? The American Catholic Sociological Society had been founded in the 1930s on the explicit premise that there was such a thing as "Catholic sociology." By the early 1960s, Catholic scholars repudiated that belief.

Such identity crises became commonplace in the sixties. By 1970 virtually every Catholic organization had agonized over whether it had any business existing. Catholic intellectual positions that once seemed permanently established dissolved, leaving even Catholic philosophers, theologians, and moralists feeling that they had nothing distinctive to say as Catholics. What could be observed clearly in these specialized disciplines also happened in a more diffuse way among educated Catholics generally as they asked themselves: "Just what do I as a Catholic believe that others equally well-informed and well-intentioned do not also believe, and what grounds have I for believing it?"

It should be emphasized that this development was under way as a result of indigenous processes internal to American Catholicism even before the Council. But the Council accelerated the movement tremendously. It called into question old attitudes and beliefs and reformulated doctrines hitherto thought of as fixed. Above all, it dramatized the startling fact that the unchangeable Church could change, and was indeed calling upon its faithful to change. This naturally had the effect of reinforcing the disposition, brought on by assimilation, for Catholics to question their habitual assumptions and ask themselves why they were acting as they did.

But beyond that, the kind of changes the Council mandated seemed to be of the same general sort as those brought on by the indigenous processes of assimilation. The effect of assimilation, after all, was to bring Catholics into more intense interaction with the non-Catholic world, and into closer conformity with its spirit and outlook. And one of the main thrusts of the Council—especially in the Pastoral Constitution on the Church in the Modern World—was precisely that Catholics should break away from their old exclusiveness and self-absorption, and go out to meet the modern world in a spirit of openness, ministering to its needs, and cooperating with all the movements for good at work within it.[9] They were not to lose their identity as Catholics in doing so, of course; but just what that Catholic identity consisted in became increasingly problematic.

This brings us to the second general category of domestic influences on the contemporary Catholic scene—the pressures exerted by the ferment in American society at large. This aspect of the situation has been neglected by commentators on the Catholic upheaval, and it deserves much fuller analysis than I can give it here. In a nutshell, this was the situation: Catholics whose old beliefs were severely jolted by the Council were told to involve themselves actively in the world; but the world they were encouraged to plunge into was being torn apart by radical denials of its basic assumptions and passionate efforts to bring about fundamental change. The religious doubts and uncertainties of Catholics, and the confusion that marked the release of pent-up energies, were more than matched by the social and political tumults raging across the land in those days of racial violence, campus disruptions, antiwar protests, street demonstrations, defiance of authority, and the setting aside of traditional norms in respect to sexual behavior and gender roles.

Experiences of this sort interpenetrate one another. We are all involved in each other's spiritual crises, and the sixties were rife with spiritual crises. On the one hand, Catholics heard it said that their Church was corrupt and its leaders bankrupt. On the other, they heard that their country was a racist, imperialist monster, its leaders war criminals. From other quarters sounded the cry: Let us be done with all this! We can build a new heaven and a new earth! The rhetoric of revolutionary politics merged with that of religious prophecy. The tactics of militant confrontation were carried into solemn ecclesiastical assemblies. Gestures of ritual sacrifice accompanied political dissent.

Everything became intermingled, confounded together, chaotic. What could one catch hold of? Some were gripped by a vision, or seized by a passion, and committed themselves to a clear-cut cause. Others stood by in bewilderment, pulled now in this direction, now in that. Some wearied of the hubbub and turned away to cultivate their own gardens. Still others continued to watch in fascination, trying to hang onto something solid amid the clashing winds of doctrine. New theologies came and went like flashes of summer lightning as churchmen strove to read the signs of the times and speak to modern man's condition. When the storm abated, a kind of spiritual exhaustion overspread the scene.

This picture may seem too lurid, overdone. Admittedly, it is partial and impressionistic. Yet the sixties were a decade of frenzied agitation, whose intensity was heightened for Catholics by the merging together of the religious crisis and the society-wide political and cultural crises. Not all Catholics were equally affected, however. The conjunction of forces struck with greatest impact on young people and religious professionals.

Groups in the Eye of the Storm

Almost everything happening in American society in recent years hit hardest among young people, even unemployment. The modern civil rights/ Black revolution began with a Supreme Court decision affecting school-age children, and young people furnished the vanguard of freedom riders and other militant activists. Young men were most directly affected by the Vietnam War; they had the draft cards it meant something to burn. Turmoil on the campuses, the drug scene, the sexual revolution, experiments in aquarian age life-styles — all of these were phenomena primarily centered in the more youthful segments of the population. Accompanying these developments, our traditional national preoccupation with youth blossomed into a full-blown cult of youth. Young people were proclaimed the best educated, most sensitive, most idealistic, most committed generation America had ever produced. The message seemed to be that salvation lay with the young — all power to the kids!

Young people of Catholic background could not help but be caught up in all this. Indeed, given the high Catholic birthrate in the previous generation, there was probably a larger proportion of Catholics among young people than in any other age segment of the population. More of them than ever before were in college, right in the eye of the storm. They were at the point of their personal life cycles where they had to grapple with the tasks of self-discovery and ideological identity formation. Like all young people, they were ripe for experimentation, idealistic, impatient with the past, intolerant of half measures, and a trifle smug about their own sincerity and general virtuousness. Most of them came from politically conservative backgrounds, and were perhaps slower than those from other traditions to move into the forefront of political radicalism. But they moved with the radical tide.

As far as religion was concerned, young Catholics were caught in a real maelstrom. The seas of faith are always troubled for adolescents and young adults, but those who matured in the 1960s encountered a veritable hurricane. They were peculiarly susceptible to all the influences discussed earlier. They were the most assimilated of any generation of American Catholics; the Vatican Council and its aftermath left them without established religious guidelines; the society around them was seething with rejections of the past and new affirmations for the future. No one should have been surprised that many of them failed to practice their religion as traditionally understood, preferred to think of themselves as Christians or humanists rather than Catholics, and sought new ways to meet their spiritual needs, new goals around which to orient a life of service to the good, the true, and the beautiful.

Many in the younger ranks of Catholic religious professionals—that is, priests, nuns, and brothers—were subject to the same pressures that affected all young people. Both casual observation and the available sociological research suggested that younger priests and members of religious communities were most discontented and most likely to resign from the priesthood or leave the religious life.[10] But leaving aside the factor of age, there were two other reasons why clerics were particularly affected by the turmoil of the sixties.

The first was quite obvious: these people were religious professionals; their whole lives were bound up in the Church. Religious concerns were much more a full-time preoccupation with them than with any other group, except perhaps a small minority of Catholic lay activists, journalists, or professional observers of the religious scene. Hence they were the first to be moved by the surges of change in the Church. They were also particularly apt to respond to the moral appeal of idealistic movements at work outside the Church—the civil rights movement, the grape-workers strike, or the peace movement. Indeed, the failure of the official Church to take sufficiently strong action against the evils of our society was one of the most common complaints made by her discontented clerical professionals.

Secondly, because these people were professionals, they were subject to the direct administrative authority of ecclesiastical officials to a far greater degree than is the case with lay folk. Rigid and oppressive authoritarianism in the Church existed largely by reputation for laypeople; but not for priests and religious! A layman, let us say, reads in the newspaper about an arbitrary or stupid action on the part of a bishop or superior of a religious order. He may groan inwardly. He may say to himself, how absurd. He may become indignant. He may write letters or join protests. Yet ninety-nine times out of a hundred, he can continue his activities absolutely as though that act of ecclesiastical authoritarianism had never occurred. This was not the case for the curate who was told to be within the doors at the rectory at 10 p.m.; the pastor who was summarily reassigned; the sisters who were denied permission to engage in some activity they wished to carry on; or the theologian who was ordered to stop publishing on a sensitive topic.

When priests and religious complained of authoritarianism and oppressive structures, they knew whereof they spoke. Hence they welcomed with particular warmth the prospect raised by the Council that greater flexibility, openness, and collegial exercise of authority was to be introduced into the Church. These changes were not just theoretically desirable: they meant that the bosses would have to work within new rules. And when the bosses showed little disposition to create the new, flexible, democratic structures; when they tried to go right back to business as usual, there was bound to be enormous disappointment, resentment, and frustration.

These feelings no doubt played a significant role in the decisions of many of the professionals who resigned their priestly office or left their convents. But the effect goes beyond that, for many of those who stayed simply quit paying attention to the voices of official leadership in the Church and followed their own rules whenever they could. Not everyone did this, of course; yet respect for authority was undermined.

In setting aside the authority of those above them, however, the professionals weakened their own. Why should they be taken seriously as moral and religious guides? By what authority did they pronounce judgment on the pope, the bishops, the American government, or the attitudes of their parishioners? Why shouldn't the laity in the pews set up their own authority against the professionals? It wouldn't be such a novelty either, since the laity were well experienced in enduring clerical scoldings without changing their minds about anything.

A good many laypersons, indeed a sizable majority in all likelihood, were not so severely shaken by all this upheaval as the foregoing discussion would suggest. Most of them went to Mass regularly as they always did, depended on their faith to give meaning to their lives, and sought salvation through it. Yet even in this great mass of traditional Catholics, unsophisticated Catholics, mediocre Catholics, if one wishes to call them that, a sense of malaise was widely diffused. It was perhaps most closely linked with the crisis of authority, which meant, at the level of ordinary experience, a weakening of confidence and an uneasiness about the direction in which things were going, or a vague fear that no one knew which way they ought to go.

Andrew M. Greeley, a consistently knowledgeable and penetrating commentator on American Catholicism, described the early 1970s as "a period of emotional exhaustion." "Powerful currents of excitement, hope, disappointment, anger, frustration and bitterness have swept the Church," he wrote. "Now our energies are spent. We are weary of controversy, of stridency, of the cycle of elation and discouragement which has been typical of the last several years."[11] This description applied to the relatively small Catholic elite who were actively involved in the developments of the sixties rather than to the Catholic masses referred to above. Yet the apathy of the elite differed little in its enervating effects from the vague uneasiness of the masses. The worst of the crisis might be over, but the prospects for creative response could not be called hopeful so long as the mood of numbed indifference continued.

But perhaps the mood was only a fleeting thing, and the energies awakened in the sixties would reassert themselves. Indeed, the phenomenal growth of Pentecostalism, or charismatic renewal, in the Church revealed unsuspected springs of vitality, especially in its combining strong commitment to the ecclesiastical structure with novel forms of religious expression. And the fact that Father Greeley followed up his diagnosis of the doldrums that prevailed in 1972 by sketching out "the new agenda" for the future gave notice that, while he might be suffering from battle fatigue, he was not about to withdraw from the struggle. It was, perhaps, merely a momentary pause for regrouping.

Romanticism and Crisis

Among the tasks appropriate to such a moment the one most congenial to the historian is trying to set the developments of the present in the context of the past. After having tried, up to this point, to do that by reviewing the recent past, I cannot conclude without stepping back to call attention to a parallel with a period more remote in time, a parallel which has application to the overall national cultural scene as well as to the Catholic Church. Developments in both spheres, I want to argue, bore testimony to a profound irruption of the romantic spirit. The 1960s were a new age of romanticism![12]

The terms "romantic" and "romanticism" are vague and uncertain in meaning. Indeed, romanticism has been defined so variously that one of the greatest students of the early nineteenth-century movement, Arthur O. Lovejoy, once argued that the term had lost its usefulness as a verbal sign — it had come to mean so many things that it no longer meant anything at all.[13] Without getting into a discussion of the essential nature of romanticism, I would argue that there are enough parallels between the temper of the sixties and that of the historical romantic period to justify calling the former a new age of romanticism.

Consider first certain broad similarities. Historical romanticism was born in a revolutionary epoch.[14] Its beginnings were closely tied to the French Revolution and the millennial hopes it aroused. We always think of Lord Byron, the archetype of the romantic hero, in connection with the struggle for Greek independence, a fighter for national liberation. Revolution became the watchword of the sixties and had its Byronic heroes in men like the younger Fidel Castro and, above all, Che Guevara. Although quite a swimmer, Chairman Mao was no longer Byronesque; but he was a poet-revolutionary and the symbol of a new kind of exotic *Chinoiserie.*

Historical romanticism exalted poetic vision, the power of imagination, and quasi-mystical intuition over the discursive processes of reason. Feeling and instinct took priority over rational analysis. Romanticism was strongly tinged with an antiscientific spirit, at least insofar as science was thought of in eighteenth-century mechanistic terms. It was anti-urban and abhorred the dark Satanic mills of nascent industrialism. All these attitudes were widely prevalent around 1970, and were given quite explicit statement in works like Theodore Roszak's *Making of a Counter Culture* (1969) and Charles Reich's *Greening of America* (1970). So also the newly emergent vogue of the American Indian corresponded to the vogue of the noble savage that marked early romanticism.

The original romantics were enemies of routine, discipline, and restraints on the individual. They rejected the forms of classicism and the institutionalized patterns of the past. They championed individual freedom and personal authenticity. But this did not mean they slighted the need for mutual concern and fellowship. On the contrary, they were committed to fraternity, and deeply concerned with communal solidarity. It was simply that they depended upon love and brotherhood, rather than external authority or forms of law, to maintain order and coherence in society. Like so many in the sixties, they believed that true community was a natural outgrowth of man's capacity for goodness and love, that it had no need for a structure of authority and officers to enforce it, and that it was perfectly compatible with the utmost freedom for the individual.[15]

Especially in Germany, the romantic longing for community was linked with a consciousness of a people's historic group identity. The German writers spoke of the *Volksgeist*—the spirit of the nation. Historians have emphasized the importance of these ideas in the rise of German nationalism.[16] For our purposes, however, it is more relevant to note the kinship between these ideas and the recent upsurge of ethnic consciousness. Indeed, the new ethnicity is a kind of incipient nationalism. It too speaks of distinctive historical experiences shaping a people's soul—in fact, "soul" is the very term Blacks use to designate their spiritual uniqueness. It dwells on the importance of language: most obviously in the case of the Chicanos, but some writers argue that Blacks too have a distinctive utterance and that white American speech is inadequate to express the genius of their people. Even the contemporary emphasis on recovering the history of American ethnic groups has a parallel in the romantic period when national self-consciousness spurred the collection of documents and the exploration of a nation's heritage.

There are also a number of more specific parallels between the 1960s and America's antebellum age of romanticism. Today's ecologists, for example, share the reverence for nature immortally associated with the names of Emerson and Thoreau. Scholars have stressed the romantic temper of the reform movements of the 1830s and 40s,[17] and it is striking how many of them have had modern counterparts. Abolitionism was paralleled by the civil rights–Black liberation movement. Nonresistance by nonviolence. Opposition to the Mexican War by opposition to Vietnam. Women's rights by women's liberation.

Horace Mann led a crusade to reform American schools in those years, and humanitarians like Dorothea Dix fought for improvement in the treatment of the insane and prisoners. Those movements had their parallels in the era of the counterculture. The resurgence of interest in communes in the sixties was surely the greatest outburst of the utopian spirit since the days of Brook Farm. Changes in style of dress and personal adornment were similar. Beards came back in style in the 1830s and 40s; sideburns followed soon after. The apostles of what was then called "The Newness" also favored Byron collars, loose, flowing outfits, and gay, flowery blouses.[18] These stylistic novelties had their latter-day parallels, and even phrenology made a mild comeback in the sixties. The various occult and mystical tendencies of recent times are reminiscent of the more bizarre phenomena of the antebellum years, such as spiritualism, which swept the country after the rappings of the Fox sisters in 1848. Nor in these days of sexual liberation should we overlook the departures from conventional norms embodied in Mormon polygamy and the "complex marriage" system of the Oneida Community.

We are specifically concerned here with religion, and in this sphere likewise we find broad similarities. The antebellum era was also a time of religious upheaval. Its most obvious signs then were the great waves of revivalism associated with the name of Charles G. Finney. Revivals did not loom very large in the sixties—although in its early days Catholic Pentecostalism resembled the intense evangelicalism of the Finney revivals. But evangelical enthusiasm spread far beyond the revivals themselves in the 1830s and 40s. Indeed, many of the movements mentioned earlier should be understood as offshoots of the religious fervor inspired by Evangelicalism. For the sense of man's sinfulness, his need for conversion, the conviction that with God's grace he could be made holy, all had important social implications. The world itself might be made over by the outpouring of God's spirit![19]

Apocalyptic visions and expectations of the millennium permeated the religious and social scene of the 1830s, firing the efforts of multitudes of reformers. In the upheaval of the sixties, kindred visions of a world made new generally assumed the form of secular social radicalism or revolutionary politics. But there was an underlying similarity of outlook and spirit. And, as I suggested before, the religious ferment of the 1960s was profoundly affected by, and intertangled with, the prevailing social upheaval. Thus it does not seem to me to be straining things unduly to see analogies to the millennialism of the 1830s in the recent theologies of hope, of revolution, and in what is called broadly political theology. Nor would it be wholly fanciful to regard Daniel Berrigan and Philip Berrigan as latter-day counterparts to that prince of religio-social radicals, William Lloyd Garrison.

Obviously, there are vast differences between the romantic past and the neoromantic sixties. The argument is not that history "repeated itself" in any literal sense, or that one can draw precise conclusions or detailed guidelines for action from study of the past. This is expecting too much. It is bound to lead to the sort of disenchantment with history expressed by Martin Duberman, who had earlier hoped to find answers in the antebellum years to America's racial problems in the 1960s.[20] But the similarities between past and present are as real as the differences. Consideration of both serves not only to put the present in perspective, but also to suggest lines of reflection that we might otherwise have overlooked.

In the case at hand, the romantic parallel suggests a number of relevant inquiries. Take the question, "Did America go through a cultural shift in the 1960s?" Might we not pose the counterquestion: Did romanticism represent a cultural shift? If it did, and if one grants a kinship between romanticism and the present, then one must posit an invervening cultural shift in the opposite direction—otherwise there would have been nothing to shift away from in the 1960s. But if cultural shifts occur as frequently as this, do they really amount to more than changes in taste and intellectual fashion?

Cultural fashion or not, romanticism was not final. It was one moment succeeded by others in the flow of human history. The same is true of our own day, our own cultural crisis. This reflection drawn from the comparison of past and present is not without practical significance. It means, on the one hand, that partisans of whatever counterculture is being promoted would be well advised to hedge their emotional investment in its permanent realization and, on the other hand, that champions of tradition might abate their anxieties over the threatened dissolution of precious values and institutions. The task of weaving old and new together is a perennial one, and it requires the collective work and wisdom of us all.

5

THE BICENTENNIAL AND
EARLIER MILESTONES

The bicentennial of independence in 1976 was the kind of occasion when ordinary folk expect historians to have something pertinent to say. And historians, who are as much flattered by attention as anyone else, are happy to oblige by saying something. Any problems that arise in this otherwise mutually satisfying arrangement will almost surely center on the issue of pertinence. The source of the difficulty is obvious—the historian characteristically wants to understand the past for its own sake, while the lay person characteristically wants to be told what, if anything, the past has to do with the present. What seems compellingly interesting to the former may very well strike the latter as remote and irrelevant. This no doubt puts the matter in too-simple terms, but commemorative occasions bring out with special clarity the problematic issue that serves as the unifying theme of these essays—how past and present are related and how they mutually illuminate one another.

In the essay that follows, I tried to meet the need for pertinence, while honoring the historian's obligation to do justice to past reality, by restricting my attention to a very small sample of evidence—four writings produced by American Catholics on earlier commemorative occasions. My strategy was based on the premise that in writing about the past we inevitably reveal a great deal about the present within which we write. Retrospective historical assessments are thus used here in a kind of double way to see how our predecessors tried to learn from their pasts and to ask whether their efforts provide points of triangulation useful to us in understanding our own position in the stream of history.

The essay was written at the request of the editor of Communio *and appeared without footnotes in the Summer 1976 issue of that journal.*

Aside from adding sparse documentation, I have made only minor stylistic changes in the version published here.

WHEN WE MARK A SIGNIFICANT ANNIVERSARY, it is natural to look back and review the experiences that have brought us to whatever milestone we have reached. Piety toward our forefathers invites us to commemorate their struggles and honor their achievements. But commemorative piety, worthy as it is, is not the only motive that inspires such retrospective moments. To tell the truth, we are more interested in ourselves than in our ancestors, and in looking at the past we usually manage to keep ourselves right up front. Sometimes we do this simply by glorying in our progress, by measuring how far we have come from where our fathers stood in the old days. But a backward glance can also serve to drive home a lesson in humility, to chasten our pride, or to requicken a spirit of dedication. Many of the bicentennial activities stressed the latter kind of theme. The major bicentennial project of the National Conference of Catholic Bishops, to cite an example of particular interest here, aimed to reawaken our commitment to "liberty and justice for all."

Another way of keeping ourselves in the forefront of a commemorative review is to ask what the past has to tell us today. But perhaps only a historian fully appreciates just how difficult it is to sum up the "lessons" of the past. No one can really do justice to two centuries of history in a brief article, even in reporting the main lines of development. And this hardly touches the problem of extracting from American Catholic history some insights of value for the present.

But American Catholics in the 1970s were not the first to confront such a problem, and the writings produced for earlier commemorative occasions furnish a body of literature that is not only manageable in size but also particularly revealing in content. To put the bicentennial in perspective let us look briefly at four notable Catholic statements: Bishop John England's address to Congress in 1826, the golden jubilee year of American independence; two essays written at the 1876 centennial by the historian John Gilmary Shea and by John Lancaster Spalding, who was named bishop of Peoria late in 1876; and a "sesquicentennial essay" written by the historian Peter Guilday in 1926.

Bishop England's Address to Congress in 1826

Although given at a time that might seem to us an appropriate occasion for a thoughtfully commemorative statement, England's address to

Congress had nothing of that character.[1] The fact that it was unplanned may partially explain this circumstance. Almost immediately upon his being named bishop of Charleston, South Carolina, in 1820, England's great energy and intelligence, his dedication to republican principles, and above all his splendid eloquence catapulted him to preeminence among Catholic churchmen in the United States. Hence it was understandable that he was asked to speak before the members of Congress and other dignitaries when he was in Washington in January 1826, especially since a Christmas sermon he had given in the capital city had attracted much attention.

In his Christmas sermon, England had taken issue with some statements made about the Catholic Church by President John Quincy Adams; he devoted his address in the chamber of the House of Representatives (for which Adams was present) to an exposition of Catholic teaching and to answering objections frequently made by those who misunderstood the Church's position. He spoke for two hours without a manuscript, only committing the discourse to paper the following week in response to a letter signed by some twenty members of Congress asking that it be published.

Assuming that his audience would agree that all men were duty bound to worship God and to follow His will, and assuming further that they agreed that divine revelation was a reality, England identified the chief point of difference between Catholics and Protestants as centering on the role of the Church as interpreter of God's revealed truth. He therefore explained why Catholics believed that the substance of revelation itself would be dissipated without an infallibly authoritative teaching Church. The infallibility of the Church, however, did not reside in the pope alone, but in the body of bishops speaking in and through their leader, the pope.

After outlining the Catholic position on this basic point of disagreement among Christians, England turned to four persistent charges made against the Catholic Church. Insisting that his purpose was not to engage in polemics but merely to make clear what the Church's position actually was, England proceeded to deny, first, that Catholicism constituted any threat to civic freedom. Just as the state could not meddle in religious matters, the Church's authority was confined strictly to the area of religious truth and the internal discipline of her own organization. "We do not believe," said England, "that God gave to the Church any power to interfere with our civil rights, or our civil concerns." His answers to the second, third, and fourth charges were, in a way, merely elaborations of this point. In them he denied that the Church was antirepublican by virtue of its own intrinsic organizational principle; that it claimed the right to persecute those who differed from its teaching (persecution, he noted sadly, "was taught by no Church; it has been practiced by all"); and finally he denied that the Church claimed the right to depose temporal rulers.

England's discourse thus centered on substantive religious issues. Although he was obviously addressing himself to topics particularly relevant to the American situation, England made no effort to relate his doctrinal assertions to the historical experience of Catholics in America nor did he allude in any way to Catholic participation in American society since independence. Even six months later, in taking note of the "National Jubilee" of independence, Bishop England's newspaper, the *United States Catholic Miscellany* (July 22, 1826), made no attempt to link the history of American Catholicism to the civic celebration. This omission is the more noteworthy since the paper did observe that the deaths on July 4th of Thomas Jefferson and John Adams left Charles Carroll as the last surviving signer of the great Declaration. It was not even pointed out that Carroll was a Catholic and the cousin of the first bishop of Baltimore.

Centennial Reflections by Shea and Spalding

The centennial of independence was celebrated much more self-consciously by Americans than the golden anniversary of 1826. The Centennial Exhibition in Philadelphia, the first of America's major world's fairs, attracted ten million visitors despite the fact that the event took place during a severe economic depression. Catholics were among the millions who trooped out to Fairmount Park to view the wonders of the fair and, as it happens, a large fountain erected by the Catholic Total Abstinence Union was one of the few architectural features of the Exhibition to survive permanently. The occasion also prompted Catholics to reflect upon their own history since 1776 and, like the nation at large, they found ample evidence of progress in the first century of national life.[2]

Sheer growth in numbers and in institutional strength overshadowed everything else. At the time of the revolution, Catholics numbered no more than 35,000; they had no bishop; the score of priests who served them were leaderless, and there existed no regularly established churches or fixed congregations. There was not a single Catholic seminary, college, convent, or monastery in the new nation; the sacraments of confirmation and holy orders had never been conferred on American soil. And although popular feeling was to improve when the American states allied themselves with Catholic France, the Quebec Act of 1774 set off a fierce burst of anti-Catholicism at the beginning of the War for Independence.

A century later immigration had swelled the Catholic population to about seven million, and the organizational structure of the Church had grown apace. The continental United States was covered by ecclesiastical jurisdictions presided over by a cardinal (McCloskey of New York, named to the sacred college in 1875), ten archbishops, and fifty-four bishops and vicars-apostolic. This was but the tip of the institutional iceberg; it rested upon a base consisting of some 5,000 priests who ministered to the faithful at 6,500 churches and chapels, sixty colleges for men and a greater number of academies for girls, thirty-three seminaries, 1,600 parochial schools, and hundreds of convents, hospitals, orphanages, and other establishments.

Two literary events of 1876 signified that Catholics had reached a new level of maturity and confidence. The first was the appearance of *Faith of Our Fathers,* doubtless the most popular and effective apologetical work ever written by an American Catholic. Its author was Bishop James Gibbons of Richmond, who was elevated in 1877 to the premier see of Baltimore where he began the forty-four year reign that made him the most widely admired churchman in the history of American Catholicism.[3]

The second event was the launching of the *American Catholic Quarterly Review* in January 1876.[4] It was an ambitious thing, this journal whose complete run fills forty-nine impressive volumes, and there is an unmistakable note of self-assurance in the first sentence of the "Salutatory" statement: "Our Review, as its name implies, is to be Catholic and American." Yet alongside the confidence, the contents reflect a feeling of embattlement, not merely against explicit anti-Catholicism, but also against the materialistic irreligion of the prevailing intellectual culture. All of these motifs can be found in John Gilmary Shea's "The Catholic Church in American History," which appeared in the first issue of the *Review.*[5]

Although it was later referred to as a "centennial article," Shea's piece was not inspired simply by the historic anniversary. Rather it was prompted by public statements made by President Ulysses Grant on education and the church/state issue which Shea interpreted as being animated by anti-Catholic bias. He alluded in passing to the centennial, but Shea's principal aim was to vindicate the place of Catholics in American life.

Shea was well equipped for the task.[6] Fifty-two years old in 1876, he was at the height of his powers as a historian. While supporting himself as a journalist, he had already written several scholarly works; between 1886 and his death in 1892 Shea published a four-volume history of the Catholic Church in the United States that has never been superseded. The article under consideration here was but the first of almost fifty essays that he contributed to the *American Catholic Quarterly Review.*

After touching on the discoveries and explorations of the Catholic Spanish and French, Shea divided the history of the Church in the American republic into two epochs of a half-century each. The period from 1776 to 1826 was one of beginnings and was characterized, in general, by friendly and harmonious relations between Catholics and their Protestant fellow countrymen. By contrast the half-century from 1826 to 1876 was marked by bigotry, intolerance, and fanatical attacks upon the Church. President Grant's statements indicated to Shea that the country stood on the threshold of another outburst of the "decennial madness" against all things Catholic.

Since he was preoccupied by the wrongs inflicted on Catholics, it is perhaps understandable that Shea adopted a harsh and belligerent tone in his references to Protestantism and its influence on American life. But while polemical and defensive, Shea's approach was also what we learned in the 1960s to call triumphal. His concluding paragraph furnishes a concentrated sample:

> The Catholic Church, first to plant the cross on our soil; first to bedew it with the blood of martyrs; first to offer on it the great Christian sacrifice and administer the Christian sacraments, has a great mission before her. Persecution she expects, injustice and oppression: these are not new to her. She sees in them the tokens of approval. . . . This will not deter her from her path; they will but strengthen and unite. As things are now tending around us, in the decline of morals and religion, the substitution of secret societies for churches, in the war of natural science on faith, it is not rash to assert, that, fifty years hence, the Catholic Church will be on this soil almost the only compact Christian body, battling for the Scriptures and the revealed Word of God, or recognizing Him as the Creator and moral Governor of the Universe, a rallying point for all who shall claim to be Christians.

The theme of growth fit neatly into Shea's triumphalism, and he noted with satisfaction the contrast between the primitive situation of revolutionary times and the throngs of faithful and solid structure of his own day. But this did not mean that Shea was uncritical of the Catholic record of progress. On the contrary, he anticipated many later commentators in his remarks on weaknesses in the intellectual and cultural sphere, and on the failure of Catholics to exert a significant influence on national life. Catholics, he pointed out, had produced few statesmen, jurists, or political leaders. "In literature, science, and the arts, we have made little mark, and are behind even the modest position of the country at large. . . . Our college course is perhaps too elementary; and Catholics even more than their neighbors, perhaps, underrate literary culture. . . ." Even though many Catholics had done well in business and the professions, Shea faulted them for a lack of public spirit and of generosity toward the needs of the Church.

Shea thus combined self-criticism with a combatively apologetical approach. Notably absent from his treatment, however, was any discussion of the *interaction* between the Catholic Church and the American environment. He recounted Catholic contributions to national development, to be sure, and spent even more time on the indignities visited upon Catholics by their bigoted neighbors. But one looks in vain for evidence that Shea thought it worthwhile to reflect on how the Church's history had been shaped by such factors as the separation of church and state, religious freedom, republican self-government, social equalitarianism, and so on. Shea's focus rather was on the Church itself. The Church had its own springs of life, its own inner vitality; America was merely the theater in which the drama of its history was enacted, not a determinative influence upon that drama.

Shea's insensitivity to this dimension of Catholic history stands out clearly in contrast to the approach taken by John Lancaster Spalding, the author of the second Catholic centennial essay.[7] Although not a historian, Spalding probably had a better education than Shea. He was born in Kentucky of an old Catholic family and, after receiving his early schooling in this country, was trained for the priesthood at Louvain. Thirty-six years old when his article appeared in the *Catholic World,* Spalding was appointed bishop of Peoria in November of the centennial year; from that improbable location he guided the campaign to establish the Catholic University of America. He is generally considered the most thoughtful member of the American hierarchy in his day, and his centennial essay supports such a judgment.[8]

Approaching the subject in a more detached and analytical manner than Shea, Spalding set out to explore a problem—namely, what prospects the Catholic Church could look forward to in the modern world. Since "what are called the principles of modern civilization" were most completely realized in the United States, Spalding reasoned that its history here could illuminate the Church's future outlook. In short, Spalding looked to the history of American Catholicism in the centennial year for an answer to the question: "What will be the influence of the new society upon the old faith?"

Reviewing the American Catholic past with this question in mind, Spalding stressed the importance of the separation of church and state and religious freedom because he regarded these points as crucial hallmarks of modernity. He turned first to the problem of how these features of the American system had come into being after independence, given the earnest Protestantism of the colonial pioneers and their intolerance of religious error, particularly that of popery. The roots of separation and religious freedom were not to be sought in any mellowing broad-mindedness in Protestantism, according to Spalding, but rather in a set of concrete social and political circumstances. A commitment to limited power in the hands of the central authority was one such circumstance, and it accounted for the wall of separation erected between the federal government and the churches. Separation and religious freedom were slower in coming at the state level, Spalding rightly observed; but eventually growing religious indifference, increasing diversity of sects, and other factors led the states also to adopt the principles of separation and freedom of religion. His conclusion was that "the Catholics of this country owe the freedom which they now enjoy to the operation of general laws, the necessary results of given social conditions, and not at all to the good-will or tolerant temper of American Protestants. Let us, however," he added in an effort at generosity, "be grateful for the boon, whencesoever derived."

Having shown how the modern situation of religious freedom had developed, Spalding then asked how the American Church had fared when free to act without official favor or disfavor. He reviewed the parlous circumstances in which John Carroll and his comrades had begun their organizational work, and the numerous difficulties which caused multitudes of the early Catholic immigrants to drift away from the faith. In spite of the trials and losses, however, the Church established itself slowly but surely. Before rehearsing the impressive statistics of progress in 1876, Spalding permitted himself this rhetorical flight:

> In the midst of losses, defeats, persecutions, anxieties, doubts, revilings, calumnies, the struggle has been still carried on. . . . New churches were built, new congregations were formed, new dioceses were organized. On some mountainside or in a deeply wooded vale a cloister, a convent, a college, a seminary arose, one hardly knew how, and yet another and another, until these retreats of learning and virtue dotted the land. The elements of discord and disturbance within the Church grew less and less active, the relations between priest and people became more intimate and cordial, the tone of Catholic feeling improved, ecclesiastical discipline was strengthened, and the self-respect of the Catholic body increased.

Spalding thus emphasized, as did Shea, the theme of Catholic growth, but he associated it with an implicit thesis absent from Shea's discussion—namely, that the Church's magnificent progress indicated that Catholicism could flourish under the conditions of modern civilization. He also linked the development of the Church to that of the nation more explicitly than Shea had in discussing another topic treated by both authors, the weak showing made by Catholics in the realm of ideas and culture. The problem, according to Spalding, was that for a hundred years the Church, like the nation itself, had been growing so fast that it had no energies to spare for anything else. Thus Spalding discussed both the remarkable record of Catholic growth *and* the less positive features of that record in the light of American circumstances.

Evidently Spalding believed that conditions were ripe for more rapid cultural advances, for he outlined an ambitious program for the future.

In the century that was dawning he called for an improved Catholic educational system and especially for the creation of Catholic universities as "intellectual centers in which the best minds of the Church in this country" could be trained. Improved educational programs, and the "more vigorous and independent press" that Spalding also advocated, were means to achieve a new level of Catholic participation in American life.

> We must prepare ourselves to enter more fully into the public life of the country; to throw the light of Catholic thought upon each new phase of opinion or belief as it rises; to grapple more effectually with the great moral evils which threaten at once the life of the nation and of the Church. All this and much more we have to do, if our God-given mission is to be fulfilled.

And just what was the "God-given mission" of Catholics? Spalding concluded his article by identifying three areas in which Catholicism had made, and would continue to make, a distinctive contribution to American civilization.

First, he pointed out that Catholics had led the way in establishing religious liberty in Maryland and that they were deeply committed to this fundamental principle of American life. Whatever others might think, Spalding declared, "we have the most profound conviction that, even though we [Catholics] should grow to be nine-tenths of the population of this country, we shall never prove false to the principle of religious liberty, which, to the Catholics of the United States, at least, is sacred and inviolable. For our own part," he added in personal testimony, "we should turn with unutterable loathing from the man who could think that any other course could ever be either just or honorable."

Secondly, Spalding claimed a commitment to the rights of individuals as a Catholic contribution to the national culture. This claim ran directly contrary to the popular impression that Catholicism was a thoroughly authoritarian system, and it must be said that Spalding did not explain it satisfactorily. But it is clear from what he wrote that he had in mind the Church's role as defender of the rights of the individual against the encroaching powers of the state. For the separation of church and state made the Church a jealous guardian of the sphere of conscience, and in the case of the Catholic Church this expressed itself in resistance to federal infringement in a number of areas, especially education. Spalding's comment that federal control of education would be a step toward the old pagan theory of state absolutism indicates that he shared the prevailing Catholic view in this matter.

Spalding's third point was more conventional for it stressed the Church's role as a bulwark to duly constituted authority. By its teaching on the virtue of obedience, on respect for authority, and on the importance of unity, the Catholic Church contributed immensely to cementing together the great national family. Without the Church, "the greatest school of respect the world has ever seen," Spalding feared that the unbounded individualism promoted by the social and political institutions of the nation — and abetted by the inherently fragmentizing tendency of Protestantism —"would fatally lead to anarchy."

Spalding and Shea thus agreed on a number of points in their centennial assessments. Both were impressed with the record of Catholic growth and seemed to feel the Church had done well in the immense task of providing for the basic spiritual needs of the faithful by building churches, recruiting missionaries, and so on. They agreed as well in singling out the intellectual and cultural sphere as the weakest area in Catholic development. Both were self-confident and triumphalist in their assurance that the Church had come far, vindicated her claims, and had something vital to contribute to America's future. And finally both were conservative in the sense that they exalted the Church's role in buttressing constituted authority.

They differed mainly in their approach to the relationship of the Church to American society. Shea was uninterested in this relationship as an intellectual problem — or, more precisely, he apparently did not perceive it as an intellectual problem: America was simply the locale where the story he was telling took place. But in telling that story Shea in fact stressed the *negative features* of the relationship, especially the hostility of American Protestants to the Catholic faith. Spalding, on the other hand, was quite self-consciously interested in the relationship, and made it the central concern of his essay. He, however, stressed the *positive elements* in the interaction between the Church and America, while mentioning the intolerance of the dominant Protestants only in the context of the rise of religious liberty. And since he explicitly related the history of American Catholicism to the larger question of "the influence of the new society upon the old faith," Spalding's favorable discussion of the Church's progress under conditions of American modernity implied a much more positive judgment of the modern world than could be inferred from Shea's article. In this respect, Spalding's approach can be called liberal; Shea's, conservative.

Peter Guilday's "Sesquicentennial Essay"

The latent conflict between the views of Shea and Spalding on the relationship between Catholicism and the American environment burst into the open in a series of bitter controversies among Catholics in the

1880s and 1890s.[9] The liberals in these battles became known as "Americanists" because they argued that, in order to assure the triumph of the faith, the Church should adapt to the modern world and align itself with the American principles of freedom, tolerance, democracy, and so on. To the conservatives, this was a minimizing policy, one that watered down Catholic doctrine in the vain hope of making it acceptable to a basically irreligious world. They distrusted anything that smacked at all of compromise and eventually came to the conclusion that the Americanist position deviated so far from orthodoxy as to be a formal heresy. The quarrels that developed from these divergent viewpoints became so embittered and confused that finally, in 1899, Pope Leo XIII intervened with a condemnation of "the opinions which some comprise under the head of Americanism."

The liberals denied that they held the theological positions condemned by the Pope, while Leo disclaimed any intention of pronouncing judgment against the laws, customs, or institutions of American society—which is what the liberals said their Americanism embraced. Because of these ambiguities, the papal letter did not settle the question of what the relation of Catholicism to American life really should be. It did, however, end debate on the question for many years. Even in 1926, when Peter Guilday, the greatest Catholic historian of his generation, wrote his "sesquicentennial essay" as the lead article in the first issue of *Thought,* he passed over in discreet silence the controversies of the late nineteenth century.[10]

Despite this omission, Guilday had a good deal to say about the relation of Americanism to Catholicism. Unfortunately, his remarks are analytically unrewarding and the article as a whole is exasperatingly diffuse. It is possible, nevertheless, to identify some salient motifs and to speculate about what he was getting at.

First of all, we should note that Guilday's self-consciously commemorative approach was closely related to his linking together of Catholic history and the history of the American nation. By subtitling his piece "A Sesquicentennial Essay," he took advantage of the fortuitous circumstance that the year 1926 was the 150th anniversary of independence to underscore both the commemorative quality of his article and the interconnection between the history of the Church and that of the nation. The latter point was further emphasized in his opening sentence: "No more misleading perspective can be given to any institution in a nation than to regard it as something distinct from national life and progress." But besides being understood in the context of national life, the Catholic Church should be seen as a significant influence upon national life. Indeed it was an influence even before American history began, for the country owed its discovery and exploration to the missionary spirit that was rooted in medieval

Europe. Hence Guilday could make the startling claim that: "The heart of the Middle Ages was the Catholic Church; and it was from the heart of the Middle Ages that America was born." The insistence on assimilating Catholic and American elements to each other runs through the essay, a point to which we shall return shortly.

Guilday's historic-commemorative emphasis was further reflected in the fact that he mentioned and quoted from England's 1826 discourse, Shea's "centennial essay" (as Guilday called it), and Spalding's 1876 article. From Shea he adopted the organizational device of treating Catholic history in fifty-year spans. He likewise followed Shea in emphasizing anti-Catholicism as the dominant feature of the period 1826–1876, but his discussion lacked Shea's fiercely polemical quality. Rather Guilday's tone is "dignified, lofty, and serene," to use the terms he applied to the response made by the American hierarchy to charges that the Church was unAmerican. Despite the fact that "no less a personage" than President Grant initiated the third fifty-year period in a "strikingly anti-Catholic manner," Guilday intimated that antipathy toward Catholics was no longer a serious problem after 1876. He made no reference at all to the Ku Klux Klan or other manifestations of anti-Catholic hostility in his own time.

The "third quinquennium" of American Catholicism (1876–1926) is handled very sketchily, but the structure of the discussion, so far as there is any, is derived from Spalding's program for the future, which Guilday quoted from the 1876 essay. Thus American Catholics were said to have responded nobly to Spalding's challenge to build up their educational system. In this connection Guilday took note of continuing pressure on Catholic schools from "rationalistic and irreligious" forces, and he expressed misgivings as to how long Catholics could bear the burden of double taxation imposed upon them by their educational efforts. He likewise associated the Catholic University of America and the National Catholic Welfare Conference (both founded in the period under consideration) with Spalding's exhortation that Catholics engage themselves more actively in the public affairs of the nation. And in an interesting slip, Guilday misquoted Spalding as calling upon Catholics to grapple with the "social evils" —rather than the "moral evils"—of the day.

Guilday thus borrowed liberally from his predecessors in the genre of anniversary assessment. His peroration on Catholic contributions to the nation also shared the triumphalist perspective of Shea and Spalding:

> America can never forget God with one-fifth of its citizens holding a supernatural aim as their chief purpose in life. America can never be effectually divided so long as these millions who adore God in the same spirit, partake of the same sacramental life, and are all children of the one true God and brethren of the one Christ, remain faithful to the teaching of the great

Church of the ages: obedience in spiritual matters to Jesus Christ, the King of the Universe, and steadfast loyalty to the Republic in national and civic concerns.

But while he agreed with Shea and Spalding in stressing a distinctive Catholic mission to the nation, Guilday differed from both in his interpretation of the relationship between the Church and American society. Shea viewed society as the theater in which the drama of Catholic life unfolded itself, and Spalding inquired how the new society had influenced the old faith, but for Guilday the subject was neither dramatic nor problematic. His theme rather was the perfect harmony that existed between Americanism and Catholicism. "To understand the Catholic Church in America," he declared, "one must see how naturally and integrally the spiritual allegiance of its members knits into the national allegiance so as to round each other out." And in introducing his three fifty-year periods, Guilday claimed that each had a distinctive character "when regarded in the light of [the] assimilation of American ideals with the supernatural purposes of life as taught and practised by the Catholic Faith. . . ."

Unhappily, Guilday failed to specify just how Catholic religious commitments dovetailed so perfectly with American political principles, and his comments on the history of the American Church in no way substantiate the claim that each of the fifty-year periods elucidates a different phase of the assimilation of Catholic to American principles. What he actually presents is mélange of categorical assertions, reports of anti-Catholic sentiment, apologetical responses by Catholic authorities, other information on various aspects of Catholic history, and some portentous but undeveloped hints such as the following: "[The period 1876–1926] can only be justly estimated in the balance of distintegrating [sic] Protestant doctrines and in the realization that morality and religion are closely interwoven with the survival of the Republic."

Guilday was a busy scholar in the mid-1920s, and perhaps some of the loose ends in his sesquicentennial essay are simply the result of hasty composition. We can confidently assume, however, that bypassing in silence the controversies of the Americanist period was a deliberate choice on Guilday's part. Although he was only a boy when they took place, he knew how passionately the battles had been fought and how cautiously one had to approach them.[11] And since he wanted to emphasize the harmony between Americanism and Catholicism, it made no sense to resurrect a buried quarrel that had led the Pope to condemn something called "Americanism," even if that Americanism was a very special — and perhaps nonexistent — kind.

But besides the tactical consideration, Catholic intellectuals of Guilday's generation could well regard the controversies of the 1890s as definitely passé—obscure contests that had little bearing on the situation of the 1920s. After all, a lot had happened since the period of the controversies. Three developments were especially important, and their effects may be discerned in Guilday's essay.

The first and second of these developments—World War I and the Scholastic Revival, respectively—might seem a very odd combination, but together they shaped Guilday's understanding of the relationship between Americanism and Catholicism. Catholic participation in the war effort, and the sense of national unity produced by the common struggle, heightened patriotic feeling and gave Catholics a more lively sense of belongingness as Americans. Guilday was closely associated with the newly formed National Catholic War Council, which was set up in 1917 and headquartered in Washington; hence he felt with special force the identification of Catholic and national energies and loyalties. His stress on the natural harmony of Catholicism and Americanism grew in part from this experience, and one can find precisely the same emphasis in Michael Williams's *American Catholics in the War* (1921), a book telling the story of the National Catholic War Council.[12]

The emotional fusion of religious and patriotic convictions that was forged in the wartime experience was reinforced on the philosophical level by Neoscholasticism. The Scholastic Revival, which had been gathering momentum for two generations, attained the status of a popular ideology among American Catholic intellectuals in the 1920s. This breakthrough was signalized not merely by the appearance of technical philosophical journals like *The Modern Schoolman* (1925) and *The New Scholasticism* (1927), but also by the appearance of more popular articles in magazines like *America,* arguing, among other things, that American political principles jibed perfectly with the teachings of St. Thomas. The same claim was implied by the following statement made by Maurice de Wulf, the leading historian of medieval philosophy: "The main theories of Thomism—such as pluralism, the horror of monism, respect for personality, the prestige of abstract ideas, the central place of God elevated above world and distinct from it—express the deepest aspirations of . . . [modern Western] civilization."[13]

The combined influence of wartime experience and Neoscholastic teaching can be seen both in Guilday's insistence on the pre-existing harmony between Catholic doctrine and American principle and in his assurance that Catholicism had been, and would continue to be, an indispensable bulwark to the American system. The third development shaping his approach was a negative one—the resurgence of virulent anti-Catholicism in the 1920s—but its effect was to lend greater urgency to Guilday's efforts to bring home to Americans that, far from being opposed to American principles, Catholicism was really the matrix from which those principles sprang and the best guarantor of their continued vitality. Guilday evidently considered it unwise to refer directly to the bigotry of his own day, but no one could mistake the prominence he gave to earlier anti-Catholic movements or the contemporary pertinence of his insistence on how misguided they were.[14] In looking back on 150 years of American Catholic history, Guilday thus employed the perspectives of his own day and attempted to meet a contemporary need while at the same time commemorating the past.

A Bicentennial View

What of our most recent milestone? I will not attempt to review what Guilday might have called the "fourth quinquennium" (1926–1976), much less the whole two-hundred-year span of American Catholic history. Yet some conclusions are in order, for by looking at these anniversary assessments together we may see both past and present in a clearer light.

We see first that two centuries of history have made us more self-conscious about taking note of the milestones and reflecting on our experience. Bishop England failed to do so in 1826, but the later writers seized an anniversary occasion to generalize freely on the state of the American Church. Running parallel to this development is an increasing self-consciousness about, and emphasis upon, the relation of the Church to American society as one of the subjects deserving of attention in these anniversary assessments. This point we must examine more carefully.

Bishop England's discourse stressed what he thought an audience of American Protestants most needed to hear. In refuting the common charges that Catholicism constituted a threat to civic freedom and that it was antirepublican, he clearly had the American situation in mind. These points, however, are all made in the context of a doctrinal exposition which follows a basically *a priori* approach rather than a historical one. Moreover, England's *a priori* method actually militates against sensitivity to the interaction of Church and society because it posits so sharp a disjunction between the religious and the political spheres. Church and state may coexist peacefully under such an arrangement, but we can hardly think of them as interacting intensely.

Shea's article was historical rather than systematic; unlike England he therefore dealt explicitly with the Church's experience in the specifically American setting. But his conceptualization of the relationship of Church and society resembles that of England in being strongly disjunctive. As was pointed out before, Shea's focus was on the Church, which he thought of as developing according to its own inner principle rather than being significantly molded by interaction with its environment.

With Spalding we have something quite different: a self-conscious curiosity about how American society and the Catholic Church have mutually influenced each other and what the record of that interaction implies for the future of the Church. Spalding's approach thus illustrates historicist and Americanist tendencies. At the same time, the Church remains in Spalding's thinking a concrete spiritual entity whose institutional structure, though sturdily developed, still requires further elaboration. The Church also retains its own distinctive character and its capacity to exert an identifiable positive influence on American society. In short, Spalding's interest in the relationship of Church and society has not blurred the boundaries between the two nor rendered problematic the identity or role of the Church.

Guilday too was deeply interested in the relationship of the Church and American society. But though he was a great historian who meant to deal with that theme historically, Guilday's essay actually rests on a fundamentally ahistorical view of the relationship. According to this view, Catholicism and Americanism were in profound harmony because both shared the common ground of natural law.[15] It was unimportant that the founding fathers had not directly derived their understanding of basic natural-law principles from the Catholic schoolmen of the Middle Ages, who had articulated them most adequately. The American founders had worked in the same tradition and penetrated to the same truths; hence the Catholic view of reality had been basic to American society from the outset. Unfortunately, earlier generations of Americans had failed to perceive that fact and had even persecuted the Church that was the surest foundation and best ally of American principles. In the 1920s, however, the revival of Scholasticism made it possible to demonstrate irresistibly what had been true all along—namely, that true Americanism found its fullest realization in the Catholic faith.

These were the unstated premises of Guilday's discussion. Since they posit a substantial *identity* between Catholicism and Americanism, it is understandable that there were few mutual *influences* of the one upon the other, especially of American society upon the Church. Guilday's actual discussion of the interaction between Church and society consists for the most part of mere assertions of harmony and is less historically interesting than that of Spalding. It is, however, a most revealing document of American Catholic thinking of the 1920s, illustrating as it does the emotional fusion of Catholicism and Americanism and implying the rationale that was understood as explaining the fusion.

The Neoscholastic model of Church/world relations which is implicit in Guilday's article is also important because it is the one that dominated the American Catholic mind until the era of Vatican II. The line of thinking adumbrated in Spalding's essay, with its historicist and immanentist tendency, was abruptly cut off by the condemnations of Americanism and Modernism. Neoscholasticism held uncontested sway in Catholic colleges, universities, and seminaries through the 1950s. It provided a complex and nuanced intellectual system for interpreting relations between the Church and society; and in the hands of a man like John Courtney Murray, S.J., it proved capable of assimilating American experience to the tradition in such a way as to lead to new insights. Yet its emphasis on perennial wisdom and eternal truths betrayed its ahistorical bias; and its careful differentiation of nature from grace, Church from world, seemed to many Catholics overly rationalistic and dualistic when the influence of historicist thinking began to make itself felt once more.

The newer currents were already at work in Europe by 1950, but in the United States the Neoscholastic interpretation of relations between the Church and society was hardly challenged until the upheaval of the sixties. Then it was swept away overnight by the combined influence of the Second Vatican Council, the postconciliar confusion, and the transvaluation of values that occurred in intellectual circles on the subject of America. These events brought home with a vengeance that the Church is involved in history and cannot avoid being shaped — and shaken — by interaction with the society in which it lives. The bicentennial thus found American Catholics attempting to reorient themselves in a landscape that had been transformed by a spiritual earthquake. The recent past had simultaneously given them a keener awareness of the importance of the Church's relationship to the world and had shattered the way of thinking by which they had made sense of that relationship for two generations.

To connect these generalities with a pertinently concrete example, let us look briefly at the Catholic bishops' major bicentennial project and compare it with our earlier anniversary assessments. The "Liberty and Justice for All" campaign sponsored by the National Conference of Catholic Bishops aimed to bring the resources of the Church to bear on the task of realizing freedom and justice for all Americans and in the world community at large. This goal was to be reached through a three-phase program: (1) nationwide parish discussion sessions and five major regional "hearings" in 1975; (2) a national conference the following year to formulate policy; and (3) a follow-up period (1977–81) during which the policy would be put into action.[16]

Although this ambitious program assigned no significant attention to history as such, it was profoundly historicist in the sense that it placed overwhelming emphasis on the Church's involvement in what was formerly known as the "temporal order," but which is now often called the "historical-political process."[17] The very name "Liberty and Justice for All" fixed the focus on the Church's relation to American society. Like the earlier commentators who stressed this relationship, the organizers of the program were convinced that Catholics had something distinctive to contribute to the nation. It is doubtful, however, that they would have agreed with our earlier writers on the content of the Church's contribution. They might have endorsed Spalding's listing of a commitment to religious freedom and individual rights; but the Church as reinforcer of national unity and bulwark of constituted authority was not calculated to arouse their enthusiasm. Nor did the bicentennial program place any emphasis on the contribution the Church made merely by mobilizing a large body of communicants who were firm believers in a supernatural faith, although that point was stressed by both Shea and Guilday.

The religious contributions that were prized in the mid-seventies dealt with "liberty and justice." But what precisely was it that the Church was supposed to contribute? What was the content of its distinctive impulse or message? The very fact that a year-long series of local discussions and "hearings" preceded any attempt to formulate a policy testified to uncertainty. This loss of certitude as to the Church's position, and the "listening process" employed in trying to reach a consensus on what that position should be, strikingly symbolize the distance that separated American Catholics at the bicentennial from Guilday, Spalding, and Shea—to say nothing of England.

What had happened can be stated simply. Catholic ideas about the Church had changed; Catholic ideas about the world had changed; Catholic ideas about the relation of Church and world were therefore understandably in flux. Since the relation of Church to world is also the relation of faith to life, trying to clarify it was an important matter. It was, indeed, a fitting task to undertake at the bicentennial, but five years were hardly enough time to complete the job.

6

THE SCHOOL QUESTION:

A CENTENNIAL RETROSPECT

Like the preceding essay, this one was originally written with an anniversary in mind. It was one of three historical papers delivered before a gathering of "Historians and Bishops in Dialogue," which was held in 1984 to mark the centenary of the Third Plenary Council at Baltimore. It might be described as a more distinctively "historical" investigation than the preceding one since, rather than analyzing what earlier writers said about American Catholicism in general, it focuses on what a definite set of historical actors did at a certain time and place with respect to the specific issue of Catholic education. As between past and present, the overwhelming weight of attention is thus devoted to the past.

As the introductory section of the paper suggests, however, this particular portion of the past was quite recently regarded as being highly relevant to the present. During the controversies of the 1960s, critics of the parochial schools often alluded to the Third Plenary Council as having been the decisive influence in shaping the subsequent development of Catholic educational efforts. Even so, relatively little was done in those days to discover why the Council fathers of the 1880s took the action they did. Their motives were usually disposed of by stock references to "immigrant defensiveness" or "the ghetto mentality." In discussing the Council's action a century later, my hope is to deepen present-day understanding of the perennial "school question" by looking more carefully into the late nineteenth-century context.

The paper as presented here is slightly revised and abbreviated from its original published form in the U.S. Catholic Historian *(nos. 3–4, 1984). It does not alter the conventional picture of Baltimore III in any fundamental way, but it brings certain matters into sharper focus—the widespread Catholic support for "denominational schools," for example; the*

115

*fact that Rome exerted a moderating influence on the American bishops
on the matter of requiring attendance at parochial schools; and the role
played by school issues in Europe in alerting American churchmen to the
dangers of "secularism." Although it is perhaps the most purely "historical" of the essays brought together in this volume, this one is also among
the most relevant to the present.*

THE EDUCATIONAL FRONT IS RELATIVELY quiet at the moment, but few
topics have been more hotly debated over the past thirty or forty years than
the status and prospects of the Catholic schools. Most Protestants, Jews,
and liberals have generally regarded them with misgivings, the degree of
which varies according to circumstance. Among Catholics themselves, the
scope and intensity of controversy has been unprecedented.[1] There was
a good deal of criticism even before the Second Vatican Council, most of
it centering on the allegedly low educational quality of parochial schools
(overcrowded classrooms, poorly prepared teachers, etc.) and on the so-
cially questionable consequences of maintaining such "separatist, ghetto
institutions." With *aggiornamento* and the Council, these lines of criticism were reinforced and blended with the general feeling that all the older
institutional features of the preconciliar Church needed root-and-branch
reform — or that they should be eliminated entirely. In 1964 Mary Perkins
Ryan brought the issue of quality to a new level of urgency by arguing that,
aside from their other drawbacks, parochial schools were not even the best
means of providing religious education, which was, of course, supposed
to be the fundamental reason for their existence.[2]

Ryan's book, *Are Parochial Schools the Answer?* — a rhetorical question to which she responded with an unqualified negative — opened the
"great debate" phase of intra-Catholic controversy over the schools. It raged
through the mid-sixties, producing a sizable literature of polemics as well
as several ambitious social-scientific studies of Catholic schooling and its
religious, educational, and social effects.[3] A five-day national symposium
held in Washington in November 1967 served, in the words of a recent
investigator, "as a Catholic educational summit, a kind of watershed in
which new ideas were expressed and serious problems were met head on."
While it did not settle any of the major issues, the Washington symposium
"seemed to act as a catharsis for troubled educators" and pointed in the
direction of constructive long-range efforts at reform.[4]

The relationship of past and present was not overlooked in the controversy for, although they were not the primary focus, certain historical
points kept coming up in the discussion. The most basic one was whether

parochial schools had outlived their historical usefulness; but this, of course, raised a number of other questions — such as whether Catholic schools had come into being strictly as a result of nativist bigotry in the nineteenth century, or whether there were more positive, and presumably more enduring, reasons for their existence. Beginning with Robert D. Cross in 1965, several writers stressed the lateness and incompleteness of the hierarchy's commitment to the parochial school as a requirement; took note of the degree to which the laity dragged their feet on this matter; and implied that there were many other equally satisfactory educational modes that the Church could and should have pursued, instead of allowing itself to become so overcommitted to parochial schools.[5]

Although the literature on Catholic educational history is sparse, everyone acquainted with the historical dimension of the school question recognized that the Third Plenary Council of Baltimore in 1884 was a major milestone, and there were many references to what was done at that gathering, the last of the great collegial meetings of the American bishops held in the nineteenth century.[6] That makes the centenary of Baltimore III an appropriate occasion to explore with some care the Council's action in the educational field and to inquire into its background. That is what I endeavor to do in the pages that follow, although I do not claim to have covered every aspect of the subject. To establish the basic groundwork, let us begin by reviewing what the Council actually provided for in respect to education and by identifying what emerges from the conciliar documents as the primary motivation for those provisions.

Conciliar Action and Its Motivation

The best-known action taken by the Council was to shift from the language of exhortation in respect to parochial schools to that of command. It laid down explicit rules *requiring* the erection within two years of a parochial school near each church where one did not already exist and *mandating* the attendance of Catholic children at these schools. The bishops left room for exceptions but underlined the seriousness of the obligation by warning pastors that they were subject to discipline if they persistently neglected to build a school and by adding that congregations which failed to support the school were to be "reprehended by the bishops and . . . induced to contribute the necessary support."[7]

The foundation for these rules had been laid in five dense decrees that explained the need for Catholic schools, set forth the general obligation to patronize them, cited the appropriate ecclesiastical authorities, and indicated where exceptions could be justified. The bishops also cautioned against "excessive zeal" in enforcing the rules, and especially against denying the sacraments to parents who didn't send their children to Catholic schools. Since they were requiring attendance, the bishops acknowledged that Catholic schools should be second to none in quality. Hence they enacted eight decrees "Concerning Ways and Means of Improving the Parochial Schools." Few could be put into practice immediately, but they helped to shape the systematization of parochial school education that took place over the next generation.

All the foregoing dealt with parochial schools, but Title VI of the decrees also included a chapter headed "On Higher Catholic Schools." The tone was hortatory, and the ideal set forth was a system whereby Catholic youth could be accommodated at every stage of education in schools that would preserve them from the dangers to faith and morals they might encounter at secular institutions. The bishops also called for special precautions in Catholic schools whose student bodies were "mixed," in order to forestall the development of religious indifferentism, to shield the Catholic students from being harmed by contact with non-Catholics, and to make sure that the latter were not scandalized by the conduct of their Catholic classmates.

Clerical education got even more attention than schools for the laity, and Baltimore III is as much a landmark in the development of seminaries as it is in respect to parochial schools. The fifty-nine decrees fixing the organization, discipline, and course of studies of minor and major seminaries were largely confirmed in the 1918 Code of Canon Law and set the basic character of priestly formation in the United States until the Second Vatican Council. The Baltimore decrees also mandated a type of continuing education for priests by prescribing quarterly clergy conferences and periodic examinations for recently ordained priests. Concern for clerical education also led to the momentous decision to establish a superior-grade national seminary that would in time become a full-fledged university. This was the special project of John Lancaster Spalding, who persuaded the Council to authorize the undertaking and appoint a committee to carry it out. This marked the official beginning of the Catholic University of America, the establishment of which constituted a genuine breakthrough in the field of Catholic higher education in the United States.

Comprehensive as these actions were, they did not exhaust the Council's educational concerns. The need for Christian schooling for Negroes and Indians was touched upon under Title VIII, "Zeal for Souls," while the preceding title, headed "Christian Doctrine," took into account the formative influence of educational factors beyond the range of formal schooling. Here the Council fathers laid down guidelines for preaching and prayer books, and expatiated on the need for Catholic books, magazines, and newspapers. But the most significant action in this area was the appointment of an episcopal committee charged to see to the preparation of a popular catechism. This action led a few months after the close of the Council to the publication of the famous Baltimore Catechism, which, in its various revisions, remained the basic instructional manual for the next half-century and more. Interestingly enough, John Lancaster Spalding, who was so concerned about university studies, was also the bishop most actively involved in the preparation of the catechism.[8]

As this reveiw makes clear, the Third Plenary Council's concern for education was broad in scope and long-lasting in impact. The basic reason the fathers regarded the subject as so important was their conviction that differing views as to the meaning and purpose of life entailed different approaches to education. The conciliar decrees left no doubt that the bishops saw a fundamental split between the Catholic view and the secular view. The subchapter dealing with the "absolute necessity" for parochial schools begins: "If ever in any age, then surely in this our age, the Church of God and the spirit of the world are in a certain wondrous and bitter conflict over the education of youth." Under the influence of those "most ruinous movements of indifferentism, naturalism and materialism," the world had drifted away from religious truth and adopted a purely secular outlook on the meaning and purpose of life.[9] Preservation of the faith was thus the key issue. At the root of all the Council's legislation on education, from catechism and parochial school through seminary and university, lay the conviction that the faith was threatened by dangers more insidious than any previously encountered, and that new measures were necessary to meet them.

This theme runs through the pastoral letter issued as the council closed. Taking note of the problem at the very outset, the letter conceded that the situation was worse in Europe. The bishops could not, however, "close [their] eyes to the fact that teachers of skepticism and irreligion are at work in our country. They have crept into the leading educational institutions of our non-Catholic fellow-citizens, they have (though rarely) made their appearance in the public press and even in the pulpit." The religious disposition and good sense of the American people offered reassurance that "wild theories" destructive of Christianity would not take root; but, the bishops continued, "when we take into account the daily signs of growing unbelief, and see how its heralds not only seek to mould the youthful mind in our colleges and seats of learning, but are also actively working amongst the masses, we cannot but shudder at the dangers that threaten us in the future."[10]

Against this background, the pastoral explained how the various matters dealt with at the Council fit into the overall religious picture. Turning first to clerical education, it pointed out that deeper learning was required of priests "in our age, when so many misleading theories are put forth on every side, when every department of natural truth is actively explored for objections against revealed religion. . . ." The same was true of education intended for the laity: "In days like ours, when error is so pretentious and aggressive, every one needs to be as completely armed as possible with sound knowledge — not only the clergy, but the people also that they may be able to withstand the noxious influences of popularized irreligion. In the great coming combat between truth and error, between Faith and Agnosticism, an important part of the fray must be borne by the laity, and woe to them if they are not well prepared."[11] And more than the spiritual welfare of individuals was at stake; solid religious education was essential for the future of civilization itself. The pastoral made its case by calling attention to the brutalizing consequences of a naturalistic view of life. "A civilization without religion would be a civilization of 'the struggle for existence, and the survival of the fittest,' in which cunning and strength would become the substitutes for principle, virtue, conscience and duty."[12]

Other aspects of life besides education were linked to the pervasive threat of irreligion. The theme recurs in the pastoral's treatment of the Christian home, the press, forbidden secret societies, and the need for sodalities and other Catholic associations. In discussing family life, the bishops stated the danger in global terms: "Beloved brethren, a great social revolution is sweeping over the world. Its purpose, hidden or avowed, is to dethrone Christ and religion. The ripples of the movement have been observed in our country; God grant that its tidal wave may not break over us."[13]

The pastoral's emphasis upon this theme and the language in which it was expressed convinces me that more was at work here than the ordinary pastoral concern one might expect in any gathering of responsible ecclesiastics. The fathers of the Third Plenary Council were persuaded that the Catholic faith was exposed to greater dangers than it had ever confronted before in the history of the American Church and that these dangers required, among other things, a new mobilization of educational resources. Their anxieties could, of course, be dismissed as symptoms of "the siege mentality," as proof that the bishops were hopelessly imprisoned in defensive, post-Tridentine modes of thought. But besides betraying an offensively arrogant kind of present-mindedness, this interpretation fails utterly to advance our understanding of the situation as the Council fathers saw it in their own day. If we want to apprehend the problem as they did, we must set Baltimore III within the context of the times, both in terms of American developments and in relation to the school question as it existed in Europe.

The American Background

Concern for Catholic education was not new in 1884. It had been warmly encouraged and systematically promoted since the days of John Carroll, first at the level of academies, colleges, and seminaries; increasingly since about 1840 at the level of parochial schools. By the time the Council met, there were already some 2,400 such schools in operation. Parochial schools had also been a source of almost continuous controversy with Protestants from their earliest days. Bishop Hughes's epic struggle in New York in 1840–42 was the first great landmark. Two years later, the issue of Bible-reading in the common schools was deeply implicated in the anti-Catholic riots that rocked Philadelphia. Efforts to get public funds for Catholic schools fueled Know-Nothing nativism in the 1850s, and after the Civil War the smoldering "school question" flared up again with great bitterness. By calling for a constitutional amendment to prevent public money from being used for religious purposes, President Grant in 1875 set the stage for a debate in Congress and in various state legislatures.[14] The so-called Blaine Amendment, which embodied Grant's suggestion, failed in Congress, but the important state of New York adopted its own version. The matrix of controversy is important, not only because it showed how sensitive an issue Catholic schools were, but also because it tended to produce extreme statements from both the Catholic and non-Catholic side. And extreme statements are always taken by the other side as revealing what its opponents *really* have in mind. Hence the anxieties and suspicions of both sides were fed by the tradition of controversy itself.[15]

Religion was the most basic factor in these controversies. The public schools had intimate links with evangelical Protestantism and they strongly reflected a pan-Protestant mentality. In the middle decades of the century it was not unusual for Protestant ministers to serve on state school boards, as superintendents of public instruction, district examiners, or officers of teachers' organizations. Church-related colleges regarded the preparation of public school teachers as one of their chief functions; and a generalized Protestant piety suffused the common schools.[16] In these circumstances, the bishops had reasonable grounds for looking upon the public schools as proselytizing agencies. In practice, a great deal depended on local conditions and attitudes, but there were enough widely publicized atrocity stories—children being ridiculed for their faith, expelled for staying out of school on holy days, etc.—to lend credibility to the most jaundiced view of the common schools as centers of organized bigotry.[17]

Classroom reading of the King James version of the Bible was an explosive issue from the first. For Catholics, requiring children to take part in these exercises was equivalent to mandating Protestant religious worship as part of the school routine. To Protestants, however, this scruple could not be credited as sincere. The Bible was not sectarian; it was pure Christianity. If Catholics objected to its being read that simply proved their perversion and made it clear that their goal was to destroy American society by undermining its religious foundation. An effort in 1869 to make the public schools of Cincinnati more attractive to Catholics by banning Bible-reading set off a furious three-cornered row between Protestants, Catholics, and those committed to secularized schooling. This so-called "Bible War" put the school question on the front pages nationally, embittered Protestant-Catholic feeling, and at the same time hastened the secularization of public education.[18]

Political and ideological issues were inseparable from religious ones. The purely partisan angle—i.e., the Democratic party allegiance of the Catholic masses—was of secondary importance, but the school question was sometimes used to mobilize voters.[19] The most explosive issue, however, concerned the use of public funds for religious schools and reflected basic differences in social policy and religio-cultural outlook. Catholics consistently argued that true education involved moral formation and had to be based on religion—and religion here was understood to involve the full doctrinal basis of belief, not a diluted, least-common-denominator moralism. But the only way this could be done in a religiously diverse society was for each religious group to have its own schools; and if the state supported any of those schools, it was obligated in justice to support all of them impartially. Catholic spokesmen advanced this argument from the 1840s through the 1880s—not just hard-liners on the schools but also liberals like Father Isaac Hecker, and Bishops Spalding and John J. Keane.[20] Indeed, the thing that surprised me the most in going through the literature of the time was the extent to which Catholic spokesmen were agreed on the theoretical desirability of the "denominational schools" approach. By the 1880s, however, it had taken on the quality of a "thesis," in the thesis-as-unattainable-ideal sense, and the Third Plenary Council did not mention it, although the pastoral letter hinted obliquely that public schools could be organized in such a way as to permit them to teach religion.[21]

The Council fathers were wise not to propose denominational schools as a solution. The plan had long been a red flag to the great majority of non-Catholic Americans, who regarded it as a genuine threat to the nation's social and cultural cohesion.[22] If the idea itself was anathema, the spectacle of Catholics organizing themselves politically to press openly for a share of the school fund set off paroxysms of opposition. The experience of Bishop Hughes, who tried it in the 1840s, convinced him that Catholics would have to go it alone in respect to school support, and the reaction that greeted similar efforts by several bishops in 1852–1853 pointed to the same conclusion. After the Civil War, Catholics continued to complain of double taxation and argued for state-supported denominational schools, but in the practical order they relied mainly on voluntary parochial schools, with occasional local compromises with public school authorities along the lines of what were later called "released time" or purchase-of-service arrangements.[23]

The Protestant view of the school question embraced four propositions of special relevance to this discussion. In the first place, most Protestants held that it was indeed possible for the public schools to teach those elements of the Christian religion essential to the formation of personal morality and civic virtue, and to do so without transgressing on the doctrinal territory disputed among various sects of Christians.[24] From this it followed that Catholics had no valid religious grounds for objecting to public school education.

Secondly, most Americans in the nineteenth century were convinced that public school education was in fact based on this kind of nonsectarian Christianity, that this arrangement was entirely appropriate, and that charges of "Godlessness" leveled against the public schools were therefore unfounded and, indeed, slanderous.[25]

Thirdly, almost all non-Catholics were convinced that common school education of this kind rested on the bedrock of national ideals and was an essential constituent of American nationality. Those who criticized the common schools, or refused to make use of them, inevitably, by the very fact of acting in this manner, placed their own Americanism in question.[26]

From all this it followed as a fourth point that the idea of state-supported denominational schools simply could not be entertained. Such an arrangement would destroy an excellent system that was already in place, substitute for it a fragmented confusion of clashing sectarian schools, and benefit chiefly a church that was basically anti-American in its inherent character and in the policies it pursued.[27]

It is impossible to review here the evidence on which these generalizations rest, but let me quote a rather lengthy passage to illustrate how they merged together in the thinking of nineteenth-century commentators. The remarks were made at the 1888 convention of the National Education Association in which criticism of the public schools was being discussed. The speaker, Thomas J. Morgan, a Baptist minister who held a number of responsible positions having to do with public education, rose to respond to the criticism that the common schools failed to inculcate sound morality.[28] This charge, Morgan said,

simply means that the public schools of this country are not Roman Catholic. . . . [it] is the club that is designed to knock our public-school system
into pieces. I have traced this matter to this source. I have studied it, and
it simply means that it is a challenge to our civilization, it is a challenge to
our Christianity, it is a challenge to our political life, it is a challenge to
everything that we Americans cherish to-day. To say that the common schools
are godless, that they do not teach morality, and that they do not teach religion, and therefore they must be set aside, stirs up a deep sentiment within
us. We will be asked at no distant day to recognize that there is no religion
except Catholicism; that there is no worship except that of the Cathedral;
that the state has no right to exist except as a servant of the church. In other
words . . . if you accept that criticism [of the public schools] as just, you
yield everything that we prize in the civilization of the nineteenth century,
represented by Martin Luther, and represented in its outflowering by American ideas; you recognize that all that is a sham and a pretense, that it is to
be thrown aside, and that we are to go back to mediaevalism, with all that
condition implies.[29]

This remarkable outburst illustrates vividly how closely Protestantism was identified with the national ideology and dramatizes the sense of
outrage engendered by what were perceived as aggressive actions on the
part of American Catholics. Morgan's ominous reference to the threat of
medievalism also hinted at the larger ideological context within which the
school question has to be situated. This brings us to the European background, for the clash between Catholic reactionism and enlightened secularism was centered there.

Secularism and the European Background

Morgan did not elaborate on the ideological point in his *ex tempore*
remarks, but other writers did. A certain M. C. O'Byrne, for example,
used as a springboard the favorable stand on democracy adopted by the
Third Plenary Council. Implying that it was merely a tactical ploy, O'Byrne
developed his argument as follows:

From the stand-point of the Syllabus [of Errors] the common schools of this
country are not to be trusted with the education of the children of Catholic
parents. They are, like the elementary schools of Belgium, Germany, etc.,
'godless' places. . . . They teach morality, but not as a pendant to the Ni-
cene Creed; they endeavor to lay the foundations of good citizenship, but
not in connection with the postulates of any catechism of theology. Conse-
quently, the Roman Church — bound as it is to oppose to the uttermost those
principles of progress, liberalism, and the new civilization which are condemned in the Syllabus — cannot look with favor on our common school

system, and, as was long since foreseen, the conflict between Clericalism and Secularism, begun in Prussia and continued in Italy, Belgium, and elsewhere, has yet to be waged in the United States. It will be a serious conflict, because one of antithetical principles.[30]

Although disagreeing with the stand he took, many Catholics would have accepted the way O'Byrne stated the issue, for they too tended to see the American situation as an instance of the larger conflict of antithetical principles. This was much more the case in the era of Baltimore III than in the days of Bishop Hughes, and the shift had important implications. It may be summed up by saying that whereas *Protestantism* in public education had been the chief problem in the 1840s, it was *secularism* in the public schools that worried Catholics in the later decades of the century. In the first instance, the faith of Catholic youngsters was endangered by their exposure to religious error; in the second, by exposure to influences of an irreligious, or even antireligious, nature. The older "sectarian" issues carried over into the later period, to be sure; but despite continuities with the older version of the school question, observers at the time were not imagining things when they discerned a new challenge to religious faith in the educational implications of secularism.

American Catholics today tend to be gun-shy on the subject of secularism; they are skittish about using the term because the evils of secularism were so much exaggerated in the preconciliar past. At least that's what they were assured by writers of the 1960s, who insisted that secularity was really a good thing and that Catholics ought to align themselves with the forces at work in the secular city. In view of the uncertainties that persist from this semantic hangover, it is important to make the point that the term "secularism" came into use in the nineteenth century, was widely applied to the elimination of religious influences from education, and was intimately associated with the Victorian crisis of faith. It was, in fact, introduced into the language by a midcentury English freethinker named George Jacob Holyoake, who was looking for a term that would raise fewer hackles than "atheism" or "infidelity" while implying the same negative stance toward supernatural religion and the social influence of the churches.[31] Holyoake was an obscure figure, but the term (and derivatives like "secularization") caught on quickly and always carried some trace of their doctrinaire origins.

For O'Byrne and most American Catholic observers of the day, "secularism" carried much more than a trace of its origins in freethought; it was a battle cry. To the champions of science, enlightenment, and progress, secularization of the schools was a key element in the advancement of society, which was leaving behind the outmoded machinery of ecclesiasticism and clearing the cobwebs of superstition from the minds of young people.

To the most extreme Catholic viewers-with-alarm, the public school movement (which was inseparably linked with secularization) seemed a demonically inspired Masonic plot, which had for its purpose to drive out every trace of Christian belief and implant in its place the rival worldview of scientific naturalism. Even American Catholic liberals spoke sharply of secularism. The optimistic Father Hecker, for example, called secularists "the worst sect of all," and Archbishop John Ireland thought Protestants and Catholics should work together to prevent the public schools from falling completely into the hands of "unbelievers and secularists," whose position amounted to a religion too, "and usually a very loud-spoken and intolerant religion."[32]

Few Protestants, however, could be persuaded that they had more in common with Catholics than with secularists. When they cast their gaze across the Atlantic, their natural sympathies did not go out to the embattled papacy, though it claimed to be defending Christian belief against the onslaughts of atheism. On the contrary, they tended to align themselves with the forces of secularism, who associated their cause with values Americans had always cherished — freedom for the individual, republicanism in government, and democracy in social relations. Education was a central issue in the European contest between the Catholic Church and the modern secular state; as the comments of Morgan and O'Byrne suggest, observation of that contest reinforced the opposition of American Protestants to Catholic claims in respect to the schools.

For American Catholics, the principal effect of the European struggle was to sharpen the apocalyptic, religion-against-atheism quality of the school controversy. Especially in traditionally Catholic countries where the Church wielded great influence, liberalism had become something of a rival religion. Many of its adherents frankly hated the Church, those who served it, and all the beliefs and values for which it stood. We cannot pause to inquire why this came about, or whether it could have been avoided.[33] The point is that, as matters actually stood at the time, liberals of this stripe really *were* enemies of the Church, and the kind of secularization they promoted really *was* intended to inculcate a set of beliefs and values different from those represented by traditional Christianity. Catholic observers in the United States were naturally affected by this spectacle, and it is perhaps understandable that they sometimes failed to make the appropriate distinctions in pointing out the lessons to be drawn from it.

The literature of condemnation produced by the European conflict was well known to American Catholics. Thomas J. Jenkins, a priest-pamphleteer from Kentucky, reviewed the field in a tract entitled *The Judges of Faith: Christian vs. Godless Schools,* which went through several editions and won a certain notoriety among Protestant critics of the Catholic position.[34] Besides scores of American pronouncements, Jenkins included passages from papal statements and pastoral letters or synodal decrees emanating from Ireland, England, Belgium, the Netherlands, France, Austria, and Prussia. An especially important document was Pius IX's 1864 letter to the archbishop of Freiburg in Breisgau, which concluded by saying that Catholics could not in conscience patronize schools where their faith would be endangered.[35] This letter figured prominently in a campaign waged by James A. McMaster, the ultra-Catholic editor of the *New York Freeman's Journal,* to get a formal Roman condemnation of American public schools. McMaster succeeded to the extent of eliciting from Propaganda an 1875 "Instruction" to the American hierarchy that was the most stringent yet on the subject and that sanctioned refusing absolution to parents who disregarded pastoral guidance on the school question.[36] The Instruction was coolly received by most of the bishops, but its existence guaranteed that the school question would be on the preliminary agenda Rome prepared a few years later for the Third Plenary Council of Baltimore.

Even as preparatory work for the Council was under way, the Catholic press carried stirring reports of conflicts in several European countries. In Germany the *Kulturkampf* was clearly abating, and an article on "Prince Bismarck's Conflict with the Catholic Church" was markedly triumphalist in tone.[37] In Belgium Catholics had won a notable victory on the educational front. In 1879 a liberal government abrogated existing arrangements for religious education in the state schools; the bishops responded by setting up a system of Catholic free schools that drew multitudes from the state system. Only a few months before the anticlerical government fell in the summer of 1884, a New York priest was moved to exclaim: "How the zeal and perseverance of these Belgian Catholics should stimulate American Catholics in the same holy cause of resisting a system which is contrary to Christianity, and in the light of this glorious example how gross appears the indifference of the Protestant sects to the decay of Christian convictions which are melting away through the influence of the public schools."[38]

In France the outlook was much grimmer. The liberals, having won control of the government in 1880, launched a program of secularization whose spirit was captured in the sardonic dictum of Georges Clemenceau: "The clergy must learn to render to Caesar what is Caesar's . . . and must also learn that everything belongs to Caesar."[39] Anticlericalism remained virulent in French civic life over the next generation, culminating in the early years of the twentieth century in drastic laws suppressing religious congregations and terminating the Concordat that had regulated the relations of church and state since Napoleonic times.

In Italy the papal struggle against liberalism and nationalism had ended in defeat years before the Third Plenary Council met. Ecclesiastical control over education was swept away through most of the country by 1860; when Rome itself was occupied by armies of the Kingdom of Italy ten years later, Pius IX withdrew to become "the prisoner of the Vatican." As a kind of reminder of these sad events, a flurry arose in 1884 when the Italian government threatened to confiscate and sell the North American College, the residence for American seminarians in Rome. A timely appeal to Washington led to diplomatic pressure that averted this seizure, but the pastoral letter of Baltimore III took note that "the ruthless hand of spoliation" was still poised to strike.[40]

Taking the European picture into account, one did not have to be a fanatic to conclude that the distinctive quality of irreligion in the late nineteenth century was that it had become politicized. The threat, in other words, did not arise simply from the fact that leading scientists, philosophers, and other men of learning were atheists or agnostics, that their views were given wide circulation in the popular press and were beginning to penetrate the level of mass public opinion. That was all true, of course, but what concentrated the threat and gave it immediacy was the fact that these naturalistic tendencies had become identified with the political programs of well-organized groups which sought to gain control of the coercive instrumentalities of state power to reshape society in keeping with their irreligious worldviews. Secularization of the schools obviously fit into the program of these groups, and they had had considerable success in certain times and places in shaping national educational policies to their own ends.

Against this background, it is not surprising that the American bishops were particularly sensitive to the dangers of secularization. They knew perfectly well—and so stated in the Baltimore decrees—that many Americans who advocated secularization of the schools were not in any way anti-religious. In responding to such persons, who usually argued that secularization was demanded by the religious diversity of American society, the bishops stressed the inherent defects of education that left God out, insisting that it tended inevitably to become "irreligious and wicked," and was therefore dangerous to Christian faith and morals.[41] They were undoubtedly convinced of the validity of this argument. But one can hardly doubt, either, that the bishops' familiarity with European anticlericalism and its fondness for schemes of secularization helped to make them apprehensive of secular education, no matter what motivated its advocates.

The same inference applies to the uneasiness felt by American Catholics over the increasing role of the state in education. The assumption of this responsibility by the state was, in fact, a new thing in the nineteenth century, and Catholic thinking had not yet reached the point of according public authorities a legitimate role in education. But beyond that, state control over schools in Europe was often associated with open hostility to the Church and a determination to eliminate her educational influence. Admittedly, matters were not so bad in the United States, but even here Catholic schools were frowned upon and there were occasional mutterings about the need for a European-style campaign against "clericalism." Considerations like this help to explain why many churchmen were hostile to state involvement in education and why bitter conflicts erupted a few years after Baltimore III over compulsory-attendance laws and state inspection of schools.[42]

Disagreement among Catholics over such legislation was one of the issues in the great "school controversy" that raged in the early 1890s. Archbishop Ireland's sympathy for laws requiring some use of English in parochial schools was particularly offensive to German Catholics, but willingness to concede any regulatory right to the state seemed to all conservatives a betrayal of the Catholic cause. That was what made Thomas Bouquillon's *Education, To Whom Does It Belong?* (1891) such a bombshell. For this short treatise by the Catholic University theologian was the first serious theoretical work by a Catholic to affirm that the state did, indeed, have a legitimate sphere of authority in educational matters. The pamphlet war that followed Bouquillon's publication, along with the protests set off by Archbishop Ireland's Faribault plan (a compromise arrangement with state authorities), divided the American hierarchy more openly than ever before.[43] The historian John Gilmary Shea was dismayed at the "great split" that shattered the unity of the American Church; years later bishops still spoke of the scandal it provoked.[44] Today we are perhaps less easily scandalized, but the eruption of controversy over the schools so soon after Baltimore III suggests that we ought to look more closely at the nature of the consensus existing then.

Agreement and Disagreement at the Council and After

Up to now, I have spoken as though all the bishops were in perfect accord on matters educational. That requires qualification, for there were naturally differences of view, especially as one moved further from fundamentals toward practical applications of principle. The bishops were virtually unanimous in thinking that the times were especially perilous from the religious point of view and that new efforts were required in education. The conviction was almost as widely shared that, since religion was the true foundation of all education, it should permeate the entire school program, especially in the grammar schools, where the child's moral and religious character was most malleable. True, Bishop Edward Fitzgerald of Little Rock argued at Baltimore that "We were ordained to teach catechism not to teach school. If we know that children are learning the catechism it is enough." But he found no explicit support for this view, and he was probably animated as much by the practical difficulties of establishing parochial schools as by the theoretical adequacy of catechism as an alternative.[45]

Most members of the hierarchy probably regarded the state-supported denominational system as the ideal solution to the financial difficulties of maintaining Catholic schools.[46] But it was clear that this system was not going to be adopted on any significant scale. Hence most of the bishops had reached the conclusion that voluntarily supported parochial schools were the only realistic means of providing the kind of religious education they regarded as necessary. This view was far from novel in 1884 — we have seen that Bishop Hughes proclaimed it in the 1840s; the plenary councils of 1852 and 1866 exhorted Catholics to establish parochial schools; and such schools actually existed in great numbers, there being upwards of a half million pupils in more than 2,400 of them in 1884.[47]

Certain bishops stood out as special champions of the parochial school. As a group, prelates of German background fell into this category. Ethnic and linguistic distinctiveness reinforced religion in their case, but there were also outstanding English-speaking advocates of parochial schools — notably John Lancaster Spalding, an old-line American; Bernard J. McQuaid, a second-generation Irish American; and Richard Gilmour, a Scottish-born convert.[48] Other bishops were daunted by the practical difficulties, or placed a lower priority on Catholic schools; perhaps the leading example here was John J. Williams of Boston.[49] Lack of uniformity, to the degree that it existed, seemed a more serious defect to the strong advocates of the parochial school than to the less committed. Archbishop Michael Heiss of Milwaukee, for example, apparently wanted a uniform national requirement as a means of reinforcing the commitment of his own flock, who were already supporting an extensive system.[50]

Whether to establish such a requirement was the major point of disagreement at Baltimore III.[51] The only other significant disagreement about schools concerned the use of spiritual sanctions to enforce the requirement. The Council fathers also spent a good deal of time worrying over the question of what constituted a Catholic school. But that somewhat theoretical issue served primarily to muddy the debate and distract the participants from substantive points on which practical action had been proposed. In the end it was left up to each bishop to rule on the Catholicity of any particular school when the question arose in concrete terms.

In analyzing the conciliar debate, the first point to be emphasized is that the language of requirement originated with the American bishops and not with Rome. A group of American prelates had been called to Rome a year before the Council and presented with a preliminary schema for discussion. But neither in this form, nor in the revised schema that emerged from the Roman discussions, was the language of command employed. Parochial schools were "urged" and "commended," but not required.[52] And when Archbishop Charles J. Seghers of Oregon City pointed out in the Roman consultations that some bishops thought well of a decree requiring that parochial schools be erected within a specific time limit, the curial Cardinals very clearly responded that such a decree would not be expedient.[53] The schema actually debated at Baltimore III, however, did require parochial schools to be built within two years, and it used the language of command in respect to the pastors who were to erect them, the congregations who were to support them, and the parents who were to patronize them. All of this was inserted into the schema at some indeterminate point *after* the Roman consultations and in clear disregard of the guidance offered there by curial officials.

In the debate itself, Fitzgerald of Little Rock was much the most active opponent of imposing a requirement. He had gained some notoriety at the First Council of the Vatican as one of the two bishops of the Church universal who voted against papal infallibility. This time, however, he either forgot or didn't know that he could have called upon Roman authority in objecting to what he called "new and formidable legislation . . . legislation unknown to any country in the world."[54] Ryan of Philadelphia, who is usually classified as a conservative strongly committed to parochial schools, also counseled moderation in imposing requirements, and Feehan of Chicago believed that exhortation might be more effective in practice. McCloskey of Louisville had misgivings, and Patrick W. Riordan, coadjutor of San Francisco, wanted to bury the whole business in committee because he thought parochial schools impracticable in the West. Joseph S. Alemany, soon to resign from the see of San Francisco, may have felt the same way for he too favored exhortation over command.

Fitzgerald's opposite number as the most vociferous proponent of stringent requirements was Joseph Dwenger of Fort Wayne, who had the support of his fellow bishops of German background, Heiss of Milwaukee, Borgess of Detroit, and Flasch of LaCrosse. But Gilmour of Cleveland played a more active role than any of these except Dwenger, and McQuaid of Rochester held forth on the evils of public schools, among which was the fact that they encouraged friendships that led to mixed marriages. Other prelates who supported the requirement were Hennessy of Dubuque, Janssens of Natchez, and Watterson of Columbus. The decisive vote came on a motion offered by Bishop James A. Healy of Portland, Maine, which was apparently intended as a compromise. The specific issue related to the obligation of parents to send their children to parochial schools. Healy's motion stated this obligation, then added the words, "unless the Ordinary judges that otherwise it may be done."[56] The motion was approved by a vote of forty-one to thirty-three (41/33), which was fairly close; but since the language left plenty of leeway for exceptions, it is difficult to interpret the vote. One commentator believes that the negative votes were about equally divided between those who thought the requirement too severe and those who objected to the built-in loophole.[55]

The other major issue — spiritual punishments — arose in two places. As presented to the Council, the rule requiring congregations to contribute to the support of parochial schools explicitly provided for "spiritual punishments"— understood to mean interdict — for parishes that were "supine" in their negligence and "contumacious" in refusing to mend their ways. When Healy suggested dropping this language because no bishop would resort to interdict for so trivial a matter, he was promptly rebutted by Chatard of Vincennes and his episcopal neighbor, the formidable Dwenger, who announced that he had already chastised recalcitrant parishes in just this manner. "Spiritual punishments" therefore remained in the decree until it reached Rome for approval; there the language was toned down to read that seriously delinquent congregations were to be "induced to contribute the necessary support" by the bishop's reproaches and "by the most efficacious and prudent means possible."[57]

The second place the matter came up was in the rule calling on parents to send their children to Catholic schools. At some point in the proceedings, a phrase had been appended to the rule stating that those who were contumacious in this regard were to be denied absolution. Since the phrase was quoted from Propaganda's Instruction of 1875, the addition seemed to enlist Rome in behalf of the rigorists' position. Bishop Spalding, although a staunch school man, became concerned about the addition and called upon the Council to reconsider its action. A number of bishops took part in the debate that followed, including John Ireland, who argued that the phrase had been taken out of context. When it was over, the vote was thirty-seven to thirty-two (37/32) to drop the explicit threat to refuse absolution to parents who willfully sent their children to public schools.[58]

Disagreement on school matters thus obviously existed at Baltimore III. But what was it about? Not about whether the state had a right to educate, or whether some compromise could be reached with public authorities, or whether supplemental religious instruction might suffice for Catholic children. The first two points were not debated at all, and Fitzgerald's assertion that the catechism was enough was not taken up as a serious matter for consideration. Disagreement focused, rather, on how

far the Council should go in requiring the erection and support of parochial schools as a part of the universally binding law of the American
Church, and in providing severe ecclesiastical penalties for those who
disobeyed that law. By majority vote, the Council fathers adopted a stance
on these questions that was more rigorous than that indicated by Roman
guidelines.[59] At the same time, however, great leeway was left for episcopal discretion in determining whether a school was Catholic (which might
permit compromises with the state), in disciplining pastors and congregations, and in allowing exceptions to parents who wished to send their children to non-Catholic schools. This degree of practical flexibility probably
mollified the opposition, few if any of whom were opposed to parochial
schools on principle.

Considering the nature of the debate and its outcome, we are certainly justified in saying that a broad consensus on education existed among
the bishops at the time of Baltimore III. This degree of unity is all the more
striking when contrasted to the deep divisions that opened up a few years
later.[60] The obvious question is, what happened? Why did the consensus
break down? It is too complicated a question to enter upon in detail, but
let me make a few general observations before closing.

In the first place, it didn't help that bitter conflict over schools flared
anew between Catholics and non-Catholics in the late 1880s, especially
in Massachusetts, Ohio, Wisconsin, and Illinois. The American Protective
Association, which came into existence in those years, also made defense
of "the little red schoolhouse" a leading theme in its program of anti-
Catholicism.[61] In these circumstances, some Catholics thought new departures advisable, while others were sensitized to anything that seemed a
weakening of the Church's position.

Much more important was the fact that the school controversy was
inseparably linked with a whole series of other issues that divided the
bishops into two opposing camps.[62] The first rumblings began soon after
Baltimore III, as difficulties arose over the establishment of the Catholic
University and as German Catholics complained to Rome about treatment
at the hands of the Irish-dominated hierarchy. The nationality question—
or "Cahenslyism," as it was called after 1891—was interwoven with the
controversy over education because critics of the Germans accused them
of using the parochial schools to perpetuate ethnic identity, while the
Germans charged the Americanizers with having abandoned Catholic
schools. Other splits developed before the school question reached its climax, overlapping with it in one way or another. The most important dealt
with secret societies, particularly the Knights of Labor, the theories of
Henry George, and the handling of the rebellious New York priest, Edward McGlynn, who flatly opposed parochial schools. As the interlinked

battles over the schools and German nationality raged on, still more new issues arose—over the appointment of an apostolic delegate, over participation in interfaith gatherings, and finally over "Americanism" as a theological aberration.

Those who remember the 1960s can testify that the ground shifts rapidly in a time of ideological conflict. The dynamic of history takes over— which is only a grandiose way of saying that the understanding people have of public issues, and the stands they take, are transformed by the very process of change that is going on. Action taken demands counteraction; that in turn must be met by still further action in continuing ding-dong fashion. Opinion stated prompts immediate rebuttal, and that requires counter-rebuttal in the same manner. Attitudes, beliefs, and institutions that seemed firmly fixed are questioned, discredited, toppled over. Ideas that would have been called extreme a short time before, now attract wide support and become platforms for action. As ideological factions crystallize, a person feels obligated to take a stand, to choose up sides, perhaps more on the basis of what he opposes and fears than on the basis of what he favors and hopes for. And once one adopts a position—throws in intellectually and emotionally with the liberals, the conservatives, the radicals, or whomever—it is difficult not to impute the worst motives to the opposition, not to portray their thinking in terms of its direst possible consequences.

This is the sort of context within which the school controversy of the 1890s has to be set. The actual points of difference between liberals and conservatives with respect to parochial schools were insignificant by comparison with what each side thought those differences revealed about the hidden motives and ideological purposes of the opposition. After all, the Faribault plan, which brought down such a storm around Archbishop Ireland's head, did not differ materially from dozens of other compromise arrangements that had existed for years.[63] The point was that Ireland was a liberal and Americanizer; *his* promotion of such an arrangement was interpreted as the first step toward complete abandonment of the parochial schools, which the conservatives regarded as a precious, and precariously maintained, institution.

Attitudes toward the school question were thus largely derivative from a more basic orientation toward liberalism or conservatism. But what did these terms really mean? What kind of content did they embody? To attempt answering those questions would be to embark on another paper, which I have no intention of doing. Let me just draw attention to two dimensions of the answer that are not without contemporary relevance. The first has to do with the relation of the Church to the modern world; the second, with the place of America as a part of the modern world.

A key element in the formation of the liberal faction of the hierarchy was the change of direction in thinking about the modern world introduced by Pope Leo XIII. Whereas Pius IX seemed to be calling for flat rejection of the modern world, Leo urged Catholics to *redeem* the modern world. This oversimplifies, of course, but there was a definite shift after Leo assumed the papal throne in 1878.[64] Neither pontiff accepted modernity as it was, but the Leonine strategy had two great advantages over that of Pio Nono. First, it was more nuanced, calling for discrimination between the positive and negative tendencies of modern life; secondly, it was dynamic, summoning Catholics to tasks more constructive than anathematizing the evils of the day. Leo also laid down concrete guidelines for action, most notably in respect to the revival of Thomism, which he was sure offered an adequate intellectual basis for overcoming modern error, and also in respect to the social question and modern democracy. There were definite limits to Leo's flexibility, as the Americanizers learned to their sorrow. It is certainly understandable, however, that as the overall thrust of his policy emerged in the mid-1880s, the more forward-looking members of the American hierarchy were encouraged to begin thinking along bold new lines.[65]

This was especially the case because of the conviction, held in greater or lesser degree by many American churchmen, that the social, political, and economic system of the United States embodied just about everything that was positive in modernity, and relatively few of its worst features. Even the separation of church and state—a bitter pill indeed to Rome and most Continental ecclesiastics—proved in practice to be a very favorable arrangement for American Catholics. From their lived experience Catholic leaders in this country were apt to entertain more benign views of modernity than their European counterparts. This Catholic version of American exceptionalism—the conviction that America was different from, and better than, Europe—was held most self-consciously by the small group of liberal Americanists who pushed things too far for many of their colleagues in the turbulent 1890s.

Were they really pushing too far? Or were the conservatives just unduly nervous? Without attempting to adjudicate those questions further, I would urge that American Catholics take to heart the realization that the school question today, as it was a century ago, is inseparable from the larger question of how religion should relate to life. In certain respects, there are surprising similarities between the school question of the 1880s and that of the present—the issue of public aid, for example, or the uncertainty as to how to respond to secularism.[66] But one cannot find a master key to the solution of today's problems in what the fathers of Baltimore III did or failed to do. What can be found there is the example of men who cared deeply about the values at stake and who tried to do justice to the realities as they saw them. Perhaps that is as much as we should hope for from the study of history.

7

THE SEARCH FOR UNITY
AND ITS SEQUEL

This paper, which served as my presidential address to the American Catholic Historical Association in 1978 and appeared in the Catholic Historical Review *the following year, is the most personal of the essays collected in this volume. It may also be the best illustration of what I described in the Introduction as the psychologically "marginalizing" effect of living through a period of profound religious change. We are, of course, notoriously unreliable authorities on matters in which we are deeply involved personally. Nonetheless, I am convinced that having witnessed at first hand the spiritual earthquake of the sixties, and having experienced it as the disintegration of a previously internalized religious worldview, were crucial factors in suggesting to me the topic treated here as the subject for a presidential address and in leading me to approach it as I did.*

Since the theme of integration—the unification of faith and life—figures so prominently in the discussion, it will perhaps not seem presumptuous for me to add that the paper attempts to integrate what I felt from my own experience and what I learned from historical study of twentieth-century American Catholicism, especially in the area of higher education. In other words, my aim here is to marshall historical evidence and argumentation in support of a general interpretation of preconciliar American Catholic culture that would help to explain why a person formed by that culture would react as I did—and as I believe many others did—when it was challenged and in large part repudiated. For myself at least, the results validate the claim made on behalf of historical study that a deeper understanding of the past in a sense liberates us from its grip and not only illuminates the present but also enables us to deal with it in a more realistic and critical manner.

In revising the essay, I have not attempted to eliminate the personal

136

quality or remove references appropriate to the occasion for which it was originally composed. I have, however, expanded certain passages and added a few citations.

THERE IS SOMETHING ABOUT THE OCCASION of a presidential address that tempts one powerfully toward autobiography. Being elected to high office is a most consoling experience; it naturally tends to confirm a person's good opinion of his own wisdom and to persuade him that others would rejoice to learn how it was acquired.

Although I found this line of reasoning seductive, you will be reassured to learn that I do not intend to act upon it. Two considerations in particular deter me. In the first place, my predecessors in this office have resisted the temptation admirably, and I would not wish to introduce a precedent that might well become a matter of universal regret if followed too faithfully. Secondly, we belong to a tradition in which there is an uncomfortably close relationship between autobiography and confession. Upon reflection, it seemed to me just as well to leave all such penitential exercises undisturbed in the desuetude into which they have fallen.

While thus foregoing autobiography, I cannot repress the feeling that I — and all American Catholics of middle years and older — have lived through extraordinary times from the religious point of view. I refer, of course, to the dramatic changes that overtook the Church in the 1960s, for which the aptest image that I have been able to devise is that of a spiritual earthquake. These events cry aloud for historical treatment, and it seems to me that we historians have an obligation to examine them and to offer whatever enlightenment our studies may afford to a community still dazed and disoriented by what has happened. But because we have lived through these times, our attempts to understand them cannot help being profoundly shaped by our own personal reactions to the developments in question. Hence an element of personal testimony — if not of autobiography proper — is necessarily implicated in any effort to analyze and interpret what happened in the 1960s. This is especially the case for a person like myself who was of mature years and settled religious disposition when the whole thing began.

No single term can adequately capture the sense one has of a great social movement while it is in progress, but the predominant impression I can recall feeling in the midst of the Catholic upheaval of the 1960s was the impression of *disintegration*. This word inevitably carries evaluative connotations, but I mean it more as a descriptive term. That is, the strongest sense I had was of a Church, a religious tradition, that was coming undone, breaking apart, losing its coherence. Aside from idiosyncrasies of personal temperament, there are more general considerations that help explain why an American Catholic of my generation would have such a reaction. Considerations of this sort will be the main topic of my remarks, but first let me run quickly through some of the symptoms of disintegration as they appeared to me.[1]

The great exodus from the priesthood and religious life was perhaps the most visible and dramatic symptom. Without impugning in any way the motives or integrity of any who resigned from the priesthood or left their religious communities, it must still be said that such a phenomenon on such a scale was a profound shock. To adult Catholics of the 1960s, the idea that one could "resign" from the priesthood was unheard of—a priest was a priest forever, and that was all there was to it. This belief, which people certainly regarded as part of the Church's traditional teaching, accounted in good part for the shock. But there was something else. Priests and religious constitute an elite, the group regarded as most expert in and dedicated to matters religious. Wholesale withdrawal from the priesthood and religious life thus seemed to signify that those best qualified to assess such matters no longer had confidence in what they were doing, no longer believed in it—and perhaps simply no longer believed.

Other aspects of institutional disintegration are too well known to require elaboration—the falling off of vocations, the closing of Catholic schools, the breakdown of respect for ecclesiastical authority, and the erosion of traditional moral norms, especially in the area of sexual conduct. At the same time, one Catholic society after another went through an "identity crisis." Catholic philosophers, formerly so self-assured, asked themselves, "Who Are We?" And Catholic theologians were no longer certain what their position was, or whether they had anything distinctive to say on dogmatic or moral questions as "Catholic" theologians.[2]

Even more striking were the instances in which reformers of the 1960s explicitly repudiated the goals toward which reformers in the same areas had bent their efforts ten or twenty years earlier. Thus a lay liturgical leader of the 1960s declared that it was precisely the idea of "worship" that had to be eliminated from religion.[3] A leader of what was formerly called catechetical renewal reached the conclusion by 1968 that "the problem of catechetics is that it exists."[4] The Catholic Art Association had always stood for *Good Work;* in fact, that was the name of its official organ. Yet the last publication sponsored by the Association was a pathetic attempt to emulate the hippie counterculture that regarded "work" as one of the few truly dirty four-letter words in the language.[5] And whereas upgrading Catholic intellectual life was the name of the game in the 1950s, a decade later we were told that a Catholic university was a contradiction in terms, and that the expression "intellectual apostolate" was a recruiting slogan for "holy panderers." No less prophetic a teacher than Daniel Berrigan assured collegians at Notre Dame that learning was no substitute for moral action. Pure scholarship, so highly prized by the Catholic "self-critics" of the fifties, he dismissed as "raw sewerage."[6]

These were some of the more lurid extremes, to be sure; and there were contrary tendencies and evidences of fresh life and growth. But for me the overall impression was one of demoralization and collapse rather than renewal or revitalization. I am aware that some found the 1960s religiously exhilarating. I suppose one should admire such folk, but the best I can do is marvel at a religious mentality so different from my own. For, to come right out with it, I found the sixties pretty devastating—devastating because what was threatened with utter decomposition was faith itself. American Catholics seem gripped by a kind of collective reticence on this subject, perhaps because of an instinctive sense that some things are better left unsaid, but two writers who operate from very different perspectives —James Hitchcock and Garry Wills—have said enough to convince me that a good many others besides myself experienced the sixties as deeply unsettling to their faith.[7]

It would have been remarkable had this not been the case, given the contrast between what happened in the sixties and what had gone before. Indeed, Catholics who had absorbed the mentality predominant in the generation before the Council had about the worst possible preparation for the sixties, because the main thrust in those years was toward an organically unified Catholic culture in which religious faith constituted the integrating principle that brought all the dimensions of life and thought together in comprehensive and tightly articulated synthesis.

My thesis, therefore, is that the stress on unity and integral Catholicism from the 1920s through the 1950s heightened the disintegrative impact of changes in the postconciliar years and made those changes particularly unsettling to the faith of persons whose religious character had been formed during the earlier period. In arguing this thesis I will first review in a general way a number of facets of the drive for unity and then look more closely at how it affected the area of Catholic higher education.

The Drive for Unity

A characteristic pronouncement on the general subject was made in 1928 by the founder of the American Catholic Historical Association, Peter Guilday. Catholics should rejoice at the widened scope of historical studies, Guilday told the ninth annual meeting of the ACHA in 1928, since their "belief in God, in the purpose of creation, in man's original fall with its consequences, and in man's final destiny, enables them to see, even as in a glass darkly, the magnificent unity of life, the stupendously intricate weave of the warp and woof of human existence, and the all-embracing divine guidance of a world which we Catholics hold and hold most firmly was created to know God, to love God and to serve God in this life in order to be happy with Him in the world to come."[8]

Statements even more florid than Guilday's could be cited from an earlier period, but it was only in the 1930s that terms like "organic unity," "synthetic vision," "integral Catholicism," and "Catholic culture" became buzz words of American Catholic discussion. The magazine *Integrity* announced its theme in capital letters in the first issue (October 1946): "WE MUST MAKE A NEW SYNTHESIS OF RELIGION AND LIFE." And the same editorial statement noted that the expression "integral Catholicism" was gaining in popular acceptance and that it did "not mean piety so much as wholeness."

In the cognitive sphere, an integrated vision had been achieved by St. Thomas, and the Thomistic synthesis was the official philosophy of Catholics, which meant that everything had already been brought together at the highest level of abstraction. In the more strictly spiritual realm, the Church was the authoritative teacher and embodiment of the salvific truth, and the growing emphasis in the 1930s on the theology of the Mystical Body of Christ unified the Church and the faithful as members of Christ Himself.[9] Catholics were therefore spiritually united in the closest possible way. Because integral wholeness thus already existed as speculative and spiritual realities, the main task as perceived by Catholics in those years was the essentially practical one of bringing home to the faithful the full realization of what this unity meant to them personally, and the further task, likewise practical, of working out its implications and applying them to various spheres of social and cultural life.

The carrying out of these practical tasks inspired a plethora of Catholic movements and the organization of a wide range of specialized Catholic societies. The liturgical movement, for example, was directed primarily toward awakening among the faithful a more lively sense of their being members of a corporate body, the Church, which was one with Christ and whose great act of worship was the renewal of Christ's redemptive sacrifice. Liturgical renewal, which emerged as an organized national movement in the American Church in 1940, was not a strictly "churchy" affair. On the contrary, liturgical leaders like Virgil Michel saw a close connection between the liturgy and social reform because the Church's social teaching, too, stressed corporatism. Like the Church itself, society was to be understood as an organism, a living unity, whose members were interdependent, not as a collocation of privatized individuals who interacted only on the basis of self-interest. True social reform, as Catholics understood it, therefore required displacement of liberal individualism and the restoration of a communal order characterized by organic unity and solidarity.[10]

To translate this Catholic social vision into concrete practical action was the task of the lay apostolate—in particular, of "Catholic Action." Stress on the lay apostolate went back to Pope Pius X, who sought to enlist the laity in the campaign to "renew all things in Christ," but Catholic Action was the special enthusiasm of Pius XI, sometimes called the Catholic Action Pope. In both cases, the point of emphasis was that lay people were full-fledged members of Christ's Mystical Body, the Church, and as such they had their appropriate responsibility, which was to apply Catholic principles in the secular world—with the approval of the hierarchy, naturally, and under the guidance of the clergy. Catholic Action really came into its own in the American Church only in the 1930s, when it represented the cutting edge of the drive for unity on the practical level.[11]

Somewhat analogous in function were the many Catholic professional associations set up in the first half of the twentieth century. There were differences among them of course, but all had the eminently practical aims of improving Catholic performance in, and applying Catholic principles to, the concerns of their various areas. Each had the general function, one might say, of showing how its field of specialization related to Catholic truth, where it fit into the Catholic synthesis. The Catholic Educational Association, formed in 1904, was the oldest such organization, but the American Catholic Philosophical Association, established in 1926, was the most important, since philosophers were regarded as the special custodians of the Catholic vision. The Catholic Theological Society of America, founded in 1945, was a relative Johnny-come-lately. By that time Catholic workers in the fields of history, anthropology, poetry, sociology, biblical studies, art, literature, and economics all had their own societies, and so did those engaged in more practically oriented fields such as journalism, social work, and medicine.[12]

Many of the activities touched on in this quick glance at the drive for unity impinged directly on Catholic higher education. The great majority of those active in Catholic professional associations, for example, were college or seminary professors, and college students were much involved in Catholic Action. Moreover, Catholic colleges confronted a number of practical problems related to the realization of the Catholic vision. Hence a closer look at this area will perhaps give us a clearer insight into the dynamics of the search for unity.

A very obvious practical problem in the 1920s was simple growth.

The average annual rate of increase in enrollments at Catholic colleges in the decade was 19 percent, and almost half (43 percent) of the students attending Catholic colleges for women in 1930 were enrolled in schools founded within the same ten-year span.[13] This massive increase of numbers reflected changes both in the Catholic population and in the role of higher education in American society. Hence, responding to it required not just a simple enlargement of Catholic facilities, but also institutional reorganization and modernization. For that reason matters like standardization (or accreditation, as it was later called), adoption of the departmental and credit-hour systems, and the introduction of new programs incorporating more electives were developments still in process, or were still very new, in the 1920s.[14]

But precisely this process of modernization, which was indispensable if Catholic institutions were to survive, created grave problems of curricular integration, because it involved significant departures from the traditional liberal arts program. As new subjects were added to the course of studies, and departmentalization of knowledge increased, the old unity of vision and purpose departed. The more conservative Catholic college men branded such changes as the death of true education. They were heartened by the criticism of fragmentation and electivism mounted by reformers like Abraham Flexner and Robert M. Hutchins, but they also maintained that curricular fragmentation was the inevitable product of a secularist outlook and that Catholics should therefore be particularly on their guard against it.[15]

Now of course Catholics were not in the situation described by Alexander Meiklejohn, who said that American educators were "lost and mixed up and bewildered . . . [because] we haven't got a gospel, a philosophy . . . a religion" to hand on to students. As a result, he went on, "We don't know what to say about life as our fathers did. We haven't got the whole body of the curriculum bound together in terms of a single enterprise in which we are engaged. . . . The old structure of interpretation of human life is wrecked, it has lost its unity, it has lost its power."[16] Catholics had all of the things Meiklejohn said secular educators lacked. Their problem was simply how the task of integration was to be handled. The answer that emerged in the midtwenties and was not effectively challenged for over a decade was that philosophy, rather than religion itself, was the crucial element in integrating Catholic higher education.

This development was intimately linked to the revival of Scholastic philosophy. With the formation of the American Catholic Philosophical Association, the publication of its journal *The New Scholasticism* (1927), and the appearance of *The Modern Schoolman* (1925), Neoscholasticism attained the level of a popular ideology among American Catholic educators. The seminary section of the National Catholic Educational Association devoted all its sessions to St. Thomas in 1924, and three years later James A. Burns, C.S.C., perhaps the most progressive and enlightened Catholic educator of his generation, laid it down that "Philosophy with all its branches is the most important study in the [Catholic] college and deserves first consideration in the arranging of the curriculum, the practical control of the various educative factors at work, and above all, [in] the selection of teachers."[17] In 1929 the graduate dean of Marquette University listed Scholastic philosophy first among the subjects the teaching of which "should have precedence . . . from the viewpoint of [creating] a Catholic civilization in America." After philosophy came the classical languages, education, sociology, biology, and history. Theology was not mentioned at all.[18]

Scholastic philosophy recommended itself as the unifying discipline because it was closely associated with the Catholic faith, supporting and elucidating it, and yet was rational rather than fideistic. In philosophy the student learned a great deal of his religion on the basis of reason rather than as straight doctrinal teaching based on authority. Hence philosophy was the most appropriate way for collegians to learn their faith, since they were thinking adults rather than immature schoolchildren. And since Scholastic philosophy and natural law had applications in politics, social teaching, the family, and ethics generally, it not only presented the fundamental truths in the most cogent form, it also spelled out their implications for other areas of knowledge. It served, in other words, as the rational core of a comprehensive synthesis of knowledge.[19]

Religion, Theology, and Integral Unity

But what of theology? you ask. Where did this leave the queen of the sciences? Her day had not yet dawned. Indeed, the teaching of religion as an academic subject was still in its infancy in the 1920s. The Reverend John Montgomery Cooper, who began teaching religion courses to undergraduates at the Catholic University of America in 1909, was probably the first to teach it as a formal academic subject in an American Catholic college or university.[20] Up until then it had been simply a matter of the catechism. Only with the general adoption of the departmental and credit-hour system in the 1920s was there a movement to upgrade the teaching of Catholic doctrine into a regular curricular offering on a par with other academic subjects. In the twenties Catholic educators debated whether religion courses should receive academic credit, and many of them were highly impressed with the work of Father John O'Hara, the Prefect of Religion (and later president) of the University of Notre Dame, who eschewed the academic approach in favor of a high-pressure campaign to promote frequent reception of Holy Communion and a general intensification of piety and devotion.[21] As late as 1937, only three Catholic colleges out of eighty-four surveyed offered an academic major in religion.[22]

In the meantime, Father Cooper was busily engaged in publishing materials for classroom use, arguing for the teaching of religion, and building up what was to become the Catholic University of America's Department of Religious Education. Cooper insisted from the outset that collegiate instruction in religion had to be quite different in content and approach from seminary courses in theology. His idea was that religious instruction should deepen the student's existential grasp of his faith and quicken his sense of its relation to life. In other words, Cooper's aim was to integrate the Catholic collegian's life around faith, not on the basis of a conceptual grasp of its doctrines and their interrelations, but on the basis of a more profound appreciation of the spiritual riches of the Christian message and a more personal appropriation of its key insights.[23]

In 1929, Fulton J. Sheen, who had won his philosophical credentials by a brilliant career at the Catholic University of Louvain, endeavored to bring together Cooper's religious emphasis and the more intellectualist Neo-scholastic approach. Catholics, Sheen said, had to be educated for two worlds: the world of Peter, which was the Church, and the world of Pan, by which he meant secular society. *Vitalization* was the principle to be followed in the former case, according to Sheen, who cited Cooper's work as illustrating how education for the world of Peter should aim at making young Catholics aware of their faith as a living reality, the vital center of their personal lives. But as preparation for the world of Pan, these same Catholic students needed an education organized around the principle of *integration*. The purpose here was to convey the realization, not merely that Catholic truth constituted a coherent and rationally grounded system, but also that it meshed perfectly with the needs of modern society and fulfilled the inchoate spiritual longings of modern man. In this manner Sheen proposed that the two approaches to unity to be unified—or at least brought into a coherent relationship with each other.[24]

Sheen's address to the National Catholic Educational Association, which was entitled "Educating for a Catholic Renaissance," struck a dynamic evangelical note in the sense that it called for an education that would make Catholics apostles to a world in need of the religious vision and human understanding that only the true faith could provide. This note grew more pronounced in the 1930s. In the miseries of economic depression at home and with storm clouds rising in Europe and Asia, Catholic educators not only promoted papal social teaching and Catholic Action, but also insisted more emphatically than ever on the organic wholeness of Catholic truth and contrasted it more sharply to the prevailing secularist order that was plunging mankind headlong to destruction. In these circumstances it became a matter of the greatest urgency to implant in young Catholics an understanding of the integrated worldview that was their heritage and to inspire them to carry this vision with them into the marketplace of ideas and action.

One could easily multiply quotations illustrating this development, but two statements from the mid-thirties will suffice. In 1935, the Catholic Educational Association formally approved the report of its Committee on Educational Policy and Program, which included the following language:

> The Catholic college will not be content with presenting Catholicism as a creed, a code, or a cult. Catholicism must be seen as a culture; hence, the graduates of the Catholic college of liberal arts will go forth not merely trained in Catholic doctrine, but they will have seen the whole sweep of Catholicism, its part in the building up of our western civilization, past and present. . . . They will have before them not merely the facts in the natural order but those in the supernatural order also, those facts which give meaning and coherence to the whole of life.[25]

The degree to which "integration" and "unity" had become shibboleths is suggested by the remarks made a year later by Mother Grace C. Damman, president of Manhattanville College and a leading personage among Catholic educators. Affirming that all the key issues of college administration were summed up in "the problem of integration," Mother Damman ticked off the dimensions of its ideal solution as follows:

> The integration of the curriculum through a carefully chosen and trained faculty, the integration of the members of that faculty so that each functions as a cell in an organism for the good of the whole, the integration of faculty and students into a unified college with Catholic culture as its objective, the integration of all activities, social, extra-curricular, scholastic, religious—so that an atmosphere results in which this culture can flourish, and finally the integration of the educational efforts of each institution with the great aim set before us by our Holy Father Pius XI in his Encyclical on Catholic Action.[26]

As Catholic educators embarked on the practical implementation of these goals, a number of problems came to light. It rapidly became evident, for example, that developing the right kind of faculty would be a problem—and one that almost guaranteed a high level of institutional inbreeding, for where else could teachers be found who not only knew their specialities but also how to integrate them with religion and philosophy?[27] In 1936, a professor of educational psychology at Fordham University pointed out how difficult it was to integrate the factual data amassed by experimental methods with the conceptual scheme of Catholic philosophical psychology. To meet the difficulty, he urged upgrading the standards of Catholic scholarship; other educators who called for more and better Catholic graduate schools had the same problems in mind. But in 1938, another Fordham Jesuit, George Bull of the philosophy department, warned that Catholic graduate schools could not accept research as their primary aim because research was an activity whose fragmentizing tendency was inevitably destructive of the Catholic intellectual synthesis and the culture it inspired.[28]

Despite these complications, Catholic educators remained strongly committed to the goal of organic integration, and in 1939 a new approach was suggested: Theology was to be the integrating study. This idea was offered very tentatively at the April meeting of the Catholic Educational Association; six months later it was propounded much more forcefully at a two-day symposium sponsored in New York by the National Catholic Alumni Federation.[29] The general theme of the meeting was "Man and Modern Secularism," and the published version of the sessions carried the significant subtitle, "Essays on the Conflict of the Two Cultures." In proposing to combat secularism by teaching theology as the unifier of knowledge and the inspiration of an integrally Catholic culture, the sponsors of the symposium seemed to think that they were calling American Catholic colleges back to a tradition from which they had somehow strayed. That view was quite incorrect.[30] Theology, as an academic specialization, had never been taught to Catholic undergraduates in this country, and teaching it had never ever been suggested until 1939!

And as soon as the subject was broached disagreement arose over how theology should be taught. The two principal speakers on this matter were the Reverend Gerald B. Phelan, director of the Pontifical Institute of Mediaeval Studies in Toronto, and Francis J. Connell, C.SS.R., then at the Redemptorist seminary in Esopus, New York, and later to move to the Catholic University of America. Phelan first distinguished between religious instruction and "the formal teaching of theology as the *science* of Divine Faith," and then argued that theology should be taught: (1) because it was the highest and noblest of all sciences; (2) because it was "essential for the proper ordering of knowledge" gained from all the other sciences; and finally (3) because the special needs of the times made theological formation necessary for educated Catholics. Connell's talk was less systematic, but he referred to the Mystical Body and Catholic Action and indicated that apologetics was the aspect of theology that should be particularly stressed. He added, however, that the college theology course should also cover dogmatic and moral theology.[31]

After these two had finished, John Courtney Murray, S.J., took the floor (apparently at his own request) to present what the printed proceedings call "Necessary Adjustments to Overcome Practical Difficulties." Since the "practical difficulties" derived from the fact that seminary theology was in no way adapted to the goals outlined by Phelan and Connell, it is not surprising that the "necessary adjustments" Murray had in mind amounted to a thoroughgoing reform of theology. The problem was that the formal object of seminary theology was "the demonstrability of truth from the revealed word of God," whereas what Catholic collegians actually needed was a theology geared toward "the liveability of the Word of God." In simpler terms, Murray called for a theology "wholly orientated toward life" and designed to help lay people in relating the truths of faith to the secular world in which they dwelt.[32]

Murray's challenge set off a debate in subsequent years. After laying out his position more fully in a two-part article in *Theological Studies* in 1944, Murray did not contribute further to the debate, having moved on to the even more sensitive topics of intercredal cooperation and church and state (where, incidentally, he again encountered Father Connell as an antagonist).[33] Murray did, however, sketch out a plan for a college course in theology which several Jesuit confrères elaborated into a strongly Christocentric and kerygmatic four-year program with its accompanying textbooks.[34]

Murray's approach rested on the premise that pluralism was legitimate in theology, for he argued at length in *Theological Studies* that the distinctive *purpose* to which lay people would put their theological understanding required that they learn a different kind of theology from that taught to priests. This argument is of interest for two reasons. First, it constituted a remote American echo of the debates over "new theology" that were being carried on at the same time in Europe. And secondly, Murray's argument implied the following fundamental question: How could theology function effectively as an integrating principle in Catholic higher education if theology itself could be understood in diverse ways?[35]

The Scholastic Synthesis and the "Corpus doctrinae"

Despite the amount of ink that was spilled on the question of theology for lay students, the problems implicit in theological pluralism were not very clearly articulated or addressed. One reason for this omission was probably the fact that Murray was the only major figure calling for a new approach who used the term "theology" to designate what he was proposing, and his involvement in the debate, although quite important, was brief. His position was similar in substance to that of John Montgomery Cooper and other champions of the "religion" or "religious education" approach, who were frankly hostile to "theology."[36] Murray's intervention did not convert them to the use of the term "theology" to describe what they wanted; hence the contest continued to be one in which theology (as traditionally understood) was pitted, not against a new form of theology, but against something other than theology (religion or religious education) that was explicitly characterized as "nontheological."

The debate has not been studied in detail except at the Catholic University of America, where there was a sharp renewal of the border warfare that had long been chronic between the Department of Religious Education, founded by Cooper, and the theologians of the School of Sacred Sciences.[37] Two investigations made in the late 1940s showed that some Catholic women's colleges had introduced "scientific theology" (i.e., strict Thomism) into their undergraduate programs, although most had not, and that men's colleges were moving toward the more pastorally oriented "religious" approach. Roland Simonitsch, C.S.C., who studied the men's colleges, added, however, that there was great diversity in the kind of courses taught and a "rather widespread state of confusion" concerning appropriate course content.[38] And because the teachers of these courses could not be expected to agree on whether they were teaching "theology" or "religion," the organizers of their new professional association in 1953 adopted the somewhat grandiose title, "Society of Catholic College Teachers of Sacred Doctrine," as a compromise designation.[39]

Despite these uncertainties, one may say with some confidence that the strict Thomists, mainly Dominicans, carried the day on the rhetorical and controversial level. It is difficult today to read some of these authors without impatience, for their self-assurance was sublime and their manner in debate apodictic to the point of insolence. Consider, for example, the 1946 exchange between Walter Farrell, O.P., author of a four-volume *Companion to the Summa* that was widely used in Catholic colleges, and William H. Russell of the Catholic University of America's Department of Religious Education. Farrell's presentation was almost contemptuously short and schematic; he settled much of the argument in a footnote definition of terms; and he implied that there could be no real debate about whether "the divine wisdom" (by which he meant Thomistic theology) should be taught to Catholic collegians.[40] From the viewpoint of men like Farrell, Cooper's religious education emphasis simply could not be taken seriously, and Murray's project was almost equally frivolous. How could there be more than one theology when there was only one God, and, hence, only one truth about Him? The *Summa Theologica* of St. Thomas was not just one theology among others; it was an exposition of the mind of God. St. Thomas's work therefore prescribed not only the content of theology, but its order of presentation as well, for the treatment of topics in the *Summa* followed "the order of divine reality, an order of things in themselves in terms of their relationship of dependence."[41] This being the case, there hardly seemed room for disagreement with the proposition that strictly Thomistic theology must guide the way in integrating Catholic higher education.

This general view seems to have predominated in the many discussions of curricular integration carried on by Catholic educators around 1950.[42] I say "this general view" because the consensus was not that any specific formulation of St. Thomas was the answer, but that Neoscholastic theology understood in a generic sense was the ultimate wisdom and that a way would eventually be found to bring everything within its aegis and to communicate the resulting synthesis adequately to students.

Even those who disagreed with the Dominican version of Thomism worked in the Neoscholastic tradition and were equally convinced of the importance of synthesis and the close connection between religious truth and intellectual unity. Thus Murray's article on the need for a new lay theology was as insistent as the most dogmatic Thomist's on the crucial importance of Scholasticism's "synthesis of all revealed truth, and of revealed truth and philosophical truth." By virtue of this synthesis, "the certainty and value of each truth is confirmed by that of all the others and by the solidity of the whole edifice itself." To grasp the Catholic faith "in its splendid organic wholeness" was, according to Murray, in itself a "formative" religious experience, for it put a person "in possession of that tightly integrated system of motives" needed to inspire consistent moral action and at the same time revealed the faith "in its uniqueness and transcendence as the supreme and universal *mystique* whose inner dynamism is of the Holy Spirit of God."[43]

But every virtue has its corresponding defect, and the defect here is that so tight an integration—so comprehensive a binding up of everything into one synthesis—inevitably put the whole system at hazard if any part of it was challenged. Indeed, Murray himself pointed out that error, "if admitted . . . would shatter not only a particular truth but the whole Catholic *corpus doctrinae*."[44] He dropped this bombshell, the implications of which seem devastating in hindsight, in the calmest possible manner, for to him it was obviously an impossible hypothesis—error would never make good its entry into the synthesis of Catholic truth to set off its chain reaction of destruction! Being true, the body of Catholic doctrine would stand forever inviolable. Confidence on this point remained strong over the next decade, despite the growth of theological and philosophical pluralism and despite the great chorus of self-criticism that arose after Monsignor John Tracy Ellis delivered his famous blast on the deficiencies of

Catholic intellectual life in 1955. Paradoxically, the self-criticism in a sense testified to confidence, for much of it was animated by the belief that Catholics were not doing justice to the richness of their own intellectual tradition and must try harder to bring the world around to their own vision of things.[45]

The intellectualism debate did, however, indicate that something fundamental was amiss, and eventually, as we have seen, it reached the point of diagnosing basic flaws in the American Catholic mentality as such. But confidence in the existence and validity of the Catholic synthesis of religious faith, intellectual understanding, and moral vision did not really give way until the postconciliar upheaval. Then it vanished almost overnight amidst the symptoms of disintegration mentioned at the beginning of this essay. Religious educators at the Catholic University of America, formerly so confident of their ability to "integrate" and "vitalize" the student's faith (although disagreeing among themselves about how to do it), now came to question whether the student *could* be given, or even *should* be given, a comprehensive knowledge of his faith. Shifting from what they had come to regard as an outmoded "custodial or apologetic" approach, they adopted an "academic" understanding of religion, one that stressed the history of religions and "man's search for meaning."[46]

For a generation that had internalized the conviction that Catholicism was a comprehensive and integrated system of religious *truth,* the collapse of the synthesis could not occur without shaking faith itself to its very foundation. No longer did what Murray called "the solidity of the whole edifice" reinforce the interlocking network of truth, natural and supernatural. On the contrary, the virtual disappearance of consensus on basic dogmatic, moral, and disciplinary issues discredited the whole structure of teaching. For if everything was bound up together, it could hardly be maintained that "the whole Catholic *corpus doctrinae*" was still in place after so many errors were admitted—and "admitted," not in the sense of being permitted entry into the system, but in the sense of being acknowledged as having been there all along and only now being targeted for elimination! But if the teaching was discredited, so were the teachers. Persons who had been urged to find in their Catholic faith the integrally unifying principle of their lives, and who had just witnessed the repudiation of that ideal, could hardly be blamed for regarding with healthy skepticism those who presented themselves in the late 1960s as trustworthy guides to a new "search for meaning"—no matter how up-to-date and academically respectable they claimed to be.

Looking back from the mid-1980s on the developments reviewed here, it is easy to observe that American Catholics in the preconciliar era were guilty of a premature closure on truth. We might also be forgiven for wishing that they had displayed a fuller measure of intellectual humility on such matters as integrating visions, an organic Catholic culture, and the synthesis of natural and supernatural truth. Once again pride had gone before a fall—and what a fall it was!

But if we have learned that lesson, let us try not to overlearn it—although overlearning things sometimes seems our specialty. Surely we can sympathize with the desire to integrate all the dimensions of existence—to "get it all together," as the popular expression has it. We also understand the yearning for organic community and the impulse to harmonize thought, belief, and feeling. And we acknowledge that faith has to be integrated meaningfully with life. That, after all, is what our predecessors were trying to do. Even though they overdid it, we should honor their attempt, try to understand it, and endeavor to profit from it.

American Catholics were not alone in their yearning for unity, nor in their overstraining to compass it. *The Education of Henry Adams* testifies to the same yearning on the part of one of the greatest of American historians. Near the end of the book, Adams refers to himself as "the weary Titan of Unity."[47] It is an affecting image and one we might apply to American Catholics. Let us hope we would be justified in adapting it slightly by calling American Catholics "weary titans of unity, chastened but not despairing."

8

KEEPING THE FAITH IN AMERICA

This essay, which is the expanded version of a previously unpublished lecture, does not require much by way of introduction. It picks up the faith-in-crisis theme from the preceding essay and, while elaborating certain aspects of the contemporary situation, enlarges the perspective by inquiring what "keeping the faith" meant to earlier generations of American Catholics. In attempting to cover a very broad subject in a few short pages, it moves at a high level of generalization and offers a necessarily personal interpretation. Comments from persons who heard the lecture, or read the essay in draft form, seem to indicate that its most distinctive, even controversial, feature is the emphasis I place on the centrality, in the preconciliar era, of "faith in the Scholastic synthesis" and on the importance of its collapse in the aftermath of Vatican II. The argument presented here will perhaps leave some readers unconvinced that such emphasis is justified. My own convictions on the subject rest on what I recall of the preconciliar mentality, as well as on the evidence my researches have turned up. I hope that what is said here (and in other essays in this book) will stimulate other historians to explore more systematically the cultural effects of Neoscholasticism on American Catholic life in the first half of the twentieth century.

In its original form, "Keeping the Faith in America" was the Catholic Daughters of the Americas Lecture. It was given in March 1982 while I was Visiting Professor at the Catholic University of America in the Chair of American Catholic History sponsored by that organization of Catholic lay women. It gives me pleasure to express my gratitude to the Catholic Daughters of the Americas, not only for having made possible my stay at the University but also for what their benefactions have done for the study of American Catholic history. I hope that this essay in some measure vindicates their belief that knowledge of the past can become a powerful resource to assist us in understanding the present.

Has the immigrant kept the faith? This question, which caused concern and occasioned controversy among Catholics for many years, was answered reassuringly in a 1925 study that took the question as its title.[1] Losses, Gerald Shaughnessy concluded, had indeed occurred, but they had been the losses of normal attrition, not massive defections that could be traced to the disruptions of migration and resettlement in a new land. Four decades after Shaughnessy wrote, the issue arose in new form. The "immigrant era" of American Catholicism, everyone agreed, was over. Its ending coincided with, if it was not caused by, the Second Vatican Council, whose reforms marked a fundamental turning point in Catholic self-understanding and whose "spirit" seemed to require a rethinking from the ground up of what it meant to be a Catholic. No such rethinking could take place, however, without calling faith into question, for faith was what *made* one a Catholic. The process set in motion by the Council inevitably made "keeping the faith" problematic, for it was no longer so clear what the faith comprised and how one should go about keeping it.

But precisely because faith was at the very core of being a Catholic—Catholics being, as Garry Wills put it, "the last believers"—there was considerable hesitancy at first about acknowledging how deeply faith was implicated in the revisions and reforms of Vatican II.[2] The faith itself, the essential dogmas, were untouched by the reforms, it was said; all that was being modified were the forms in which those truths were expressed. But such a formulation could not persuade indefinitely, could not still the doubts even of those who wished to be persuaded. Conservatives were alarmed for the integrity of the faith from the beginning, and as early as 1966 Donald J. Thorman, publisher of the progressive *National Catholic Reporter,* discerned the onset of an "age of unbelief" among American Catholics, a radically new phenomenon "not created by the Vatican Council, but certainly unleashed by it."[3] Thorman's frankness in speaking of a "crisis of faith" was rare at the time; the locution favored in the late sixties was "identity crisis," an expression of invincible vagueness then at the height of its general popularity that enabled Catholics to mask the depth of their apprehensions in the modish jargon of pop psychology.[4]

In the next decade, however, the situation of faith was confronted more openly. In 1972, a widely noted report on Catholic beliefs and practices—whose title asked the ominous question, "The End of American Catholicism?"—indicated clearly that although the immigrants had kept the faith, the loyalty of their grandchildren was highly questionable.[5] At almost the same moment, the conservative James Hitchcock and the radical Garry Wills made the issue of faith central in two books that offered quite divergent interpretations of what was happening to American Catholicism.

Hitchcock's approach was straightforward: his *Decline and Fall of Radical Catholicism* (1971) argued that, far from renewing and deepening the faith, the reformers had, by their immoderate criticism of the preconciliar Church, severely weakened both the Church and the religious faith inextricably associated with it. "Many individuals of deep intelligence, virtue, and good will," he wrote, "now find themselves beset by the greatest uncertainties, the barest glimmer of what they once serenely called their faith." And virtually all Catholics had experienced "a weakening of belief—a loss of certitude, a diminution of joy and serenity, an unaccustomed cynicism and vague spiritual malaise, an embarrassment about expressing beliefs."[6]

Wills handled the issue of faith with greater personal reticence and with a certain overall ambiguity in his *Bare Ruined Choirs* (1972). Indeed, a hasty reader might well infer that the book was written by a man who had not only lost his faith, but who had also concluded that he had never had any genuine faith in the first place. Yet Wills's real message, as I read him, was that destruction of the old Church, and eradication of the faith Catholics cherished under its regime, was a work of purification essential to the attainment of authentic faith. For the great enemy of faith was not doubt, as preconciliar Catholics had mistakenly assumed; it was pretense, and they had been guilty of the systematic pretense that nothing about their faith was open to doubt. "Doubt is the test," Wills asserted. "Faith is rooted in it, as life in death. Faith, unless it is mere credulity . . . is a series of encounters with doubt, perpetual little resurrections; cynicisms met and transcended, never evaded. . . ." There were no shortcuts of the sort offered by the old Church: "The only way is the long way, through indirection, doubt, and a faith that survives its own death daily."[7]

These two books gained wide attention and doubtless helped bring the issue of faith out in the open. It would exaggerate to say that a spate of publications followed, but there was certainly an increase and by 1983 a writer in an Irish journal could refer (somewhat insouciantly) to "[t]he currently in-phrase 'crisis of faith.'"[8] The works of Hitchcock and Wills, as well as the writings published since, also demonstrate how wide a range of disagreement and controversy can exist over how faith is to be understood, how personal faith is related to "the faith" considered as the ensemble of beliefs and dispositions corporately held by Catholics, and how that corporately held faith is to be articulated by the magisterium, or teaching authority of the Church. The extent of disagreement and the air of crisis surrounding the whole subject lend new relevance—indeed a kind of urgency—to the perennial emphasis in American Catholic history on "keeping the faith" and make it worthwhile to inquire how Catholics in the past understood that responsibility and went about meeting it.

The scope of such an inquiry is vast; the story of how Catholics kept the faith is, in a sense, the whole story of American Catholicism under an alternate designation. And since Catholics conceived of "the faith" so broadly, and took it so much for granted as that around which everything else revolved, there are no histories (known to me) that focus on keeping-the-faith as a specialized and analytically distinct subject. Shaughnessy's work is only a partial exception to this statement, since it is a relatively narrow study of Catholic population statistics undertaken to determine whether claims that millions of Catholic immigrants fell away from the Church were factually accurate. In these circumstances, all I can offer here is a sketch of the subject; a sketch that is highly interpretive and necessarily comprised in large part of broad generalizations. It must also focus on the collective dimensions of the subject rather than the personal spiritual travail of individuals. The latter is lost to history anyhow, in all but the most exceptional cases, and even those were shaped by the ecclesiological and socio-cultural contexts in which they took place.

Another reason for the collective focus is that keeping the faith for Catholics has always been closely associated with adherence to the Church —"leaving the Church" was traditionally equated with abandoning the faith. In looking at the history of American Catholicism from this perspective, we can discern four epochs, or phases, each of which had its characteristic challenges and tasks in respect to keeping the faith. The periods of course overlap and shade into each other rather than having clear-cut boundaries. Leaving aside the colonial era and beginning with the establishment of an autonomous "national" Church after the American Revolution, the first period stretches into the middle decades of the nineteenth century. In this epoch devoted primarily to establishing and defending the faith, emphasis on the role of the Church is especially pronounced.

Establishing and Defending the Faith

The basic task in this era was to make the faith present and available to the Catholic people by building up the Church in the physical and institutional sense, and by recruiting the ministry needed to offer worship, dispense the sacraments, instruct the immature, and defend all the faithful against attacks from without. It is difficult for us today to appreciate fully how arduous a work this was, or even how needful it was. Having enjoyed for generations all the basic necessities that our pioneering forefathers lacked, we tend to underestimate the enormity of their task and its intimate relation to the perpetuation of the Catholic faith. We stand today in the same relation to the pioneers as did those European Catholics of his own time to whom Bishop John Hughes of New York addressed these words in 1840: "Happy Christians of Europe, you have had but to receive from the faith of your ancestors those religious edifices and institutions which have been handed down to you as a rich inheritance. But for us [in America] the past has done nothing. It is [left] for our weakness to undertake all, create all, at the same time that we must preserve and maintain."[9]

Overwhelming as the lack of physical resources was—and it included not only church buildings but minor items like altar stones, vestments, chalices, missals and prayer books, holy oils, and so on[10]—it was not as serious as the lack of personnel. Many were the bishops who could echo the words that appeared in 1828 in the first Catholic newspaper published in this country: "It is painful to reflect on the situation of those Catholics who seek for the bread of life, and there are but few to break it to them."[11] Not many faced conditions quite so parlous as those confronting Richard P. Miles, who went to Nashville as its first bishop in 1838 without a single priest to help him, and who ministered alone to the Catholics of Tennessee for a year before one arrived to assist him.[12] But if this was one of the worst cases, it illustrated the general situation: the shortage of clergymen was the single most serious problem for a number of years. The example of Miles also illustrates the point that being a bishop in the early days involved labors that seem to us heroic. Most of them responded in a spirit well expressed by Bishop Michael Portier of Mobile, who informed Roman authorities in 1827: "There is but one way to establish religion and that is to be campaigning always in the field, to preach everywhere, to destroy the prejudices of the Protestants, to confirm Catholics in the faith, and to render respectable the august character in which we [bishops] are vested by word, example, and independence."[13]

The lack of priests to minister to the widely scattered Catholic flock was one of the chief reasons assigned for the widespread loss of faith that contemporary observers lamented. It is true that many discussions were grossly exaggerated—including Bishop John England's influential, but wildly overinflated, estimate that more than three-and-half million Catholics had already lost the faith by 1836.[14] Yet there was such widespread agreement that the problem was real that we must assume the people of the time were speaking from experience when they said it was generally expected that multitudes of the second generation would leave the Church.[15]

Besides losses arising from inadequate spiritual care, additional damage was done by the confusion, quarrels, and disruptions that punctuated the work of establishing the Church in many localities. The internal strife that goes by the name of "trusteeism" was endemic in the first half-century of the Church's existence in this country, and it persisted into the twentieth century among the later waves of Catholic immigrants. These broils were destructive of faith. Many a parish was laid under interdict, its people deprived of the sacraments, until order was restored. Some went into schism, usually short-lived, and the faith of not a few embittered Catholics was sacrificed. Even that of innocent bystanders could be affected, as is shown by a story told by Simon Gabriel Bruté. While teaching theology at Mount Saint Mary's Seminary, the future bishop of Vincennes enlivened a class dealing with the sacraments for the dying by recounting the case of an old gentleman whom he had reconciled to the Church on his deathbed. The man had been bewildered by trustee uproars in Philadelphia, couldn't make up his mind which faction to support, and simply drifted away from the Catholic faith for a number of years.[16]

Besides their internal quarrels, Catholics had external foes. Even though organized anti-Catholicism did not become a major force until the 1830s, living in a religiously alien, and sometimes hostile, milieu no doubt took its toll from a much earlier date. While Catholic apologists did not overlook the dangers of rationalistic infidelity, their main effort had to be directed toward defending the faith of Catholics against attacks by Protestants who regarded the Church's teaching and practice as corruptions of the true gospel of Jesus Christ.[17] Especially after the great evangelical awakening that swept across American Protestantism in the late 1820s, the strongest currents of anti-Catholic feeling were fed by religious sources and had to be met by religious argumentation.

This accounts for the prominence in that era of the formal public controversy that pitted Catholic and Protestant champions against each other. The most famous of these encounters were John Hughes's two exchanges with John Breckinridge, a Presbyterian minister, which occurred while Hughes was still a parish priest in Philadelphia, and the debate between Bishop John B. Purcell of Cincinnati and Alexander Campbell, a major figure in nineteenth-century Protestantism and a founder of the denomination known as the Disciples of Christ.[18] But there were many other instances of a similar sort. John England's controversial writings fill several volumes of his collected works, and we have the testimony of the famous Kentucky missionary, Stephen Theodore Badin, that there were lay people in every congregation who studied works of controversy so as to be able to hold up their end in disputes with Protestants.[19]

Bitter though they often became, these controversies were family quarrels among Christians. Protestants and Catholics, after all, shared a belief in the existence of God, the fact of revelation, the saving mission of Jesus, and the essential need for faith in the gospel He proclaimed. The most important difference between them centered on the nature and function of the Church — and that accounts for the prominence in the controversies of that era of what was called "the rule of faith."

Perhaps this expression is still a familiar one among theologians, but it strikes the layman as exotic, and I confess to being puzzled for some time as to what it meant and why it loomed so large in Catholic apologetics in the first half of the nineteenth century.[20] The explanation is actually quite simple. Catholics and Protestants alike accepted St. Paul's admonition that without faith it was impossible to please God. What they disagreed about was how faith was to be understood, and here the key difference concerned the standard or norm—the rule of faith—to which Christians were to resort in order to settle questions as to what faith involved. For Protestants, the rule of faith was Scripture, read and interpreted by the individual believer. For Catholics, the rule of faith included tradition as well as Scripture, with both being authoritatively interpreted and taught by the Church. In practical terms, then, the Catholic rule of faith was "the authority of the Pastors of the Church, successors of the apostles, to whom the sacred deposite [sic] of faith has been entrusted by our Lord."[21]

This formulation is taken from a controversial pamphlet published in 1822 by John B. David, coadjutor bishop of Bardstown, Kentucky, which argued the Catholic position effectively. He pointed out that oral tradition, rather than the written word, had guided the faith of the earliest followers of Christ. Calling the roll of the fathers of the Church, David showed that in the first centuries of Christian history appeal was always made to what was believed and taught in the churches, as well as to Scripture, in determining how the faith was to be understood. Thus for Catholics, tradition and Scripture were coequal elements in the rule of faith.

David's positive argument, presented with learning and moderation, had much cogency. In terms of rhetorical emphasis, however, it was outweighed by his critique of the Protestant rule of faith. Forty of the fifty-six printed pages of his discourse analyzed the flaws in the principle of private interpretation of Scripture, showing that it led inevitably to disunity, rationalism, skepticism, and ultimately to unbelief. In this respect, David's pamphlet was a relatively early example of the conviction, repeatedly expressed by Catholics in the nineteenth century, that Protestantism was crumbling—giving way inexorably to stark infidelity—by virtue of its own intrinsic principle of private interpretation. This conviction highlights the logical connection in the Catholic tradition between faith as such and the authority of the Church. For without the teaching Church as its authoritative interpreter, faith itself would be fragmented, dissolved by a hundred clashing opinions, and in the end extinguished altogether in the sea of skepticism and indifference.

But the power and subtlety of David's analysis also tacitly implanted a psychological, as well as a logical, motivation for emphasizing the teaching authority of the Church, or if such a motivation already existed, reading his pamphlet would reinforce it. The psychological point is simply that few could read a critique such as his without being assailed by the question, "If others have been so mistaken in their religious views, what warrant do I have for thinking that my own are securely grounded?" If private judgment—or the unacknowledged influence of cultural forces, which, as David held, actually shaped "private interpretation"[22]—led directly to the shipwreck of faith, one had to rely all the more unquestioningly on the authority of the Church.

Thus the need to defend the faith against other Christian believers, who actually agreed with Catholics on much of the content of faith, reinforced an intimate linkage between faith and the Church, and inculcated acceptance of the Church's teaching authority as the only alternative to religious ruin. This was understandable enough in the circumstances, but it also involved drawbacks for Catholics existing in a society that placed a high premium on personal freedom and on the dignity and responsibility of the individual. The linkage of faith with the institutionalized procedures of an authoritative teaching Church also entailed a certain rigidity that made it more difficult for Catholics to respond to new challenges to the faith. This brings us to the second phase of our story, for between 1850 and 1900 a new challenge did emerge—that of adjusting the faith to the changing modern world.

Adjusting the Faith to a Changing World

Meeting the basic pastoral needs of the ever-expanding household of faith continued to impose heavy burdens, but by the 1850s the Church was sufficiently well established to assure its survival. That permitted attention to other kinds of problems. At the same time, the older type of controversial apologetics was becoming outmoded, as Protestantism continued on what Catholics regarded as its course of inevitable decline. It was no longer sufficient to defend the authentic rule of faith against misguided fellow Christians. The task of the Catholic apologist in the new era was to justify religious faith itself to unbelievers, to present the Christian message in ways appropriate to changing circumstances, and to suggest ways in which the Church should respond to the needs of a world being reshaped by the forces of modernity.

Several of these connections were brought out explicitly by Isaac T. Hecker, founder of the Paulists, a religious community whose purpose was to present the Catholic faith in a manner suitable to American circumstances. Writing in 1864 to Richard Simpson, a liberal English Catholic who collaborated with Lord Acton in publishing *The Rambler,* Hecker described the religious situation in the United States as follows:

> The primary questions with us are the Trinity, the Fall, and Hell. For our Protestantism is rapidly going over to Unitarianism, and this is fast becoming Universalism. These points must be thoroughly ventilated in order to meet the objections of intelligent non-Catholics. The work of our day is not so much to defend the Church against the attacks of heresy, as to open the way for the return of those who are without any religion, true or false. We have to begin the conversion of these people *de radice,* and to do this in our day and civilization, theology requires to be entirely recast. This conviction has forced me to take a new standpoint from the start, and to bring it out on all occasions.[23]

There were controversies aplenty in this era, as in the previous one. But now they usually featured Catholics at odds with each other; for what some prescribed as desirable reforms that would enhance the prospects for faith seemed to others concessions tantamount to its abandonment. This scenario will strike today's postconciliar Catholics as a familiar one, and it was by no means unique to American Catholics in the late nineteenth century. As Avery Dulles observes in his history of apologetics, revisionist efforts to forge a new synthesis between religious faith and secular thought in the modern age have repeatedly become "sources of scandal and conflict within the Churches themselves."[24]

The challenge of responding to modernity existed on the practical level, as well as on the speculative. Practically speaking, the question was how the Catholic Church should adjust itself to such developments as representative government, social equalitarianism, separation of church and state, universal education, and an unprecedented degree of liberty of thought, speech, press, and artistic expression. On the speculative plane, the great problem was to reconcile the dogmas of faith with the findings of modern science, biblical scholarship, comparative religion, history, philosophy, and psychology.

American Catholics were much more actively engaged with the practical dimensions of modernity than with the speculative. This came about not because of any alleged "pragmatic strain" in the national character, but simply because modernity was a condition, not a theory, in the political and social order of the nation and had to be dealt with as such. Freedom, equality, democracy, separation of church and state, liberty of conscience—all of these things existed in the United States in a far more advanced state than anywhere else in the world, and Catholics had to respond to them as realities, not as visionary possibilities or as hypothetical perils. Reflective persons naturally thought about these matters and generalized from their experience. But the Catholics who did so were far from being in perfect agreement among themselves. On the contrary, definitely opposed liberal and conservative orientations soon emerged concerning the appropriate strategies to be followed. Since the disagreements centered on how the Catholic Church should respond to the American form of modernity, controversies over Americanization usually involved, at least implicitly, disagreements about how to deal with the more basic issue of modernity.

The first explicit controversy of this sort developed in the 1850s when Orestes A. Brownson scolded the Irish Catholic immigrants for failing to distinguish sufficiently between their Catholicity and their being Irish. Here was a case, the great convert publicist believed, where immigrants were endeavoring to keep the faith in a wrongheaded way. The problem was that by identifying being Catholic with being Irish, they were reinforcing the prejudices of the Protestant majority who took it for granted that the Catholic religion was irredeemably foreign and intrinsically opposed to the principles of American civilization. The Catholic faith could never prosper in the United States, Brownson insisted, until it took root here and developed an indigenous life in harmony with the character and spirit of American institutions.[25]

The need for "indigenization," as contemporary theorists of evangelization might put it, meant among other things that Catholic children should not be cut off from Protestant youngsters any more than necessary. For that reason, Brownson had reservations about Catholic schools. If the common schools in any locality were really anti-Catholic, he agreed that Catholic schools would be necessary. But he did not feel that this was universally the case, and wherever it was at all possible, Catholic children should be educated alongside other Americans. Above all, Brownson opposed the use of Catholic schooling to perpetuate the nonreligious features of imported immigrant cultures on American soil. This, in Brownson's view, was actually being done, and he denounced schools which, "under the pretext of providing for Catholic education . . . train up our children to be foreigners in the land of their birth."[26]

Alerted by the ethnic issue, Brownson became convinced that "Catholic tradition" was not necessarily the same thing as "the traditions of Catholics."[27] If the faith was to be truly universal, it had to make itself at home in all ages as well as in all climes. For that reason, old forms of Catholic life and thought had to be re-examined when the Church found herself confronting new social, intellectual, and cultural circumstances. The conditions of American life in the mid-nineteenth century called for precisely this sort of revaluation of Catholic thinking, Brownson was convinced, and between 1854 and 1864 he grew increasingly radical in calling for a positive alignment of the faith with the spirit and outlook of American republicanism, which he considered perfectly compatible with the true genius of Catholicity.[28]

Brownson, who died in 1876, recanted his liberalism in the last few years of his life. In poor health and disheartened by personal tragedies—two of his sons died in the Civil War—he lost hope in the modern world and reverted to rigid orthodoxy and bitter antimodernism. But his friend and fellow convert Isaac Hecker steadfastly maintained that God's providence was at work in the evolution of modern civilization. Catholics should therefore welcome and endorse the positive characteristics of modernity, such as the value it placed on human intelligence and on personal freedom and responsibility. Since these features of modernity were nowhere more at home than in the United States, Hecker continued to believe that the Church in this country had a pioneering role to play in reconciling Catholicity to the new age that was coming unmistakably into its own in the late nineteenth century.[29]

Besides these two outstanding individuals, there was a small coterie of New York priests—some well known in their own day but now forgotten—whose thinking revealed the lengths to which the premises of liberal Americanism could carry Catholics in the Civil War era. It was very much a private group, known as the "Accademia," whose existence was recently brought to light by the researches of R. Emmett Curran.[30] Originally influenced by Brownson, and having occasional contact with Hecker, the Accademia flourished briefly in the late 1860s, meeting informally, but on a fairly regular basis, to exchange views on topical issues. Its members opposed the temporal power of the papacy and the belief that infallibility appertained to the office of the papacy rather than to the Church as a whole. They longed for a vernacular liturgy, questioned the need for private auricular confession, criticized mandatory celibacy for priests, and regarded religious orders as outmoded. They differed among themselves on the matter of biblical inspiration and inerrancy, with the most radical maintaining that the inspiration of Scripture was on all fours with that of Dante's *Divine Comedy*. The best-known member of the Accademia, Father Edward McGlynn, opposed parochial schools, preached what he called the "American Idea," and championed social reform and the single-tax socialism of Henry George, activities that made him notorious in the Archdiocese of New York and led to his suspension from the priesthood and temporary excommunication in the 1880s.

John Lancaster Spalding took a more moderate, but definitely liberal, position in the 1876 article marking the centennial of American Catholicism, which was earlier discussed in detail.[31] He believed that the experience of the American Church was of universal significance because its history could shed light on the question he made the explicit theme of his article: "What will be the influence of the new society upon the old faith?" The answer he drew from ten decades of Catholic growth was unambiguously affirmative: despite all the hardships encountered, Catholicism had flourished as a bay tree under the conditions of American modernity. The conclusion was clear that "the old faith" had nothing to fear from political and religious freedom, from the separation of church and state, or from "the new society" considered in the most general terms. The policy implications were equally clear—American Catholics should embrace the spirit and institutions of their national culture and thereby bring the faith to its fullest realization in the new world.

This became the platform of the churchmen who became known as Americanizers, or Americanists, in the controversies that rocked the Catholic Church in this country from the mid-1880s to 1900.[32] It is impossible to do more than hint at these tangled issues here, but the approach espoused by the Americanists had much in common with the stance Brownson had adopted thirty years earlier, except that now it was German Catholics, rather than Irish Catholics, whom the Americanizers accused of religious nationalism and whose schools were suspect as agencies designed to perpetuate a foreign nationality on American soil. Father McGlynn's rebelliousness made him a storm center; he was anti-German and generally identified with the Americanists, but the leading figures in that faction did not really sympathize with his social radicalism or his ecclesiastical insubordination. The school question, also discussed in an earlier chapter, became an explosive issue in the controversies, and there were other conflicts over temperance reform, Catholic membership in secret societies, especially in the Knights of Labor, and over participation by Catholics in interfaith gatherings.

In all of these disputes about socio-ecclesiastical policy, the Americanizers advocated an irenic adjustment to American ways in everything that did not affect the substance of Catholic doctrine as such. They believed that the American social and political order embodied genuine values —values that were not as fully realized in Europe, nor as fully appreciated by European Catholics, including Roman authorities—and that the Church should embrace those positive values and make them her own. Above all, they deprecated anything that created—or appeared to create—unnecessary opposition between the Church and American civilization. The conservatives, on the other hand, were more impressed by features of American society, and of modern culture generally, that were, in their view, irreconcilable with Catholicity—such matters as the deepening agnosticism of modern thinkers, the "Mammonism" and materialism of American society, and the undisguised hostility which many Protestant Americans felt

for the Catholic religion. From the conservative perspective, the Americanizers were simply too liberal—they were watering down the Catholic faith
in a dangerously misguided effort to make it more palatable to Protestants
and secularists.

The doctrinal implications of the Americanists' program were brought
decisively to the fore in 1897 by the publication of a French translation
of a biography of Isaac Hecker, who had died in 1888. Like their American co-religionists, the French Catholics were bitterly divided in the 1890s
between liberals and conservatives. The liberals, who sponsored the French
edition of Hecker's life, made the founder of the Paulists into a partisan
figure by hailing him as the prophet of a new approach to evangelization
and apologetics—"Americanism"—that would reconcile the faith and modern culture. French Catholic conservatives, unsympathetic by nature to the
upstart republicanism of the New World, naturally responded by attack-
ing Hecker, "Heckerism," and "Americanism" as symbols of everything
dangerous, deluded, and heretical in the ideas of their opponents.

The conflict in France overlapped and reinforced the one already raging between Americanists and their critics in this country. The situation
grew so confused and embittered that Pope Leo XIII finally announced
he would personally look into the matter and make a ruling. His judgment
was delivered in a papal letter to Cardinal Gibbons in January 1899. Here
the pope condemned as unacceptable "opinions which some comprise under the head of Americanism." The principle underlying these opinions
was the Church should "adapt herself somewhat to our advanced civilization" and relax "her ancient rigor," not only with respect to discipline, "but
also to the doctrines in which the *deposit of faith* is contained."[33]

Upon receiving this letter (known from its opening words as *Testem
Benevolentiae*), the Americanists immediately denied holding the condemned positions and protested against the implication that they had any
intention of diluting the faith. Leo had specifically exempted from his
censure the kind of Americanism associated with "the condition of your
commonwealths, or the laws and customs which prevail in them," and
"the characteristic qualities which reflect honor on the people of America." This left the status of Americanism rather unsettled, since the liberals
claimed that their "Americanism" was of precisely this nature and thus did
not imply any doctrinal deviations. But if there was some uncertainty as
to where permissible Americanism left off and the reprobated version began, it was nevertheless quite clear that a severe rebuke had been admin-
istered to those who proclaimed that the American Church was called to
blaze a new trail in the reconciliation of the faith and modern culture. As
a distinctive religious idea or policy, "Americanism" had been stopped cold,

and nothing further was heard of it until it became the subject of historical inquiry two generations later.[34]

Compared to the tempest of Americanism, the papal condemnation
of Modernism in 1907 raised scarcely a ripple in the United States.[35] The
main reason was that American Catholic scholarship in the most sensitive
areas — biblical studies and philosophy—was too negligible to be much of
a factor in the developments which Rome regarded as heretical in fact or
in tendency. Only a handful of individuals were directly affected by the
condemnation, most of whom were associated with the *New York Review.*
This high-level theological publication, put out by the priests of the New
York archdiocesan seminary at Dunwoodie and subtitled "A Journal of the
Ancient Faith and Modern Thought," fell victim to the conservative reaction that followed the condemnation of Modernism. It was closed down
in the third year of its existence, and the reputation for orthodoxy of those
who edited it or wrote for it passed under a cloud.

But the fewness of those directly touched by the condemnation did
not mean that American Catholics were unaffected by the ferment of new
ideas about the relation of the faith to modern thought that characterized
the European Catholic scene at the turn of the century. Merely dipping
into the periodical literature of that era reveals that such was not the case.
On the contrary, the literate American Catholic of those days probably
knew as much about the ideas of George Tyrrell and Alfred Loisy as his
counterpart today knows about the theology of Karl Rahner or Hans Küng.

As the new century opened, there was much discussion of the intellectual needs of the emerging class of educated laity. Indeed, the publish-
ers of the *American Ecclesiastical Review* established a new journal, called
The Dolphin, which was intended to meet precisely those needs. It sur-
vived for five years, and occasionally printed letters from readers who praised
the policy it followed of confronting the difficulties for faith created by
modern currents of thought.[36] The *Catholic World,* which had been
founded by Father Hecker in 1865, also published many articles of the same
tenor and evidently intended for the same audience.[37] In one of the most
interesting, Joseph McSorley, a young Paulist who was to become one of
the grand old men of the community in the twentieth century, called boldly
for greater open-mindedness on matters of faith.[38] If the early Christians
had been as narrow-minded as certain contemporaries, he observed, they
would have excommunicated anyone who predicted in patristic times that
the laity would ever be denied the cup at communion! Prudence was required to be sure; but one had to be cautious in rejecting novelties as well
as in accepting them. Indeed, it was positively dangerous to faith to adopt
a stance of blind conservatism. For what would be the effect when the

conscientious Catholic layman learned that charges rashly denied were in fact true, or that arguments dismissed with contempt were actually well grounded?

McSorley also deprecated the tendency to overspecify the content of Catholic faith. Here he used an illustration that must have caused him some discomfiture not long after the article was published in 1906. The Catholic student was apt to find his confidence in the magisterium weakened, McSorley wrote, when, upon reading Cardinal Newman's *Grammar of Assent,* he "laughs at himself for ever having believed the details of Scholastic philosophy to be akin to revelation."[39] McSorley was soon to learn that Scholastic philosophy was far from being a laughing matter. Indeed, his comment can serve as an ironic epilogue to the period dominated by concern to adjust the faith to a changing world—ironic because in the epoch about to open Neoscholasticism furnished the foundation for the whole edifice of Catholic faith.

Faith in the Scholastic Synthesis

The third epoch in the story of keeping the faith in America stretches from the condemnation of Modernism in the first decade of this century to the Second Vatican Council in the seventh. But even to cover it in a hop, skip, and jump we must look back for a moment at the earlier development of the Scholastic Revival. Its emergence as an incipient movement can be dated from the 1850s, when Roman authorities, enthusiastically abetted by the Jesuits' newly founded journal, *Civiltà Cattolica,* made Scholasticism the basis from which the errors of Catholic philosophers and theologians could be corrected, or (as happened with increasing frequency) condemned. By 1869, when the First Council of the Vatican met to reaffirm the Church's teaching against the "rampant errors" of the day, the Revival was well begun. Scholastic premises underlay the formulation of the faith embodied in *Dei Filius,* the "Dogmatic Constitution on the Catholic Faith," the approval of which was one of the two most important actions taken by the Council before it was broken up by the political upheavals set off by the outbreak of the Franco-Prussian war.[40]

The other important action taken by the Council was the definition of papal infallibility. This enhancement of the prestige of the pope's teaching authority lent additional weight to the encyclical *Aeterni Patris* (1879), in which Leo XIII mandated the study of St. Thomas Aquinas as the official philosophy of the Catholic Church. Leo had long been committed to the revival of Scholasticism; in issuing the encyclical he was responding in a quite self-conscious way to the challenge of modernity. The fundamental challenge, as he saw it, was philosophical: it had to do with the relation of supernatural faith and natural reason. Scholastic philosophy, as perfected by St. Thomas and applied to the data of revelation, provided the ideal articulation of the realms of grace and nature, faith and reason. In so doing, the Thomistic version of Scholasticism triumphantly refuted the claim that modern science and scholarship had completely discredited orthodox teaching and reduced traditional Christian faith to the same level as primitive superstition.[41]

Pope Leo's mandating of St. Thomas was, in its own way, as much an effort to adjust the faith to changing circumstances as were the new departures called for by Brownson, the Americanizers, and the Modernists. But it differed from these efforts at adjustment in two important respects. First, it was more traditional than the others, for what Leo prescribed was not a new philosophical-theological approach, but the revival of an old one that had been allowed to fall into disuse in recent centuries. Secondly, Thomism was not just another intellectual position championed by a particular group of thinkers that would have to win its way among Catholics by virtue of its intrinsic merits. Rather, with *Aeterni Patris* it was designated the *official* philosophy of the Church, and the immense authority of the papacy was mobilized to establish it as the only system orthodox believers could employ in elaborating the cognitive dimensions of the faith.

But despite Pope Leo's exhortations and direct pressure exerted on individuals and institutions here and there, Catholic scholars did not immediately fall in line behind the banners of Thomism. On the contrary, there was considerable foot-dragging and even active resistance to the imposition of Neoscholasticism. In the United States, for example, John Lancaster Spalding spoke condescendingly of the thought of Aristotle and St. Thomas in a speech given at the cornerstone-laying of the Catholic University of America, and in Europe several of those later associated with Modernism were flagrantly disrespectful.[42] All of this helps explain why it was not until after the condemnation of Modernism that Neoscholasticism was imposed in a really ironclad way.

In his encyclical on Modernism, *Pascendi Dominici Gregis* (1907), Pope Pius X said that the whole poisonous system—"the synthesis of all heresies"—sprang from "the union between faith and false philosophy." Contemptuous of Scholasticism, the Modernists had embraced modern philosophy "with all its false glamour" and thereby placed the faith in grave jeopardy. To limit the damage, their ideas were vehemently proscribed, and bishops were admonished to be zealous in stamping out their influence. To make sure that nothing of the kind ever happened again, the pope "strictly ordain[ed] that scholastic philosophy be made the basis of the sacred sciences." To guard against any possible misinterpretation, Pius continued:

And let it be clearly understood above all things that when We prescribe scholastic philosophy We understand chiefly that which the Angelic Doctor [St. Thomas] has bequeathed to us, and We, therefore, declare that all the ordinances of Our predecessor [Leo XIII] on this subject continue fully in force, and, as far as may be necessary, We do decree anew, and confirm, and order that they shall be strictly observed by all. In seminaries where they have been neglected it will be for the Bishops to exact and require their observance in the future; and let this apply also to the superiors of religious orders. Further, We admonish professors to bear well in mind that they cannot set aside St. Thomas, especially in metaphysical questions, without grave disadvantage.[43]

Although this seemed comprehensive enough, the remedy was further elaborated in subsequent decrees. In 1910, for example, Thomistic assumptions concerning faith and reason underlay the positive portion of the "Oath against Modernism" to which all clerics had to subscribe before being raised to the dignity of the diaconate. And only weeks before his death in 1914, Pius X made it clear that when he had earlier said St. Thomas was to be studied "particularly," he really meant "exclusively." The "capital theses" of Thomism, he now asserted, were not debatable; professors of philosophy and theology were solemnly warned that they were exposed to grave peril "if they deviated so much as a step, in metaphysics especially, from Aquinas."[44] Soon thereafter the Congregation of Studies in Rome helpfully issued a list of twenty-four Thomistic theses, adherence to which would guarantee orthodoxy; and the new code of canon law, promulgated in 1917, laid it down as a formal requirement that professors of the sacred sciences were "to hold and teach the method, doctrine and principles of the Angelic Doctor."[45]

In view of these guidelines, and the draconian way in which the post-Modernist crackdown was prosecuted, it is not surprising that Neoscholasticism quickly attained universal sway in Catholic institutions of learning.[46] This is not to say that the leading Thomistic thinkers were simply following orders in philosophizing as they did. They accepted the premises of the system internally and held their views with genuine intellectual conviction. But because Neoscholasticism was imposed on the entire Catholic body by fiat, there were many others—the great majority, in all likelihood—who did simply accept it on authority, not because they had appropriated its principles and methods by deep personal reflection.

This was particularly the case in the United States, for, as Catholic colleges and universities expanded rapidly from the 1920s through the 1950s, Neoscholasticism was taught on a mass basis to collegians as well as to seminarians.[47] No system of philosophy could be purveyed on so vast a scale without being denatured in the process—and that is what happened to Thomistic Scholasticism. For the great majority of those who came into contact with it in the classroom, Neoscholasticism was simply a body of given content to be mastered as well as one could. As a result, it played the role in American Catholic culture of an *ideology* rather than that of a philosophy properly understood. In other words, it functioned primarily as an ensemble of agreed-upon answers to various kinds of speculative questions, the validity of which one accepted on authority, which provided a rational grounding for Catholic beliefs and attitudes and served as the source of organizing principles for practical action. This is an admittedly loose application of the term "ideology," but I can think of nothing better to get the point across that what I have in mind here is not Neoscholasticism as a technical philosophical system, but the worldview or intellectual outlook its authoritative inculcation inspired.[48]

The implications of this development for faith as it was understood by two generations of American Catholics were enormous. In the first place, it meant that faith itself was conceived in highly rationalistic terms. It was largely a matter of assent to propositions, the reasonability of which could be demonstrated philosophically. Leo XIII, we must recall, had promoted the revival of Thomism primarily as a way of vindicating the claims of faith against the pretensions of modern science and philosophy. The problem of faith and reason was naturally of central importance, and the great strength of Neoscholasticism was that it was said to *prove* that faith was perfectly compatible with reason.[49] The quality of faith as a supernatural virtue, freely given through the grace of God, was carefully preserved. But the breathtaking assertion was made that the power of human reason alone was sufficient to establish with certainty that God exists, that the divine nature was such that God always spoke the truth and had in fact spoken to humankind, proposing definite truths for their belief. All this was not faith as such, but merely the "preambles of faith." And it was, to repeat, accessible to unaided human reason—most of it being, in the words of one of the better college theology textbooks, "scientifically proven in our course of Philosophy."[50]

To prove this much from reason was surely a consolation, since the great issue now was the existence of God as such, not some relatively marginal question like the legitimacy of tradition as an element in the rule of faith. It was, of course, a troubling point that most non-Catholics were unconvinced by the process of reasoning that led to God's existence as a conclusion. And Catholics themselves were usually a little hazy about the step-by-step argumentation. But strict reasoning required a long apprenticeship, and non-Scholastics were sure to go astray by using faulty methods or starting from false premises. Since most of those exposed to Neoscholasticism in the classroom did not intend to become professional philosophers, they were willing to settle for the conviction that the faith was rationally demonstrable, even though they might personally be unable to demonstrate it. [51]

The conviction that the Catholic faith was rationally grounded, and that there were appropriately certified specialists somewhere who could perform the required demonstration of that fact, became a hallmark of the American Catholic mind in the generation before the Second Vatican Council. Indeed that conviction itself took on the quality of faith. We shall return to this point shortly, but first we must look quickly at certain other features of American Catholic culture and how they are related to the Neoscholastic understanding of faith.

Consider, for example, the intense devotionalism, the piety, the drive for personal sanctity—all coupled with deep loyalty to the Church—that was so conspicuous a feature of Catholic life in the preconciliar era. [52] Many other factors no doubt played a role in the development of this vigorous spirituality: the devout traditions of an immigrant-derived people; the reforms of Pius X regarding frequent reception of Holy Communion; systematic efforts to stimulate piety through parish missions, novenas, public recitation of the rosary, and so on. But putting faith on so solid a footing surely contributed, perhaps indispensably. Knowing what they believed, having confidence in the truth of those beliefs, and seeing an intimate connection between their faith and the Church with her treasury of grace, Catholics could throw themselves with loving abandon into the search for personal holiness through assistance at Mass, reception of the sacraments, attendance at devotional exercises, spiritual reading, and of course private prayer. A highly rationalistic understanding of faith thus paradoxically made possible, indeed encouraged, an emotional, even fideistic, practice of the faith.

Another cultural consequence of the Neoscholastic version of faith concerns the imperative toward synthesis, the drive to integrate all aspects of Catholic life that was examined at length in the previous chapter. This flowed very naturally from Neoscholastic premises. [53] Since Thomism brought faith and reason into harmony, it also ordered supernatural wisdom and human understanding into a coherent whole—or at least it was capable of doing so if worked out with sufficient care. From this it followed that the application of faith to virtually every sphere of life could be determined in some detail. Catholicism came to be viewed as a culture, a total way of life. There was a "Catholic viewpoint" on everything, a Catholic way of doing everything, even, I remember hearing, of tying one's shoes—but that was perhaps facetious.

This outlook underlay the formation of dozens of Catholic societies in various professions and fields of learning. These associations, to which we have also alluded before, were the famous—or infamous—"ghetto organizations" that came in for so much abuse in the 1950s.[54] Other factors contributed to their development, but they rested at bottom on the conviction that the Catholic faith had some bearing on how a person should interpret the findings of scholarly investigation in a certain field, or discharge his or her professional responsibilities as a journalist, a physician, or, for that matter, a trade-unionist. In the present ecumenical-minded age, American Catholics may find little to admire in these artifacts of an earlier "separatist mentality." For that reason, it is worth emphasizing that the ghetto organizations of old were not exclusively, or even primarily, defensive in purpose. Ideally, they were apostolic and outward-looking; they were intended to embody and further Catholic truth in a world that sorely needed the message of salvation they offered.

Since postconciliar American Catholics are not accustomed to hearing the institutional Church of the ghetto era spoken of in positive terms, I should perhaps make clear that I intend no irony in speaking of the salvation offered by Catholic truth. Apostolic Catholics of that era were as much convinced that the world needed saving as are their more recent counterparts who specialize in prophetic witness against the evils of poverty, racism, and war. It is true, of course, that important differences exist between the ways these two generations of American Catholics interpret(ed) worldly evils and the appropriate remedies for them; but the present generation has no guarantee that its diagnoses and prescriptions enjoy an absolute superiority over those of the ghetto generation. And the work of John Courtney Murray stands as testimony to what a first-rate intelligence could do with Neoscholastic materials. For though he was far from being ghetto-minded, Murray was very much a man of Neoscholastic formation, and he worked within that tradition to fashion a vindication of religious freedom and church/state separation that has enduring value.[55]

Despite the fact that it induced in Catholics a lamentable intellectual complacency—after all, didn't we already know the answers to the questions that really matter?—Neoscholasticism and the mentality it inspired are thus not to be despised. But there was another problem, and it was even more serious than smugness, maddening as the latter could become. The deeper problem was that the faith became terribly overextended. This, we must remember, was a synthesis. Everything was tied up together. And it all rested on the assurance that human reason could establish the fact of God's existence and the implications of that fact for every sphere of life. Very few, however, could actually perform for themselves the rational operations that proved God's existence. And no one claimed to be in full possession of the total synthesis. No one, that is, boasted of having mastered the philosophical-theological foundations and of knowing enough about every other sphere of learning to be able to explain in detail just *how* everything fit together. Not even a new St. Thomas could have done that; despite their merits, none of the leading Neoscholastics was even an old St. Thomas.

What this meant was that belief in the reasonability of faith itself, and belief in the existence of a coherent synthesis of faith and natural knowledge, were *collective assumptions* on the part of American Catholics — or, more accurately, on the part of that portion of the Catholic community concerned about the intellectual dimensions of their faith. And to say that they were collective assumptions really signifies that they became secondary objects of faith themselves. It was in this sense that the Catholic faith had become terribly overextended: religious faith in the strict sense had become authoritatively identified with a particular philosophical articulation of faith and with the comprehensive ideological system that was elaborated to show how the faith impinged on all the important dimensions of existence. This inevitably put the faith at great hazard. For if the distinctive mark of the Catholic faith was the way it unified everything, then it followed logically that the denial of particular elements in the synthesis called the whole structure into question. And if collective confidence in the Neoscholastic synthesis once began to weaken, that would inevitably weaken religious faith itself, since everything was so closely tied together.

Erosion of confidence in the Neoscholastic synthesis began almost imperceptibly in the 1950s, but in the next decade the whole structure collapsed with stunning speed and impact. Which brings us to the point where we began, the contemporary crisis of faith, the latest of the four phases of keeping the faith in America.

The Contemporary Crisis of Faith

Historians are not very comfortable talking about the present or the very recent past, and I am not competent to say anything useful about the contemporary crisis of faith as a philosopher or theologian. But I am convinced that the interaction of past and present play a very important role here, so let me try to round out the story by listing the main factors in the collapse of the Neoscholastic synthesis as the cognitive foundation of the Catholic faith and by commenting on the consequences of that event.

As a preliminary point, I should stress that in speaking of the "collapse" of the Neoscholastic synthesis what I have in mind is the evaporation of the collective assumption that Catholics had their own proven philosophical system, one that furnished a rational grounding for faith and showed how it applied to personal morality, social ethics, and so on. Whether Neoscholasticism as a speculative system has actually been shown to be invalid is an entirely different question, and one on which I have no opinion one way or the other. All I wish to affirm is that Neoscholasticism, understood in a crude ideological way, fulfilled an important cultural function for American Catholics between World War I and the Second Vatican Council, that it does so no longer, and that as a result the faith has become far more problematic than it was regarded as being in the era of the Neoscholastic synthesis.

One of the reasons for the collapse of the synthesis was that divergent schools of thought developed within Neoscholasticism itself. Historical scholarship had revealed that the thought of St. Thomas and the other medieval schoolmen was far richer and more complex than the nineteenth-century pioneers of the Revival had suspected.[56] By the 1950s, an undeniable diversity existed among philosophers and theologians who drew their inspiration from Aquinas, and there were still others who associated themselves with non-Thomistic traditions, such as existentialism or linguistic analysis. The philosophical layman might not know much about the different varieties of Thomism, but their very existence—to say nothing of the degree of mutual suspicion felt, for example, between philosophers trained at Laval University and followers of Jacques Maritain—made the assumption of a unified Catholic synthesis harder to sustain.

Similar strains began to show up in other areas. The tension between Thomists and proponents of "religious education" touched on in the last chapter persisted unresolved in the 1950s. In the same decade, theologians of the traditional sort became aware of the need to ward off incursions of their territory on the part of Catholic Scripture scholars who were beginning to talk about "biblical theology."[57] Researchers in other fields found it more and more difficult to discern how the results of their labors were to be fitted into any overall synthesis; after the Ellis-inspired "great debate" on Catholic intellectual life broke out, most of them probably gave up the attempt, feeling that they could contribute more to the search for "excellence" by pushing back the frontiers of knowledge in their own specialized areas.[58]

Accompanying these stresses and strains in the realm of the intellect, related shifts were taking place in the social sphere. Upward mobility and the assimilation of second- and third-generation immigrants were processes that tended to make Catholics more like other Americans in their ways of thinking as well as in educational background and occupational status.[59] The more closely Catholics came to resemble their fellow citizens in experience and outlook, the more self-critical they became about their "ghetto organizations" and their "siege mentality." Was it really necessary, was it even desirable, they began to wonder, for Catholics to have their own distinctive "viewpoint" that marked them off from others in American society?

It is a moot question how soon these social and intellectual shifts, acting alone, would have brought down the Neoscholastic synthesis. For the fact is that the Second Vatican Council intervened, as it were, to topple the Thomistic edifice almost overnight. Except that "topple" may not be the best verb to use in this context because it too strongly suggests some kind of direct blow delivered to that which topples. That is not what happened, as I see it. The Neoscholastic synthesis did not fall as a result of being pushed. Rather it collapsed because of the withdrawal of an element that was vital to its stability. That element was consensus among the Church's authoritative leaders as to what the faith was, how it was to be conceptualized, and what it implied for practical life. Two generations of Catholics, we must remember, had been assured that these matters *were settled* and that the Neoscholastic synthesis embodied the terms of the settlement. But the spectacle that presented itself during and after the Council of theologians, bishops, and curial officials in almost furious disagreement over the most fundamental questions of discipline, worship, and doctrine forced even the dullest Catholic to realize that these matters *weren't settled at all*. In these circumstances the Neoscholastic synthesis came down like a house of cards.

The expression "like a house of cards" perhaps suggests a touch of cynicism, an intimation of guilty knowledge that the celebrated synthesis had been kept in place all along by a tacit agreement not to look too carefully at how it was put together. Disturbing as it may be to confront these questions squarely, I suspect that many loyal Catholics would admit that suspicions of precisely this sort were at least temptations (as we used to say), for they are quite in line with the phenomenology of faith-in-crisis sketched by the conservative Hitchcock, who speaks of "unaccustomed cynicism," and by the radical Wills, who portrays preconciliar faith as largely "pretense."[60] And if it were merely a matter of taking satisfaction in the come-uppance meted out to the know-it-all Thomists of yore, one would have to be mean-spirited indeed to begrudge traditional Catholics formed in the Neoscholastic era the meager consolations of *Schadenfreude*. But there is more to it than that. We are dealing here with the kind of situation in which, as Wills puts it, cynicism must be "met and transcended."

It will not do, in other words, to treat the collapse of the Neoscholastic framework of faith as a kind of joke—or even to interpret it as a belated emergence from adolescent "innocence," or to introduce the subject with condescending references to people who inhabit walled-in villages. Nor does it do full justice to the seriousness of the issues to draw a facile distinction between "the faith" and "faith"—the former understood as an impersonal "deposit . . . forever enshrined in the 'Credo'," while the latter is presented as "a biblical concept" that "gives life and gives it more abundantly," the spring from which flows forth "an eschatological hope and a dynamic love."[61] I would not deny that such a distinction is legitimate. The problem is that this kind of airy allusion to a "biblical understanding" of faith tends to make it ineffable and thus to sidestep the demand that one should be able to give faith some kind of concrete content, and should be willing to give reasons for holding it.[62]

There is, in my opinion, no way of getting around the fact that the Catholic religion makes what philosophers call a "truth-claim." "The faith" is the content of that truth-claim, insofar as it has been formulated as "story," history, or doctrine; "faith" understood as a personal quality is an orientation of the entire personality by which an individual grasps, accepts, and identifies himself or herself with the truth-claim embodied in, or pointed toward by, "the faith." Much more than intellectual assent to propositions is admittedly involved. But because of the intimate relationship between "the faith," and personal "faith," it seems to me to border on a new kind of "pretense" to talk as though the latter can endure in any meaningful sense if the former is discredited or dismissed as of little consequence.

That is why the collapse of the Neoscholastic synthesis brought on a crisis, and why it must be taken seriously. It raised the issue of the *truth* of faith in the starkest possible way. The intellectual system by which the truth-claims of Catholic faith had been spelled out, and their congruence with the requirements of reason shown, was suddenly abandoned. It was not overthrown in direct debate, nor was it expressly repudiated. Least of all was it replaced with another system of comparable elaboration. It was simply abandoned! But no such abandonment could take place without its discrediting the faith that was articulated by the system. And discrediting "the faith" in this manner inevitably unsettled the personal faith of Catholics on a massive scale, for adherence to truth-claims made available through the collective tradition is central to personal faith, "biblical concepts" notwithstanding. If American Catholics learned anything by experience in the sixties, surely it was that we are all involved in each other's crises of faith!

The crisis was most acute for the generation of American Catholics who had been formed by the Neoscholastic outlook. That is the thesis argued in the previous chapter, and the longer view of keeping-the-faith sketched in this one supports the same conclusion. This was a generation whose members internalized the conviction that Catholic truth was changeless, perennially the same; moreover, they grew up in an era that saw little actual change in Catholic life. Growth and development there were in full measure, along with the flourishing of a Catholic literary and intellectual awakening; but of significant change in religious teaching or in the overall tendency of developments there was little or nothing. Small wonder, then, that the sudden changes of the 1960s hit the Neoscholastic generation with an impact recently likened by a progressive theologian to that of "a massive surgical operation carried out without anaesthesia on a patient who thought he was in the best of health."[63] Judging from its effects on the Church's "official" mode of thinking, and some of the bizarre twitchings since observable, we might add that the operation seems to have been performed on the patient's central nervous system.

The deeper understanding it affords of the nature of the crisis set off by Vatican II is the first of three benefits to be derived from this historical review of what keeping the faith has meant in America. The second is in a way the obverse of the first. For if looking at the situation as it was experienced by those formed in the Neoscholastic era makes it easier to understand the trauma of that generation, stepping back to take a longer view brings out the historically conditioned factors that went into their formation. Such a perspective discloses that, despite the important positive features of American Catholic life in the Neoscholastic era, there was something fundamentally unhealthy about the authoritarian way Thomism was imposed, and something fundamentally unnatural about the way it tried to put a stop to change, and did put a stop to earlier efforts to respond to change. The longer view suggests, in other words, that the Church erred grievously in permitting—indeed, in causing—the faith to become overidentified with a particular philosophical system and then in overspecifying and overextending the reach of that system. This point has been made many times before, but setting it within the context of our own national history gives it greater pertinence and force.

The final benefit—if that is the right word—to be derived from this account is the rueful comfort American Catholics can take in the realization that the opportunities for heroic struggle were not all used up in earlier phases of keeping the faith in America. For reasons already sufficiently elaborated, it is legitimate to speak today of a crisis of faith. The breakdown of consensus in the Catholic community on how the faith is to be understood and how it applies to practical life inevitably throws the individual believer back on his own, or her own, resources to a greater extent than before and requires, on the part of serious Catholics, a more self-conscious personal grappling with fundamental issues. The heroic-struggle quotient in keeping the faith is thus surely as high now as it has ever been in American Catholic history.

Indeed, American Catholics today might understandably be persuaded that it is higher than ever before. Simply because they are our own—the ones we experience at first hand—the difficulties of our own time loom much larger in our consciousness than those of earlier generations. We are tempted to look back with envy on the happy days of old, telling ourselves, in the case at hand, how much easier it was to be a believer in those times. But that is a delusion. Being a believer has never been easy. No generation of American Catholics has been without its doubts and difficulties, its divisions among the faithful, its contradictions, betrayals, and losses. None has wholly escaped the obligation of rethinking the faith. If this is a sobering realization, it can also be a source of encouragement and inspiration. What the postconciliar generation confronts is but the most recent phase of a perennial struggle. And in keeping the faith today, we also keep faith with those who went before.

PART II

9

LITERARY LANDMARKS OF
AMERICAN CATHOLICISM IN TRANSITION

Several years ago I taught a two-week, summer-session minicourse on American Catholicism since Vatican II. Readings are always a problem in such short courses, and since there was no really satisfactory survey available, I decided to draw up a reading list of works produced in the period being studied and let students choose from it whatever they wished to read. My bibliographic approach was quite unscientific—I simply began listing books that stood out in my recollection, or that I remembered hearing about in the course of living through those years. The mode of presentation was to be as casual as the method of compilation. All I planned to do was list the titles under a few general headings. But so many of them seemed to require some comment that I soon found myself embarked on a bibliographical essay, although I had not started out with any intention of writing one.

After using it in class, and supplementing the background section on 1950s, I submitted the essay to Theology Today, *where it appeared in October 1981 under the title "A Browser's Guide to American Catholicism, 1950–1980." The present version is somewhat revised and includes mention of some more recently published works, but it remains an impressionistic retrospect rather than a systematic bibliography. Despite its informal character, I found that sorting out in my mind the principal writings of the period helped me to grasp the development of events. I hope that reading it will help others do the same.*

R ETROSPECTIVELY, TWO THEMES STAND OUT in American Catholicism in the immediate preconciliar era. Although labels inevitably distort, we

181

can call them the *Catholic mobilization* theme and the *anti-ghettoism* theme. The former was older, but reached a climax in the forties and fifties; anti-ghettoism was in part a reaction against some of the aspects of Catholic mobilization, but the two should not be thought of as flatly opposed to each other. Anti-ghettoism will be treated more fully because it feeds directly into developments of the 1960s, but first a few words about Catholic mobilization.

Catholic Mobilization and the Catholic Revival

The most obvious dimension of Catholic mobilization was the tremendous build-up of institutional Catholicism (churches, schools, Catholic organizations, etc.) that took place after 1900 and became especially marked after World War I. The establishment in 1919 of a national organization by the Catholic bishops, with a permanent headquarters and staff in Washington — the National Catholic Welfare Conference — symbolized the dominance that Catholic mobilization was to have in the following decades.[1]

Catholic mobilization was clearly inward-looking in the sense that it implied the elaboration of intragroup structures, the formation of new Catholic associations, and so on. But it was also outward-looking because the purpose of all of this organization was not only — or even primarily — to preserve the faith of Catholics; rather it was to enhance the influence that Catholics might exert on the larger society and culture. That was the goal enunciated by Pope Pius X as "To redeem all things in Christ"; Pope Pius XI systematized it in the program known as Catholic Action, which envisioned the collaboration of all the faithful, under episcopal guidance, in the work of Christianizing the social order.

This evangelical, outward-directed impulse in Catholic mobilization was usually designated as "apostolic," and the term "apostolate" was applied to the various specialized areas in which apostolic zeal found its focus — as in the social apostolate, apostolate of the press, etc. The Catholic Worker movement is the only facet of this apostolic ferment to have received much attention from historians, but it was by no means the whole story.

The apostolic orientation developed within the context of the great Catholic intellectual and cultural revival of the interwar period. This was primarily a European phenomenon and was closely linked to the revival of Neoscholastic philosophy and theology. American Catholics looked to Europe for inspiration and gloried in the achievements of philosophers like Jacques Maritain and Etienne Gilson; theologians like Romano Guardini and Karl Adam; writers like Sigrid Undset, Paul Claudel, François Mauriac,

Graham Greene, and Evelyn Waugh; cultural critics like G. K. Chesterton and Christopher Dawson; artists like Georges Rouault and Ivan Mestrovic, and other lesser figures in a variety of fields. Against this background it is understandable that apostolically inspired American Catholics began to speak of a Catholic renaissance, of creating a Catholic civilization, of building a Catholic culture integrated around faith and radiating outward into all the realms of life and thought.

This whole phenomenon is only beginning to attract the attention of historians. Various aspects of the mentality are touched upon in certain of the essays collected in this volume, and William M. Halsey's *The Survival of American Innocence* (1980) is a more systematic treatment from a different perspective. James Hitchcock's "Postmortem on a Rebirth" (*American Scholar,* Spring 1980), and Arnold J. Sparr's doctoral dissertation, "The Catholic Literary Revival in America, 1920–1960" (Wisconsin, 1985) are very helpful; chapter two of Garry Wills's *Bare Ruined Choirs* (1972) portrays the late stages of the revival mentality in the 1950s. Recent studies of the Catholic Worker—especially Mel Piehl's *Breaking Bread* (1982); two books by William D. Miller, *A Harsh and Dreadful Love* (1972) and *Dorothy Day* (1982); and Marc H. Ellis's *Peter Maurin* (1981)—help set that movement in the context of the times, and David O'Brien's *American Catholics and Social Reform* (1968) covers the broader topic of Catholic social teaching in the 1930s.

This is not the place to enlarge on the Catholic Revival, but we must note three points about it and the Catholic mobilization which it complemented. The first is that several movements later regarded as progressive and therefore putatively at odds with the preconciliar mentality, actually originated within the matrix of Catholic mobilization and reflected its inspiration. This is most notably the case with the liturgical movement, as is shown in a work written in the 1950s—Paul Marx's *Virgil Michel and the Liturgical Movement* (1957). The same is true of the movement for catechetical reform, but we are without a satisfactory general account of its early stages in this country.

Secondly, the Catholic Revival accustomed American Catholics to taking their intellectual cues from Europe. Hence, when new impulses began to flicker across the European Catholic scene after 1945, they soon attracted attention in this country. Only a handful of specialists really knew much about these matters, but general works by prominent progressive theologians—like Henri de Lubac's *Catholicism* (1950) and the same author's *The Splendor of the Church* (1956)—were made available to English-language readers. English translations of such works as Yves Congar's *Lay People in the Church* (1957) and Karl Rahner's *Free Speech in the Church* (1959) were harbingers of what was to come in flood a few years later. At the close of the fifties, Pierre Teilhard de Chardin's *Phenome-non of Man* (1959) and *Divine Milieu* (1960) enjoyed a great vogue.

The third point is that Catholic mobilization was dialectically related to anti-ghettoism because, despite its being theoretically directed toward renewal of society generally, its main effect was to cut Catholics off from the larger world by recruiting them into strictly Catholic organizations, which the critics began calling "ghetto organizations" sometime around 1950. Usually the critics simply overlooked (or were unaware of) the apos-tolic purpose that Catholic mobilization presumed, and interpreted its goal as the purely defensive one of protecting the faithful from religious peril, which was certainly also present. But they likewise believed that separate Catholic organizations represented the wrong strategic approach if one wished to influence the larger world. They prescribed instead that Catho-lics *as individuals* should bring the influence of their religion to bear on society by joining forces with persons of other (or no) religious background in "pluralistic" organizations defined by function or goal rather than by denominational commitment.

This new emphasis, which emerged clearly in the early fifties, was very "American." Those who spoke for anti-ghettoism were interested in liberal Catholic stirrings in Europe—e.g., the French worker-priests—but this influence was negligible in comparison to the way their thinking was shaped by American social and cultural forces. This was, after all, the epoch of the "American celebration," when even *Partisan Review* intellectuals looked favorably upon national values and institutions, and when the ef-fort to understand the American character preoccupied social scientists as well as humanistically oriented scholars. In these circumstances, younger Catholic liberals were especially concerned about the relation of their re-ligion to the national culture, and topics like Americanization, pluralism, ghettoism, and the contribution of Catholics to the intellectual life of the nation loomed large in their thinking. We will begin our survey of Catho-lic writings on these matters with a look at some general studies of the relation of Catholicism to the national culture.

Catholicism, Americanism, and Anti-ghettoism

In the first place, it is noteworthy that the historical recovery of the episode of "Americanism" took place at this time. John Tracy Ellis's magis-terial *Life of James Cardinal Gibbons* (1952), Robert Cross's *The Emer-gence of Liberal Catholicism in the United States* (1958), and Thomas T. McAvoy's *The Great Crisis in American Catholic History* (1957) were the outstanding landmarks in this outpouring of scholarship on the controversies over Americanization of the Catholic Church in the 1880s and 1890s.[2] McAvoy had already introduced in the forties the concept of "the Catholic minority," adapted from the social science of the day, which highlighted the relationship of Catholicism to the majority culture. Similar perspectives were employed by other writers in the fifties. In *The American Catholic Family* (1956), for example, John L. Thomas used the minority concept in analyzing the impact of American cultural norms on an institution central to the Catholic mobilization approach—namely, the family.

Will Herberg's *Protestant-Catholic-Jew* (1955) was the most influential book on American religion published in the decade. It drew on the Catholic Americanism scholarship and McAvoy's minority thesis in a brilliantly provocative treatment of the so-called revival of religion and in an incisive critique of the role religion was assumed to play in buttressing the "American Way of Life," which Herberg saw as the real religion of Americans.

Two collections of essays by Walter Ong also attracted attention: *Frontiers of American Catholicism* (1957) and *American Catholic Crossroads* (1959). Thomas T. McAvoy, ed., *Roman Catholicism and the American Way of Life* (1960) made available the papers presented at two symposia dealing with various aspects of the subject indicated by the title. Two earlier volumes took a more internalist approach, providing information about Catholic population groups and Catholic activities, Louis J. Putz, ed., *The Catholic Church, U.S.A.* (1956), and Leo R. Ward, *Catholic Life, U.S.A. Contemporary Lay Movements* (1959). Jacques Maritain's *Reflections on America* (1958), and Raymond Bruckberger's *Image of America* (1959), were very favorable assessments of American civilization by European Catholic observers.

There was a good deal of tension between Catholics and others, especially over the school issue, censorship, and related matters. Paul Blanshard's books, and Catholic replies, made the issues highly visible in the late 1940s. They are reviewed from an enlightened Protestant point of view by George H. Williams, Waldo Beach, and H. Richard Niebuhr in the journal *Religion in Life* (vol. 23, Spring 1954), and from a Catholic viewpoint by John J. Kane, *Catholic-Protestant Conflicts in America* (1955).

The church-state issue was especially crucial. John Courtney Murray's work on this problem attracted favorable attention from liberals and aroused a very critical reaction from Catholic conservatives, including Roman authorities who required Murray to stop writing on the subject. Donald E. Pelotte's *John Courtney Murray* (1976) covers the controversy well. At least one book—Waldemar Gurian and M. A. Fitzsimons, eds., *The Catholic Church in World Affairs* (1954)—had to be withdrawn from circulation because it contained a church-state essay by Murray. Most of Murray's work appeared in articles, but Jacques Maritain's *Man and the State* (1950) represented a liberal Catholic statement early in the decade, and in 1960 Murray's *We Hold These Truths* brought together a collection of his writings on church-state, secularism, and other subjects. Murray also propounded a forthrightly Catholic, yet irenical, position in the symposium sponsored by the Fund for the Republic and edited by John Cogley as *Religion in America* (1958). By the end of the decade, the beginnings of a self-consciously "ecumenical" approach could be noted in Gustave Weigel's *A Catholic Primer on the Ecumenical Movement* (1957) and in the exchange between Weigel and Robert McAfee Brown published under the title *An American Dialogue* (1960). Jaroslav Pelikan's *The Riddle of Roman Catholicism* (1959) was described by a Catholic reviewer as "the best fruit of the new American encounter between Protestant and Catholic thought." In the early 1960s both "dialogue" and "encounter" became buzz words.

The main thrust of Catholic liberalism in the fifties was unquestionably that Catholics should abandon separatism, outgrow their siege mentality, and break out of their Catholic ghetto. This message was often accompanied by praise for American pluralism, which was interpreted as requiring everyone to mix indiscriminately "as Americans." The liberal Catholic journal *Commonweal* was the principal organ of the break-out-of-the-ghetto school of thought, and the volume, *Catholicism in America* (1953), consisting of articles from the magazine, is the most convenient collection of pieces embodying that viewpoint. For the magazine itself, see Rodger Van Allen, *The Commonweal and American Catholicism* (1974). After the mid-fifties, anti-ghettoism came to focus primarily on the question of Catholic intellectual life.

As noted earlier in chapter 3, the great debate about Catholic intellectual life was touched off in 1955 with the publication of John Tracy Ellis's essay, "American Catholics and the Intellectual Life." Ellis's critique, which was published as a book in 1956, reviewed the meager record of Catholics as contributors to American science, scholarship, and creative literature, and listed a number of factors that might explain their weak showing. Its appearance prompted an outpouring of articles, the most important of which were excerpted (along with much earlier material) in Frank L. Christ and Gerard E. Sherry's *American Catholicism and the Intellectual Ideal* (1961). Especially important was the only full-scale book on the question to come out in the fifties, Thomas F. O'Dea's *American Catholic Dilemma* (1958). Ellis emphasized Catholics' self-imposed ghetto attitude as a cause of intellectual backwardness; O'Dea added several other aspects of Catholic life—clericalism, formalism, authoritarianism, moralism, and defensiveness—as explaining the deficiencies of Catholic intellectual life, or what was often simply called Catholic anti-intellectualism. Hence it seemed all the more important for Catholics to break out of the ghetto and enter the mainstream of American life, for by doing so, it was asserted, they would be able to compile a more respectable intellectual record and become a more vital element in Amerian society. In this sense, the controversy fit into the general Americanist emphasis of the 1950s; it also reflected the American environment more directly in that it paralleled the broader concern over "anti-intellectualism" in American life that was touched off by McCarthyism.

The Early Sixties: Kennedy, the Council, and Continuing Themes

John F. Kennedy's election marked a breakthrough and a new stage in the relationship of American Catholics to the life of the nation. It did not, however, produce any really notable publications. Francis J. Lally, *The Catholic Church in a Changing America* (1962), was organized around the Kennedy breakthrough, and Lawrence H. Fuchs, *John F. Kennedy and American Catholicism* (1967), provided an academic analysis by a professor of American civilization at Brandeis University. Andrew M. Greeley suggested in *The Catholic Experience* (1967) that JFK might be regarded as a "Doctor of the Church," but that opinion was looked upon as somewhat extravagant by the time the book came out.

If John F. Kennedy represented the continuation in a new way of the theme of Catholic participation in American life, Pope John XXIII (whose name was often coupled with that of Kennedy, as in "two men named John") became the symbol of the new spirit in the Church and brought the influence of European currents of thought to bear on American Catholic developments in an earthshaking way through the Second Vatican Council.

The literature on the Council and its consequences is immense. I will simply mention a few of the books that were best known even among those who didn't try to keep up with their reading on the Council. Hans Küng's *The Council, Reform and Reunion* (1961) came out before the first session met and was the most widely noted volume to discuss the needs the Council might address. It also marked the first appearance on the American Catholic horizon of a man who became one of the leading luminaries of the theological scene. Küng's lecture tour of the United States in the spring of 1963 featured the issue of freedom in the Church and dramatized the clash between liberal theologians and the Roman Curia with its conservative theological allies.

Xavier Rynne's *Letters from Vatican City* (1963), originally serialized in *The New Yorker* during the first session of the Council, had already brought the liberal curial/split out in the open, as did Robert B.

Kaiser's *Pope, Council, and World: The Story of Vatican II* (1963). Michael Novak's *The Open Church* (1964) analyzed the second session of the Council; Rynne continued to chronicle the latter sessions as well, and Gary MacEoin, *What Happened at Rome?* (1966) offered a succinct summing up. Walter Abbott and Joseph Gallagher's paperback edition of *The Documents of Vatican II* (1966) circulated widely; while John H. Miller's *Vatican II: An Interfaith Appraisal* (1966) made available the proceedings of a conference in which most of the theologians who had been leading advisors or observers at the Council took part. John G. Deedy, ed., *Eyes on the Modern World* (1965) is a collection of American Catholic reactions to the Council schema dealing with the relationship of the Church to the modern world.

In the meantime, the semipopular works of the European theologians sold well in the United States, with Karl Rahner's *The Christian Commitment* (1963) being, perhaps, the best example of the genre. The frequently issued, topical volumes of the series called *Concilium* (est. 1965) provided a way of keeping up to date on the rapidly changing theological scene.

The concerns that emerged in the 1950s continued into the sixties, but were also affected by the newer currents associated with *aggiornamento*. Donald J. Thorman's *The Emerging Layman* (1962) seemed to herald a new age, but in looking back into it again, one is struck by how old-fashioned it now seems. The apostolic lay action it calls for goes back to the Catholic-Action tradition of Pope Pius XI and the 1930s; its family emphasis is distinctly that of the 1950s, and in general it reveals relatively little of the temper that was soon to dominate. By 1967 Thorman was speaking of "Today's Layman: An Uncertain Catholic" (*America*, January 14, 1967), and his *American Catholics Face the Future* (1968) shows how drastically things had changed in the half-dozen years since the earlier book had marked the laity's emergence.

Daniel Callahan's *Mind of the Catholic Layman* (1963) stressed the issue of lay freedom, but it too revealed a strong carryover of the preoccupations of the fifties. Michael Novak's *A New Generation* (1964) was self-conscious about youth and newness, but concerned itself primarily with the intellectual and cultural issues that mattered to educated Catholics in the late fifties rather than with the radical questions that were to be raised a few years later. *The Generation of the Third Eye* (1965), a collection of essays edited by Daniel Callahan, presents the views of a score of younger Catholics at the end of the Council.

Mary Perkins Ryan's *Are Parochial Schools the Answer?* (1964) represented a blending of the old and new. Her subject (Catholic education) was a perennial, but her prescription (de-emphasize the Catholic schools) was radically new. Her approach was doubtless reinforced by the Council, but she was a veteran of the preconciliar liturgical movement, and she argued that Christians should be formed by the liturgy, not by classroom teaching. Her book raised quite a furor and was blamed for contributing to the weakening of the parochial schools in the later 1960s. The same author's *We're All in This Together* (1972) offers an interesting comparison and contrast to her 1964 book, of which she says, for example, that her reliance on the liturgy alone as educator was "astonishingly naive."

The Catholic intellectualism controversy revived momentarily in the early 1960s, having been somewhat complicated in the meantime by the appearance of Gerhard Lenski's *The Religious Factor* (1961), a sociological analysis of the effects of religious belief and affiliation, not merely on intellectual activity, but on the more general question of "achievement orientation." Lenski found Catholicism a generally negative factor, and his findings reinforced the position of the critics of Catholic intellectual life and thus became an issue in the debate. Andrew M. Greeley's *Religion and Career* (1963) was a major challenge to the Lenski thesis and to the critics of Catholic intellectual performance, since Greeley discovered, through a national sample survey, that the Catholics in the collegiate graduating class of 1961 were every bit as intellectual and achievement-oriented as non-Catholics. At about the same time, John Donovan brought out another sociological study, *The Academic Man in the Catholic College* (1964), that agreed with the more pessimistic appraisals of Lenski and the earlier Catholic critics. Exchanges on these matters seemed to generate more heat than light, but they reflected important differences both as to *why* Catholics had done poorly heretofore and whether they might be expected to do better in the future. The optimistic position (Greeley's) implied that improvements in Catholic social and educational status would take care of the problem more or less automatically. The pessimistic position of the so-called self-critics seemed to be that there were deep-rooted Catholic attitudes and practices that had to be eradicated by purposeful reform before any significant improvement could be expected in "Catholic intellectualism."

Mid- and Late-Sixties

So many things happened so fast from 1965 to 1970 that one can offer only a highly selective sampling. Moreover, books were less influential than actions, and some of the most important developments took place without calling forth notable writings; for example, Catholic participation in the Civil Rights movement was more a matter of example and action than of literary influence. But despite the radical changes that occurred, there were certain lines of continuity, and we will begin with one of these, the controversy over education and intellectualism.

Mary Perkins Ryan's book, already noted, had made parochial schools a major focus of controversy. As one of the chief "ghetto" institutions closely identified with the authoritarianism, clericalism, etc., that were regarded as hindrances to intellectualism, the schools were targets for the liberal critics; they had long been viewed as "divisive" by non-Catholics; and as nuns and brothers turned their attention to new forms of apostolic work, the schools lost some of their attractiveness to the group that had been essential to staffing them in the past. The growth of lay faculties not only increased costs, but eventually led to problems about freedom and autonomy for teachers, and to the question of unionization. By the late 1960s, Catholic school people were seriously demoralized; many parochial schools were being closed, and the future of the institution seemed highly questionable.

In these circumstances, two social-scientific surveys of the situation attracted great attention. The so-called Notre Dame study, Reginald A. Neuwein, ed., *Catholic Schools in Action* (1966), was widely regarded as a disappointment from the viewpoint of method and results, but *The Education of Catholic Americans* (1966), by Andrew M. Greeley and Peter Rossi, was a solid study and had greater impact. The Greeley-Rossi study was positive in the sense that it showed Catholic education did make a difference, not only in respect to loyalty to the Church, but also because those with Catholic education tended to develop better (more liberal, tolerant, open-minded) attitudes on social and political issues. Greeley became the chief champion of the Catholic schools in the controversy that followed, and continued to argue in subsequent years that they should be maintained. His *Catholic Schools in a Declining Church* (1976; written with William McCready and Kathleen McCourt) is a follow-up survey and analysis. Other informative works for the 1960s are: George N. Shuster, *Catholic Education in a Changing World* (1967), and Neil G. McCluskey, *Catholic Education Faces Its Future* (1969).

Meanwhile the field of catechetics was undergoing drastic reconsideration. Mary Perkins Ryan's previously mentioned *We're All in This Together* gives some indication of how far catechists had come (or gone) by 1972. Gabriel Moran, one of the most prominent American leaders, had reached the conclusion by the late 1960s that "the problem of catechetics is that it exists," as he put it in his *Design for Religion* (1970).

After 1965, the Catholic intellectualism problem was absorbed into the issue of academic freedom in Catholic higher education, and that in turn soon disappeared in the more generalized identity crisis of Catholic institutions, which itself took place against the chaotic background of campus revolution in the nation at large. Edward Manier and John W. Houck, eds., *Academic Freedom and the Catholic University* (1967), and Robert Hassenger, ed., *The Shape of Catholic Higher Education* (1967), offer the best entry into these subjects. Neil G. McCluskey, ed., *The Catholic University: A Modern Appraisal* (1970), is an important collection that reveals how matters stood by the end of the sixties.

Robert Hoyt's *Issues that Divide the Church* (1966), originally a symposium that appeared in the *National Catholic Reporter,* reproduces a discussion among representatives of six different positions and gives some notion of the range of newer issues that began to attract attention in the mid-sixties. (The *NCR* itself began in the fall of 1964 and soon became the principal vehicle of criticism, controversy, and reform.)[3]

Daniel Callahan's *Honesty in the Church* (1965) anticipated the widespread concern over "credibility gaps"; the implication that honesty had been lacking in the Church before indicated the degree of alienation from the "institutional Church" that had already taken place by the end of the Council.

Harvey Cox's *Secular City* (1965) reinforced the Council-inspired turn toward involvement in the world. The book was widely hailed by Catholics, and Callahan edited a collection of reactions (not just Catholic) entitled *The Secular City Debate* (1966). Cox's secularity was at least a first cousin of the Death-of-God theology; both were premised on a demythologized understanding of religion in a "world come of age." Themes of immanentism and humanism were also prominent. These and related emphases may be found in Jackson Lee Ice, ed., *The Death of God Debate* (1967), and Bernard Murchland, ed., *The Meaning of the Death of God* (1967). John A. T. Robinson's *Honest to God* (1963) provided a link between the honesty theme and the death of God. Leslie Dewart's *The Future of Belief* (1966) announced the end of the Hellenic mentality with its essentialist understanding of religious truth, again indicating that, if not dead, God certainly could not be understood in the old way. Joseph Fletcher's *Situation Ethics* (1966) popularized an approach to morality that seemed more in keeping with the humanized and de-mythologized understanding of religion called for by the radical theologians.

Incomparably the most important moral problem for Catholics was birth control, and the evolution of this question also threw the issues of honesty and authority in the Church into bold relief. The reaction to Charles Curran's handling of this issue, and the Catholic University of America's handling of him, also created an academic freedom crisis. The literature here is very large, but John Noonan's *Contraception: A History of Its Treatment by the Catholic Theologians and Canonists* (1965) was a great landmark in the debate; chapter 15 also provides an excellent summary of the discussion up through the early 1960s. Two works edited by the man who became the central figure in the crisis following the publication of *Humanae Vitae* are Charles Curran, ed., *Contraception: Authority and Dissent* (1969), and Curran et al., *Dissent In and For the Church: Theologians and Humanae Vitae* (1969).

William DuBay's criticism of Cardinal McIntyre for backwardness on the racial issue gave him relatively early prominence as a dissenting priest. His book *The Human Church* (1966) shortly preceded his leaving the priesthood. Even more spectacular was the departure from the priesthood of James Kavanaugh, announced before a large audience at Notre Dame. His general critique was presented in *A Modern Priest Looks at His Outdated Church* (1967). Almost equally sensational, but at a more serious level, was the departure from the priesthood of Charles Davis, a well-known English theological writer and editor of the respected *Clergy Review*. Davis's apologia, *A Question of Conscience* (1967), was highly critical of the Church.

These were perhaps the most widely reported instances of what became a massive exodus from the priesthood. It caused much concern and occasioned the publication of several books. Two books by priest-sociologists came out in 1968: Joseph Fichter's *America's Forgotten Priests* and Andrew Greeley's *Uncertain Trumpet: The Priest in the United States*. Greeley also published *New Horizons for the Priesthood* in 1970 and directed the large-scale sociological survey sponsored by the Catholic bishops, which appeared in 1972 as *The Catholic Priest in the United States: Sociological Investigations*. Greeley's *Priests in the United States: Reflections on a Survey* (1972) gave his own interpretation of the findings. At the same time, John Tracy Ellis edited another volume of the series sponsored by the bishops: *The Catholic Priest in the United States: Historical Investigations* (1971).

The corresponding exodus of religious women from their communities was less well reported as it occurred and has received less study. Leo Cardinal Suenens's *The Nun in the World* (1963) was an early example of a new spirit concerning the work of religious women; according to one authority, it was read by virtually every American nun. Sister Charles Borreomeo Muckenhirn's selection of short pieces entitled *The New Nuns* (1967) was relatively tame. Chapter 6 of Garry Wills's *Bare Ruined Choirs* (1972) is a merciless exposé of the fatuities of the best known "new nun" of the period, "Sister J." (Jacqueline Grennan), president of Webster College in St. Louis, who resigned her position and left her community to become more actively involved in the secular city. Helen Ebaugh's *Out of the Cloister* (1977) is an informative sociological study of the changes the sisterhoods have undergone and the dilemmas they face. A more recent treatment by a respected sociologist is Marie Augusta Neal, *Catholic Sisters in Transition: From the 1960s to the 1980s* (1984).

The Catholic charismatic movement, which surfaced (to use a sixties word) in 1967, was perhaps the most surprising development in an epoch of surprises. It was primarily a lay movement, although priests, religious, and some bishops have also identified themselves with it. The early stirrings occurred in Pittsburgh, but the movement first gained national visibility at Notre Dame, and two of the most informative early accounts were written by persons who became involved in it there—Kevin and Dorothy Ranaghan's *Catholic Pentecostals* (1969) and Edward D. O'Connor's *The Pentecostal Movement in the Catholic Church* (1971). Also by an early participant is Ralph Martin, *New Wine, New Skins* (1976). More detached in approach are: Joseph Fichter, *The Catholic Cult of the Paraclete* (1975) and Killian McDonnell, *The Holy Spirit and Power* (1975).

The explosion that rocked the Catholic Church attracted wide attention (and caused some alarm) among non-Catholics; it became a contributing cause to the wider cultural turmoil that prevailed in American society in the late 1960s. Of course Catholic developments were also profoundly affected by the upheaval in the wider society. The books mentioned here do no more than suggest the various kinds of connections that existed.

Catholics, or persons of Catholic background, played very prominent roles in several spheres, but Marshall McLuhan was in a class by himself as constituting a one-man cultural revolution, a prophet of the global village and media consciousness. His views defy brief summary but can be gotten at through his *Understanding Media* (1964), or more painlessly (if more bewilderingly) through the picture-book with captions, *The Medium is the Massage* (1967)—and "massage" here is not a misprint for "message."

The background of Timothy Leary, high priest of the psychodelic revolution, was Catholic; and Theodore Roszak's *The Making of a Counter Culture* (1968) argued for an extreme form of romanticism that found many Catholic sympathizers. My article, "Our New Age of Romanticism" (*America,* October 10, 1967) called attention to the phenomenon, which is stringently criticized in Andrew Greeley's *Come Blow Your Mind with Me* (1971). The title of Michael Novak's *A Theology for Radical Politics* (1969) suggests greater sympathy for this sort of cultural radicalism. Rosemary Ruether's *The Church against Herself* (1967) and *The Radical Kingdom* (1970) applied eschatological and millennialist perspectives to ecclesiology. James Colaianni's *The Catholic Left* (1968) is a potpourri dealing with "the crisis of radicalism within the Church."

I know of no general survey of Catholic participation on the Civil Rights-Black movement, but there are few snippets in Colaianni, and journalistic reporting of the activities of Father James Groppi of Milwaukee, who first gained national prominence in 1965, gives some notion of its extent and character. In the anti-Vietnam movement, the brothers Daniel and Philip Berrigan were the outstanding figures (and Philip, a Josephite priest, had long been active on the racial front). On the Catholic antiwar movement, see Francine du Plessix Gray, *Divine Disobedience: Profiles in Catholic Radicalism* (1970); *The Berrigans,* edited by William VanEtten Casey and Philip Nobile (1971), and three studies of broader scope: Patricia McNeal, *The American Catholic Peace Movement* (1978); Charles A. Meconis, *With Clumsy Grace: The American Catholic Left* (1979); and William A. Au, *The Cross, the Flag, and the Bomb: American Catholics Debate War and Peace, 1960–1983* (1985). Dorothy Dohen, *Nationalism and American Catholicism* (1967), is a critique of the Church for allowing itself to become uncritically committed to nationalist political aims and ideology. Thomas Merton's activities as a critic of American foreign policy stimulated new interest in him which is reflected, for example, in Monica Furlong's *Merton* (1980) and Michael Mott's *The Seven Mountains of Thomas Merton* (1985).

New Interests after 1970

While there is no sharp demarcation between phases of the postconciliar upheaval, the turmoil was most intense between about 1965 and 1970. A calmer atmosphere gradually prevailed in the seventies, but many of the movements begun in the sixties continued to make themselves felt and there were also some new developments.

One such new development was the revival of ethnicity dealt with in chapter 2. Since the most important literature is discussed there, I will simply add that, although the ethnic revival is over as a popular movement, scholarly interest continues to be very strong, resulting, to give but one recent example, in such excellent works as Robert Orsi's *The Madonna of 115th Street* (1985), which examines Italian-American life through the prism of popular religion. It should also be emphasized that ethnicity remains an important reality in American Catholic life. Works like Andrew Greeley's *The American Catholic* (1977) and Harold Abramson's *Ethnic Diversity in Catholic America* (1973) demonstrate the general significance of ethnicity, but it is particularly important in the case of Hispanic Catholics. Although much has been written about this group (or rather the various groups included under the label "Hispanic"), there is still relatively little that focuses primarily on the religious aspect of their experience. *Hispanics in the United States* (1985), edited by Pastora San Juan Cafferty and William C. McCready, is a recent overview that includes an essay on "Culture and Religion." Three other works that deal more directly with religion are *Prophets Denied Honor* (1980), a valuable anthology edited by Antonio M. Stevens-Arroyo, and two books by Virgilio P. Elizondo: *Christianity and Culture* (1975) and *Galilean Journey: The Mexican-American Promise* (1983).

Sixties social concern and commitment to radical restructuring of society carried over in the seventies in the form of sympathy for the Third World and liberation theology, advocacy on behalf of the poor and oppressed, promotion of peace and justice, and in a largely unacknowledged, but quite obvious, gravitation toward some form of Christian socialism as the most desirable ideal of political-economy. Indigenous tendencies of a social-justice sort accounted for the peace-and-justice emphasis of the bicentennial "Call to Action" observance sponsored by the National Conference of Catholic Bishops. As noted in chapter 5, Joseph A. Varacalli's *Toward the Establishment of Liberal Catholicism in America* (1983), is the only full-length study of this event, but David J. O'Brien, a leading participant in the Call to Action, co-edited with Thomas G. Shannon a volume entitled *Renewing the Earth* (1977), which makes available a number of Church statements dealing with "peace, justice and liberty." More recent works valuable for what they present in themselves and for the leads they provide to the literature of the field are: John A. Coleman, *An American Strategic Theology* (1982); Joseph Gremillion, ed., *The Church and Culture since Vatican II* (1985); and especially, Charles E. Curran and Richard A. McCormick, eds., *Readings in Moral Theology No. 5: Official Catholic Social Teaching* (1986).

Latin American liberation theology powerfully reinforced the indigenous U.S. social-justice movement. Gustavo Gutierrez's *A Theology of Liberation* (1973) established the importance and visibility of this school of thought, and the Maryknoll-sponsored Orbis Press has since poured forth a torrent of liberation theology works in English translation. A conference in Detroit in 1975 marked the first widely noted effort to apply the Latin American perspective to the social situation in this country. For this event, see Sergio Torres and John Eagleson, eds., *Theology in the Americas* (1976). Liberation theology gained wider notice and acceptance in the 1980s, but it also generated opposition that brought forth a critique, not only from Rome, but also from so-called neoconservatives like Michael Novak. The viewpoint of these Catholics, who object not only to liberation theology but also to the position taken by the American hierarchy on nuclear policy and the economy, may be found in works like

Novak's *Freedom with Justice* (1984) and in the columns of *Catholicism in Crisis,* a monthly journal founded in 1982 by Novak and Ralph M. McInerny of the University of Notre Dame. (The name of this journal changed to *Crisis* in August, 1986.)

Women's liberation, which has obvious affinities with liberation theology, may turn out to be the most important of all the legacies of the 1960s. Catholic women have been profoundly affected. Indicative of the influence exerted by the new feminism is the fact that a supplemental volume to the *New Catholic Encyclopedia* issued in 1979 devoted no fewer than twelve separate articles to the role of women in the Church and in society. Mary Daly's *The Church and the Second Sex* (1968) was a pioneering work, the highly critical tone of which foreshadowed the author's later withdrawal from the Catholic Church. Daly's work—along with that of three other Catholic feminist theologians: Anne Carr, Elisabeth Schüssler Fiorenza, and Rosemary Radford Ruether—is discussed in Mary Jo Weaver's *New Catholic Women* (1985). This book, written by a Catholic feminist trained in theology at Notre Dame who teaches religious studies at Indiana University, provides an invaluable overview of the impact of the women's movement on American Catholicism. In addition to feminist theology, it covers new developments among religious communities of women, the campaign for women's ordination, the "Womanchurch" movement, and the emergence of new forms of feminist spirituality. Of particular relevance to the past-and-present theme that interweaves through the essays collected in this volume is Weaver's thoughtful discussion of women in American Catholic history and her insistence that the whole field must be reconceptualized to do justice to the role of women.

Weaver's book does not confront the issue of abortion directly, although there is growing tension between Catholic feminists and ecclesiastical authorities over "freedom of choice" and whether any "pluralism" of views is possible concerning the permissibility of abortion. Such tensions were exacerbated by debates set off during the 1984 presidential campaign, especially by statements on abortion made by Geraldine Ferraro, Mario Cuomo, and Cardinal O'Connor of New York; by the appearance in the *New York Times* (October 7, 1984) of "A Catholic Statement on Pluralism and Abortion," and by disciplinary action initiated against certain of the nuns who were among the ninety-six signers of the statement. Abortion has thus become a divisive issue among Catholics, as well as being a central focus of recent church/state controversies.

Since the issue only emerged in the 1970s, the literature (aside from strictly controversial pieces) is not large. Daniel Callahan's *Abortion: Law, Choice and Morality* (1970) is an early major work by a Catholic who was traditionally opposed to abortion, but was led to reconsider the question by contemporary shifts in American liberal thinking. John Noonan, whose book on contraception contributed to Catholic acceptance of birth control, became the outstanding scholarly opponent of abortion. *The Morality of Abortion* (1970), which Noonan edited, appeared before the Supreme Court decision that removed virtually all legal limitations on abortion; his *A Private Choice: Abortion in America in the Seventies* (1979) argues powerfully against the situation that resulted from the Court's action. James T. Burtchaell, who edited *Abortion Parley* in 1980, contributed a major work of his own two years later: *Rachel Weeping: The Case against Abortion.* Mary T. Hanna includes a chapter on abortion as a "Catholic issue" in her *Catholic and American Politics* (1979), but that book appeared too soon to cover the more embittered church/state clashes that arose in the presidential election year of 1984.

General Studies and Histories

Besides the writings that dealt with one or another aspect of the changing scene, there have been efforts since the mid-sixties to describe and assess the overall situation. An early and very defective attempt to paint the big picture was Edward Wakin and Joseph F. Scheuer's *The De-Romanization of the American Catholic Church* (1966). Barrett McGurn's *A Reporter Looks at American Catholicism* appeared in 1967. Donald Thorman's already-mentioned *American Catholics Face the Future* came out the next year, as did *American Catholics Exodus,* a collection of essays edited by John O'Connor, nearly all of which were written by liberals. A somewhat similar volume that I edited, *Contemporary Catholicism in the United States* (1969), brought together fourteen original essays, mainly by academics, who placed near the middle of the spectrum, ideologically speaking. Thomas F. O'Dea's *The Catholic Crisis* (1968) is a fine analysis of the overall impact of the Council by a scholar prominent in the sociology of religion. George H. Tavard's *Catholicism U.S.A.* (1969), an interesting and historically informed commentary, is the English-language version of a book published for a French audience in 1966.

A trio of important books published in 1972 represent three different positions on the ideological spectrum. James Hitchcock's *Decline and Fall of Radical Catholicism,* a conservative critique, argued that the excesses committed by enthusiasts of change in the sixties defeated the goals of renewal and reform which had originally inspired Pope John XXIII's calling of the Council. David J. O'Brien's *Renewal of American Catholicism,* on the other hand, approved the general direction taken by postconciliar developments, but believed that they had to be carried much further to achieve true renewal. In contradistinction to O'Brien, who stood squarely in the classic tradition of American Catholic liberalism, Garry Wills, formerly an outspoken conservative of the *National Review* variety, set forth in his *Bare Ruined Choirs* an idiosyncratic form of radicalism. Flaying liberal heroes like John Courtney Murray with the same zest that he exhibited in demolishing the traditional Catholic position on birth control, Wills intimated that the whole rotten structure had to be brought down. Given the radical lexicon of the day, the last line of his book—"It is time to join the underground"—seemed a muted call to the barricades.

Langdon Gilkey's *Catholicism Confronts Modernity* (1975) offers a review of the situation by a critically sympathetic Protestant theologian. James Hitchcock's *Catholicism and Modernity* (1979), is, like his earlier book, a conservative critique. Hitchcock's *Recovery of the Sacred* (1974) is also critical, but concentrates on changes in the liturgy. George A. Kelly's *The Battle for the American Church* (1979) presents a great deal of information in a tone of dismayed conservatism. *American Catholicism: Where Do We Go From Here?* (1975) by George Devine, moderate in outlook and textbookish in flavor, was perhaps written with classroom use in mind. Much more pastoral in intention is Leonard Urban's *Look What They've Done to My Church* (1985), which belies its alarmist-seeming title by offering a reassuring wrap-up of postconciliar Catholic teaching for the benefit of those who need reorienting.

Andrew Greeley remains a host unto himself even though he has devoted his talents primarily to fiction writing in the 1980s. *The American Catholic,* which came out in 1977, synthesizes the results of social-scientific studies of American Catholicism carried out over more than a decade when the pace of change was most feverish. His popular history of American Catholicism was widely read; his writings on ethnicity made him a leading figure in the ethnic revival; and the importance of his books on Catholic education and the priesthood have already been noted. Besides all this, Greeley's topical works, of which *The Communal Catholic* (1976) is a good example, were consistently original and thought-provoking. His fiction also treats religious themes and reaches a vast new audience. I cannot assess the impact of Greeley's work in that genre; whatever it might turn out to be, he had already established himself as the leading commentator on American Catholicism before he turned to writing novels.[4]

Joann W. Conn's doctoral dissertation, "From Certitude to Understanding: Historical Consciousness in the American Catholic Theological Community in the 1960s" (Columbia, 1974), discusses the work of two other prolific commentators on the Catholic scene, Daniel Callahan and Michael Novak. Callahan's focus shifted away from explicitly Catholic matters when he left the editorship of *Commonweal* in 1968; Novak's personal testament, *Confessions of a Catholic* (1983), provides insight into his changing view on developments in the Church. Garry Wills's autobiographical *Confessions of a Conservative* (1979) throws only limited light on the intellectual peregrinations of this dazzling, but hard to pin down, conservative-radical. John Cogley's *A Canterbury Tale* (1976) is a tantalizingly laconic memoir by a leading liberal Catholic of the preconciliar era who joined the Protestant Episcopal Church in the mid-seventies. The collection *Journeys* (1975), edited by Gregory Baum, brings together autobiographical reflections by ten prominent Catholic writers, all theologians except for Andrew Greeley and David O'Brien. Charles A. Fracchia's *Second Spring* (1980) combines personal reminiscence with a review of developments since the days of "ghetto Catholicism."

The changes of the recent past have stimulated greater interest in American Catholic history and clearly affected the way historians approach the subject. This assertion is too sweeping to be documented here,[5] but it is appropriate to bring this discussion to a conclusion by looking very briefly at the half-dozen general surveys that have appeared in the past two decades.

Three such surveys have been written by persons who are not professional historians. Andrew Greeley's previously mentioned work, *The Catholic Experience* (1967), was prompted by the author's conviction that the current state of American Catholicism could not be understood without deeper knowledge of its history. As I pointed out earlier (in the headnote to chapter 2), Greeley's subsequent involvement in the ethnic revival led him to disavow the "Americanist" interpretation advanced in this book. His new "pluralist" interpretation was developed in a bicentennial article in *The Critic* (Summer 1976).

The second nonprofessional survey—Robert Leckie's *American and Catholic* (1970)—a popularized narrative, remained firmly Americanist in its treatment of the past, but betrayed dismay at what acculturation to American norms was bringing about in the 1960s. The traditional God of Catholic faith had become "the Permissive One," who was to be worshipped with great daintiness. In its preoccupation with the social gospel, its obsession with sex, its slack discipline, and its overall surrender to modernity, "the American Church [had] already taken on much of the protective coloration of the environment." It was thoroughly American; whether it would remain Catholic was, in Leckie's view, an open question.

The conclusion to John Cogley's *Catholic America* (1973), the third survey by a nonhistorian, showed that the author took seriously the challenge of reconciling Catholicism and modernity. But while his book, commissioned for a bicentennial series, was readable and judicious, it was carelessly done (the original edition was riddled with factual errors) and disappointing because it conveyed so little of the special insight expected of a longtime spokesman for Catholic liberalism.

The dean of professional historians of American Catholicism, John Tracy Ellis, brought out in 1969 the second edition of his brief survey, *American Catholicism.* The importance he accorded to the changes that had taken place since the book first appeared in 1956 is indicated by the fact that he devoted more than a third of the revised version to the events that had occurred in that span of thirteen years. In fact he declared that one had to look back to the Reformation of the sixteenth century to find "a parallel to the revolutionary transformation" still in process.

Thomas T. McAvoy, who was Ellis's only peer as a master of American Catholic history, dealt with the 1960s in more matter-of-fact terms. His *History of the Catholic Church in the United States* also appeared in 1969, and it too included a chapter on the *aggiornamento.* That chapter, however, was one of the shortest—and blandest—in the book. McAvoy did not portray the events of the sixties as indicative of profound shifts. Rather he wove them into his overall interpretive scheme, suggested that they were more the result of developments long under way than they were results of the Council, and insisted that problems regarded as serious in the fifties (e.g., the quality of Catholic intellectual life) had not been fundamentally altered. Since McAvoy died just before the book came out, we do not know how he would have reacted to later phases of postconciliar change. As it stands, his treatment contrasts strikingly with that of Ellis.

David O'Brien's *Renewal of American Catholicism* is not a survey but an interpretive essay centering primarily on twentieth-century developments. It is quite self-consciously philosophical in approach and reflects the existentialist premise that we must forge an understanding of the past that will enable us to master the present and shape from it a better future. The book is (as noted before) an important statement of postconciliar liberalism. O'Brien could not fully endorse the Americanism of earlier generations of Catholic liberals because he shared the late-sixties conviction that America itself was profoundly flawed; but neither could he fully endorse the position of their conservative opponents, even though he accepted much of the critique of Americanism they mounted. The results of his struggle to transcend the categories bequeathed by the past have, perhaps inevitably, a high abstruseness-quotient, and the position he finally reaches does not admit of succinct formulation. It will suffice to note here that O'Brien would definitely agree with Ellis rather than McAvoy as to the depth and seriousness of the changes of the sixties.

James Hennesey, author of *American Catholics* (1981), a comprehensive and informative general history, likewise shares Ellis's view. Not only does he mark the beginning of the third major epoch in American Catholic history in the 1960s, "when fissures opened wide in the church which the immigrants had built," but he also adds that future historians will probably see the present era as "a major turning-point in the story of human affairs." While fully alert to the "revolutionary moment" through which we are passing, Hennesey exercises great interpretive restraint in his judgments, and his description of events since 1960 is admirably balanced. His book is likewise of interest because he aspires to apply the People-of-God perspective to American Catholic history, and he notes that it coincides with the kind of "people history" so much favored by social historians today. His ambitions in this regard have not been realized with complete success, and some reviewers have suggested that Hennesey's book should be read simply as a superior specimen of old-fashioned institutional history. But that advice is not altogether on target either, for Hennesey rescues his subject from institutional insulation by embedding the history of the Catholic community firmly within the outlines of the larger national story, and he gives us far more information about the Catholic people—including Indians, Hispanics, Blacks, and ordinary laymen and laywomen—than any previous writer. If his account falls short as People-of-God history, it is perhaps because we do not yet have enough models of such an approach to know quite how to carry it off.

The need for exemplary works lends added importance to Jay P. Dolan's *The American Catholic Experience* (1985), the most recent general history of American Catholicism. This book is notable for two reasons. First, the author operates from a postconciliar perspective in the sense that he clearly approves the direction taken by change in the Church over the past quarter-century, and he portrays the American Catholic past in the light of that perspective. Secondly, Dolan has broken the traditional mold of American Catholic history-writing more decisively than any previous scholar—perhaps because his postconciliar ecclesiology merges so harmoniously with his professional commitment to social history. He covers the whole span, to be sure, and does justice in his narrative to the main lines of development. But Dolan's great new contribution is his synthesis of the recent scholarship in social history, which is blended with his own original research in the sources, in topical chapters dealing with the groups that compose the Catholic population—their ethnic background, migration and settlement, family life, group ethos, educational strivings, mobility patterns, and so on. It will take time to assimilate the new approach Dolan has pioneered, but his book has already been recognized as a major achievement. One can confidently predict it will remain a landmark in American Catholic historiography—which makes it a good place to end this retrospect of literary landmarks of American Catholicism in transition.

10

HISTORY, HISTORICAL CONSCIOUSNESS, AND PRESENT-MINDEDNESS

Unlike the others, the essay that follows is not an example of historical work, but a theoretical discussion of historical work itself as a form of intellectual activity. It also differs from the others in being the only essay that was written specifically for this volume. That came about because I realized early on that any collection of essays dealing with American Catholicism in transition and purporting to be organized around the theme of past and present would have to confront the issue of "historical consciousness," which is often described as a characteristic feature of postconciliar Catholic thought.

Realizing that I would have to say something about historical consciousness was easy; pinning the subject down and actually getting the essay written was anything but. "Historical-mindedness" (a term used interchangeably with historical consciousness) proved highly elusive and terribly perplexing. Its elusiveness derives in large part from the fact that most of the times one hears it spoken of, or runs across it in reading, historical consciousness is merely alluded to, without being explained or developed with any theoretical fullness. The assumption seems to be that its meaning is sufficiently obvious not to require explication. Sometimes, it is true, one does get the general point without difficulty—as when the "nonhistorical orthodoxy" of preconciliar days is contrasted to the more historical-minded approach of contempory theologians. But—and here we come to the perplexing part—I consider myself more historical-minded than most people, yet I have often been bewildered by the implication, which is not at all unusual in references to the subject, that historical consciousness somehow means that the past is completely irrelevant to the present.

In the face of these obscurities, the first requirement was to find treatments of historical consciousness that were sufficiently concrete and de-

tailed to permit critical analysis. *The search for discussions meeting these criteria was complicated by the fact that philosophers and theologians are the ones most apt to talk about historical consciousness, and the characteristic mode of thinking employed by persons in those disciplines is anything but congenial to most historians, myself very definitely included.*

Eventually I came upon three article-length statements that were almost ideally suited to my needs. Each was written by a Catholic scholar who is a historian professionally concerned with one aspect or another of the history of the Church. Each of the statements explicitly addresses the philosophical issues of historical understanding as they bear on the situation of postconciliar Catholicism, but does so in a manner relatively accessible to the laity's apprehension. Having found statements I could come to grips with intellectually, I was able to clarify the reasons for my dissatisfaction with the understanding of history and its relation to the present which is implicit in many of the more informal allusions to historical consciousness that one encounters.

Much of this essay is given over to an exposition and critique of the views advanced by these three historians. But since I have much fault to find with their way (or rather, ways) of dealing with the theoretical and methodological issues related to historical study, it seemed incumbent on me to venture out from behind the role of critic and hazard a positive formulation of my own. Thus the concluding section sets forth my personal "methodological confession of faith." No one could be more conscious than I am of its inadequacy to the scope and complexity of the matters with which it deals. But that is one form of historical consciousness with which I am quite familiar—as I suspect most historians are when they contemplate the fragility of their efforts to reconstruct the past.

To launch into the speculative seas of theorizing about history is to move out upon vasty deeps that terrify the ordinary historian. And in truth many a rash adventurer has been swallowed up in these treacherous waters—lost forever in the fog-banks of existential hermeneutics, or mired hopelessly in the Sargasso Sea of relativism, or swept away without a trace in the gales of dialectical *praxis*. Yet if history is too important to be left to historians, as the philosophers and theologians seem to have decided, it surely makes sense for those who consider themselves simple practitioners of the craft to pay some heed to what the theorists are up to. Indeed, a few such practitioners from time to time report to their colleagues on what the theorists are saying, or even prescribe how history should be pursued if it is to be truly up-to-date. In the pages that follow, I will analyze the views of three such historian-commentators before outlining my own position.

Let me begin, however, with two relatively noncontroversial generalizations. The first is that a great deal has been written in recent years, not only about the philosophy of history, but about the relation of history to religion and theology, and about historical consciousness as a distinctive feature of the modern religious mentality. Documenting this statement would be a major task in itself; perhaps it will suffice to call attention to Robert North's "Bibliography of Works in Theology and History" (1973) which listed 179 titles for the decade of the fifties and 516 for the sixties.[1] Secondly, it has become a commonplace to affirm that Catholic thinking since the Council has been marked by historical-mindedness, whereas it was caught in an unhistorical "classicism" before the Council. The authority of Bernard J. F. Lonergan and John Courtney Murray can be called on in support of this view, and a 1974 doctoral dissertation argues that it suffused the theological journalism of Michael Novak and Daniel Callahan.[2]

A third and more contentious generalization is that the literature dealing with these matters is so filled with obscurities that uninitiated readers are apt to lose their way. In part this is because the issues are complex; a greater source of bewilderment, however, is the fact that words like "history" and "historical consciousness" are frequently used with special philosophical meaning without the reader's being put on notice that these apparently familiar terms mean a good deal more in the context in question than they do in ordinary usage. It would, of course, be unreasonable to expect philosophers to spell out the premises of their systems every time they use a term that takes on special meaning in the light of those premises. But confusion is bound to result when terms that people think they understand actually carry connotations about the nature of reality that are not at all manifestly entailed in the meaning of the terms as they are generally understood. This blurring of the boundaries between history and philosophy makes category mistakes almost inevitable, since it becomes very difficult, for example, to discern that "the doctrine of historicity is not an empirical generalization but a metaphysical thesis."[3]

We must pause on this point a moment longer, for it is both elusive and important. A few quotations from an article by the Louvain professor, Albert Dondeyne, may be helpful. Entitled "The Historicity of Man According to Modern Philosophy," it was published in a catechetical journal intended for teachers of religion and illustrates the philosophically top-heavy understanding of historical consciousness to which literate American Catholics were exposed. Dondeyne begins with the statement that man is a historical being, and that "the *modern world,* or let us say, *modern humanism* . . . is characterized by the sense of the historical dimension of human life."[4] Well and good, the historian might say; nothing here to suggest philosophical profundities. These are commonplaces of cultural commentary, and without Dondeyne's subsequent explication the reader would have no reason to suppose that accepting them implied acceptance of any particular philosophical position on the nature of reality and human existence. The value of Dondeyne's exposition is that he reveals what historicity *really* means according to "modern philosophy."

Negatively, he tells us, historicity or "the historical character of existence" is not to be identified with transitoriness, or with an awareness of the fugitive quality of things. Neither is it synonymous with becoming or evolution; and finally historicity is not the same thing as *"history in the sense of historical sciences."* How different it is from the latter is made clear by the three positive characteristics "which together make historicity." The first of these is *"incarnation,* in the philosophical sense of the word," which means that man must be understood as "incarnate and situated liberty, having to realize himself in time and progress." Secondly, there is *"temporality,"* or human time, which encompasses past, present, and future in such wise that the present "envelopes and contains the past and the future in a certain way." The third mark of historicity is *"being-with-others,* or *intersubjectivity,"* which means, according to Dondeyne, that "I am in relation with others always and everywhere."[5]

This is vague enough in Dondeyne's article, which is merely a brief popularization, and it may seem altogether meaningless in this drastic summary. But we need not inquire further into how it all hangs together, since the validity of the philosophical system he outlines (clearly some species of existentialism) is not our concern. What is pertinent for us is simply to observe that he is outlining a *philosophical* system, and that terms relating to history take on a quite distinctive, although by no means transparent, meaning within the context of that system. Thus when Dondeyne and others who operate within this framework speak of history, or the historical dimension of human life, they are not speaking of history as the term is commonly understood; rather, they are making philosophical statements about the nature of things, the human condition, reality as such. Such statements can neither be established nor refuted by historical evidence or historical inference as practiced by historians. Since they are really philosophical statements, they can be appropriately evaluated only by philosophical analysis of the speculative basis on which they rest.

Three Versions of Historical-Mindedness: A Critique

To insist on the point just made is not to belabor the obvious because the characteristic terminology employed by those influenced this kind of thinking almost systematically confuses discussion where history is concerned. John W. O'Malley's essay, "Reform, Historical Consciousness, and Vatican II's *Aggiornamento*," illustrates the problem and suggests the practical consequences that flow from looking at "history" in this manner. It is worth examining in detail, for O'Malley is a respected historian of the Renaissance, and his article was published in the leading American Catholic theological journal and received wide notice.[6] It is, indeed, an impressive piece of work; but it does not escape the pitfalls created by blurring the boundaries between history and philosophy.

O'Malley begins by saying that the "almost despairing confusion [that] has hallmarked Catholicism" since the Council derives from the inadequacy of our notions of reform; that defect, he adds, flows from a mistaken understanding of the relation of past to present. More specifically, it results from a failure to grapple directly with "the problem of contemporary historical consciousness." In launching an "*aggiornamento*," O'Malley continues, the Council actually set in motion a fundamental transformation of the Church. Unfortunately, such a transformation could not be admitted since it violated what was thought to be historically acceptable change. Because Catholics have not absorbed the "emphasis on discontinuity with the past" and "subjectivism" that are among the most characteristic features of "contemporary historical thinking," they found themselves trying to adjust to changes that in fact exceed what they regard as historically legitimate developments.[7]

This is the problematic, as our theological colleagues might put it. To elucidate it more fully, O'Malley reviews the history of Church councils, showing how different approaches to reform can be linked to different "styles of historical thought or philosophies of history which were operative in the councils." This review yields five varieties of history: classicist or substantialist, providential, ethical (history teaching by example), primitivist, and developmental. All of them are "traditional or conservative as regards the past." For while they permit reform by excision, by accretion, by revival, by accommodation, and by development, they make no provision for "reform by transformation or even by revolution," which implies "at least a partial rejection of the past in the hope of creating something new." This has created an urgent need to understand—indeed, to adopt—"an adequate contemporary philosophy of history," for that alone will open up the "possibility of the 'new'" as a theoretical option and thus enable us to come to terms with what has actually been going on since Vatican II.[8]

At this point it is clearly time for O'Malley to explain just what this "modern historical consciousness" amounts to, and it is precisely here that we run into trouble. In the first place, the phenomenon is presented in generic terms: although the authorities he cites belong for the most part to the tradition of neo-idealism and existential hermeneutics, the position has no party name. It is simply called "modern historical consciousness" or "contemporary philosophy of history."[9] Even though O'Malley speaks of its "presupposition," this global way of referring to it suggests that the position he is about to sketch is the universal conclusion of all educated people rather than being a distinctive philosophical position that involves specific metaphysical and epistemological assumptions.

Much more serious is the fact that in discussing the contemporary philosophy of history O'Malley vacillates between two quite different ways of interpreting that expression. Under one aspect, "contemporary philosophy of history" seems to refer primarily to the set of methodological guidelines within which historians must operate in their efforts to understand and explain the past. Then, with no warning of a shift, these methodological guidelines suddenly assume the aspect of a substantive theory of the nature of things. In the first instance, the philosophy of history is presented as dealing with that which the historian is competent to ascertain; in the second, that which is ascertainable by the historian looms as the sum total of what is there to be ascertained. Let us look more closely at this subtle shift.

O'Malley's exposition proceeds as follows: "Contemporary philosophy of history is based upon one fundamental presupposition: history as a *human* phenomenon." Hence the historian's inquiry, "insofar as he is a historian," is restricted to the past "as it resulted from human passions, decisions, and actions." This means that "for the historian the past is radically contingent and particular." Everything in the past must be understood in terms of its own circumstances, which are not repeatable; thus the past is "understandable as history only insofar as it is unique and the result of man's more or less free action and decision." Since man is capable of reversing himself, discontinuity is thereby injected into history and it is desacralized or "deprovidentialized," for "God may have hardened Pharaoh's heart, but the historian is interested only in the contingent social, economic, and psychological factors which were at work on Pharaoh."[10]

Although the language is ambivalent and the logical transitions rather abrupt, the argument thus far can be interpreted as dealing primarily with the philosophy of history as it refers to methodological assumptions and the consequences they entail for doing history, *insofar as one is a historian.*[11] Considered in this light, the main point is that the historian must confine his explanation to human factors, because they are all that are accessible to historical analysis. Then, without seeming to be aware of any shift in perspective, O'Malley writes: "The historian, accordingly, becomes deeply aware of the discontinuity of the past, and he is forced to remove from his consideration any overarching divine plan. . . . The past is human. This means it is to be understood in terms of man, who is free and contingent. . . ."[12]

But how can this be? The historian is not forced to remove overarching divine plans by what he learns about discontinuity from studying the past. Divine elements were excluded by the hypothesis with which he began, and discontinuity is not a conclusion from the evidence but a corollary of the original stipulation. How can the humanness of the past be announced as though it were a discovery, when it was postulated as the one fundamental presupposition of the whole enterprise? Clearly, we are no longer being instructed about what the historian must assume in order to operate as a historian; rather, we are being told *what is actually the case*. We have shifted, in other words, from an exposition of methodological axioms and their theoretical implications to a series of ontological affirmations about the way things are, the nature of reality itself.

Now it is true, of course, that the expression "contemporary philosophy of history" can be used to refer either to an ontology or a methodology. But the two are not the same thing—or if one thinks they are, that surely requires explicit mention and some theoretical justification. O'Malley's mode of treatment guarantees confusion because he fails to distinguish at all between the two senses in which he is actually employing the formula "contemporary philosophy of history." Then to make matters worse, he speaks of "modern historical consciousness" as though it were interchangeable with "contemporary philosophy of history," thus equating a broad cultural outlook with an already equivocal designation for two different kinds of technical theorizing.

Reading on, one suspects that O'Malley may have unconsciously avoided a clear-cut confrontation with ontological issues because of his uneasiness over what historicist ontology might entail. Thus while he speaks of "relativizing" and "demythologizing" our history, of accepting "man's radical historicity," of being freed from the past and of creating the future, he draws back from the most drastic interpretation of these formulations. He assures us, for example, that "purifying" our historical thinking of older outmoded forms does not mean we are to "jettison the truth which these forms of historical thinking tried to express but could do so only in an unhistorical way." For instance, he goes on, there really *is* continuity in history, just as these older outlooks maintained. He even states that the data of Scripture constitute a limit on the discontinuity that may arise from new interpretations. He likewise asserts that continuity is assured because "the basic operations of the human mind do not radically change from culture to culture." Now whatever one thinks of the validity of these qualifications, they certainly place O'Malley among the more restrained expounders of "man's radical historicity."[13]

The reservations are a minor theme in the article as a whole, and are inconsistent with its overall thrust, but they offer reassurance that nothing essential to the Christian faith will be lost in the acceptance of discontinuity and relativism as prescribed by modern historical consciousness. Hence we can welcome change that transforms and revolutionizes, that rejects the past "at least in part." Understanding ourselves as "beings of radical historicity," imposes on us "a new way of thinking and acting about 'reform,'" and frees us to remake religion in order to bring it more closely into line with our present needs.[14]

This is surely a consequential result of accepting "modern historical consciousness." But we must ask: Does O'Malley really make clear what modern historical consciousness is, and does he demonstrate that it will light the way out of our "almost despairing confusion"? In my opinion, he does not. Modern historical consciousness, as he uses the expression, actually refers to a specific philosophical position, and it must be analyzed in philosophical terms if it is to be adequately understood. But O'Malley's whole treatment conveys the impression that what he is talking about is a generally recognized phenomenon of human experience, simply the way modern man thinks about history; it therefore fails to bring out the systematic philosophical content implied by this understanding of the formula "modern historical consciousness." When he does take up the "contemporary philosophy of history," O'Malley fails to differentiate clearly between the methodological and the ontological dimensions of the subject, or to explain how they are related to each other. In so doing, he raises to the level of a metaphysical principle the ancient equivocation between history understood as the study of the past, and history understood as the past itself. This kind of conceptual ambiguity can only multiply the confusions that beset our efforts to understand what is going on in the Church today and to decide what actions we should take.

We must deal more briefly with David J. O'Brien's discussion of "history and the present crisis," which constitutes chapter two of his *Renewal of American Catholicism*.[15] Like O'Malley's essay, it reflects a basically existentialist understanding of history and historicity. O'Brien also shares O'Malley's conviction that a rethinking of our ideas about history is essential to the reform of the Church, but his approach is less systematic and far more hortatory. He is not so much concerned to lay out the theoretical basis for a new conception of history as he is to persuade historians to reorient their work in the light of that conception. But since the implications of his view of history are quite drastic, O'Brien's failure to confront the theoretical issues detracts seriously from the force of his exhortation.

For O'Brien, "the historical process" embraces all of reality. Everything is thereby made historical, and at the same time relativized, for everything is continually being transformed in itself and in its relationship to everything else. Truth cannot therefore be thought of as stable and fixed. This holds for historical truth too, since the historian, like everyone else, is "stranded in the raging current of time, unable to speak meaningfully of its origins or ends." But the historical process is open-ended, not predetermined in its course; this means that humankind can influence the direction it takes, and all are therefore obligated to work for a better future. For Christians, God too is somehow located in the historical process, and for them shaping a better future means working for the coming of the Kingdom of God. Whether conceived in distinctively Christian terms or not, striving for a better future can legitimately be called "making history," and it is a universal moral obligation. The way in which a person is to fulfill this obligation is specified by his or her station in life, area of professional expertise, and so on; for the historian, the appropriate way to "make history" is through the activity of studying, researching, and writing history. For that reason, O'Brien insists that historians must be as concerned about the future as they are about the past. "Rather than telling the story of the past for its own sake," he declares, "they must tell the present and the future as history."[16]

At this point one may legitimately ask for clarification. What precisely would "telling the future as history" amount to? Is O'Brien reopening the whole issue of relativism? He cites Charles A. Beard favorably, but he does not enter into any of the problems raised by relativism, nor does he make clear just what degree of relativism he himself espouses, or how he would avoid the self-stultification that even Beard recognized was entailed in its most radical version.[17] There are other basic questions. What, for example, is the philosophical grounding for O'Brien's "vision of the new history [in which] man is 'man becoming,' open to the past and the future in his own experienced present, able if he will to resign himself to the absurdities of the chaos around him or to forge his life in an effort to shape the world to the realization of his deepest hopes and aspirations." Johannes Metz is cited here as an authority, but the position is not argued, it is simply proclaimed.[18]

The homiletic tone is even more pronounced in O'Brien's treatment of historicity as it affects the Church. Catholic acceptance of "a more dynamic and humble conception of history" was, he writes, a liberating force at first, but it soon "threatened to erode all stable values and institutions. . . . History in all its stark, bleak force caught up with the Catholic." But it is futile to "seek an escape from history," to try to seal off "essential" doctrines from "the realities of change and historicity." Rather a "consistent, honest commitment to history" requires the Church to accept its place within the historical process and to embrace its mission in history, which is to hold out "the promise of the Christ-event to a world in flux," to remind humankind of its responsibility to shape the course of human history. For the world can be changed; and it is only by changing it that we can throw off the burden of history and enter into the freedom and unity of the Kingdom of God.[19]

This is a moving exhortation, and the remainder of O'Brien's book is a courageous attempt to act upon it. But few historians are likely to accept the implications of his theoretical position. For however much one may admire O'Brien's prophetic intensity, it is disconcerting that he recommends what looks like partisanship in scholarly work and that he seems to equate the traditional ideal of objectivity with a "wholly abhorrent" lack of concern for contemporary problems. And it is more than disconcerting that he refers twice in a few pages to the "dead past" from whose grip historians must disengage themselves in order to contribute more directly to the needs of "the living present and the hoped-for future."[20]

Something has gone seriously awry when a historian can speak of the "dead past" and imply disparagement of historical work that does not relate directly to contemporary issues or contribute to the shaping of a better future. The past, after all, is the historian's metier; it is where his or her skills are deployed in the search for truth. What justifies historical research is the truth, or approximation to truth, it attains, and not, as O'Brien would have it, whether it helps to "make history" in the sense of influencing the direction of future developments.[21] Of course historians believe that the understanding of the past that their work makes possible has value in the here and now. But few of them would agree with O'Brien that they should go about their work with one eye cocked on present needs and future hopes. On the contrary, most historians would say that such an approach erects bias in favor of the researcher's values into the central organizing principle of whole activity and thus invites moralizing, polemicizing, and special pleading. That is not what David O'Brien had in mind, to be sure; but his position is open to the same criticism that the distinguished Renaissance scholar, Eric Cochrane, leveled against traditional "Catholic historiography," namely, that it subjects the practice of history to the prescriptions of a religio-philosophical worldview and by doing so makes distortion inevitable.[22]

Cochrane's strictures apply with even greater force to the historical ideas of certain writers on liberation theology. I claim no expertise in this highly controversial area, but merely dipping into the literature brings to light examples of the same doctrinaire mentality and readiness to resort to metahistorical verities that Cochrane found so lamentable in the practice of Catholic historians of the old school. For an illustration of how this familiar mindset adapts itself to a new idiom, we turn for a moment to Enrique Dussel's discussion of "Theology and Liberation History."[23]

According to Dussel, an Argentine scholar who has been called "liberation theology's principal historian and ethicist," there is only one history —the history of salvation, which is at the same time the history of liberation. This is not something distinct from, or over and above, secular history, "the concrete history we live each day." Rather, history as such is sacred history, "the history of messianic liberation, the history of salvation." History, in a word, is God revealing himself to us in time, and for that reason, neither faith nor theology can be separated from history. Properly understood, faith is "day-to-day interpretation of history," and since history is the locus of God's revelation, it is also of necessity the locus of theology. From this it follows that if we are to comprehend God's revelation, we must discover "the *sense and import* [sic] of history" from the earliest of God's transactions with man to the present moment.[24]

The kind of historical understanding we need, in other words, is the kind that gives us the "big picture," enabling us to grasp "the historical process as a history of liberation and a 'pasch' of justice and liberation." Fortunately, we may infer from Dussel, such a comprehensive vision has recently been attained, after long centuries in which the correct historical understanding of revelation and theology was lost to view because of the baneful influence of the Hellenic mentality and other secularizing forces. Under those unhappy circumstances, history was impoverished to the point that even Church historians carried on their work in the spirit of "profane history." Now, however, the theologians—especially liberation theologians —have rescued history from the level of the "merely anecdotal" and brought out its *meaning* for the present.[25]

Discerning the total meaning of history is something the ordinary Christian must be able to do, not just the scholar. Faith, we must remember, is the day-to-day interpretation of history, and its appropriate expression is right action (orthopraxis) rather than right belief (orthodoxy). But how is the simple Christian to act in accordance with the divine impulse in history if he or she doesn't know what God is driving at? Obviously, all believers have to be attuned to the "eschatological thrust toward the future" which comes through only to those who have grasped the meaning of history as a whole. And precisely this is what liberation theology both makes possible and requires as the test of true faith. For to feel bewildered by the confusion and complexity of events is to be weak in faith. "When I open the morning paper," writes Dussel, "I should know how salvation history is working itself out through everything that is happening." Hence he endorses Hegel's observation that reading the newspaper is a form of worship for the modern person. A person who "comprehends God's revelation in the concrete course of salvation history" as it is laid out in the daily papers "is really praying."[26]

As a specimen of intellectual hubris, Dussel's version of history surely ranks with the more extravagant productions of Catholic historiography in the good old days of triumphalism. Indeed, it goes even further by opening before us the prospect of an era when everyman will have become his own Brooklyn *Tablet*—with a very different editorial slant, to be sure! The content is quite novel, but how much does this differ in spirit from the approach of the old-fashioned Catholic militant for whom Church history was a branch of apologetics? Do we not find in Dussel and other spokesmen for liberation theology the same pretension to a monopoly on truth, the same conflation of theology and history, the same readiness to condemn, the same manipulation of black-and-white categories—good and evil, truth and error, liberation and oppression? Do we not, in a word, find history ideologized—that is, employed as a weapon in the struggle to advance a certain set of beliefs—just as it was in the embattled days of the siege mentality?

Strangely enough—or perhaps not so strangely, in view of the dogmatic mindset they both exhibit—we even find among the liberation theologians an antihistorical animus at least equal to, although of a different quality from, that of the Catholic champions of what Michael Novak called "nonhistorical orthodoxy." This is true despite the fact that liberation theologians proclaim their historical-mindedness. For them, as for the modern philosophers described by Dondeyne, history is more a metaphysical category than it is past reality, knowledge of past reality, or a method for exploring past reality. The historical-mindedness of the liberation theologians is thus to be understood as a way of interpreting the present in the light of what they already know about the past. Since, as Dussel's exposition makes clear, what they already know about the past is its *total meaning,* liberation theologians obviously have little incentive to engage in further historical work. The interpretive template of oppression/liberation can be imposed on whatever historically conditioned situation is under consideration; it will yield its predetermined results, thereby enabling the liberation theologian to get on with his real task, which is identifying the forces of good and evil in the present situation and pointing out how liberation is to be achieved. This "dialectic," as we might venture to call it, explains the paradoxical present-mindedness of theologians who claim, in the words of Juan Luis Segundo, to be "deeply committed to history," but whose method (to quote Segundo again) "completely rules out applying any theological criterion to history *except the direct and present evaluation of happenings here and now*" [sic].[27]

If we step back at this point to review the positions of O'Malley, O'Brien, and Dussel, we find two common elements in their theoretical views on history as it relates to the present situation of the Church. Getting a firm grip on these two elements will help clear away the mystifica-

214 / HISTORY, HISTORICAL CONSCIOUSNESS

tion that attends much recent talk about "history." The first is a tendency to blur the boundaries between history and philosophy, even to merge the two together, by overloading historical terms with philosophical connotations, thereby tacitly conveying the impression that to be "historically minded," to think "historically," automatically entails acceptance of specific substantive views about the nature of reality, the meaning of human existence, and the relation of past, present, and future. This is a deplorable tendency because it confuses two distinct cognitive realms, each of which requires a method of investigation and a mode of argumentation quite different from that employed in the other. Nor will it meet the objection to say that all historians operate from philosophical premises, either implicit or explicit. That may very well be the case; but the problem here is that the philosophical content is, as it were, disguised by being embedded in ostensibly historical terminology in such a way as to obscure the fact that what is being said has a markedly speculative quality over and above its seemingly transparent historical meaning. The language used, in other words, keeps people from recognizing that what they are reading —or writing—is more philosophy than it is history.

The particular philosophical positions adopted by O'Malley, O'Brien, and Dussel reinforce, if they did not induce, the emphatic present-mindedness that constitutes the second common theme to be found in their writings. O'Malley's present-mindedness accounts for his stress on discontinuity, the historical legitimacy of which he is bent on establishing so that current efforts to reform the Church will not be limited by historical precedents hitherto regarded as normative. The purpose of O'Brien's discussion is to persuade historians that they are morally obligated to write history in such a way as to illuminate contemporary issues and guide the way to a brighter future. With Dussel we reach the point where present-mindedness caricatures itself—the ordinary Christian is to grasp the meaning of history as a whole so that he can interpret current events "correctly"!

I would be the last to argue that all forms of present-mindedness either can be or should be eliminated from historical work. Some degree of present-mindedness is unavoidable, and, if adequately disciplined, a good thing. But in the words of a leading manual of methodology, "for it to be fruitful and not damaging, it must be held in check by an awareness—almost a suspicion—of its power to distort."[28] Such self-critical vigilance would find little encouragement in O'Malley's cordial acceptance of present-mindedness; it could hardly survive O'Brien's passion for telling the present and future as history; and it would have no chance at all among the categorical certitudes of Dussel's historical world. On the contrary, the increasingly uncritical present-mindedness represented by these three writers is almost certain to produce distortions in historical work. The reason is that it assumes that the past can be *forced* to speak to us on our terms, that all we need to do is formulate "relevant" questions and address them to the past in a sufficiently peremptory manner. But that is no way to get a bygone age to yield its secrets. If we insist on blustering into the past, waving our search warrants of relevance and announcing that we intend to "ransack" it for our present needs, we will encounter nothing there but our own reverberating obsessions.[29]

Appreciation of this point comes easier to conservatives, who feel a spontaneous piety toward the past, than it does to liberals, who are naturally disposed to look toward the future and to welcome change. Thus it is not surprising that James Hitchcock's conservative critique of the postconciliar mentality includes a chapter on "The Loss of History," in which he speaks feelingly of the importance of tradition and excoriates the "unflinching present-mindedness" of liberal reformers. "When it is asserted that the only meaningful questions we can ask the past are those which arise from our present needs," he writes, "the appropriate Catholic response (albeit one whose aptness is not limited to Catholics) is that an attention to the past in its own terms can alter our basic understanding of who we are and what our needs are."[30] I am in thorough agreement with Hitchcock here. Paradoxical as it may seem, I am convinced that, once embarked on a historical investigation, we must strive to forget our own preoccupations and study the past for its own sake if we are to learn anything from it that will enrich our understanding of the present.

Lest it seem that this conviction reflects nothing more than temperamental conservatism, on my part as well as Hitchcock's, let me cite the views of Bernard J. F. Lonergan, a thinker not usually regarded as a conservative, and a pioneer in converting Catholic theologians to historical-mindedness. Lonergan's superb discussion of history and historians in his *Method in Theology* (1972) is too comprehensive and subtle to permit summary. He explores what we have been calling present-mindedness in a variety of its dimensions, treating it under such headings as "perspectivism" and "horizons," and reserving part of his analysis for the chapter on "dialectic," since the issues are more properly philosophical than historical.[31] In other words, by respecting the intrinsic complexity of the subject, Lonergan has made it impossible to pick out any single quotation and present it as an adequate representation of his views on the whole issue of present-mindedness. He does, however, insist that the task of the historian is to grasp and explain what was happening *in the past;* and he is equally insistent that the historian must strive for *detachment* in this work. For to approach the study of the past with a concern to promote apologetical, political, or social goals is a purpose extraneous to the task of history properly considered as such, and it "can exercise not only a disturbing but even a distorting influence on historical investigation." Or, as Lonergan puts it more picturesquely, one who brings these consciously held social, political, or religious aims directly into historical work "is attempting to serve two masters and usually suffers the evangelical consequences."[32] Recalling O'Brien's language about the "dead past" and the "living present and hoped-for future," can there be any doubt as to which of the two masters the historian who is present-minded on principle will cherish and which he will despise?

A Methodological Confession of Faith

For Lonergan, the past is the historian's proper and exclusive master in the sense that its explication must be the purpose to which the historian is committed—insofar, that is, as he or she is engaged in the work of history as such. That is also my own position. And with that avowal, I would willingly bring the discussion to an end, simply referring the reader to Lonergan for an exposition of the philosophical grounding on which this conception of historical activity rests. But having criticized at length what seem to me the mistaken views of others, I feel a certain obligation to say something in a more positive way about my own understanding of the nature and value of historical work—without, however, explicitly relating my views to the contemporary religious situation.

To some extent, my views have already emerged in the critical discussion, or are implicit in what was said there; making them more explicit is not a congenial task. Like most historians, I find it difficult to bring to the level of conscious articulation the assumptions that guide the work I do as a historian—to say nothing of its seeming a little pretentious even to talk about making the attempt! As to offering a full theoretical justification for the position to be outlined, that is out of the question. Even if I were intellectually and temperamentally equipped to provide it, such a treatise would be misplaced here. What follows should therefore be understood as a methodological confession of faith—a series of affirmations about history that I believe to be theoretically justifiable, but that I offer here as a personal statement as to the purpose, possibility, and value of historical work.

In the first place, let me repeat my conviction that explicating the past is the defining purpose of history as an intellectual activity. Lonergan adds a further specifying element in saying that the historian must grasp and explain "what was going forward in particular groups at particular places and times" in the past.[33] This brings out the historian's characteristic interest in *what was happening* in the past—the dynamic aspect of history. But while this aspect may be implicitly present even in works that portray a moment frozen in time, it is not always equally prominent. The crucial point is that understanding and explaining the past (or, more precisely, some portion of it) must be the historian's primary purpose if he or she is to be true to the intrinsic nature of the discipline itself. The contemporary "relevance" of history is a function of how good a job the historian does in understanding and explaining the past.

At another time and place, it might be otiose to insist on this point, for it surely seems the most natural thing in the world that historians should concern themselves with the past. But the degree of principled present-mindedness we have already observed among recent Catholic commentators on history makes it impossible to take that natural assumption for granted. Hence the importance of getting the fundamental starting point right: history is of its very nature oriented toward the past, and so therefore must the historian be as well.

Accepting the purpose of history as the explication of the past immediately raises a host of other questions, the most important of which are: Does this mean that there is a "truth" about the past, and if there is, that the historian can attain it? Obviously, we are in deep water already! But every historian operates on tacit beliefs about the answers to questions like these; all that I have engaged to do is report what my own beliefs are. I suspect, however, that most historians would agree with me that the appropriate answer to the first question is "Yes," and to the second, "No . . . but in a way Yes."

To answer Yes, there is a "truth" about the past, amounts to affirming the kind of common-sense realism on which the professional activity of historians is clearly premised.[34] It means that one believes the past had a determinate structure, that such and such actually was the case at time X, was affected by an unknowably great number and variety of conditions and changed into something different, but also determinate, at time Y. This common-sense realism excludes the sort of relativism that would make the past whatever we say it is. It rules out the claim that since we know it only relatively, the past cannot, even in theory, provide a norm by which statements about it (i.e., the past) can be judged. And it denies the assertion that history is a fiction on all fours with every other sort of fiction because historical statements have no knowable objective referent. In short, believing that truth is something that can be affirmed about the past makes a difference. Unless one held this belief, it would make no sense to say that the historian's task is to explicate the past for there would be nothing real to be explicated. More practically, if there were no truth about the past, neither could there be any falsity; the most sober and responsible version of history would have no better claim on our intelligence than the most fanciful.

What has just been said does not mean that the historian can attain the full truth about the past or explain it in an ultimate way. Only God could do that, for to do it would require omniscience—absolute knowledge of every pertinent action, intention, relationship, accident, and circumstantial condition. No human mind can attain this level of knowledge about even the most ordinary affairs of everyday life, much less about large-scale historical happenings which are inherently more complex and concerning which our sources of information are necessarily indirect and often sparse. But just as we make judgments of truth or falsity about matters of everyday life without having absolute knowledge, so also are we justified in regarding truth as a quality that can responsibly be predicated of historical accounts. Hence the answer to the question "Can the historian attain truth about the past?" must be a qualified one. If we mean by truth complete adequacy to the past in every particular—that is, a statement embodying absolute knowledge of every pertinent action, intention, etc.—then the answer is No. But if by truth we mean a faithful likeness to certain aspects of what was actually the case in the past, then the answer is Yes, the historian can attain that kind of truth.

Limitations on the truth attainable about the past do not arise exclusively from its pastness; to some extent, they are simply a function of what we are trying to find out. We do not, after all, expect the same degree of certitude when we seek to discover *why* something occurred as when we are trying to establish that it did, in fact, occur. This holds for the present as well as for the past. If I hear, for example, that married friends of mine have gotten a divorce, I can reasonably hope to ascertain the truth of that report in a more or less unequivocal way. But I would not expect to arrive at the same kind of unambiguous truth as to the *reasons* for their getting a divorce (assuming that is what they did). Nor should I be surprised if the conclusions I reach on that matter differ from those reached by others acquainted with the couple in question. Too many factors affecting judgments like these are, as we say, "relative"—relative to how well one knows the people involved; relative to how much care one devotes to the investigation; relative to the views one holds about the kind of factors most apt to be decisive when marriages break up. The point of view of the investigator, in other words, enters more significantly into explaining why an event occurred than it does into ascertaining that it did or did not occur. That simple consideration obviously affects the degree of certitude, the approximation to truth, one can hope to attain in explaining why events take place as they do in the here and now—and in explaining why historical events took place as they did.

We can take the example one step further. Since my divorced friends need names at this point, let us suppose that some third party, a mutual acquaintance, inquires of me: "Don't you think it was really for the best that John and Mary decided to call it quits?" Here point of view becomes decisive, for what I am being asked to pronounce on is not whether something occurred, or why it occurred, but what I think of its having occurred. If a dozen people were asked the question, it is conceivable that all the replies would be different. How would one adjudicate the truth in such a case? Actually, *truth* isn't really the appropriate word to use in this context, for what is at issue is the moral and philosophical soundness of the various evaluative frameworks being applied, and their fitness to the case in question. The situation is strictly analogous when we are dealing with evaluative judgments in history. Here we confront relativism in history, to be sure; but the relativity derives from the diversity of perspectives from which events are viewed, not from any indeterminacy in the events themselves. Indeed, the fact that John and Mary's divorce *becomes a historical event immediately after it occurs* suggests that the way we come to know about history does not differ essentially from how we come to know about human affairs in our own times. Historical knowledge, then, differs from knowledge of contemporary affairs primarily in respect to the relative accessibility of sources of information and the way in which the passage of time changes our perspective on the significance and consequences of events.[35]

From the foregoing discussion we can distill three levels of historical inquiry and assign to each an appropriate expectation as to the degree of certitude, or approximation to truth, attainable at that level. At the first or "factual" level, the characteristic question is "What happened?" Here the expectation of reaching a high degree of certitude is much better than at the next two levels, although the nature of the event in question and the sources of information available are crucial limiting circumstances. Establishing what happened in the case of John F. Kennedy's assassination, for example, is a very different matter from establishing what happened in the case of John and Mary's divorce. But at the most basic level (*Was* Kennedy assassinated? *Did* John and Mary get a divorce?), the historian can generally expect to attain a fairly high degree of certitude.

Certitude, truth, and agreement among historians is inherently less attainable at the second or "explanatory" level of inquiry, where the characteristic question is "Why did it happen?" The reason is that answers to this question depend, not on what we might call the historian's direct inspection of events in themselves, but on inferences about the relationships between events. These relationships are not, so to speak, directly observable, and a great variety of factors come into play in drawing inferences about them—the historian's beliefs about human motivation in general, his intuitions as to the temperamental makeup of the historical actors, his sense of how large social forces impinge on events, his acceptance of an overall explanatory paradigm such as Marxism, or any number of other possibilities. The interaction of all these variables cannot help but make the degree of certitude less secure at this level of historical inquiry. As to the third or "evaluative" level—whose characteristic question is "Was its having happened good or bad?"—certitude is least secure of all because the historian's perspective, the value system from which he or she operates, obviously determines the answer. Here the formulation that springs so readily to the lips of undergraduates is fully justified: "It's all in your point of view!"

Distinguishing these three levels of historical inquiry is worthwhile because it helps us pick our way through the intellectual minefields surrounding the subject of truth in history. But the threefold model cannot be applied simplistically either in writing history or in assessing how others have written it. The reason is that although the three levels may be distinguished for analytical purposes, they fuse together in the actual work of the historian. The "facts" the historian is interested in, for example, are seldom discrete events, the occurrence or non-occurrence of which is of central moment. Rather, events are usually apprehended by the historian in linkage with, or as embracing under a single designation (e.g., Kennedy's assassination), a whole constellation of other events and circumstances. Discrete events can hardly be dealt with at all in isolation, outside the framework of some larger interpretive scheme. And what we conventionally call the historian's "interpretation" typically melds the second and third levels of inquiry by including both an explanation *and* an evaluation, either explicit or implicit.

That the threefold model has limitations is no cause for dismay. All such conceptual devices are of limited utility in analyzing historical work; as guides to the actual practice of historical research and writing, their value is even less, if, indeed, they do not constitute a positive distraction. As an activity, historical work is guided by something like Pascal's intuitive mind—it depends upon the kind of intellectual sensibility that enables the historian to accumulate, hold in mind, and perceive the relationships between seemingly disparate bits of information, and ultimately to weave the myriad of details into an intelligible whole. Despite the familiarity of the term, there is no such thing as "historical method" in the strict sense—that is, understood as a clear-cut set of distinctive procedures that the historian must follow in order to produce acceptable results. Jacques Barzun's statement, "history has no method or methods," was made in a polemical context and lends itself to misinterpretation. But he is certainly on solid ground in asserting that, for the historian, method "is only a metaphor to say that he is rational and resourceful, imaginative and conscientious. Nothing prescribes the actual steps of his work. . . ." George C. Homans, who turned to history because he was assured that its having a "method" made it the most scientific of the social sciences, discovered in the course of producing a book on medieval English village life that historical method is nothing but "the commonest of common sense."[36]

This formulation too is open to misunderstanding. It cannot, of course, be taken to mean that everyday knowledge will get us very far in interpreting medieval court records or other highly technical kinds of historical evidence. Nor does it mean that a "common-sense view" of how things happen in human affairs automatically suffices to explain historical events. Homans intended nothing so obviously simple-minded as that. What he clearly meant was that the mode of reasoning the historian employs in reaching conclusions is *nontechnical,* does not differ in kind from the mode of reasoning one employs in reaching judgments and making decisions in daily life. Lonergan, who shares the view that historical explanation "is a sophisticated extension of common-sense understanding," elaborates the point in a passage worth quoting:

> [T]he historian finds his way in the complexity of historical reality by the same type and mode of developing understanding as the rest of us employ in day-to-day living. The starting-point is not some set of postulates or some generally accepted theory but all that the historian already knows and believes. The more intelligent and the more cultivated he is, the broader his experience, the more open he is to all human values, the more competent and rigorous his training, the greater is his capacity to discover the past.[37]

This passage reinforces the point made earlier that there is no essential difference between historical knowledge and knowledge of human affairs in general, and it suggests two further reflections. The first has to do with bias on the part of the historian; the second with the problem of how the reader is to make qualitative judgments about historical work.

Accepting Lonergan's assertion that the historian's starting point is everything that he or she "already knows and believes," brings us directly up against the problem of bias. Nor is much reflection required to convince us of its intractability. For the historian clearly must know and believe *some* things before starting to work; and it is equally obvious that knowing and believing certain things, and *not* knowing and believing other things, will inevitably color the work he or she produces. Barzun and Graff tackle the problem by making a distinction between "bias" and "interest," with the latter being understood as pretty much the same thing Lonergan spoke of as "all that the historian already knows and believes," while "bias" is defined as "an uncontrolled form of interest."[38] This is a helpful distinction—so long as we don't allow ourselves to fall into the error of thinking that bias is radically different from interest and that it is possible for the historian to be "completely unbiased." Rather, we must keep reminding ourselves not only that bias and interest are related as points along a spectrum, but also that there is a gravitational tendency for interest to edge further and further in the direction of bias unless we struggle actively against it. The same "sophisticated extension of common sense" that characterizes the historian's overall approach has a role to play in this effort to keep interest from degenerating into bias; so also do the criteria of professionalism that he or she internalizes in the course of graduate training and scholarly practice.

The application of common sense on the reader's part can also help to control for bias. We are all accustomed to making allowance for bias in the opinions we hear expressed every day on matters ranging from the federal budget to the personal mannerisms of our acquaintances. Extending the same discriminating allowance for bias to the reading of historical works will help control it, at least in the sense of mitigating its effects. This brings us to the second reflection, which has to do with how the reader is to make qualitative judgments about historical work. Briefly, the point is that what Lonergan says of the historian holds equally for the reader: in evaluating history, just as in producing it, a person must bring into play everything that he or she already knows and believes. And the more intelligent, experienced, and humane the reader is, the greater will be that person's capacity to learn from reading historical works and to evaluate them critically. In the overwhelming majority of cases, the historian will know much more about the subject of the book than the reader, but that in no way disqualifies the serious reader from making judgments about how well the information is conveyed, how pertinent it is to the interpretation offered, how balanced the author's conclusions are, and how generally impressive the book is as a product of human intelligence.

To my way of thinking, the most palpable indication of excellence in historical work is originality—which comes across to the reader as the unexpectedness of what the work tells us about the past. Predictability, by contrast, robs history of interest, and may even give rise to suspicion if it seems to result from the author's riding a thesis too hard. Good history can take us by surprise in a number of ways—by opening to our mind's eye the richness of an unfamiliar subject; by setting before us telling new evidence on a subject already well studied; by inviting us to look at an old problem from a new angle and thereby bringing to light hitherto unrecognized significance in familiar materials. In all these cases the past is made more intelligible; we understand it more fully than we did before. But the vision that is laid out, or the explanation set forth, must be apprehended by the reader as growing organically from the evidence. Not that the past speaks for itself. It does not. It speaks only through the historian's interpretation, and here we encounter all the difficulties associated with the issues of interest and bias. What the reader has to decide, as best one can, is whether the historian's interpretation seems to have been *derived from* the evidence, or whether it gives the impression of having been *imposed upon* the evidence. The interpretation that speaks with the authentic inflection of the past will, I believe, nearly always have the quality of unexpectedness, while predictability will be a mark of what is reported through the voice of a historical ventriloquist's dummy.

But why should we trouble ourselves to decide who speaks with the true accent of the past? It's over and done with, isn't it? What is the good of historical knowledge anyhow, no matter how nearly it approaches being the truth about the past?[39] These questions bring us to the fundamental objection of the history-is-irrelevant school — including the "historical-minded" members of its "dead past" sub-branch. Volumes have been written about these issues, but for me the key points are that historical knowledge has intrinsic value as a genuine form of knowledge and that acquiring it enriches us by deepening our self-understanding.

Historical knowledge is worth having, first of all, because it shares in the quality Cardinal Newman affirmed of all true knowledge, namely, that it is capable of being its own end. "Such is the constitution of the human mind," Newman wrote in the beautiful fifth discourse of his *Idea of a University,* "that any kind of knowledge, if it be really such, is its own reward." He called on Aristotle and Cicero to witness that he was only stating what "has ever been the common judgment of philosophers and the ordinary feeling of mankind."[40] We can summon a more modern authority in the person of Richard Hofstadter, whose untimely death in 1970 removed one of the most thoughtful and highly respected historians of his generation. Hofstadter was but echoing Newman when he spoke of "the ultimate value in existence of the act of comprehension," and his own work exemplified the self-perfecting action of the contemplative intellect that "examines, ponders, wonders, theorizes, criticizes, imagines."[41] This simple delight in knowing and understanding for their own sake accounts for most of the attention devoted to history, both by professional scholars and amateur readers, and it validates the worth of historical knowledge regardless of any other usefulness that knowledge might possess.

But because we are social beings who exist in time, whatever of truth we learn about the human past cannot help but deepen our self-understanding at the same time that it satisfies the mind in its appetite to know. This endows historical knowledge with a tremendous potentiality for personal and social usefulness, not by supplying "alternative models of what the future might become,"[42] but by enlarging the store of practical wisdom on which prudential judgments must be based.

No one would claim that history is the only mode of knowing that gives us self-understanding as social beings who exist in time. But it makes a unique and indispensable contribution, because history is the only one that focuses directly and in concrete terms on the interaction between man's sociality and his temporality. The social sciences take one aspect or another of man's social nature as their special provinces, but they characteristically neglect the temporal dimension or treat it schematically in their search for law-like regularities. Some philosophers lay great emphasis on temporality, or "historicity," but their theorizing lacks the actuality that history provides through the depiction of real persons enmeshed in networks of relationships that shift and reshape themselves in response to actions taken and the passage of time. By means of such portrayals, history builds upon and enriches the understanding we gain of the human condition through our own lived experience. This enrichment of knowledge is as real—and as difficult to articulate—as that acquired by living through a family crisis or sharing a friendship over the years. In short, history deepens our self-understanding as social beings existing in time by opening to our vicarious experience the lives of others like ourselves, showing us how they reacted to the issues of their world and how time modified that world. History thus becomes, in Burckhardt's memorable words, "the guide of life" because it helps "to make us, not shrewder (for the next time), but wiser (forever)."[43]

This is already a great deal, but history deepens self-understanding in yet another way. Precisely because we are social beings existing in time, there is a carryover from past into present. The past isn't over and done with; it is still with us. As one of William Faulkner's characters says, "The past is never dead. It is not even past."[44] Language is the paradigmatic example: none of us invented the language we speak; it comes to us as a social inheritance from the past. It has been subject to modification throughout its history, of course, and may be used in original ways by speakers and writers today. But it is saturated with history, and those who would use it well ought to have some self-conscious awareness of where they stand with respect to that history. The same is true, *mutatis mutandis,* of our legal codes, our political institutions, our social values, and, what is most pertinent here, our religious systems and churches. Given the massive reality of tradition, of historical continuity, it seems superfluous to argue that historical knowledge can deepen our understanding of ourselves and of the world around us here and now.[45]

Thus we are brought round again to the relation of past and present. Much more could be said on the subject, for it is an inexhaustible theme. Let me conclude this methodological confession of faith—and this book—by elaborating briefly on my conviction that the historian must stick to his last, striving to understanding the past on its own terms, if he wishes to shed any really useful light on how past and present are related.

I begin with the assumption that, just as the past had a determinate structure, so also real and determinate linkages exist between past and present, which take the form, for example, of institutional continuities, persisting attitudes and beliefs, and consequences of earlier actions. At the same time, however, there are genuine differences between past and present because discontinuity is also a reality and because change can take place even within the framework of basic continuity. Now if, as we saw earlier, the actuality of the past is too multitudinous to be grasped by any but an omniscient intelligence, it ought to be even more obvious that the precise interaction of continuity and change between past and present will elude full comprehension by observers in the present—which is, of course, the venue of all observers when they are doing any observing. What this means is that all attempts to understand how the present differs from the past, or was shaped by it, are bound to be partial and incomplete.

But this built-in limitation is massively reinforced, and given a particular character, by the simple fact that we know more about our own world than we know about the past, and we know it in a more lively and urgent manner. This sharp imbalance inevitably skews our efforts to understand the relationship of past and present; it overdetermines them in the direction of *our* concerns, *our* presuppositions, *our* assumptions about what is and isn't relevant to the inquiry. Though the analogy is imperfect, our situation vis-à-vis the past might be likened to that of American policy-makers who are called upon to determine the nation's stance with respect to affairs in distant and exotic locales, such as Vietnam. We know our own interests and priorities so much better than we know those of such remote peoples that we are in peril of misconstruing the whole set of relationships. The historian, to continue the analogy, is the area-studies specialist whose expertise is the world of peoples removed from us in time. We depend on him or her to tell us what things look like from that side, what those people really had on their minds, what constraints they operated under, and what kind of perspective their world affords on that of our own day. Naturally we want our area-studies experts to provide information that will help us understand what our relationships with those people really are and on how our policies should be shaped in the light of those relationships. But we want them to provide this information from their immersion in the world of the past. And surely we are right in thinking that only an immersion in the world of the past for its own sake can equip the historian to tell us anything of real value about how that world is related to our own.

NOTES

INTRODUCTION

1. James Hennesey, *American Catholics: A History of the Roman Catholic Community in the United States* (New York, 1981), chap. 21; Jay P. Dolan, *The American Catholic Experience: A History from Colonial Times to the Present* (Garden City, N.Y., 1985), chap. 25.

2. James Hitchcock, *Catholicism and Modernity: Confrontation or Capitulation* (New York, 1979), 15–30.

3. This statement is reported by James Hennesey in James E. Biechler, ed., *Law for Liberty: The Role of Law in the Church Today* (Baltimore, 1967), 78. I myself heard virtually the same thing at a mid-sixties meeting of the Catholic Commission on Intellectual and Cultural Affairs.

4. For fuller discussion of this book see my review in *Review of Politics* 30 (January 1968), 111–14.

5. John Saville, "The Radical Left Expects the Past to Do Its Duty," *Labor History* 18 (Spring 1977), 267–74. Van Wyck Brooks was interested in the past from the viewpoint of its usefulness as a source of inspiration for literary creativity. See his original article, "On Creating a Usable Past," *Dial* 64 (April 11, 1918), 337–41. David J. O'Brien recently wrote of a symposium on "the United States experience" of the Catholic Church: "This conference characteristically professes to be in search of a usable past, but one suspects that the past which is discovered will be determined largely by the real quest, which is 'the search for a usable future.'" O'Brien, "Some Reflections on the Catholic Experience in the United States," in Irene Woodward, ed., *The Catholic Church: The United States Experience* (New York, 1979), 6.

6. See Robert E. Park, "Human Migration and the Marginal Man," *American Journal of Sociology* 33 (May 1928), 881–93; Everett V. Stonequist, *The Marginal Man* (New York, 1937), and Milton M. Gordon, *Assimilation in American Life* (New York, 1964), 56–57.

7. See Avery Dulles, *Models of the Church* (Garden City, N.Y., 1974).

1. AMERICAN CATHOLICS AND THE MYTHIC MIDDLE AGES

1. Dana C. Munro, *The Kingdom of the Crusaders* (New York, 1936), 174.

2. Ernst Robert Curtius, *Gesammelte Aufsätze zur romanischen Philologie* (Bern and Munich, 1960), 28. For the development of medieval scholarship in the United States see Hans Rudolph Guggisberg, *Das europäische Mittelalter im amerikanischen Geschichtsdenken des 19. und des frühen 20. Jahrhunderts* (Basel and Stuttgart, 1964); S. Harrison Thomson, "The Growth of a Discipline: Medieval Studies in America," in *Perspectives in Medieval History,* edited by K. D. Drew and F. S. Lear (Chicago, 1963); and Karl F. Morrison, "Fragmentation and Unity in 'American Medievalism,'" in *The Past Before Us: Contemporary Historical Writing in the United States,* edited for the American Historical Association by Michael Kammen (Ithaca, N.Y., 1980), 49–77.

3. Barbara Probst Solomon, "Back to Madrid," *Harper's Magazine* 209 (August 1969), 76.

4. Jacques Maritain, *True Humanism* (New York, 1938), esp. 1–8. See also G. G. Coulton, "The Historical Background of Maritain's Humanism," *Journal of the History of Ideas* 5 (1944), 415–33, and William J. Grace, "Jacques Maritain and Modern Catholic Historical Scholarship," ibid., 434–45. On widespread admiration for the Middle Ages in the 1920s see H. I. Marrou, *Time and Timeliness* (New York, 1969), 156–57.

5. Edward Ingram Watkin, *Catholic Art and Culture* (New York, 1944); Martin R. P. McGuire, "Mediaeval Studies in America; A Challenge and Opportunity for American Catholics," *Catholic Historical Review* 22 (April 1936), 17–18.

6. The thesis on Claudel was done by Sister Kathryn Marie Gibbons in 1930; the one on Undset by Sister Lelia Mahoney in 1941.

7. Hilaire Belloc, *Europe and the Faith* (New York, 1920), 201.

8. Eugene Bianchi, "Resistance in the Church," *Commonweal* 90 (May 16, 1969), 257–60; Donald J. Thorman, *American Catholics Face the Future* (Wilkes-Barre, Pa., 1968), 177–78. See also critical comments on the Middle Ages in John G. Deedy, ed., *Eyes on the Modern World* (New York, 1965), 31, 33, 124–25.

9. Don Hynes, "The Knight," Notre Dame *Observer,* March 7, 1969.

10. Norman F. Cantor, "Medieval Historiography as Modern Political and Social Thought," *Journal of Contemporary History* 3 (April 1968), 55–73.

11. Arthur O. Lovejoy, *Essays in the History of Ideas* (New York: Capricorn paperback, ed., 1960), essays 10 and 11, esp. pp. 205, 215n. See also Gottfried Salomon, *Das Mittelalter als Ideal in der Romantik* (Munich, 1922).

12. For aspects of preromantic interest in the Middle Ages see: Nathan Edelman, *Attitudes of Seventeenth-Century France toward the Middle Ages* (New York, 1946); Arthur Johnston, *Enchanted Ground: The Study of Medieval Romance in the Eighteenth Century* (London, 1964); B. Sprague Allen, *Tides in English Taste,* 2 vols. (Cambridge, Mass., 1937), II, chap. 16; Paul Frankl, *The Gothic: Literary Sources and Interpretations through Eight Centuries* (Princeton, N.J., 1960), 329–447; Kenneth Clark, *The Gothic Revival* (Harmondsworth, England: Pelican paperback ed., 1964), chap. 1; David C. Douglas, *English Scholars* (London, 1939); Samuel Kliger, *The Goths in England* (Cambridge, Mass., 1952); J. G. A. Pocock,

The Ancient Constitution and the Feudal Law (Cambridge, 1957); Werner Krauss, "Das Mittelalter in der Aufklärung," in *Medium Aevum Romanicum: Festschrift für Hans Rheinfelder,* edited by H. Bihler and A. Noyer-Weidner (Munich, 1963), 223–31. Lionel Gossman, *Medievalism and the Ideologies of the Enlightenment* (Baltimore, 1968), 332 ff., 349–53, 357–58, provides a judicious commentary on the differences between medievalists' interests before and after 1800.

13. Quoted in Herbert Butterfield, *Man on His Past* (Cambridge, 1955), 212.

14. From Heine's *The Romantic School,* reprinted in *Romanticism,* edited by John B. Halsted (New York: Harper Torchbook, 1969), 62.

15. Clark, *Gothic Revival,* chap. 6; Franz Schnabel, *Deutsche Geschichte im neunzehnten Jahrhundert: Die katholische Kirche in Deutschland* (Freiburg im Breisgau: Herder-Taschenbuch ed., 1965), 295; Agnes Addison, *Romanticism and the Gothic Revival* (New York 1938), 114; Roland Behrendt, "Joseph von Eichendorff's Romantic Concept of History and the Restoration of Marienburg Castle" (Unpublished M.A. thesis, University of Minnesota, 1953).

16. Dorothy Doolittle, *The Relation between Literature and Medieval Studies in France from 1820 to 1860* (Bryn Mawr, Pa., 1933), 56. For Germany, see W. D. Robson-Scott, *The Literary Background of the Gothic Revival in Germany* (Oxford, 1965).

17. Butterfield, *Man on His Past,* 33. On romanticism and history see Thomas P. Peardon, *The Transition in English Historical Writing, 1760–1830* (New York, 1933), chap. 5. On the *Monumenta* and its background, see David Knowles, *Great Historical Enterprises* (London, 1963), and M. T. Gamble, "The *Monumenta Germaniae Historica:* Its Antecedents and Motives," *Catholic Historical Review* 10 (1924–25), 202–33.

18. Quoted in Butterfield, *Man on His Past,* 69–70.

19. Rudolph Stadelmann, "Grundformen der Mittelalterauffassung von Herder bis Ranke," *Deutsche Vierteljahrschrift für Literaturwissenschaft und Geistesgeschichte* 9 (1931), 70–71. On Hurter see also: J. Martinoff, "Frederick Hurter," *Catholic World* 3 (April 1866), 115–21. On Voigt, see: G. P. Gooch, *History and Historians in the Nineteenth Century* (Boston: Beacon paperback ed., 1959), 68; and Thomas Oestreich, "The Personality and Character of Gregory VII in Recent Historical Research," *Catholic Historical Review* 7 (April 1921), 35–43.

20. Detlev W. Schumann, "Aufnahme und Wirkung von Friedrich Leopold Stolbergs Uebertritt zur katholischen Kirche," *Euphorian* 50 (1956), 271–306. Schumann notes that Catholics had astonishingly little to say about Stolberg's conversion at the time, so completely were they out of the mainstream of German intellectual life in 1800.

21. In his *Apologia,* Newman described Hurrell Froude as "powerfully drawn to the Medieval Church, but not to the Primitive." He adds: "from Froude I learned to admire the great medieval Pontiffs." And in explaining the background to the Oxford Movement, Newman wrote in 1839 of "the literary influence of Walter Scott, who turned men's minds in the direction of the middle ages." Newman, *Apologia Pro Vita Sua* (New York: Modern Library ed., 1950), 53, 79, 117.

22. A. Welby Pugin, *A Treatise on Chancel Screens and Rood Lofts, Their*

Antiquity, Use, and Symbolic Signification (London, 1851) is a polemic directed against the Italianizers. Louis Allen, ed., "Letters of Phillipps de Lisle to Montalembert" *Dublin Review* 228 (1954), 443–44, reveals Phillipps' disgust with the Oxford converts. On Pugin, see Benjamin Ferrey, *Recollections of A. N. Welby Pugin . . .* (London, 1861); Michael Trappes-Lomax, *Pugin: A Mediaeval Victorian* (London, 1932); Denis Gwynn, *Lord Shrewsbury, Pugin and the Catholic Revival* (London, 1946); Clark, *Gothic Revival,* chap. 7; and Phoebe Stanton, *Pugin* (New York, 1971). On Phillipps, see Edmund S. Purcell, *Life and Letters of Ambrose Phillipps de Lisle,* 2 vols. (London, 1900), and the letters to Montalembert, edited by Allen, cited above, which run through volumes 228 and 229 of the *Dublin Review.*

23. Phoebe B. Stanton, *The Gothic Revival & American Church Architecture: An Episode in Taste, 1840–1856* (Baltimore, 1968), 61 ff.

24. On Digby, see Bernard Holland, *Memoir of Kenelm Digby* (London, 1920); George N. Shuster, *The Catholic Spirit in Modern British Literature* (New York, 1922), chap. 2; and Mark Girouard, *The Return to Camelot: Chivalry and the English Gentleman* (New Haven, Conn., 1981), chap. 5.

25. For reprints from Digby see *Catholic Telegraph* (Cincinnati), March 21, 28, April 4, 11, 18, 25, May 2, 1840; *Catholic Cabinet and Chronicle of Religious Intelligence* (St. Louis) 2 (1844–45), 727–34. For the 1842 edition see Mary Peter Carthy, "English Influences on Early American Catholicism," *Historical Records and Studies* 46 (1958), 106. Pugin was also reprinted by Catholics in the United States; see *Catholic Telegraph* (Cincinnati), August 14, 28, September 4, 11, 1841; and *The Metropolitan Catholic Almanac and Laity's Directory for the Year 1844* (Baltimore, n.d.), 13–38.

26. *Catholic Digest* 6 (October, 1942), 49–57.

27. Peter Guilday, *The Life and Times of John Carroll,* 2 vols. (New York, 1922), I, 131–32. (Guilday calls this letter "one of the most significant documents of this period.") Wilfrid Parsons, *Early Catholic Americana: A List of Books and Other Works by Catholic Authors in the United States, 1729–1830* (New York, 1939). The only titles I can associate with the Middle Ages are: Item 347, "The Knights Templars, a Historical Tragedy . . ."; item 357, "The Saracen . . . A Crusade-Romance . . ."; item 363, "William Tell; or Swisserland [*sic*] Delivered . . ."; and item 789, The Life and Acts of Saint Patrick. . . ."

28. "The Papacy and Feudalism" in *The Works of the Right Rev. John England . . . ,* edited by Hugh P. McElrone, 2 vols. (Baltimore, 1884), II, 380. England was an Anglo-Saxonist, a believer in the "Norman Yoke" theory. Thus he was a supporter of the idea of "Gothic liberty," and to that extent viewed the Middle Ages positively. On Gothic liberty, see Kliger, *Goths in England;* Pocock, *Ancient Constitution* (note 12 above) Caroline Robbins, *The Eighteenth Century Commonwealthman* (New York: Atheneum paperback ed., 1968), 3, 5, 18, 34, 35, 45, 52, 81, 89, 98, 101, 104, 109, 141, 155, 181, 182, 226, 272, 385; and Christopher Hill, "The Norman Yoke," in *Democracy and the Labor Movement; Essays in Honour of Dona Torr,* edited by John Saville (London, 1954), 11–66.

29. Charles Constantine Pise, *A History of the Church, from Its Establishment to the Present Century,* 6 vols. (Baltimore, 1827–30), I, xiv–xv; V, 29–31.

30. F. E. T[ourscher], *The Kenrick-Frenaye Correspondence* (Philadelphia, 1920), 232.

31. "The Church in the Dark Ages," from *Brownson's Quarterly Review,* July 1849, in *The Works of Orestes A. Brownson,* edited by Henry F. Brownson, 20 vols. (Detroit, 1882–87), X, 239–66.

32. Brownson, *Works,* XI, 238.

33. "The Pope's Supremacy," *United States Catholic Miscellany* (Charleston, S.C.), October 9, November 6, 13, 1822; "The Dark Ages," ibid., December 11, 18, 25, 1822; "The Inquisition Examined," ibid., December 14, 1825, July 22, 1826. See ibid., August 4, 1827, for a review, taken from a Catholic newspaper of London, of a book on chivalry which shows an awareness of the changing attitudes toward the Middle Ages.

34. Quotation from John Lancaster Spalding, *The Life of the Most Rev. M. J. Spalding . . .* (New York, 1873), 110–11. The elder Spalding's principal apologetical writings were his *The History of the Protestant Reformation . . . ,* 2 vols. (New York, 1860), which has a seventy-page review of the medieval background and a similar review of the background of the English reformation, and his *Miscellanea: Comprising Reviews, Lectures, and Essays, on Historical, Theological, and Miscellaneous Subjects,* 2nd ed. (Louisville, 1855). See also, Thomas W. Spalding, *Martin John Spalding: American Churchman* (Washington, D.C., 1973), chap. 4.

35. See Spalding, *Reformation,* I, 19–21, 37, 39; and Spalding, *Miscellanea,* chaps. 4–8. Francis Patrick Kenrick also touches on a number of these points in his *The Primacy of the Apostolic See Vindicated,* 3rd ed. (New York, 1848), part III, "Literary and Moral Influence [of the Papacy]." A passage from this work (381 ff.), maintaining that "the Popes were uniformly favorable to popular rights and liberty," was published in *United States Catholic Magazine* 7 (December 1848), 621–24. Kenrick was somewhat uneasy dealing with certain medieval subjects, however. He wrote to his brother in 1844: "But when I speak of the power of the Pope over civil rulers in the middle ages, and the Crusades expeditions, and the Inquisition, I fear some danger of misunderstanding when the book [*The Primacy*] is published, for these all can be interpreted in a sense that is wrong." Quoted in Hugh J. Nolan, *The Most Reverend Francis Patrick Kenrick, Third Bishop of Philadelphia, 1830–1851* (Philadelphia, 1948), 234.

36. *The Vickers and Purcell Controversy* (Cincinnati and New York, 1868), 15, 28–29, 37, 42 ff., 52, 63 ff., 82–83. Quotation from p. 43.

37. See "The Middle Ages," *Ave Maria* 4 (April 11, 1868), 232–34; "The Monks and Priests of the Middle Age," ibid. 6 (November 5, 1870), 717–18; Henry A. Brann, *A Political-Historical Essay on the Popes as the Protectors of Popular Liberty* (New York, 1875) 19 ff.; Charles G. Herbermann, "The Myths of the 'Dark' Ages," *American Catholic Quarterly Review* 13 (1888), 589–614.

38. For a defensive Catholic reaction to the obscurantism charge, see R. S. Dewey, "The Inquisition Mythology," *American Catholic Quarterly Review* 12 (1887), 691–704.

39. See Harry W. Kirwin, "James J. Walsh—Medical Historian and Pathfinder," *Catholic Historical Review* 45 (January 1960), 409–35; Mary Marcella Smith, "James J. Walsh, American Revivalist of the Middle Ages" (Ph.D. diss., St.

John's University, Brooklyn, 1944). Guggisberg, *Europäische Mittelalter,* 150 ff., (note 2 above) discusses historians of medieval science; on page 159 he comments on Walsh.

40. An English text may be found in H. S. Reiss, ed., *The Political Thought of the German Romantics, 1793–1815* (New York, 1955), 126 ff. *The Catholic Cabinet* (St. Louis) 2 (1844–45), 692–98, published an English version of Novalis's fragment taken from the London *Tablet.* J. E. D., "The Bible in the Middle Ages," *Catholic Expositor* (New York) 6 (July 1844), 251–52, includes the following passage obviously inspired by Novalis: "There was a time when the whole Christian world bowed down before the same altars . . . when the rising Sun, shedding his refreshing rays over half a world, shone upon . . . one kneeling mass of millions . . . on whose tongues the same words and the same prayers . . . all went up together . . . to the throne of the Almighty."

41. Quoted in John Dixon Hunt, *The Pre-Raphaelite Imagination, 1848–1900* (Lincoln, Neb., 1968), 19–20.

42. "Letters from Abroad," *The Metropolitan* (New York) 2 (March 1854), 106–7, 108, contains a labored description of the beauties of a Gothic cathedral. Among other things, the author says: "Leave the glare of the outer world, and . . . contemplate the triumph of religious art. The eye, springing to that airy, fretted vault, seems to reach beyond it, a remote holier realm; the mysterious twilight calms the heart and disposes the mind for meditation. . . ." And further on: "The graceful curves of the arches, the delicate profiles of the mouldings, the lightness of the lateral walls grooved into almost continous windows and carved into crocketted flower work . . . the rose and ogive lights, with their soft, tremulous and dreamy lustre, and dim and solemn triforium, the paintings and bas-reliefs, and *boiseries* and marble groups with multiplied forms and representations . . . the colossal and deep-toned organ which resounds through the vast enclosure, in unison at times with peals of the sonorous *Bourdon,* or enormous bell of the southern tower, attract, captivate and thrill the heart with strange emotions."

For an excellent contemporary discussion of the aesthetic appeal of medievalism see, "The Artistic and Romantic View of the Church of the Middle Ages," *The Christian Examiner* (Boston) 46 (May 1849), 345–83.

43. *United States Catholic Magazine* 4 (February 1845), 89–92; ibid. *5* (February 1846), 79–81.

44. Ibid. 6 (January 1847), 39 et seq. For comments on this novel, which was republished in book form in 1871, see Willard Thorp, "Catholic Novelists in Defense of Their Faith, 1829–1865," *Proceedings of the American Antiquarian Society* 78, pt. i (April 1968), 66.

45. Shuster, *Catholic Spirit* (note 24 above), esp. viii, and chaps. 1–2. See also Alice Chandler, *A Dream of Order: The Medieval Ideal in Nineteenth-Century English Literature* (Lincoln, Neb., 1970).

46. Raymond Williams, *Culture and Society, 1780–1950* (New York: Harper Torchbook, 1966); see also Margaret R. Grennan, *William Morris, Medievalist and Revolutionary* (New York, 1945); E. P. Thompson, *William Morris, Romantic to Revolutionary* (London, 1955; 2nd ed., 1977); Robert A. Nisbet, *The Sociological Tradition* (New York, 1966), chap. 1; Alfred Cobban, *Edmund Burke and*

the Revolt Against the Eighteenth Century, 2nd ed. (London, 1960), 197 ff., 263–64. Chandler, *Dream of Order* (note 45 above), is also relevant to the social critique theme.

47. William Cobbett, *History of the Protestant Reformation in England and Ireland,* 2 vols. in 1 (New York, 1895), I, 256. This work appeared originally in the late 1820s. Catholics in the U.S. promoted it industriously. See *Kenrick-Frenaye Correspondence* (note 30 above), 172; *Catholic Expositor* 5 (March 1844), 442; and Brownson, *Works,* X, 451.

48. Grennan, *Morris,* 8; Cobbett, *History,* II, 325–26.

49. *Contrasts,* originally published in 1836, was reprinted by the Humanities Press (New York, 1969) as part of "The Victorian Library."

50. These two plates are also reproduced in Clark, *Gothic Revival* (note 12 above).

51. See "The Hebraisms and Catholicisms of Disraeli's Novels," *The Metropolitan* 2 (September 1854), 471. (This article is reprinted from *The Rambler,* May 1854.) Montalembert's *Monks of the West,* which appeared in English in 1861, climaxed the enthusiasm for medieval monasticism.

52. The quoted passage is from the essay reviewing *Past and Present* in *United States Catholic Magazine* 3 (September 1844), 545–59; for other references to the book, see ibid. 3 (April, June 1844), 242, 355–56.

53. Morris made this statement in his 1894 article, "How I Became a Socialist," which is reprinted in *William Morris, Selected Writings and Designs,* edited by Asa Briggs (Baltimore: Penguin paperback, 1962), 33–37. On another occasion, Morris confessed that "absurd hopes curled round my heart" when he dreamed of the destruction of London. See Philip Henderson, *William Morris: His Life, Work and Friends* (New York, 1967), 279.

54. A number of these connections can be traced in the career of Graham Carey, whose father was one of the founders of the Boston Society of Arts and Crafts and who was himself a medievalist, a worker in stained glass and allied arts, and a founder of the Catholic Art Association. He also took a sympathetic interest in the Liturgical Arts Society, the Catholic Rural Life movement, the Catholic Worker, and other Catholic social reform activities. He was acquainted with Eric Gill and other English medievalist craft workers and guild enthusiasts. See Ade deBethune and John Benson, "Graham Carey," *Catholic Art Quarterly* 6 (1942–43), 18–21. On Gill see his *Autobiography* (London, 1940), and Robert Speaight, *The Life of Eric Gill* (London, 1966). Gill is also mentioned several times in a work by the co-founder of the Catholic Worker. See Peter Maurin, *The Green Revolution,* 2nd ed. (Fresno, Calif.: Academy Guild Press paperback, 1961).

55. Franz H. Mueller, "The Church and the Social Question," in *The Challenge of Mater and Magistra,* edited by J. N. Moody and J. G. Lawler (New York, 1963), 13–154, is the best introduction to the subject which places American developments in the context of continental Catholic social thought.

56. Philip Gleason, *The Conservative Reformers: German-American Catholics and the Social Order* (Notre Dame, Ind., 1968), esp. 131–38, 188–90, 199–203, 206–8, 214–16.

57. See Joseph L. Perrier, *The Revival of Scholastic Philosophy in the Nine-*

teenth Century (New York, 1909); Maurice de Wulf, "Cardinal Mercier: Philosopher," *New Scholasticism* 1 (January 1927), 1–14; Charles A. Hart, "America's Response to the Encyclical 'Aeterni Patris,'" in American Catholic Philosophical Association, *Proceedings . . . 1929* (n.p., n.d), 98–117; James A. Weisheipl, "The Revival of Thomism as a Christian Philosophy," in *New Themes in Christian Philosophy*," edited by Ralph M. McInerny (Notre Dame, Ind., 1968), 164–85; Gerald A. McCool, *Catholic Theology in the Nineteenth Century: The Quest for a Unitary Method* (New York, 1977), chaps. 6–10; and William M. Halsey, *The Survival of American Innocence: Catholicism in an Era of Disillusionment, 1920–1940* (Notre Dame, Ind., 1980), chaps. 8–9.

58. As one writer, John S. Zybura, put it, "we must plan to build on the bed-rock of perennial principles, of absolute and transcendental values: reliance on the shifting sands of scientism and sentimentalism, or relativism and romanticism has led but to disaster. . . . [Scholastic thought is] deeply rooted in the imperishable achievements of that beautifully balanced Hellenic mind. . . ." Another, L. Noël, wrote: "Romanticists might well amuse themselves with picturesque memories of the Middle Ages; there they could find material for melancholy or truculent poetry, for theatrical scenes and for panoplies for the drawing-room. But from all this it was a far cry to calling forth out of the darkness of the thirteenth century ideas fit to merit the attention not only of fanciful, but of serious, minds." John S. Zybura, ed., *Present-Day Thinkers and the New Scholasticism* (St. Louis, 1927), viii, 215.

59. Calvert Alexander, *The Catholic Literary Revival* (Milwaukee, 1935) 19–26, 305–6.

60. Dom Olivier Rousseau, *The Progress of the Liturgy* (Westminster, Md., 1951), 7 ff., 130 ff.; Waldemar Trapp, *Vorgeschichte und Ursprung der liturgischen Bewegung vorwiegend in Hinsicht auf das deutsche Sprachgebiet* (Würzburg, 1939), 190 ff., quotation 197; Louis Bouyer, *Liturgical Piety* (Notre Dame, Ind., 1955), 15, 20, 67, 259, 261. For the commitment to Scholasticism of the leading American liturgical reformer see Virgil Michel, "The Metaphysical Foundations of Moral Obligation," in American Catholic Philosophical Association, *Proceedings . . . 1928* (n.p., n.d.), 29. For ambivalence on the Middle Ages see Dunstan Tucker, "The Council of Trent, Gueranger, and Pius X," *Orate Fratres* 10 (October 1936), 538–44; and Paul Bussard, "Liturgy in the Age of Gothic," ibid. 10 (October 1936), 545–52.

61. For a somewhat similar identification of the Middle Ages with the natural law tradition, universal rational truths, and absolute values, see the presidential address of the Catholic historian, Herbert H. Coulson, "Mediaevalism in the Modern World," *Catholic Historical Review* 26 (January 1941), 421–32. Coulson is also critical of the romantics for admiring the Middle Ages for the wrong reasons.

62. For a brief and enlightening essay on how historical studies have modified Neoscholastics' ideas of Scholasticism and its relation to theology see Anton C. Pegis, *The Middle Ages and Philosophy: Some Reflections on the Ambivalence of Modern Scholasticism* (Chicago, 1963).

63. Dawson's best known work in this area is his *The Making of Europe: An Introduction to the History of European Unity* (New York, 1932).

64. Raymond A. Schroth attests to Walsh's being required at Fordham in 1951 in a review of Halsey, *Survival of American Innocence*, in *Cross Currents* 32 (Summer 1982), 248. The book was still being used as a prize in American Catholic seminaries in 1952; see John Tracy Ellis, ed., *The Catholic Priest in the United States: Historical Investigations* (Collegeville, Minn., 1971), 380 n. 212.

65. See Robert Mane, *Henry Adams on the Road to Chartres* (Cambridge, Mass., 1971); Robert Muccigrosso, *American Gothic: The Mind and Art of Ralph Adams Cram* (Washington, D.C., 1980); T. J. Jackson Lears, *No Place of Grace: Antimodernism and the Transformation of American Culture 1880–1920* (New York, 1981), esp. chaps. 4–5, 7; and the special issue of *Studies in Medievalism* 1 (Spring 1982) devoted to "Medievalism in America."

66. On this point, see the entertaining exchange between Thomas T. Mc-Avoy, C.S.C., Notre Dame's well-known historian of American Catholicism, and Thomas J. Brennan, C.S.C., a member of the philosophy department at Notre Dame: McAvoy, "The Role of History in the Catholic Liberal College," *Catholic Educational Review* 48 (October 1950), 505–15; Brennan, "Balance That Mind!" ibid. 49 (March 1951), 159–65; and McAvoy, "Facts Versus Abstractions: A Rejoinder," ibid. 49 (April 1951), 257–259. In his "Rejoinder," McAvoy observes: "The worship of a mediaeval world that never existed hangs like a deathly pall—a kind of ancestor worship—over much thinking about Catholic education. . . . Sometimes after hearing some philosophy teachers repeating their mediaeval verbiage I expect to see them finish the class by calling for their armor and lance and rushing out to defend their ivied towers. But unfortunately they never seem to rush out from their ivied towers. . . ."

67. James Hennesey, "Leo XIII: Intellectualizing the Combat with Modernity," paper presented at the spring meeting of the American Catholic Historical Association, held at the University of Notre Dame in April 1979. See also Hennesey, "Leo XIII's Thomistic Revival: A Political and Philosophical Event," *Journal of Religion* 58 (1978, supplement), S185–S197; McCool, *Catholic Theology* (note 57 above), chaps. 3, 6, 10; Gabriel Daly, *Transcendence and Immanence: A Study of Catholic Modernism and Integralism* (Oxford, 1980), chap. 1; and, for an extreme statement of the view that the Scholastic Revival was politically motivated, William McSweeney, *Roman Catholicism: The Search for Relevance* (New York, 1980), 67–74.

68. Weisheipl, "Revival of Thomism" (note 57 above),. 177–81.

69. Pope Leo XIII, *Church and Civilization* (New York, 1878).

70. For a sketch of papal policy see Roger Aubert et al., *The Church in a Secularised Society*, volume 5 of "The Christian Centuries" (New York and London, 1978), chaps. 1 and 20. Catholic Action and Neoscholasticism are discussed more fully in chaps. 7–9 of this book. See also Halsey, *Survival of American Innocence* (note 57 above).

71. Rev. Donald J. Kanaly quoted in Dennis J. Robb, "Specialized Catholic Action in the United States, 1936–1949: Ideology, Leadership, and Organization" (Ph.D. diss., University of Minnesota, 1972), 97. See also Victor Yanitelli, "Gerald Groveland Walsh in Appreciation," *Thought* 27 (Fall 1952), 345.

72. See below, chapter 7.

73. George Bull, *The Function of the Catholic College* (Pamphlet, New York, 1933), 4–5; S. B. James, "Re-Creating Christendom," *Christian Front* 1 (July 1936), 106–8.

74. Ruth Benedict, *Patterns of Culture* (Boston, 1959, orig. pub. 1934), 247–48, 273–78; Edward Sapir, "Culture, Genuine and Spurious," *American Journal of Sociology* 29 (January 1924), 410–16; Philip Gleason, "Americans All: World War II and the Shaping of American Identity," *Review of Politics* 43 (October 1981), 486–91.

75. Peter L. Berger, *Facing Up to Modernity: Excursions in Society, Politics, and Religion* (New York, 1977), 56–69. For American Communism in the 1930s, see Harvey Klehr, *The Heyday of American Communism* (New York, 1984).

76. See Philip Gleason, "World War II and the Development of American Studies," *American Quarterly* 36 (Bibliographical number, 1984), 343–58.

77. See chapter 9 below.

78. Theodore Roszak, *The Making of a Counter Culture* (Garden City, N.Y., 1969), esp. chap. 8. Susan Sontag, *Styles of Radical Will* (New York, 1969), 202–3.

79. See Philip Gleason, "Our New Age of Romanticism," *America* 117 (October 7, 1967), 372–75; Andrew M. Greeley, *Come Blow Your Mind with Me* (Garden City, N.Y., 1971).

80. Harvey Cox, *The Secular City* (New York, 1965); Daniel Callahan, ed., *The Secular City Debate* (New York, 1966).

81. Harvey Cox, *The Feast of Fools: A Theological Essay on Festivity and Fantasy* (Cambridge, Mass., 1969), 3, 170–71.

82. The Associated Press ran a story on Father Weber that appeared in the *South Bend Tribune,* March 26, 1972; for the Society for Creative Anachronism, see *Encyclopedia of Associations,* 19th ed. (Detroit, Mich., 1985), 772.

83. *New York Times,* April 23, 1972.

84. The journal, *Studies in Medievalism,* is an outgrowth of sessions on medievalism held at the annual medieval studies conference at Western Michigan University, Kalamazoo, over the past decade.

85. Besides Williams, *Culture and Society;* Thompson, *Morris;* and Lears, *No Place of Grace;* see Eileen C. Boris, "Art and Labor: John Ruskin, William Morris, and the Craftsman Ideal in America, 1876–1915" (Ph.D. diss., Brown University, 1981); and Peter Stansky, *Redesigning the World: William Morris, the 1880s, and the Arts and Crafts* (Princeton, 1985).

2. IMMIGRANT PAST, ETHNIC PRESENT

1. For the rise of the new ethnicity, see Perry L. Weed, *The White Ethnic Movement and Ethnic Politics* (New York, 1973); Arthur Mann, *The One and the Many: Reflections on the American Identity* (Chicago, 1979), 1–45; and Philip Gleason, "American Identity and Americanization," in Stephan Thernstrom et al., eds., *Harvard Encyclopedia of American Ethnic Groups* (Cambridge, Mass., 1980), 52–55. The latter work also contains authoritative entries on the ethnic groups touched on in this essay. Joseph J. Parot remarks on the ethnic revival in the "Preface" to his *Polish Catholics in Chicago, 1850–1920* (DeKalb, Ill., 1981), xi–xii. For

a roundup of recent research, see Randall M. Miller and Thomas D. Marzik, eds., *Immigrants and Religion in Urban America* (Philadelphia, 1977). Harold J. Abramson, *Ethnic Diversity in Catholic America* (New York, 1973), is a social-scientific analysis of the persistence and significance of ethnic distinctiveness among the various elements of the Catholic population.

2. Michael Novak, *The Rise of the Unmeltable Ethnics: Politics and Culture in the Seventies* (New York, 1972). For examples of Novak's later writings on the subject see his *Further Reflections on Ethnicity* (Middletown, Pa., 1977), and his "Pluralism: A Humanistic Perspective," in *Harvard Ethnic Encyclopedia,* 772–81.

3. Andrew M. Greeley, *Why Can't They Be Like Us?* (New York, 1971); *Ethnicity in the United States: A Preliminary Reconnaissance* (New York, 1974); *That Most Distressful Nation: The Taming of the American Irish* (Chicago, 1972). Greeley, *The American Catholic: A Social Portrait* (New York, 1977), synthesizes much of Greeley's research on ethnicity as it bears on the contemporary situation of American Catholics; chapters 1 and 14 are of particular interest from the theoretical viewpoint.

4. Baroni died in 1984. For an appreciation of his work, see Gerald R. McMurray, "Remembering Geno Baroni," *America* 151 (September 22, 1984), 145–48. Baroni was an activist and an organizer rather than a writer, but for an example of his approach see his "Ethnicity and Public Policy," in *Pieces of a Dream: The Ethnic Worker's Crisis with America,* edited by Michael Wenk, S. M. Tomasi, and Geno Baroni (New York, 1972), 3–11.

5. Silvano M. Tomasi, *Piety and Power: The Role of the Italian Parishes in the New York Metropolitan Area, 1880–1930* (New York, 1975).

6. H. Richard Niebuhr, *The Social Sources of Denominationalism* (New York, 1929), chap. 8.

7. Ernest L. Tuveson, *Redeemer Nation: The Idea of America's Millennial Role* (Chicago, 1968), 20 ff. For standard works on anti-Catholicism, see Mary Augustana Ray, *American Opinion of Roman Catholicism in the Eighteenth Century* (New York, 1936), and Ray Allen Billington, *The Protestant Crusade, 1800–1960: A Study of the Origins of American Nativism* (New York, 1938).

8. Timothy L. Smith, "Protestant Schooling and American Nationality, 1800–1950," *Journal of American History* 53 (March 1967), 679–95; David P. Tyack, "The Kingdom of God and the Common School," *Harvard Educational Review* 36 (Fall 1966), 447–69; Francis Michael Perko, "A Time to Favor Zion: A Case Study of Religion as a Force in American Educational Development, 1830–1870" (Ph.D. diss., Stanford University, 1981), 38–54, 75–85.

9. For a succinct survey of the issues, see James Hennesey, *American Catholics: A History of the Roman Catholic Community in the United States* (New York, 1982), chap. 15. My essay, "Coming to Terms with American Catholic History," *Societas* 3 (Autumn 1973), 283–312, treats the late nineteenth-century controversy within the context of Americanization as a long-range theme in American Catholic history. For an excellent short discussion that considers Americanization from the Polish-American viewpoint, see Daniel S. Buczek, "Polish-Americans and the Roman Catholic Church," *The Polish Review* 21 (1976), 39–61.

10. On this point, see George F. Theriault, "The Franco-Americans in a New

England Community: An Experiment in Survival" (Ph.D. diss., Harvard University, 1951), 538 ff. See also Parot, *Polish Catholics,* 229–30.

11. See Patrick Carey, *An Immigrant Bishop: John England's Adaptation of Irish Catholicism to American Republicanism* (Yonkers, N.Y., 1982). The Irish were not always proponents of Americanization. In the first explicit controversy that arose over the matter (in the 1850s), the Irish were accused of resisting Americanization, while the principal spokesman for Americanization was Orestes A. Brownson, an American-born convert to Catholicism. See Gleason, "American Identity and Americanization," 36–38.

12. Oscar Handlin, *The Uprooted: The Epic Story of the Great Migrations That Made the American People* (Boston, 1951). Rudolph J. Vecoli, "The Contadini in Chicago: A Critique of *The Uprooted*," *Journal of American History* 51 (December 1964), 404–17, argues that Handlin exaggerated the degree of uprootedness experienced by immigrants and his contention has been supported by other recent students of ethnic history. Handlin may have overstressed the degree of uprootedness, but such a condition did exist. John Bodnar's disagreement with Handlin is implied in the title of Bodnar's new book, *The Transplanted: A History of Immigrants in Urban America* (Bloomington, Ind., 1985), esp. ch. 8.

13. Philip Gleason, *The Conservative Reformers: German-American Catholics and the Social Order* (Notre Dame, Ind., 1968), 21.

14. Ibid. See also John J. Bukowczyk, "The Immigrant 'Community' Reexamined: Political and Economic Tensions in a Brooklyn Polish Settlement, 1888–1894," *Polish-American Studies* 27 (Autumn 1980), 5–16.

15. Victor R. Greene, *For God and Country: The Rise of Polish and Lithuanian Consciousness in America, 1860–1910* (Madison, Wis., 1975), chaps. 2–3; and Timothy L. Smith, "Lay Initiative in the Religious Life of American Immigrants, 1880–1950," in Tamara K. Hareven, ed., *Anonymous Americans: Explorations in Nineteenth-Century Social History* (Englewood Cliffs, N.J., 1971), 214–49.

16. Thomas O'Brien Hanley, ed., *The John Carroll Papers,* 3 vols. (Notre Dame, Ind., 1976), I, 292, 389, 431. For a typical later complaint, see Dolores Ann Liptak, "The National Parish: Concept and Consequences for the Diocese of Hartford, 1890–1930," *Catholic Historical Review* 71 (January 1985), 58.

17. M. Timothy Audyaitis, "Catholic Action of the Lithuanians in the United States; A History of the American Lithuanian Roman Catholic Federation, 1906–1956" (M.A. thesis, Loyola University, Chicago, 1958), 26. A local history that illuminates many of the themes of this essay is Daniel Buczek, *Immigrant Pastor: The Life of the Right Reverend Monsignor Lucyan Bojnowski of New Britain, Connecticut* (Waterbury, Conn., 1974).

18. See Parot, *Polish Catholics* (note 1 above), chaps. 3–4; John Iwicki, *The First One Hundred Years: A Study of the Apostolate of the Congregation of the Resurrection in the United States, 1866–1966* (Rome, 1966), 46–110; and Anthony J. Kuzniewski, *Faith and Fatherland: The Polish Church War in Wisconsin, 1896–1918* (Notre Dame, Ind., 1980), 44, 64–65, 92, 110–11.

19. Patrick Carey's forthcoming general study of trusteeism, *People, Priests, and Prelates: Ecclesiastical Democracy and the Tensions of Trusteeism* (Notre Dame, Ind., 1987), will replace older works, among which Patrick J. Dignan, *A History*

of the Legal Incorporation of Church Property in the United States, 1784–1932 (Washington, D.C., 1933), has special value. Also valuable is David A. Gerber, "Modernity in the Service of Tradition: Catholic Lay Trustees at Buffalo's St. Louis Church and the Transformation of European Communal Traditions, 1829–1955," *Journal of Social History* 15 (Summer 1982), 655–84.

20. See, for example, Henry B. Leonard, "Ethnic Conflict and Episcopal Power: The Diocese of Cleveland, 1847–1870," *Catholic Historical Review* 62 (July 1976), 388–407; Greene, *God and Country,* chs. 4–6; Lawrence D. Orton, *Polish Detroit and the Kolasinski Affair* (Detroit, 1981); and Richard S. Sorrell, "The Sentinelle Affair (1924–1929) and Militant Survivance: The Franco-American Experience in Woonsocket, Rhode Island" (Ph.D. diss., SUNY, Buffalo, 1975), esp. chap. 4.

21. Bohdan P. Prockho, *Ukrainian Catholics in America: A History* (Washington, D.C., 1982); Victor J. Pospishil, "Ukrainians in the United States and Ecclesiastical Structures," *The Jurist* 39 (1979), 368–422.

22. Francis E. Tourscher, *The Hogan Schism and Trustee Troubles in St. Mary's Church, Philadelphia, 1820–1829* (Philadelphia, 1930); for a shorter account, Hugh J. Nolan, *The Most Reverend Francis Patrick Kenrick, Third Bishop of Philadelphia, 1830–1851* (Philadelphia, 1948), chap. 3.

23. William Galush, "The Polish National Catholic Church: A Survey of its Origins, Development, and Missions," *Records of the American Catholic Historical Society of Philadelphia* 83 (1972), 131–49; Hieronim Kubiak, *The Polish National Catholic Church in the United States of America from 1897 to 1980* (Cracow, 1982).

24. "Vietnamese Join Traditionalists," *National Catholic Reporter,* January 13, 1978. On the traditionalists, see William D. Dinges, "Catholic Traditionalism in America: A Study of the Remnant Faithful" (Ph.D. diss., University of Kansas, 1983).

25. Tomasi, *Piety and Power* (note 5 above), 62, 76 ff.; see also, Liptak, "National Parish" (note 16 above).

26. Jay P. Dolan, *The Immigrant Church: New York's Irish and German Catholics, 1815–1865* (Baltimore, 1975; rpt. Notre Dame, Ind., 1983), 21.

27. Compare Milton L. Barron, "Intermediacy: Conceptualization of Irish Status in America," *Social Forces* 27 (March 1949), 256–63. There is really no satisfactory overview of the Irish role in American Catholic history; Carl Wittke, *The Irish in America* (Baton Rouge, 1956), chap. 9, is old-fashioned but informative.

28. Francis Hertkorn, *A Retrospect of Holy Trinity Parish* (Philadelphia, 1914); Vincent J. Fecher, *A Study of the Movement for German National Parishes in Philadelphia and Baltimore (1787–1802)* (Rome, 1955).

29. A recent student of Franco-Americans in New England, who were among the bitterest resisters of Americanization, has this to say: "Finally the militant Franco-American claim of unrelenting persecution by the Irish Church hierarchy is false. It is true that the Church was often more assimilationist than civil authorities in America, something which was hard for French-Canadian immigrants to realize since in Quebec Catholicism was the bulwark of survivance. However, outward harassment by Irish bishops was the exception. Most of the New England bishops

from 1870 until the 1920s, including those of the Rhode Island diocese, were willing to allow the formation of Franco-American national parishes and the continuation of the French language, as long as bilingualism was provided for. Between 1865 and 1890 there was only one attempt (Fall River) to prevent the establishment of a Franco-American parish. But the assimilationist atmosphere was pervasive, and its veiled and sometimes insidious nature made Franco-Americans quick to seize upon any evident harassment." Sorrell, "The Sentinelle Affair," 137. See also, Liptak, "National Parish," 57 ff.

30. For resistance on the part of territorial pastors see Tomasi, *Piety and Power* (note 5 above), 80. An example of the problems sometimes created is given by James W. Sanders, *The Education of an Urban Minority: Catholics in Chicago, 1833–1965* (New York, 1977), 49, in describing the situation of a German church becoming Polish. "The crisis between St. Boniface and the encircling Polish strongholds produced a comedy of ethnic errors. First, the strongly nationalistic German pastor tried 'every promising means' to 'keep his own people clustered around the church.' The efforts included successful lobbying for newly paved streets, sewer installation, and even the 10-acre Eckert Park. Meanwhile, he spoke publicly against the Poles, snubbed them in the streets, and made them generally unwelcome in parish and school. But to no avail. The Germans departed anyway, and the parish income no longer met expenses, nor could it even pay interest on the debt. Finally, in 1916, the Archbishop appointed a new, more realistic German pastor who welcomed the Poles and laboriously learned their language. For his efforts he earned the bitter accusations of neighboring Polish pastors for enticing their parishioners into the German church."

31. Sanders, *Urban Minority,* chap. 7; Charles Shanabruch, *Chicago's Catholics: The Evolution of an American Identity* (Notre Dame, Ind., 1981), chaps. 7–9, esp. 180 ff. and 215 ff.; Edward R. Kantowicz, *Corporation Sole: Cardinal Mundelein and Chicago Catholicism* (Notre Dame, Ind., 1983), chap. 5; Parot, *Polish Catholics* (note 1 above), chap. 8; and Stephen J. Shaw, "Chicago's Germans and Italians, 1903–1939: The Catholic Parish as a Way-Station of Ethnicity and Americanization" (Ph.D. diss., University of Chicago, 1981).

32. Gleason, *Conservative Reformers* (note 13 above), is a detailed treatment of this theme in regard to German-American Catholics.

33. For the "language question" in Ireland itself, see John Edwards, "Language, Diversity and Identity," in Edwards, ed., *Linguistic Minorities, Policies and Pluralism* (London, 1984), 284–89, and the literature cited there. See also Kerby A. Miller, "Emigrants and Exiles: Irish Cultures and Irish Emigration to North America, 1790–1922," *Irish Historical Studies* 22 (September 1980), 97–125.

34. Sanders, *Urban Minority,* 67–71. See also, Rudolph J. Vecoli, "Prelates and Peasants: Italian Immigrants and the Catholic Church," *Journal of Social History* 2 (Spring 1969), 217–68, esp. 249–51.

35. The American founder of the Benedictines, Boniface Wimmer, learned this by experience; although he originally planned to serve only Germans, he found it necessary to take in English-speaking as well as German-speaking youths. See Henry A. Szarnicki, "The Episcopate of Michael O'Connor, First Bishop of Pittsburgh, 1843–1860" (Ph.D. diss., Catholic University of America, 1971), 179–80.

36. See Philip Gleason, "Immigration and American Catholic Intellectual Life," *Review of Politics* 26 (April 1964), 161–62.

37. Greeley, *American Catholic,* 40–47, esp. Tables 2.2 and 2.3; Philip Gleason, "Immigration and American Catholic Higher Education," in Bernard J. Weiss, ed., *American Education and the European Immigrant: 1840–1940* (Urbana, Ill., 1982), 161–75.

38. Gleason, *Conservative Reformers,* 48.

39. Ibid.

40. Ibid., chap. 3 and passim.

41. Greene, *God and Country* (note 15 above); for the PNA, see Donald Pienkos, *PNA: A Centennial History of the Polish National Alliance of North America* (Boulder, Colo., 1984).

42. M. Martina Tybor, "Slovak American Catholics," *Jednota Annual Furdek* 16 (January 1977), 60.

43. See Colman J. Barry, *The Catholic Church and German Americans* (Milwaukee, 1953), 98 ff.; William Galush, "Both Polish and Catholic: Immigrant Clergy in the American Church," *Catholic Historical Review* 70 (July 1984), 407–27; Gerald F. DeJong, *The Dutch in America, 1607–1974* (Boston, 1974), 200–201; Tybor, "Slovak American Catholics," 61.

44. For the Irish clerical association, see Barry, *German Americans,* 125; for the Lithuanian statement, National Conference of Catholic Bishops Committee for the Bicentennial, *Liberty and Justice for All, Newark Hearing "Ethnicity and Race"* (Washington, D.C., 1975), 20.

45. Antonio M. Stevens-Arroyo, ed., *Prophets Denied Honor: An Anthology on the Hispanic Church in the United States* (Maryknoll, N.Y., 1980), 139–40.

46. There has been a burst of publication on Hispanics in recent years but little that is focused directly on the religious dimension of the subject. Besides *Prophets Denied Honor,* see Virgilio P. Elizondo, *Christianity and Culture: An Introduction to Pastoral Theology and Ministry for the Bicultural Community* (Huntington, Ind., 1975); Elizondo, *Galilean Journey: The Mexican-American Promise* (Maryknoll, N.Y., 1983); and Isidro Lucas, *The Browning of America: The Hispanic Revolution in the American Church* (Chicago, 1981). Patrick H. McNamara, "Bishops, Priests and Prophecy" (Ph.D. diss., UCLA, 1968), covers Catholic outreach to the Spanish-speaking in the Southwest in the era before the revival of ethnicity; Lawrence J. Mosqueda, "Chicanos, Catholicism, and Political Ideology" (Ph.D. diss., University of Washington, 1979), written from a neo-Marxian viewpoint, is of limited value as history but provides useful information about current attitudes.

47. As one authority stated in 1971: "What typically took place in immigrant groups in the second generation is now occurring among third and fourth-generation Mexican Americans. . . . Also, these third and fourth-generation Americans are facing the problems of marginality and assimilation which other ethnic groups met in the second generation." Celia S. Heller, *New Converts to the American Dream? Mobility Aspirations of Young Mexican Americans* (New Haven, Conn., 1971), 14. For an excellent general survey, see Carlos E. Cortes, "Mexicans," in *Harvard Ethnic Encyclopedia,* 697–719.

48. For the emergence of an Irish Catholic middle class in the 1890s, see David N. Doyle, *Irish Americans, Native Rights and National Empires: The Structure, Divisions and Attitudes of the Catholic Minority in the Decade of Expansion, 1890–1901* (New York, 1976), 38–90.

49. The ambiguities of this term are analyzed in my essay, "Pluralism and Assimilation: A Conceptual History," in Edwards, *Linguistic Minorities* (note 33 above), 221–57.

50. It is revealing, for example, that Monsignor Bojnowski, the patriarch of Polonia in Connecticut, "argued for a cultural pluralism as the proper relationship between peoples in the United States, yet vigorously and often contemptuously dismissed Pilsudski for having propagated the same position between the Polish people and the non-Polish populations of the eastern borderlands of Poland." Buczek, *Immigrant Pastor* (note 17 above), 58. See also, Parot, *Polish Catholics* (note 1 above), 210, 217, 232; and Gleason, *Conservative Reformers* (note 13 above), chap. 7.

3. IMMIGRANT ASSIMILATION AND THE CRISIS OF AMERICANIZATION

1. Edward J. Foye, "'Adjournamento'?" *Front Line* 4 (Fall 1966), 94–96; Michael Novak, "Christianity: Renewed or Slowly Abandoned?" *Daedalus* 96 (Winter 1967), 237–66. J. S. Mattson, "Oliver Wendell Holmes and 'The Deacon's Masterpiece': A Logical Story?" *New England Quarterly* 41 (March 1968), 104–14, disputes the conventional interpretation as a satire on Calvinism.

2. Will Herberg, *Protestant-Catholic-Jew* (rev. ed., New York, 1960); Andrew M. Greeley, *The Catholic Experience* (New York, 1967).

3. See Philip Gleason, *The Conservative Reformers: German-American Catholics and the Social Order* (Notre Dame, Ind., 1968), esp. chaps. 1 and 9 for theoretical discussion.

4. Herberg, *Protestant-Catholic-Jew.*

5. Criticism of the Irish is reviewed critically in "The Myth of the Irish: A Failure of American Catholic Scholarship," *Herder Correspondence* 3 (November 1966), 323–27.

6. John J. Kane, "The Social Structure of American Catholics," *American Catholic Sociological Review* 16 (March 1955), 23–30.

7. Norval D. Glenn and Ruth Hyland, "Religious Preference and Worldly Success: Some Evidence from National Surveys," *American Sociological Review* 32 (February 1967), 73–85.

8. Andrew M. Greeley and Peter H. Rossi, *The Education of Catholic Americans* (Chicago, 1966), 28–29.

9. See John J. Kane, *Catholic-Protestant Conflicts in America* (Chicago, 1955).

10. Milton M. Gordon, *Assimilation in American Life* (New York, 1964), 23–24.

11. Some other professional societies and their dates of founding are: National Conference of Catholic Charities (1910); Catholic Press Association (1911); Catholic Hospital Association (1915); Catholic Historical Association (1919); Catho-

lic Philosophical Association (1926); Catholic Physicians Guild (1927); Catholic Economic Association (1941); Catholic Psychological Association (1946).

12. Letter to the editor, *America* 117 (August 12, 1967), 141.

13. *Linacre Quarterly* 33 (November 1966), 332–33; Alphonse F. Trezza, "Like God, CLA is Dead," *Catholic Library World* 38 (April 1967), 511–13; Daniel C. O'Connell and Linda Onuska, "A Challenge to Catholic Psychology," *Catholic Psychological Record* 5 (Spring 1967), 29–34.

14. The following discussion draws heavily upon David W. McMorrow, "The Development of Sociology as an Academic Discipline in Catholic Colleges: A Study of the American Catholic Sociological Society," an unpublished senior thesis done for the Department of History, University of Notre Dame, 1967.

15. Raymond W. Murray, *Introductory Sociology* (New York, 1946), 34. Murray is here quoting Ralph A. Gallagher, S.J., the principal founder of the Catholic Sociological Society.

16. *Sociological Analysis* 25 (Spring 1964), 1. [The ACSS changed its name to "The Association for the Study of Religion" in 1970. For an interesting review of these issues in more recent years, see Joseph P. Fitzpatrick, "Catholic Sociology Revisited: The Challenge of Alvin Gouldner," *Thought* 53 (1978), 123–32.]

17. Ernan McMullin, "Presidential Address: Who Are We?" in American Catholic Philosophical Association, *Proceedings . . . 1967* (Washington, 1967), 1–16. The quotations in the following paragraphs are taken from this source, as is the information given above about the percentages of doctorates earned in Europe.

18. "Abortion and Dialogue," *Commonweal* 85 (March 17, 1967), 667–68. The letter on abortion in the same issue from John S. Holland is also revealing. Among other things, Mr. Holland writes: "If we stick on the unrationalized premise that every foetus has an inalienable right to be born, *the rest of the world will pass us by*" (italics added).

19. Daniel Callahan, "The Quest for Honesty," *Commonweal* 80 (April 24, 1964), 137; and Callahan, *Honesty in the Church* (New York, 1965), 20–21. See also Callahan's discussion, "Theological Stew," *The Critic* 26 (June–July 1968), 10–17.

20. *Thought* 30 (Autumn 1955), 351–88.

21. Frank L. Christ and Gerard E. Sherry, eds., *American Catholicism and the Intellectual Ideal* (New York, 1961).

22. The interest of immigrant groups in creating leadership elites is discussed in Philip Gleason, "Immigration and American Catholic Intellectual Life," *Review of Politics* 26 (April 1964), 161–62.

23. Christ and Sherry, *Intellectual Ideal,* 260–61. Christ and Sherry reprint the main body of Ellis's article, and for the sake of convenience citations will be to their volume.

24. Ibid., 73, 140, 227–28.

25. Ibid., 255, 135, 130, 118.

26. John A. O'Brien, ed., *Catholics and Scholarship* (Huntington, Ind., 1938), Preface.

27. Christopher Dawson, *The Crisis of Western Education* (New York, 1961).

28. Leo R. Ward, *Blueprint for a Catholic University* (St. Louis, 1949); Ward,

"Is There a Christian Learning?" *Commonweal* 63 (September 25, 1953), 605–7; Justus George Lawler, *The Catholic Dimension in Higher Education* (Westminster, Md., 1959).

29. Christ and Sherry, *Intellectual Ideal,* 142–43.

30. Ibid., 277–78.

31. Daniel Callahan, *The Mind of the Catholic Layman* (New York, 1963), 98.

32. Thomas F. O'Dea, *American Catholic Dilemma* (paperback ed., New York, 1962), 127 ff.

33. See Andrew M. Greeley, *Religion and Career* (New York, 1963).

34. See the articles of Greeley, Donovan, and Trent in *Commonweal* 81 (October 2, 1964), 33–42. See also Joseph Scimecca and Roland Damiano, *Crisis at St. John's* (New York, 1967), 105–6, 108; and James W. Trent and Jenette Golds, *Catholics in College* (Chicago, 1967).

35. Edward Wakin and Father Joseph F. Scheuer, *The De-Romanization of the American Catholic Church* (New York, 1966), 261.

36. See Philip Gleason, "American Catholic Higher Education: A Historical Perspective," in Robert Hassenger, ed., *The Shape of Catholic Higher Education* (Chicago, 1967), 15–53.

37. John Cogley, "The Future of an Illusion," *Commonweal* 86 (June 2, 1967), 310–16.

38. William J. Richardson, "Pay Any Price? Break Any Mold?" *America* 116 (April 29, 1967), 624 ff.

39. In its draft report on academic freedom, a faculty committee of the University of Dayton was quoted as saying of the Catholic university: "Its purpose is to become secularized; for to be secularized means to come of age, to come into the time and forms of the city of man today." See also Paul J. Reiss, "The Future of the Catholic Liberal Arts College," *Holy Cross Quarterly* (Fall 1967), 15–23. [The language of the University of Dayton faculty committee quoted above from an undated clipping from the *Dayton Daily News,* headed "Faculty Group Wants a Secular UD," was confirmed by examination of a copy of the committee report, which is now in my possession. For a general review of the episode, see Erving E. Beauregard, "An Archbishop, a University, and Academic Freedom," *Records of the American Catholic Historical Society of Philadelphia* 93 (1982), 25–39.]

40. The remarks of Robert A. Nisbet in respect to the cognate demand that the American university articulate an "explicit, verbalized *purpose,*" are apropos here. Nisbet writes that "in a large-scale historical institution such as the university, purpose is given, not by rationalist assent, arrived at on the basis of 'dialogue' in conferences, but by continuous historical function, through common, if diversified, effort over long periods of time. . . ." Nisbet, "Crisis in the University?" *The Public Interest,* no. 10 (Winter 1968), 57–58.

41. Writing of a Protestant college caught in transition from religious to secular orientation, Thomas LeDuc notes: "The very acceptance of an idea operates to make exegesis needless and apology supererogatory. Only when its validity is challenged will there appear a body of definition and discussion." LeDuc, *Piety and Intellect at Amherst College, 1865–1912* (New York, 1946), vii.

42. Lionel Trilling, *The Liberal Imagination* (New York, 1950), 9. See also "Prologue: The Myth and the Dialogue," in R. W. B. Lewis, *The American Adam* (Chicago, 1955).

43. Ildefons Lobo, "Toward a Morality Based on the Meaning of History: The Condition and Renewal of Moral Theology," *Concilium*, vol. 25 (New York, 1967), 29, italics added.

44. Letter to the editor, *America* 118 (January 6, 1968), 15.

45. See the classic study by H. Richard Niebuhr, *Christ and Culture* (New York, 1951).

4. CATHOLICISM AND CULTURAL CHANGE IN THE 1960s

1. Garry Wills, "Catholic Faith and Fiction," *New York Times Book Review*, January 16, 1971, 1; Walter Laqueur, "America and the Weimar Analogy," *Encounter* 37 (May 1972), 25. Daniel Bell, "Religion in the Sixties," *Social Research* 37 (Autumn 1971), 447–97, discusses the Catholic situation in the context of a broader cultural analysis.

2. In an elegant variation of this point, Francine du Plessix Gray writes: "The Catholic Church can be compared to a zoo of wild beasts, held in captivity for over a millennium, whose bars Pope John removed. There are as many new pacifists among the rampaging animals as there are liturgical innovators and structural reformists." *Divine Disobedience: Profiles in Catholic Radicalism* (New York, 1971), 94.

3. This question appears on the cover of *National Review*, May 4, 1965.

4. Gray, *Divine Disobedience*, 52, 67 ff.

5. Robert Rouquette, "France," in M. A. Fitzsimons, ed., *The Catholic Church Today: Western Europe* (Notre Dame, Ind., 1969), 232. For the Church in Holland, see 1–28.

6. Norval D. Glenn and Ruth Hyland, "Religious Preference and Worldly Success: Some Evidence from National Surveys," *American Sociological Review* 32 (February 1967), 73–85. See also Andrew M. Greeley, *Come Blow Your Mind with Me* (Garden City, N.Y., 1971), 166–68.

7. See Andrew M. Greeley, *Religion and Career: A Study of College Graduates* (New York, 1963).

8. For fuller elaboration, see above, chapter 3.

9. Thomas F. O'Dea, *The Catholic Crisis* (Boston, 1968), lays particular stress on the importance of this conciliar document and its teaching.

10. The factor of youthfulness is related in a complex way to many other factors. See Andrew M. Greeley, *Priests in the United States: Reflections on a Survey* (Garden City, N.Y., 1972), esp. 160–61 and chap. 11. Greeley speaks of a generation "slope" rather than a generation "gap" among priests, with each ten-year age category "being more 'modern' in its religious attitudes and more 'liberal' in its sexual morality than its immediate elders." *Documentation for General Meeting of National Conference of Catholic Bishops, April 27–29, 1971. Detroit, Michigan* (Xerox), 47.

11. Andrew M. Greeley, "The New Agenda," *The Critic* (May–June 1972),

246 NOTES TO PAGES 93–94

36. Greeley's essay, "American Catholicism 1950 to 1980," is a splendid review and analysis. See *Come Blow Your Mind,* 109–65.

12. Philip Gleason, "Our New Age of Romanticism," *America* 117 (October 7, 1967), 372–75, develops this thesis, citing literature not referred to here.

13. A. O. Lovejoy, *Essays in the History of Ideas* (paperback ed., New York, 1960), 232.

14. ". . . the Romantic period was eminently an age obsessed with the fact of violent and inclusive change, and Romantic poetry cannot be understood, historically, without awareness of the degree to which this preoccupation affected its substance and form." M. H. Abrams, "English Romanticism: The Spirit of the Age," in Northrop Frye, ed., *Romanticism Reconsidered* (New York, 1963), 28–29. On this same point see Jacques Barzun, *Classic, Romantic, and Modern* (rev. ed., Boston, 1961); Ronald W. Harris, *Romanticism and the Social Order, 1780–1830* (New York, 1969); and Eugene N. Anderson, "Response to Contemporary Crisis," in John B. Halsted, ed., *Romanticism: Problems of Definition, Explanation, and Evaluation* (Lexington, Mass., 1965), 96–103. Anderson's essay originally appeared in the June 1941 issue of the *Journal of the History of Ideas,* along with several other articles on romanticism.

15. See chap. 4, "Romanticism: Community," in Ludwig Kahn, *Social Ideals in German Literature* (New York, 1938); Werner J. Cahnman, "Max Weber and the Methodological Controversy in the Social Sciences," in W. J. Cahnman and A. Boskoff, eds., *Sociology and History: Theory and Research* (New York, 1964), 104 ff. Speaking of contemporary hippie communal thinking, Bell writes: "In this Elysium, each person does his own 'thing,' and there is little compulsion to obey any rules. All men are good if they only follow their own natures, in contrast to the pressures of the social structure. In their formal ideology there is no leader; like Adam Smith's invisible hand, natural grace leads to natural harmonies. As one description of 'Drop City,' a rural commune in Colorado, puts it: 'Drop City is a tribal unit. It has no formal structure, no written laws, yet the intuitive structure is amazingly complex and functional . . . everything works itself out with the help of the cosmic forces.'" Bell, "Religion in the Sixties" (note 1 above), 493–94.

16. Hans Kohn, "Romanticism and the Rise of German Nationalism," *Review of Politics* 12 (October 1950), 443–72; Kohn, *Prelude to Nation-States: The French and German Experience, 1789–1815* (Princeton, 1967), chap. 24.

17. See John L. Thomas, "Romantic Reform in America, 1815–1965," *American Quarterly* 17 (Winter 1965), 656–81; David Brion Davis, "The Emergence of Immediatism in British and American Antislavery Thought," *Mississippi Valley Historical Review* 49 (September 1962), 209–30.

18. See Robert Carter, "'The Newness,'" *Century Magazine* 39 (1889), 129; and Thomas W. Higginson, *Cheerful Yesterdays* (Boston, 1898), chap. 3 "The Period of the Newness." Josiah Quincy, president of Harvard from 1829 to 1845, ran into trouble with the students because he was tactless enough to criticize their dress "or the whiskers which (greatly to his disgust) began to sprout toward the end of his administration." Samuel E. Morison, *Three Centuries of Harvard* (Cambridge, Mass., 1937), 251. See also Richard King, *The Party of Eros* (Chapel Hill, N.C., 1972), chap. 6, "The New Transcendentalism."

19. William G. McLoughlin, *Modern Revivalism* (New York, 1959); Timothy L. Smith, *Revivalism and Social Reform in Mid-Nineteenth Century America* (New York, 1957); Bertram Wyatt-Brown, *Lewis Tappan and the Evangelical War against Slavery* (Cleveland, 1969). Intense religiosity permeated the correspondence of leading abolitionists. See G. H. Barnes and D. L. Dumond, eds., *Letters of Theodore Dwight Weld, Angelina Grimké Weld and Sarah Grimké, 1822–1844,* 2 vols. (New York, 1934). Even temperance reformers linked their cause with millennial hopes. The American Temperance Society in 1831 wrote that, with the success of their movement, "The word of the Lord, unobstructed, will run very swiftly; and, pouring with double energy its mighty, all-pervading influence upon the whole mass of minds, will be like the rain and the snow that come down from heaven, and water the earth, and cause it to bring forth and bud. The frost and the snows of six thousand winters will be forever dissolved; and the spring-time of millennial beauty, and the autumnal fruit of millennial glory will open upon the world." *Permanent Temperance Documents of the American Temperance Society* (Boston, 1835), 53.

20. Martin Duberman, *The Uncompleted Past* (New York, 1969), 336–56. In 1968 Duberman endeavored to shed some light on the contemporary racial scene by a historical parallel between abolitionism and the Black Power movement. See his article, "Black Power in America," *Partisan Review* 35 (Winter 1968), 40–43.

5. THE BICENTENNIAL AND EARLIER MILESTONES

1. "Address Before Congress. Delivered in the Hall of the House of Representatives of the Congress of the United States, in the City of Washington, on Sunday January 8, 1926," in Sebastian G. Messmer, ed., *The Works of the Right Reverend John England, First Bishop of Charleston,* 7 vols. (Cleveland, 1908), VII, 9–43. For background and a lengthy summary of the address, see Peter Guilday, *The Life and Times of John England, First Bishop of Charleston (1786–1842),* 2 vols. (New York, 1927), II, 48–67.

2. See Arlene Swidler, "Catholics and the 1876 Centennial," *Catholic Historical Review* 62 (July 1976), 349–65. For the centennial generally, see Dee Brown, *Year of the Century: 1876* (New York, 1966); William Randel, *Centennial: American Life in 1876* (Philadelphia, 1969); John Maass, *The Glorious Enterprise: The Centennial Exhibition of 1876 and H. J. Schwarzmann, Architect-in-Chief* (Watkins Glen, N.Y., 1973).

3. For *Faith of Our Fathers* and its influence, see John Tracy Ellis, *The Life of James Cardinal Gibbons, Archbishop of Baltimore, 1834–1921,* 2 vols. (Milwaukee, 1952), I, 145–52; II, 582–92.

4. For background, see Mary Marcian Lowman, "James Andrew Corcoran: Editor, Theologian, Scholar (1820–1889)" (Ph.D. diss., St. Louis University, 1958), 342 ff.

5. John Gilmary Shea, "The Catholic Church in American History," *American Catholic Quarterly Review* 1 (January 1876), 148–73.

6. See Peter Guilday, *John Gilmary Shea, Father of American Church History, 1824–1892* (New York, 1926); Henry Warner Bowden, "John Gilmary Shea:

A Study of Method and Goals in Historiography," *Catholic Historical Review* 54 (July 1968), 235–60.

7. [John Lancaster Spalding], "The Catholic Church in the United States, 1776–1876," *Catholic World* 23 (July 1876), 434–52. The article is unsigned, but was reprinted in Spalding's *Essays and Reviews* (New York, 1877), 9–49.

8. David F. Sweeney, *The Life of John Lancaster Spalding, First Bishop of Peoria, 1840–1916* (New York, 1965), is a recent scholarly biography; see 98–99 for comments on the centennial article.

9. See James Hennesey, *American Catholics* (New York, 1981), chap. 15, and the literature cited therein.

10. Peter Guilday, "The Catholic Church in the United States: A Sesquicentennial Essay," *Thought* 1 (June 1926), 3–20. For an excellent discussion of Guilday's career and outlook, unavailable when I wrote this essay, see David O'Brien, "Peter Guilday: The Catholic Intellectual in the Post-Modernist Church," in Nelson H. Minnich et al., eds., *Studies in Catholic History in Honor of John Tracy Ellis* (Wilmington, Del., 1985), 260–306, esp. 295–97 for the sesquicentennial essay.

11. Guilday dealt with the controversies in a self-consciously restrained way in "The Church in the United States (1870–1920): A Retrospect of Fifty Years," *Catholic Historical Review* 6 (January 1921), 533–47. In a letter written at the time to Shane Leslie, editor of the *Dublin Review,* who had solicited such an essay from Guilday, he commented on the difficulty he experienced in getting a purchase on the period in question, and said that he "purposely submerged" some of the leading personalities in the controversies "because some still float above the waters of Lethe." Guilday to Leslie, February 2, 1921 (carbon), in Guilday papers, Archives of the Catholic University of America. See O'Brien, "Guilday," 285–86.

12. Michael Williams, *American Catholics and the War: National Catholic War Council, 1917–1921* (New York, 1921). See also Guilday's comments on war-related matters, *Catholic Historical Review* 3 (July 1917), 242–47; ibid. 7 (April 1921), 18. Very valuable for its treatment of World War I and the postwar era is William M. Halsey, *The Survival of American Innocence: Catholicism in an Era of Disillusionment, 1920–1940* (Notre Dame, Ind., 1980), esp. 2, 8, 37–60; for Guilday, see ibid., 40–42, 47, 48. Also valuable for the relation of World War I to American Catholicism are Elizabeth McKeown, "The National Bishops' Conference: An Analysis of Its Origins," *Catholic Historical View* 66 (October 1980), 565–83; John Sheerin, *Never Look Back: Biography of John J. Burke, C.S.P.* (New York, 1975); and Christopher J. Kauffman, *Faith and Fraternalism: The History of the Knights of Columbus, 1882–1982* (New York, 1982), chap. 8.

13. Maurice de Wulf, "Cardinal Mercier: Philosopher," *New Scholasticism* 1 (1927), 13. See also Halsey, *American Innocence,* chaps. 8–9.

14. When anti-Catholicism reached its climax in 1928, Guilday responded with a forty-three-part series for the Catholic press on "The Catholic Question in the United States." The *Catholic Review* of Baltimore, which ran the series from January 6 to October 26, 1928, headlined the first installment as follows: "Doctor Guilday Shows Bigotry Is Unchanging/Noted Historian Begins His Series of Articles on 'The Catholic Question'/Chapters on Subject to Run Through 1928/These

Contributions Will Be Among the Most Important Published by the Review." See also O'Brien, "Guilday," 298–301.

15. Guilday had an unspeculative mind and did not, so far as I know, develop this argument explicitly. We can be confident that he was acquainted with it, however, for it was quite popular with Catholics in the 1920s, and was given early expression in an article in the *Catholic Historical Review,* which Guilday edited. It is also reflected in his statement that America sprang from the heart of the Catholic Middle Ages. See Gaillard Hunt, "The Virginia Declaration of Rights and Cardinal Bellarmine," *Catholic Historical Review* 3 (October 1917), 276–89, and Halsey, *American Innocence,* 71 ff.

16. Joseph A. Varacalli, *Toward the Establishment of Liberal Catholicism in America* (Washington, 1983), is the only full-length study of this episode so far published, but David J. O'Brien, a key participant in the bicentennial project, is the author of a book-length manuscript, "A Call to Action: The Church Prepares for the Third Century," upon which Varacalli was able to draw.

17. The principal historical effort undertaken by American Catholics to mark the bicentennial was the publication in the Catholic press of sixty popular articles dealing with a wide range of historical topics. These articles, done by many different authors, were made permanently available in Robert Trisco, ed., *Catholics in America, 1776–1976* (Washington, 1976).

6. THE SCHOOL QUESTION: A CENTENNIAL RETROSPECT

1. For general overviews written near the height of the turmoil, see George N. Shuster, *Catholic Education in a Changing World* (New York, 1967); Neil G. McCluskey, *Catholic Education Faces Its Future* (Garden City, N.Y., 1969); Harold A. Buetow, *Of Singular Benefit: The Story of Catholic Education in the United States* (New York, 1970), 280–366.

2. Mary Perkins Ryan, *Are Parochial Schools the Answer? Catholic Education in the Light of the Council* (New York, 1964). For Ryan's views a few years later, see her *We're All in This Together* (New York, 1972).

3. The most important of the social scientific works were Andrew M. Greeley and Peter H. Rossi, *The Education of Catholic Americans* (Chicago, 1966); and the follow-up study, Andrew M. Greeley, William McCready, and Kathleen McCourt, *Catholic Schools in a Declining Church* (Kansas City, Mo., 1976).

4. The first quotation is from Karl Peter Ganss, "American Catholic Education in the 1960s: A Study of the Parochial School Debate" (Ph.D. diss., Loyola University, Chicago, 1978), 111; the second from Louise Mayock and Allan Glatthorn, "NCEA and the Development of the Post-Conciliar Catholic School," *Momentum* 11 (December 1980), 8. See also Michael P. Sheridan and Russell Shaw, eds., *Catholic Education Today and Tomorrow: Proceedings of the Washington Symposium on Catholic Education, November 5–10, 1967* (Washington, D.C., 1968).

5. See Robert D. Cross, "Origins of Catholic Parochial Schools in America," *American Benedictine Review* 16 (June 1965), 194–209; Vincent P. Lannie, "Church and School Triumphant: The Historiography of Catholic Education in

America," an unpublished manuscript, of which a shorter version with the same title appeared in *History of Education Quarterly* 16 (Summer 1976), 131–45; and Marvin Lazerson, "Understanding American Catholic Educational History," ibid. 17 (Fall 1977), 297–317. Much information on Catholic use of, and preference for, public schools is provided in Howard R. Weisz, *Irish-American and Italian-American Educational Views and Activities, 1870–1900* (New York, 1976), esp. 47–95.

6. McCluskey, *Catholic Education,* chap. 3, is the best-informed of these topical discussions. For a general treatment of Baltimore III, see Peter Guilday, *A History of the Councils of Baltimore, 1791–1921* (New York, 1932), 221–49; for its background and preparation, see John Tracy Ellis, *The Life of James Cardinal Gibbons, Archbishop of Baltimore, 1834–1921,* 2 vols. (Milwaukee, 1952), I, 203–51.

7. The official text of the decrees is *Acta et Decreta Concilii Plenarii Baltimorensis Tertii* (Baltimore, 1886), 99–114, for those dealing with parochial schools, academies, and colleges. These decrees are reproduced in Latin and translated into English in Bernard J. Meiring, "Educational Aspects of the Legislation of the Councils of Baltimore, 1829–1884" (Ph.D. diss., University of California, Berkeley, 1963), Appendix II, 293–318. Ibid., 190–249 discusses Baltimore III. For a detailed discussion which includes seminary education also, see Francis P. Cassidy, "Catholic Education in the Third Plenary Council of Baltimore," *Catholic Historical Review* 34 (October 1948–January 1949), 257–305, 415–36.

8. Ellis, *Gibbons,* I, 235–36; David F. Sweeney, *The Life of John Lancaster Spalding, First Bishop of Peoria, 1840–1916* (New York, 1965), 173–75; Robert N. Barger, "John Lancaster Spalding: Catholic Educator and Social Emissary" (Ph.D. diss., University of Illinois, 1976), 185–86; Francis J. Connell, "Catechism Revision," in *The Confraternity Comes of Age; A Historical Symposium* (Paterson, N.J., 1956), 189–201.

9. Meiring, "Educational Aspects," 293.

10. Peter Guilday, ed., *The National Pastorals of the American Hierarchy (1792–1919)* (Westminster, Md., 1954), 229–30.

11. Ibid., 239, 244.

12. Ibid., 246.

13. Ibid., 252.

14. See Vincent P. Lannie, *Public Money and Parochial Education: Bishop Hughes, Governor Seward and the New York School Controversy* (Cleveland, 1968); Vincent P. Lannie and Bernard C. Diethorn, "For the Honor and Glory of God: The Philadelphia Bible Riots of 1844," *History of Education Quarterly* 8 (Spring 1968), 44–106; Ray Allen Billington, *The Protestant Crusade, 1800–1860* (Quadrangle paperback, 1964), 292–95; Austin Flynn, "The School Controversy in New York 1840–1842 and Its Effect on the Formulation of Catholic Elementary School Policy" (Ph.D. diss., University of Notre Dame, 1962), 178–223; Daniel F. Reilly, *The School Controversy (1891–1893)* (Washington, D.C., 1943), 22–38.

15. The point about extreme statements and their role in heightening suspicions is taken from Owen Chadwick, *The Secularization of the European Mind in the Nineteenth Century* (Cambridge, 1975), 125–26. For an indication of how Protestants reacted to sometimes extreme Catholic statements about the school issue, see Charles L. Sewrey, "The Alleged 'Un-Americanism' of the Church as a

Factor in Anti-Catholicism in the United States, 1860–1914" (Ph.D. diss., University of Minnesota, 1955), 167–99.

16. Jerome E. Diffley, "Catholic Reaction to American Public Education, 1792–1852" (Ph.D. diss., University of Notre Dame, 1959), 73–98; Timothy L. Smith, "Protestant Schooling and American Nationality, 1800–1850," *Journal of American History* 53 (March 1967), 679–95; Smith, *Uncommon Schools: Christian Colleges and Social Idealism in Midwestern America, 1820–1950* (privately printed, 1978), 9, 14, 16, 22, 29; David P. Tyack, "The Kingdom of God and the Common School," *Harvard Educational Review* 36 (Fall 1966), 447–69; Francis Michael Perko, "A Time to Favor Zion: A Case Study of Religion as a Force in American Educational Development, 1830–1870" (Ph.D. diss., Stanford University, 1981), 38–54, 75–85.

17. A well-known atrocity story concerned the 1859 case of Thomas Wall, whose hands were beaten for half an hour because he refused to recite the Protestant version of the Ten Commandments in a public school in Boston. The parents brought the teacher to court, but he was acquitted. See Robert H. Lord, John E. Sexton, and Edward T. Harrington, *History of the Archdiocese of Boston,* 3 vols. (New York, 1944), II, 587–600. See also Weisz, *Educational Views* (note 5 above), 97–123.

18. Perko, "Time to Favor Zion," 154–91; Robert Michaelson, *Piety in the Public School* (New York, 1970), 89–106.

19. Marie Carolyn Klinkhamer, "The Blaine Amendment of 1875: Private Motives for Political Action," *Catholic Historical Review* 42 (April 1956), 15–49; John Higham, *Strangers in the Land: Patterns of American Nativism 1869–1925* (Atheneum paperback ed., 1970), 28–29.

20. For Hecker see, "What Does the Public-School Question Mean?" *Catholic World* 34 (October 1881), 84–90; for the liberals Gibbons and Keane, see National Education Association, *Journal of Proceedings and Addresses . . . 1889* (Topeka, 1889), 111–23; for similar views from John Ireland, N.E.A., *Journal of Proceedings and Addresses . . . 1890* (Topeka, 1890), 181–83; for Spalding, "Religious Instruction in State Schools," *Educational Review* 2 (July 1891), 105–22. Patrick F. McSweeny, the priest who initiated the well-known "Poughkeepsie plan," a compromise agreement with the state, also believed in denominational schools; see McSweeny, "The School Question," *Catholic World* 43 (July 1886), 505–12. The views of Protestants who agreed with Catholics on the need for religious education and denominational schools were noted by Catholics with approval. See H. H. Wyman, "President Seelye and Religious Education," *Catholic World* 43 (September 1886), 829–32; Patrick F. McSweeny, "Christian Public Schools," ibid. 44 (March 1887), 788–97.

21. The pastoral observed that public schools, "as they are now organized," could not be blamed for not teaching religion. Guilday, *Pastorals* (note 10 above), 246.

22. The prevailing non-Catholic view was well stated by Senator John Sherman in a private letter (dated December 25, 1875) to his brother, William T. Sherman, who was married to a Catholic. "The Priests from the Pope down have been so foolish as to assail our common schools. Their position is untenable. If reli-

gious teaching is admitted into them, it is an end of the system. I have no prejudice whatever against Catholics, their faith or their priests, but I can see at a glance that if they will persist in making an issue on the sharing of the school funds or upon the introduction of their forms and dogmas into any of the schools supported by general taxes they will array against themselves not only the whole Protestant population but Jews, Gentiles and Pagans also. The assumption that they will not send their children to non-sectarian schools would lead them to prohibit marriage, companionship, and even political association with other than Catholics, and thus divide society into sects and revive again the religious wars of the middle ages." Quoted in Klinkhamer, "Blaine Amendment," 26.

23. An old but informative review of such arrangements is James A. Burns, *Growth and Development of the Catholic School System in the United States* (New York, 1912), 248–73.

24. This view was stated by Senator Frederick T. Frelinghuysen (Republican, N.J.) in the debate on the Blaine Amendment in 1876: "The pure and undefiled religion which appertains to the relationship and responsibility of man to God, and is readily distinguishable from the creeds of sects; that religion which permeates all our laws . . . that religion which is our history, which is our unwritten as well as our written law, and which sustains the pillars of our liberty, is a very, very different thing from the particular creeds or tenets of either religionists or infidels." Quoted in Klinkhamer, "Blaine Amendment," 43. John Jay, "Public and Parochial Schools," in N.E.A., *Journal of Proceedings . . . 1889,* 154–55, quotes Daniel Webster and other authorities as holding that "it would be cruel and wrong to exclude the children from the knowledge of those broad and general precepts and principles which are admitted by all Christians" and can be taught apart from "clashing doctrines and sectarian controversies."

25. Michaelsen, *Piety in Public School,* esp. chaps. 1–4; Reilly, *School Controversy* (note 14 above), 36.

26. The common school, said John Jay, "is recognized at home and abroad by intelligent people of all creeds and parties as the chief basis of our government of the people, by the people, and for the people, and the chief source of our undoubted strength and unsurpassed prosperity." Jay, "Public and Parochial Schools," 152. From another writer in 1889: "The common-school system is among the fundamental bases of the American type of political and social life. It is coeval in its origin with the colonization of the country. . . . It has been universally felt to be a necessary condition, a part of the indispensable groundwork, of free, republic institutions." George P. Fisher, "Cardinal Manning and Public Schools," *Forum* 7 (April 1889), 123. Michaelsen, *Piety in Public School,* 122, quotes three prominent Protestant clergymen (Horace Bushnell in 1853, Josiah Strong in 1885, and Daniel Dorchester in 1888) as asserting that Catholics either were un-American because they excluded themselves from public schools, or that they should be *required* to attend public schools.

27. See Jay, "Public and Parochial Schools," and the companion piece by Edwin D. Mead, in N.E.A., *Journal of Proceedings . . . 1889,* 123–47. Mead argued for the enactment of laws, such as one already on the books in Massachusetts, which would forbid Catholic authorities from using "threats of religious disabili-

ties" to deter attendance at public schools. This kind of interference with the right of a church to maintain its own internal discipline justified Bishop Keane's sarcastic rejoinder: "Oh, how we love liberty when it means coercing others into what we choose!" Ibid., 131, 142, 151.

28. The question of how public schooling affected moral behavior was widely discussed and highly explosive. The most extreme Catholic charges came from Zach Montgomery, a California lawyer and political figure whose magazine, *The Family Defender,* published in the early 1880s, was filled with intemperate attacks on the public schools. The title of one of his works conveys their spirit: *The Poison Fountain or, Anti-Parental Education. Essays and Discussions on the School Question from a Parental and Non-Sectarian Standpoint. Wherein the Decline of Parental Authority, the Downfall of Family Government, and the Terrible Growth of Crime, Pauperism, Insanity and Suicide, in America, are Traced Directly and Unmistakably to our Anti-Parental Public School System* (San Francisco, 1878). See also Reilly, *School Controversy,* 35–36, 41; Weisz, *Educational Views,* 257–74.

29. N.E.A. *Journal of Proceedings and Address . . . 1888* (Topeka, 1888), 158. For Morgan's various school and church positions see the sketch of his life in *Dictionary of American Biography.* During his stint as Commissioner of Indian Affairs, Morgan clashed bitterly with Catholics engaged in missionary and school work among the Indians. See R. Pierce Beaver, *Church, State, and the American Indians* (St. Louis, 1966), 162 ff., and Francis Paul Prucha, *The Churches and the Indian Schools, 1888–1912* (Lincoln, Neb., 1979), 10–29.

30. M. C. O'Byrne, "What Is the Catholic School Policy?" *North American Review* 140 (June 1885), 521. John J. Keane replied to O'Byrne, ibid., 528–35.

31. Chadwick, *Secularization* (note 15 above), 91; Franklin L. Baumer, *Religion and the Rise of Skepticism* (New York, 1960), 133.

32. Hecker, "A New But False Plan for Public Schools," *Catholic World* 36 (December 1882), 419; Ireland in N.E.A., *Journal of Proceedings . . . 1890,* 183. For another liberal, shocked at secularists' intentions, see Walter Elliott, "Dynamic Sociology," *Catholic World* 38 (December 1883), 383–89. For an example of conservative viewing-with-alarm, see August J. Thébaud, "The Church and the Intellectual World," *American Catholic Quarterly Review* 1 (1876), 504–38, esp. 531, for reference to "secularism."

33. See Chadwick, *Secularization,* 107–39, on "the rise of anticlericalism."

34. Thomas J. Jenkins, *The Judges of Faith: Christian vs. Godless Schools* (Baltimore, 1886). Referring to this work as *The Catholic Educators' Manual on Schools* (which appeared on the title page as a kind of superscript), Edwin Mead said that for thirty cents, apparently the price of the book, one could find out what Catholics really thought on the subject of schools. N.E.A., *Journal of Proceedings . . . 1889,* 136.

35. Jenkins, *Judges of Faith,* 168–71.

36. Thomas T. McAvoy, "Public Schools vs. Catholic Schools and James McMaster," *Review of Politics* 28 (January 1966), 19–46. The Instruction of 1875, which quoted from Piux IX's letter to the archbishop of Freiburg, is reproduced in John Tracy Ellis, ed., *Documents of American Catholic History* (Chicago, 1967), II, 405–8.

37. Herman J. Heuser, "Prince Bismarck's Conflict with the Catholic Church," *American Catholic Quarterly Review* 9 (April 1884), 322–39.

38. Henry A. Brann, "The Improvement of Parochial Schools," ibid., 243. The Belgian Minister of Public Instruction who put the law of 1879 into effect was a Freemason, who was alleged to have said at some earlier time that "Catholicism was a corpse that barred the way of progress and would have to be thrown into the grave." See *Catholic Encyclopedia,* 16 vols. (New York, 1907–1914), II, 410–12.

39. Adrien Dansette, *Religious History of Modern France,* 2 vols. (New York, 1961), I, 347.

40. Guilday, *Pastorals* (note 10 above), 236–37; Bernard O'Reilly, "The Propaganda Question and Our Duty," *American Catholic Quarterly Review* 9 (April 1884), 285–303; Robert F. McNamara, *The American College in Rome, 1855–1955* (Rochester, 1956), 275–83.

41. Decree 195 of Baltimore III states: "Among those who strongly advocate this merely secular education are many who wish neither to bring any harm to religion nor to afford dangers to young people. From the very nature of the case, however, it follows that a merely secular education gradually breaks down so that it becomes irreligious and wicked, and especially dangerous to the faith and morals of the young. This point has been demonstrated from sad experience." Meiring, "Educational Aspects" (note 7 above), 294.

42. For the controversy in Massachusetts, see Lord et al., *Boston* (note 17 above), III, 111 ff., and Lois B. Merk, "Boston's Historic Public School Crisis," *New England Quarterly* 31 (June 1958), 172–99; for Ohio, Patrick F. Quigley, ed., *Compulsory Education, The State of Ohio versus the Reverend Patrick Francis Quigley, D.D.* (New York, 1892); for Illinois, Charles Shanabruch, *Chicago's Catholics: The Evolution of an American Identity* (Notre Dame, Ind., 1981), 59–73; for Wisconsin, Robert J. Ulrich, "The Bennett Law of 1889: Education and Politics in Wisconsin" (Ph.D. diss., University of Wisconsin, 1965).

43. Reilly, *School Controversy* (note 14 above), is the basic work; Colman J. Barry, *The Catholic Church and German Americans* (Milwaukee, 1953), 184–200, throws light on the German-Catholic side of the controversy; Robert D. Cross, *The Emergence of Liberal Catholicism in America* (Cambridge, Mass., 1958), 130–45, is a good brief account.

44. For Shea, see Joseph F. Martino, "A Study of Certain Aspects of the Episcopate of Patrick J. Ryan, Archbishop of Philadelphia, 1884–1911 (Ph.D. diss., Gregorian University, 1983), 426; for recollections of scandal, see Gerald P. Fogarty, *The Vatican and the American Hierarchy from 1870 to 1965* (Stuttgart, 1982), 217.

45. Meiring, "Educational Aspects," 234, is the source of the quotation; Fitzgerald was evidently concerned with the practical problem, for he cited statistics in the debate to show that parochial schools could not be built at all in some areas and were inadequate to the needs in others. See Cassidy, "Catholic Education" (note 7 above), 304.

46. Even those who supported the denominational school idea publicly might entertain misgivings privately. Bishop Keane, for example, defended the denomina-

tional approach in a controversial context at the 1889 meeting of the NEA, but in a private conversation on the eve of Baltimore III he was said to have expressed regret that the Blaine Amendment was not approved in Congress, as "it would put a stop to the agitation for getting a share in the public money for Catholic Schools —a thing he thinks would ultimately bring them under the sway of the state—as it tends to do in England. . . . On the contrary he thinks Protestants would be then led to have schools of their own and the public or state schools would lose their importance." Quoted from the entry for November 5, 1884, in John B. Hogan diary, Sulipician Archives, Baltimore.

47. Neil G. McCluskey, ed., *Catholic Education in America: A Documentary History* (New York, 1964), 78–85, reproduces the relevant passages on education from the pastoral letters issued by the First and Second Plenary Councils in 1852 and 1866. McCluskey, *Catholic Education Faces Its Future* (note 1 above), 105, provides a table showing the growth of parochial schools between 1884 and 1900.

48. On Spalding, see Barger, "Spalding" (note 8 above), 172–81, 24–37; on McQuaid, Norlene M. Kunkel, "Bishop Bernard J. McQuaid and Catholic Education" (Ph.D. diss., University of Notre Dame, 1974); on Gilmour, Michael J. Hynes, *The History of the Diocese of Cleveland: Origin and Growth (1847–1952)* (Cleveland, 1953), 127 ff.

49. See James W. Sanders, "Boston Catholics and the School Question," Cushwa Center Occasional Paper series, no. 2, Fall 1977, esp. 24–25.

50. At Baltimore III, Heiss argued that the decrees should *command,* rather than *urge,* the establishment and maintenance of parochial schools because dropping the word "command" would weaken Catholic schools where they already existed and retaining it would do no damage where such schools did not exist. Cassidy, "Catholic Education," 302. In preliminary discussions held at Rome on the agenda for Baltimore III in the fall of 1883, Heiss had asked whether the faithful could be required to attend Catholic schools for no other reason than that such schools would be weakened if they did not. He was informed that such a consideration was not, in itself, a sufficient reason to require attendance. See "Minutes of Roman Meeting Preparatory to the III Plenary Council of Baltimore," *The Jurist* 11 (1951), 424.

51. The following discussion is based on Cassidy, "Catholic Education," 300–305, 414–16; and Meiring, "Educational Aspects," 233–42.

52. Meiring, "Educational Aspects," 221–22, gives the Latin texts of the original and revised forms of the schema on parochial schools; in both cases, the word "commendanda" is used, although Meiring translates the second case "commanded" rather than "commended," probably through a typographical error.

53. "Minutes of Roman Meeting," 423. Fogarty, *Vatican and American Hierarchy,* 34, speaks of the bishops attempting to "specify and limit the original Roman schema" by requiring the building of parochial schools within two years unless the bishop granted an exception. Unless Fogarty is referring to some other document, this misinterprets the situation, because, as explained above, the bishops actually stiffened the Roman guidelines rather than limiting them. Actually, the "Minutes of Roman Meeting" and secondary works on the Council all suggest

that Rome was much less interested in parochial schools than in seminary education and in regularizing the relations between priests and bishops in the United States.

54. Meiring, "Educational Aspects," 236.

55. Cassidy, "Catholic Education," 303–4; Meiring, "Educational Aspects," 237–38.

56. Meiring, "Educational Aspects," 238.

57. Cassidy, "Catholic Education," 305; Meiring, "Educational Aspects," 240, for debate; 244, for text as approved in Rome.

58. Cassidy, "Catholic Education," 416.

59. Meiring, "Educational Aspects," 242–44, indicates the manner in which Rome "softened the harsh effect" of the Council's wording of the four rules contained in decree 199 in the final process of approving the decrees.

60. Thomas T. McAvoy noted that Baltimore III "stands out as the last great manifestation of unity of the Catholic bishops in the nineteenth century," and he adds that explaining why it was followed by fifteen years of division within the hierarchy is a problem for the historian. McAvoy, *The Great Crisis in American Catholic History 1895–1900* (Chicago, 1957), 10. A more recent work which also stresses Baltimore III as the climax of unity among the bishops, followed by deep divisions, is Robert Emmett Curran, *Michael Augustine Corrigan and the Shaping of Conservative Catholicism in America, 1878–1902* (New York, 1978), 64 ff., 78 ff., 112–19.

61. For school controversies in the states named, see the works cited above in note 42; for the A.P.A., see Donald L. Kinzer, *An Episode in Anti-Catholicism: the American Protective Association* (Seattle, 1964), 25–29, 39, 45, 50, 52, 64–72.

62. The most recent general treatment of these controversies, which cites earlier standard works and incorporates new archival material, is Fogarty, *Vatican and American Hierarchy,* chaps. 2–7. Philip Gleason, "Coming to Terms with American Catholic History," *Societas* 3 (Autumn 1973), 283–312, sets the controversies, and the historical literature about them, within the context of Catholic thinking on the relation of the Church to the American environment.

63. The most detailed study of Ireland's controversial arrangement is Timothy H. Morrissey, "Archbishop John Ireland and the Faribault-Stillwater School Plan of the 1890s: A Reappraisal" (Ph.D. diss., University of Notre Dame, 1975).

64. This follows the interpretation of Roger Aubert, *The Church in a Secularised Society* (New York, 1978), 8–15. William McSweeney, *Roman Catholicism, the Search for Relevance* (New York, 1980), 61–91, is a much less sympathetic analysis of "The Leonine Strategy."

65. For evidence of the influence of Leo on the Americanizers, see John J. Keane, *The Providential Mission of Leo XIII* (Baltimore, 1888); Isaac T. Hecker, "Leo XIII," *Catholic World* 46 (December 1887), 291–98; and Hecker, "The Mission of Leo XIII," ibid. 48 (October 1888), 1–13, which discusses Keane's lecture on Leo. See also Thomas Wangler, "Emergence of John J. Keane as a Liberal Catholic and Americanist (1878–1887)," *American Ecclesiastical Review* 166 (September 1972), 457–78.

66. For evidence of continuity on the first of these issues, see Timothy Walch, "Tuition Tax Credits: Historical and Hopeful Perspective," *Momentum* 15 (February 1984), 20–23.

7. THE SEARCH FOR UNITY AND ITS SEQUEL

1. As evidence that my sense of disintegration is not wholly idiosyncratic, let me cite John Tracy Ellis's statement in 1973 that nothing in the history of American Catholicism approximated "its present dispiritedness and disarray." Ellis, "American Catholicism in 'an Uncertain, Anxious Time,'" *Commonweal* 98 (April 27, 1973), 177. See also Ellis, "The Church in Revolt, the Tumultuous Sixties," *The Critic* 28 (January-February 1970), 12–21; and William C. McCready and Andrew M. Greeley, "The End of American Catholicism?" *America* 127 (October 28, 1972) 334–38. A well-informed and well-disposed Lutheran observer who takes a somewhat similar view is George A. Lindbeck; see his essay, "The Crisis in American Catholicism," in John Deschner, Leroy T. Howe, and Klaus Penzel, eds., *Our Common History as Christians: Essays in Honor of Albert C. Outler* (New York, 1975), 47–66.

2. See Ernan McMullin's presidential address entitled "Who Are We?" American Catholic Philosophical Association, *Proceedings . . . 1967* (Washington, 1967), 1–16. The next year Walter J. Burghardt concluded his presidential address to the Catholic Theological Society of America by asking: "In a word, can we, in hard-nose reality, justify our actual, independent, relatively unproductive existence? I say no." See Catholic Theological Society of America, *Proceedings . . . 1968* (Yonkers, N.Y., 1968), 28. A later president of the CTSA, Richard McBrien, quoted Burghardt's question and his answer and remarked that those who heard it in 1968 might well have been "stunned by so ominous a pronouncement from so insightful a critic. . . ." McBrien also noted that Charles Curran, CTSA president in 1970, had "posed the survival question but offered . . . a probationary stay of execution." McBrien himself took a more confident and positive line; but the theme of the convention in the year of his presidency was "Is there a Catholic theology?" See CTSA, *Proceedings . . . 1974* (Bronx, N.Y., 1974), 397 and *passim*. One participant, Gabriel Moran, regarded the word "theology" as the problematic term in the convention's theme, and concluded his contribution by saying: "I think that the word theology should be laid to rest." Ibid., 123.

3. James Colaianni, *The Catholic Left: The Crisis of Radicalism within the Church* (Philadelphia, 1968), 27. Colaianni, a former editor of *Ramparts,* was executive director of the Liturgical Conference when he wrote this. James Hitchcock, *The Recovery of the Sacred* (New York, 1974), reports many instances of the outlook revealed by Colaianni and provides an excellent critique of that mentality.

4. Gabriel Moran, *Design for Religion: Toward Ecumenical Education* (New York, 1970), 9.

5. The historian of the Catholic Art Association characterizes this work, entitled *The Prophetic Generation; Fourteen Essays on the Aquarian Age,* as "a dreadful publication." It was intended to be a "springboard for dialogue" at the

CAA's 1970 convention, but the old-line leaders of the Association managed to have the convention cancelled. Practically speaking, that was the end of the organization. See Maureen T. Murphy, "The Search for Right Reason in an Unreasonable World: A History of the Catholic Art Association, 1937–1970" (Ph.D. diss., University of Notre Dame, 1975), 174.

6. For intellectual apostolate and holy panderers, see Edward Wakin and Father Joseph F. Scheuer, *The De-Romanization of the American Catholic Church* (New York, 1966), 260–61. For Berrigan, *The* [Notre Dame] *Observer*, February 13, 1970.

7. James Hitchcock, *The Decline and Fall of Radical Catholicism* (New York, 1971), 112–13; Garry Wills, *Bare Ruined Choirs: Doubt, Prophecy, and Radical Religion* (New York, 1972), esp. 268.

8. "Proceedings of the Ninth Annual Meeting . . . 1928," *Catholic Historical Review*, 15 (April 1929), 16. My attention was drawn to this passage by J. Thomas Douglas, "Interpretations of American Catholic History: A Comparative Analysis of Representative Catholic Historians, 1875–1975" (Ph.D. diss., Baylor University, 1976), 76.

9. William M. Halsey, *The Survival of American Innocence: Catholicism in an Era of Disillusionment, 1920–1940* (Notre Dame, Ind., 1980), is the most useful secondary account of these developments. For general background, see James Hennesey, *American Catholics: A History of the Roman Catholic Community in the United States* (New York, 1981), chaps. 17–19. Fulton J. Sheen, *The Mystical Body of Christ* (New York, 1935), is a popular exposition of the doctrine. The importance of unity in this theological approach is indicated by the titles of chaps. 2–5 of Emile Mersch, *The Theology of the Mystical Body*, trans. Cyril Vollert (St. Louis, 1951). The titles are: "Theology as Science and as Search for Unity"; "Unity in Theology: The Whole Christ"; "Unity: The Human Consciousness of Christ and the Consciousness of Christians"; and "The Teaching of Philosophy on Man and his Unity."

10. See Paul Marx, *Virgil Michel and the Liturgical Movement* (Collegeville, Minn.: 1957).

11. The secondary literature here is virtually nonexistent. Martin H. Work and Daniel J. Kane, "The American Catholic Layman and his Organizations," in Philip Gleason, ed., *Contemporary Catholicism in the United States* (Notre Dame, Ind., 1969), esp. 354–62, gives a few sketchy hints of developments, and Dennis M. Robb, "Specialized Catholic Action in the United States, 1936–1949: Ideology, Leadership, and Organization" (Ph.D. diss., University of Minnesota, 1972), is a detailed study of a narrow but important aspect of the story. John Fitzsimons and Paul McGuire, eds., *Restoring All Things: A Guide to Catholic Action* (New York, 1938), is a useful contemporary overview. The early chapters of Abigail McCarthy, *Private Faces / Public Places* (Garden City, N.Y., 1972) recreate the atmosphere of those years and provide an insight into the way in which serious and intelligent young people perceived what was going on in American Catholicism and reacted to it.

12. See above, chapter 3; David L. Salvaterra, "The Apostolate of the Intellect: Development and Diffusion of an Academic Ethos among American Catho-

lics in the Early Twentieth Century" (Ph.D. diss., University of Notre Dame, 1983), ch. 6; Donald J. Gavin, *The National Conference of Catholic Charities* (Milwaukee, 1962); Robert J. Shanahan, *The History of the Catholic Hospital Association, 1915–1965: Fifty Years of Progress* (St. Louis, 1965); and Mary Lonan Reilly, *A History of the Catholic Press Association, 1911–1968* (Metuchen, N.J., 1971).

13. George Johnson, "Recent Developments in the Catholic College," *Catholic School Journal* 30 (March 1930), 96.

14. Philip Gleason, "American Catholic Higher Education: A Historical Perspective," in Robert Hassenger, ed., *The Shape of Catholic Higher Education* (Chicago, 1967), esp. 28, 36 ff., 44 ff. David J. Arthur, "The University of Notre Dame, 1919–1933: An Administrative History" (Ph.D. diss., University of Michigan, 1973) is an excellent study of the process of modernization at Notre Dame.

15. See Gleason, "American Catholic Higher Education," 43–47. For a representative Catholic lament over the deterioration of true education and a prescription for its reversal, see Charles Phillips, "Catholic Ideals in Higher Education," *National Catholic Educational Association Bulletin* 25 (1928), 60–74. For appreciative references to Hutchins, see ibid. 34 (1937), 129; 35 (1938), 219; 36 (1939), 85, 173. (Hereafter referred to as *NCEAB.*)

16. See *Association of American Colleges Bulletin* 9 (April 1923), 88–89. The liberal arts dean at Notre Dame characterized Meiklejohn's statement as "one of the most pitiful admissions ever made by any modern educator." See Charles C. Miltner, "Modifying the Curriculum," *Notre Dame Scholastic* 57 (January 24, 1924), 301.

17. James A. Burns, "Position and Prospects of the Catholic College," *NCEAB* 24 (1927), 128–40. For Burns's career, see Anna R. Kearney, "James A. Burns, C.S.C.—Educator" (Ph.D. diss., University of Notre Dame, 1975).

18. Edward A. Fitzpatrick, "Lay Cooperation in the Financial Administration of Catholic Colleges," *NCEAB* 26 (1929), 134–35.

19. Although not formulated so explicitly, this line of reasoning is implied in Burns's 1927 discussion. See especially *NCEAB* 24 (1927), 132 ff.

20. A sketch of the career of this extraordinary man, who was a self-taught anthropologist and the founder, in 1926, of the Catholic Anthropological Conference, is provided by Paul Hanley Furfey, "John Montgomery Cooper: 1881–1949," *Primitive Man* 23 (1950), 49–65. See also Rosemary T. Rodgers, "The Changing Concept of College Theology: A Case Study" (Ph.D. diss., Catholic University of America, 1973), esp. chap. 2. William J. McGucken, "The Renascence of Religion Teaching in American Catholic Schools," in Roy J. Defarrari, ed., *Essays on Catholic Education in the United States* (Washington, 1942), 342 ff., is a good secondary account of religious education in Catholic colleges in the 1920s and 1930s.

21. For O'Hara, see Thomas T. McAvoy, *Father O'Hara of Notre Dame: The Cardinal-Archbishop of Philadelphia* (Notre Dame, Ind., 1967), chap. 3. Representative discussions from the 1920s may be found in *NCEAB* 20 (1923), 106–11; 23 (1926), 134–42; 24 (1927), 157–65. The place of religious education at the college and university level was interwoven in the 1920s with a bitter controversy over the scope and character of the Newman apostolate being carried on at non-Catholic institutions, especially at the University of Illinois by Father John A.

O'Brien. This matter is discussed in John Whitney Evans, "John LaFarge, *America,* and the Newman Movement," *Catholic Historical Review* 44 (October 1978), 614–43.

22. *NCEAB* 34 (1937), 89.

23. See Cooper's articles on the moral, dogmatic, historical, apologetic, and ascetic content of high school and college religion classes in *Catholic Educational Review* 21 (1923), 1–13, 80–88, 153–60, 107–213, 349–56; and Cooper, "Content and Credit Hours for Courses in Religion," *NCEAB* 23 (1926), 134–42.

24. Fulton J. Sheen, "Educating for a Catholic Renaissance, *NCEAB* 26 (1929), 45–54. See also Sheen's "Organic Fields of Study," *Catholic Educational Review* 28 (April 1930), 201–7, in which he attacked the credit-hour system as "mechanistic," productive only of "a numerical unity, not an organic one." Education was not a matter of accumulating information; rather it was "so much a [matter of] reduction to intelligible unity that the Scholastics held that the fewer general ideas a man possessed the more educated he was." Hence, Sheen called for "a complete and total rearrangement of all college courses . . . [such that] some one 'vital principle' gives unity to the distinct courses in the same way the soul gives unity to the body."

25. *NCEAB* 32 (1935), 70–71. Creighton University incorporated this passage in its "Statement of Objectives" for 1936–37. See James Michael Vosper, "A History of Selected Factors in the Development of Creighton University" (Ph.D. diss., University of Nebraska, 1976), 255–56.

26. *NCEAB* 33 (1936), 231–32.

27. *NCEAB* 35 (1938), 121–22; 36 (1939), 118. Reporting on the results of a "fruitless and disappointing survey" undertaken by the Committee on Educational Policy and Program, William J. McGucken observed soberly that "the problem of vitalizing our courses in religion, philosophy, and classics is a real one." *NCEAB* 34 (1937), 90.

28. Jaime Castiello, "The Problem of Integration in Educational Psychology," *NCEAB* 33 (1936), 206–18; George Bull, "The Function of the Catholic Graduate School," *Thought* 13 (1938), 364–80. For examples of attention to graduate education and the need for more scholarship see Alphonse M. Schwitalla, "Graduate Education in Catholic Colleges and Universities," *NCEAB* 27 (1930), esp. 104–6, and Martin R. P. McGuire, "Catholic Education and the Graduate School," in *Vital Problems of Catholic Education in the United States* (Washington, D.C., 1939), 108–26. See also Gleason, "American Catholic Higher Education" (note 14 above), 40–43, 48–49.

29. Mother Grace Damman put it hesitantly at the NCEA meeting: "These [religion] courses at the college level should really be—should they not?—elementary courses in Dogmatic, Moral, and Ascetical Theology," *NCEAB* 36 (1939), 177. See also *Commonweal* 29 (April 14, 1939), 676, for notice of the call for the National Catholic Alumni Federation meeting; for the meeting itself, see Harry McNeill, "Integrating Religion," ibid., 31 (November 10, 1939), 75–77, and Raymond J. McCall, "At the College Level," ibid., 31 (December 1, 1939), 131. The presentations given at the symposium are available in National Catholic Alumni

Federation, *Man and Modern Secularism: Essays on the Conflict of the Two Cultures* (New York, 1940).

30. McGucken makes this point in his critical discussion of the 1939 symposium in "The Renascence of Religion Teaching" in Deferrari, *Essays on Catholic Education* (note 20 above), 345–48.

31. Phelan's paper was entitled "Theology in the Curriculum of Catholic Colleges and Universities"; Connell's, "Theology in Catholic Colleges as an Aid to the Lay Apostolate." See *Man and Modern Secularism,* 128–51.

32. Ibid., 152–57.

33. See Murray, "Towards a Theology for the Layman," *Theological Studies* 5 (1944), 43–75, 340–76. Donald Pelotte, *John Courtney Murray: Theologian in Conflict* (New York, 1975), does not discuss this aspect of Murray's career, although it is very informative for the controversies over intercredal cooperation and church and state.

34. For Murray's role in the Jesuit series, see the "Acknowledgement" in John J. Fernan, *Theology: A Course for College Students,* vol. 1: *Christ as Prophet and King* (Syracuse, 1952). See also the remarks of Gerard S. Sloyan in Josef Andreas Jungmann, *The Good News Yesterday and Today,* trans. W. A. Huesman, ed. J. Hofinger (New York, 1962), 218.

35. See the first part of Murray's article, which is entitled, "Towards a Theology for the Layman. The Problem of Its Finality," *Theological Studies* 5 (1944), 43–77. For the "new theology" see Robert F. Harvanek, "Philosophical Pluralism and Catholic Orthodoxy," *Thought* 25 (1950), 21–52, and the literature cited there. A good statement of the position opposed to that of Murray and John M. Cooper is Joseph Clifford Fenton, "Theology and Religion," *American Ecclesiastical Review* 112 (1945), 447–63.

36. Cooper's "Catholic Education and Theology," in Defarrari, *Vital Problems,* 127–43, is a powerful critique of the negative effects of theology in religious pedagogy. For an indication of how long an antitheological animus persisted among catechists, see Gabriel Moran, "The Time for a Theology," *The Living Light* 3 (Summer 1966), 7.

37. See Rodgers, "Changing Concept of College Theology" (note 20 above), 202–18.

38. Roland G. Simonitsch, *Religious Instruction in Catholic Colleges for Men* (Washington, 1952), 301. For women's colleges, see Mary Gratia Maher, *The Organization of Religious Instruction in Catholic Colleges for Women* (Washington, 1951), 46–51.

39. Cyril Vollert, "The Origin, Development, and Purpose of the Society of Catholic College Teachers of Sacred Doctrine," *NCEAB* 51 (1954), 247–55; Rodgers, "Changing Concept," 193–201. This group became the College Theology Society in 1967.

40. *NCEAB* 43 (1946), 215–38, 239–44. See also, Rodgers, "Changing Concept," 187–92.

41. See Thomas C. Donlan, "Theology and Higher Education," Catholic Theological Society of America, *Proceedings . . . 1955* (New York, 1955), 222–

49, and discussion, 251–58. See also Donlan's *Theology and Education* (Dubuque, 1952).

42. See, for example, Roy J. Defarrari, ed., *Integration in Catholic Colleges and Universities* (Washington, 1950), and Roy J. Defarrari, ed., *Theology, Philosophy, and History as Integrating Disciplines in the Catholic College of Liberal Arts* (Washington, 1953).

43. Murray, "Towards a Theology for the Layman," *Theological Studies* 5 (1944), 57–58, 354.

44. Ibid., 61.

45. For the Catholic intellectualism controversy, see above, chapter 3.

46. Rodgers, "Changing Concept," 250n, 267, and 232–69 *passim*.

47. Henry Adams, *The Education of Henry Adams,* Modern Library ed. (New York, 1931), 455.

8. KEEPING THE FAITH IN AMERICA

1. Gerald Shaughnessy, *Has the Immigrant Kept the Faith? A Study of Immigration and Catholic Growth in the United States, 1790–1920* (New York, 1925).

2. Garry Wills, *Bare Ruined Choirs: Doubt, Prophecy, and Radical Religion* (New York, 1972), 4. For unwillingness to acknowledge the faith problem, see James Hitchcock, *The Decline and Fall of Radical Catholicism* (New York, 1971), 26–31.

3. Donald J. Thorman, "'Age of Unbelief' Hits Church," *National Catholic Reporter,* September 7, 1966. Although Michael Novak makes reference to Vatican II in his *Belief and Unbelief: A Philosophy of Self-Knowledge* (New York, 1965), the book is a somewhat technical treatment of the philosophical problem of religious faith rather than a discussion of the general impact of the Council on the state of Catholic religious belief.

4. See Philip Gleason, "Identifying Identity: A Semantic History," *Journal of American History* 69 (March 1983), 910–31.

5. William C. McCready and Andrew M. Greeley, "The End of American Catholicism?" *America* 127 (October 28, 1972), 334–38.

6. Hitchcock, *Decline and Fall,* 185, 112–13; see also, 129, 182.

7. Wills, *Bare Ruined Choirs,* 268–69. John Tracy Ellis also stresses the issue of faith, but from a different angle, in his review of this book in *Theological Studies* 34 (March 1973), 139–45.

8. Mary Hogan, "Keeping Faith," *The Furrow* 34 (March 1983), 143. This article was the third in *The Furrow*'s year-long series, "Belief and Unbelief." Earlier special issues devoted to faith in other journals were: "Faith: The Struggle to Believe," *Commonweal* 101 (November 15, 1974); "How Do I Celebrate My Faith?" *New Catholic World* 221 (January/February 1978); "Faith in the Contemporary World," *Theological Studies* 39 (December 1979). See also Berard L. Marthaler, "To Teach the Faith or to Teach Theology: Dilemma for Religious Education," in Catholic Theological Society of America, *Proceedings . . . 1976* (New York, 1976), 217–33; Gabriel Daly, "Faith and Theology," *The Tablet* (London) 235 (April 11–

May 9, 1981), 361–62, 391–92, 446–47, and the replies it called forth, ibid. 235 (May 23–October 17, 1981), 499, 520, 640–42, 669, 1013–16. James Fowler, *Stages of Faith* (New York, 1981), sets forth a "developmental" theory of personal faith adapted from Kohlberg's scheme of the stages of moral development that has attracted considerable attention. For discussions see, C. Ellis Nelson, "Does Faith Develop? An Evaluation of Fowler's Position," *Living Light* 19 (Summer 1982), 162–73, and George McCauley, "Developments in the Theology of Faith," *Lumen Vitae* 38 (1983), 409–20.

9. "To the Members of the Central Council of the Association for the Propagation of the Faith," in Lawrence Kehoe, ed., *Complete Works of the Most Rev. John Hughes, D.D.,* 2 vols. (New York, 1864), II, 385–86.

10. For representative references to the lack of items of this nature in Kentucky in the 1790s and in Chicago in 1849, see John Tracy Ellis, ed., *Documents of American Catholic History* (Milwaukee, 1956), 188, 308–9.

11. *United States Catholic Miscellany,* March 1, 1828. My attention was drawn to this statement by Thomas J. Stritch's draft history of the Diocese of Nashville, Tennessee.

12. Victor F. O'Daniel, *The Father of the Church in Tennessee, Or the Life, Times, and Character of the Right Reverend Richard Pius Miles, O.P.* (New York, 1932).

13. Michael V. Gannon, *The Cross in the Sand: The Early Catholic Church in Florida, 1513–1870* (Gainesville, Fla., 1965), 132–33.

14. England's estimate and his valuable discussion of the causes of leakage were prepared for the Society for the Propagation of the Faith; see Sebastian G. Messmer, ed., *The Works of the Right Reverend John England,* 7 vols. (Cleveland, 1908), IV, 256–97, esp. 295. Shaughnessy, *Has Immigrant Kept Faith?* 224–31, analyzes England's estimate, noting that it became "the foundation stone of all later claims of a similar nature," but adding that it was "so utterly wide of the mark as to be actually ludicrous . . . did not so much depend on it."

15. For other discussions of the second generation's loss of faith, see Shaughnessy, *Has Immigrant Kept Faith?* 31, and Richard J. Purcell, "Missionaries from All Hallows (Dublin) to the United States, 1842–1865," *Records of the American Catholic Historical Society of Philadelphia* 53 (1942), 220.

16. Bruté's anecdote is reported in the class notes for April 1, 1829, kept by John McCaffrey. Archives of Mount Saint Mary's, Emmitsburg, Md. For trusteeism, see above, chapter 2.

17. John Carroll's sermon "Faith and Infidelity," which cannot be dated, is an attack on rationalism, but it reveals a close connection in Carroll's thinking between infidelity and the breakdown of private morals and public order. See Thomas O'Brien Hanley, ed., *The John Carroll Papers,* 3 vols. (Notre Dame, Ind., 1976), III, 375–83. For a general study covering the period we are concerned with, see Robert Gorman, *Catholic Apologetical Literature in the United States, 1784–1858* (Washington, D.C., 1939).

18. Gorman, *Apologetical Literature,* 67–68, 72–74, 75–78; Richard Shaw, *Dagger John: The Unquiet Life and Times of Archbishop John Hughes of New*

York (New York, 1977), 86–89, 94–100; Anthony H. Deye, "Archbishop John Baptist Purcell of Cincinnati: Pre–Civil War Years" (Ph.D. diss., University of Notre Dame, 1959), 166–87.

19. Stephen Theodore Badin, "Origin and Progress of the Mission of Kentucky," *Catholic World* 21 (September 1875), 82. The writings designated "Controversies" by Messmer are found in volumes II and III of his edition of England's *Works*, but much of the material in other volumes under such headings as "Doctrine" and "History" is, in fact, controversial in origin and nature.

20. See Messmer, *Works of England*, VI, 9–12; Kehoe, *Complete Works of Hughes*, II, 667–84; Gorman, *Apologetical Literature*, 17, 18, 29, 31, 32, 35, 44, 54, 67, 68, 69, 84n, 93, 95, 100, 112.

21. *An Address of the Rt. Rev. Bishop David, to His Brethren of Other Professions on the Rule of Faith* (Louisville, 1822), 5. The following paragraphs are based on this discourse, which John Baptist David, coadjutor bishop of Bardstown and rector of its seminary, offered as an elaboration of questions proposed orally to a Protestant minister.

22. "The truth is," David asserted, "Protestants are tutored from their infancy . . . they are guided by their Parents and Masters, and are influenced by the opinions and examples of those with whom they live or converse. . . . Hence, before they read the Scriptures their creed is already formed; and when they actually read it, they fancy that they see in it what they have been otherwise taught to believe. . . ." Ibid., 17.

23. "Some Letters of Father Hecker," *Catholic World* 83 (June 1906), 364–65. For a sampling of Catholic statements on the decline of Protestantism, see Alfred J. Ede, "The Lay Crusade for a Christian America: A Study of the American Federation of Catholic Societies" (Ph.D. diss., Graduate Theological Union, Berkeley, Ca., 1979), 119–21.

24. Avery Dulles, *A History of Apologetics* (New York, 1971), 202.

25. Orestes A. Brownson, "Native Americanism," and "The Know Nothings," in *Brownson's Quarterly Review* 11 (July, October 1854), 328–54, 447–87. Thomas R. Ryan, *Orestes A. Brownson: A Definitive Biography* (Huntington, Ind., 1976), 455–612, covers this phase of Brownson's life in detail; for his "liberalism" as such, see 597–612. See also Thomas T. McAvoy, "Orestes A. Brownson and Archbishop John Hughes in 1860," *Review of Politics* 24 (January 1962), 19–47.

26. Brownson, "Public and Parochial Schools," *Brownson's Quarterly Review* 16 (July 1859), 324–42, quotation at 331. See also Brownson, "Schools and Education," ibid. 11 (January 1854), 354–76; Brownson, "Catholic Schools and Education," ibid. 19 (January 1862), 66–84. Brownson's views on Catholic education shifted more than once; for a comprehensive study of his opinions, see James M. McDonnell, "Orestes A. Brownson and Nineteenth-Century Catholic Education" (Ph.D. diss., University of Notre Dame, 1975).

27. Brownson made the distinction explicit in a highly controversial article, "The Rights of the Temporal," *Brownson's Quarterly Review* 17 (October 1860), 464, and repeated it in an editorial note, ibid. 19 (January 1862), 133–34.

28. For Brownson's most enthusiastically "Americanist" statement, see "The Mission of America," *Brownson's Quarterly Review* 13 (October 1856), 409–44.

29. There has been much of recent work on Hecker; for an excellent sampling, accompanied by useful bibliographies, see John Farina, ed., *Hecker Studies: Essays on the Thought of Isaac Hecker* (New York, 1983).

30. Robert Emmett Curran, "Prelude to 'Americanism': The New York Academia and Clerical Radicalism in the Late Nineteenth Century," *Church History* 47 (March 1978), 48–65; Curran, "The McGlynn Affair and the Shaping of the New Conservatism in American Catholicism, 1886–1894," *Catholic Historical Review* 66 (April 1980), 184–204. See also Nelson J. Callahan, ed., *The Diary of Richard L. Burtsell, Priest of New York: The Early Years, 1865–1868* (New York, 1978).

31. John Lancaster Spalding, "The Catholic Church in the United States, 1776–1876," *Catholic World* 23 (July 1876), 434–52. See above, chapter 5.

32. The most recent and authoritative survey of these controversies is Gerald P. Fogarty, *The Vatican and the American Hierachy from 1870 to 1965* (Stuttgart, 1982), chaps. 2–7. Thomas T. McAvoy, *The Great Crisis in American Catholic History, 1895–1900* (Chicago, 1957), is standard for "Americanism" as such.

33. The text of *Testem Benevolentiae* is given in McAvoy, *Great Crisis*, 379–91.

34. Philip Gleason, "Coming to Terms with American Catholic History," *Societas* 3 (Autumn 1973), 283–312.

35. See Michael V. Gannon, "Before and After Modernism: The Intellectual Isolation of the American Priest," in John Tracy Ellis, ed., *The Catholic Priest in the United States: Historical Investigations* (Collegeville, Minn., 1971), esp. 326–50; and Michael J. DeVito, *The New York Review, 1905–1908* (New York, 1977).

36. For remarks relating to issues of faith and apologetics, see *Dolphin* 1 (March 1902), 329; ibid. 4 (September 1903), 371; ibid., 7 (April 1905), 485–87, the last of which includes the observation that, while some may preserve their faith by cutting themselves off from contemporary intellectual life, "to assert this as a principle of life, is to preach intellectual suicide." For the condemnation of Loisy's work, see ibid. 5 (February–April 1904), 215–18, 467–74, 482–83. George Tyrrell, later to be condemned as a Modernist himself, contributed a three-part article, "The Spirit of Christ," ibid. 8 (October–December 1905), 385–98, 519–45, 657–70, which set off a controversy that a more recent writer intimates may have contributed to *The Dolphin's* being discontinued after 1905. See John L. Murphy, "Seventy-Five Years of Fundamental Theology in America, Part I," *American Ecclesiastical Review* 150 (June 1964), 393n.

37. See "Father Tyrrell, S.J., as an Apologist," *Catholic World* 74 (December 1901), 345–56; William L. Sullivan, "Father Hogan and the Intellectual Apostolate," ibid. 74 (March 1902), 783–92; William L. Sullivan, "The Latest Word of Theology on Inspiration," ibid. 84 (November–December 1906), 219–27, 327–33. (Sullivan, a young Paulist priest, left the Catholic Church as a self-professed Modernist.) See also James J. Fox, "A Catholic and the Bible," ibid. 80 (February 1905), 569–81; and L. E. Lapham, "Fogazzaro and his Trilogy," ibid. 84 (November 1906–January 1907), 240–50, 381–87, 462–76, which is a critical, but not hostile, commentary on Antonio Fogazzaro's "Modernist novel," *Il Santo*. Even

after the condemnation of Modernism, W. H. Kent could conclude an article on "Liberalism and Faith" by asking: "Why should we desiderate a wearisome uniformity [of theological schools in the Church] which would involve a break with the past and make our modern theology something strangely unlike the spacious theological literature of our fathers." Ibid. 86 (March 1908), 719–29. For the related argument that a more vigorous organizational life would contribute to "a sturdy Catholic sense of solidarity to protect believers in this age of doubt," see William J. Kerby, "Reinforcement of the Bond of Faith," ibid. 84 (January–February 1907), 508–22, 590–606, quotation 603.

38. Joseph McSorley, "Open-Mindedness," ibid. 83 (April 1906), 18–31.

39. Ibid., 30.

40. See Gerald A. McCool, *Catholic Theology in the Nineteenth Century: The Quest for a Unitary Method* (New York, 1977), chaps. 6, 10; and Gabriel Daly, *Transcendence and Immanence: A Study in Catholic Modernism and Integralism* (New York, 1980), chap. 1. For a longer view, see Marcia L. Colish, "St. Thomas Aquinas in Historical Perspective: The Modern Period," *Church History* 44 (December 1975), 433–49. For the text of *Dei Filius*, see *Documents of Vatican Council I, 1869–1870*, selected and translated by John F. Broderick (Collegeville, Minn., 1971), 37–52.

41. See James Hennesey, "Leo XIII's Thomistic Revival: A Political and Philosophical Event," *Journal of Religion* 58 (Supplement 1978), S185–S197; and Hennesey, "Leo XIII: Intellectualizing the Combat with Modernity," paper given at the spring meeting of the American Catholic Historical Association in 1979.

42. John Lancaster Spalding, *Education and the Higher Life* (Chicago, 1890), 196. See also "Aquinas Resuscitatus," *American Catholic Quarterly Review* 16 (October 1891), 673 ff. George Tyrell, at one time an enthusiastic Scholastic, abandoned the system and gave the sarcastic title *Medievalism* (London, 1909) to a book he published in response to Cardinal Mercier's critique entitled *Le modernisme* (Paris, 1909). For the relative lack of interest in the Scholastic Revival in the United States until after the condemnation of Modernism, see William M. Halsey, *The Survival of American Innocence: Catholicism in an Era of Disillusionment, 1920–1940* (Notre Dame, Ind., 1980), 139–43.

43. For the text of *Pascendi*, see Vincent A. Yzermans, ed., *All Things in Christ: Encyclicals and Selected Documents of Saint Pius X* (Westminster, Md., 1954), 89–132; quotations from paragraphs 39, 41, and 45. For critical analysis, see Daly, *Transcendence and Immanence*, chap. 9.

44. For the anti-Modernist oath, see *New Catholic Encyclopedia*, 15 vols. (New York, 1967), IX, 995, and "Motu Proprio of Our Holy Father Pope Pius X: Establishing Certain Laws for the Driving Out of the Dangers of Modernism," *American Catholic Quarterly Review* 35 (October 1910), 712–31, esp. 723–24; for the 1914 statement, *Doctoris Angelici*, see Yzermans, *All Things in Christ*, 255–59.

45. James A. Weisheipl, "The Revival of Thomism as a Christian Philosophy," in Ralph M. McInerny, ed., *New Themes in Christian Philosophy* (Notre Dame, Ind., 1968), 180–81. Weisheipl's entire article (164–85) is valuable.

46. John Tracy Ellis says the anti-Modernist decrees set off "a veritable witch-hunt . . . in Catholic institutions of learning, the evil effects of which endured long after the close of World War I." See Ellis, "A Tradition of Autonomy?" in Neil G. McCluskey, ed., *The Catholic University: A Modern Appraisal* (Notre Dame, Ind., 1970), 237. See also Roger Aubert, *The Church in a Secularised Society* (New York, 1978), 199–203.

47. See above, chapter 7. The most extensive discussion of Neoscholasticism in American Catholic life is unrelievedly negative; see Halsey, *Survival of American Innocence,* chaps. 8–9. For a more positive evaluation by a professional philosopher who was a founder of the American Catholic Philosophical Association, see Charles A. Hart, "Twenty-five Years of Thomism," *New Scholasticism* 25 (1951), 3–45. Hart acknowledges (41–44) that Neoscholasticism won virtually no acceptance outside Catholic ranks. Also of interest are Ernan McMullin's presidential address, "Who Are We?" in ACPA, *Proceedings . . . 1967* (Washington, 1967), 1–16; and the report on a survey taken in 1966 which is provided in McMullin's "Philosophy in the United States Catholic College," in McInerny, *New Themes,* 370–409, esp. 398–401.

48. The interpretation advanced here and in the following paragraphs is based mainly on my own experience and observation of American Catholicism over four decades of adult life.

49. Daly, *Transcendence and Immanence,* chap. 1, stresses this aspect, in one place (19) characterizing the Neoscholastic approach that crystallized after *Aeterni Patris* as "supernatural rationalism." See also the article, "Faith," by Hugh Pope in *Catholic Encyclopedia,* 15 vols. (New York, 1907–1912), V, 752–59, and compare it with the articles on "Faith" and related subjects in *New Catholic Encyclopedia,* V, 782–811.

50. Bernard J. Murray et al., *Theology: A Course for College Students,* vol. IV: *Christ in His Members* (Syracuse, N.Y., 1955), 124. R. J. Buschmiller, the author of the subsection headed "Existence of God in Theology" of the entry "God" in the *New Catholic Encyclopedia,* states: "That man can actually demonstrate and prove the existence of God is certainly Catholic teaching." *New Catholic Encyclopedia,* VI, 555.

51. In 1954 a Jesuit philosopher said that one of the reasons for having undergraduates study metaphysics was that it would provide the Catholic college graduate with the conviction that "there is a metaphysics which at one time he understood (at least partially)," and thus reassure him "that there are resources if he is pressed by our unbelieving environment." G. P. Klubertanz, "The Teaching of Thomistic Metaphysics," *Gregorianum* 35 (1954), 192.

52. I know of no historical studies of this aspect of American Catholic life in general, but for the admittedly special case of seminary training for priests, see Philip J. Murnion, *The Catholic Priest and the Changing Structure of Pastoral Ministry: New York, 1920–1970* (New York, 1978), 52–90, 135–39. For the broader development of popular piety in the nineteenth-century Church, see Aubert, *Church in Secularised Society,* 117–28.

53. See above, chapter 7. Consider also the following statement: "Unless

philosophy presents a synthesis of being, its principle, its end, its exemplar, its unity, its composition, its order, its subordination, the order and relations in the life of man—the truths of religion will remain outside of life, detached and inoperative. Only by means of an integrated intellectual life, can these great truths be made to penetrate and inform and elevate and live in every greatest and least act of life. . . . Wisdom does not know and understand any reality as isolated, as in itself and absolute; but it cognizes all being in its relations with the sum total of all other reality, as related in cause and end and likeness to the Pure Act of being; because reality is related to all other being and is a participation in the truth and goodness and beauty of the Absolute." John J. O'Brien, "Problems of Philosophy to be Stressed in the Undergraduate Curriculum," *National Catholic Educational Associational Bulletin* 37 (1940), 305.

54. See above, pp. 66–71.

55. Murray's work was done in scholarly articles; some of the best are brought together in his *We Hold These Truths: Catholic Reflections on the American Proposition* (New York, 1960); for a historical account of his career, see Donald E. Pelotte, *John Courtney Murray: Theologian in Conflict* (New York, 1976); for a recent discussion by a theologian, Charles E. Curran, *American Catholic Social Ethics: Twentieth-Century Approaches* (Notre Dame, Ind., 1982), chap. 5.

56. See Anton C. Pegis, *The Middle Ages and Philosophy: Some Reflections on the Ambivalence of Modern Scholasticism* (Chicago, 1963); McCool, *Catholic Theology* (note 40 above), 241–67; and W. Norris Clarke, "The Future of Thomism," in McInerny, *New Themes,* 191–92.

57. R. A. F. MacKenzie was cautious and diplomatic in explaining "The Concept of Biblical Theology" at the 1955 meeting of the Catholic Theological Society of America, but his presentation aroused a critical reaction. See CTSA, *Proceedings . . . 1955* (New York, 1955), 48–73.

58. For the debate on Catholic intellectual life, see above, pp. 71–78. In 1953, a self-study of the undergraduate liberal arts program at the University of Notre Dame made the "integration" of the curriculum around a Thomistic approach to philosophy and theology the primary end to be achieved in curricular reorganization. By the end of the decade that goal seemed quite outdated, and hearings held by another committee set up in 1961 revealed that the integration of knowledge was not a major concern for members of the faculty.

59. See above, pp. 63–66.

60. See notes 6 and 7 above.

61. Mary Hogan, "Keeping Faith," *The Furrow* 34 (March 1983), 136–37. For "innocence," see Halsey, *Survival of American Innocence,* esp., ch. 10; for walled-in villages, Gabriel Daly, "Faith and Theology; 1) Conflicting Mentalities," *The Tablet* (London) 235 (April 11, 1981), 361.

62. I would agree with Geoffrey Scarre, who argues that all belief aspires to the condition of rational belief; see Scarre, "A Simple Argument for Faith Requiring Reasons," *New Blackfriars* 62 (April 1981), 157–68.

63. Daly, "Faith and Theology: 3) The Pluriform Church," *The Tablet* (London) 235 (May 9, 1981), 446.

9. LITERARY LANDMARKS OF AMERICAN CATHOLICISM IN TRANSITION

1. Following a reorganization in 1966, the formal organization of the American hierarchy is called the National Conference of Catholic Bishops, and the permanent staff is now known as the United States Catholic Conference.

2. This literature and its place in the larger discussion of Americanization as a theme in Catholic history is reviewed in my article "Coming to Terms with American Catholic History," *Societas* 3 (1973), 283–312. A more recent revisionist approach to the Americanist controversy is illustrated in Margaret M. Reher, "Pope Leo XIII and Americanism," *Theological Studies* 34 (1973), 679–89. McAvoy's book, incidentally, was reissued in 1963 under a new title: *The American Heresy in Roman Catholicism.*

3. Michael R. Real, *"The National Catholic Reporter:* Communications and Change in a Turbulent Era" (Ph.D. diss., University of Illinois, Urbana-Champaign, 1971) is a very valuable study which provides much information on American Catholic developments generally.

4. Greeley's writings up through 1977 are discussed at greater length in my review-essay, "Greeley Watching," *Review of Politics* 40 (October 1978), 528–40.

5. James Hennesey, *American Catholic Bibliography, 1970–1982* (Cushwa Center, Working Paper Series 12, no. 1, University of Notre Dame, 1982), lists almost five hundred books and articles published in the seventies and early eighties.

10. HISTORY, HISTORICAL CONSCIOUSNESS, AND PRESENT-MINDEDNESS

1. Robert North, "Bibliography of Works in Theology and History," *History and Theory* 12 (1973), 55–140. I accept the totals for the two decades as calculated in C. T. McIntire, ed., *God, History, and Historians: An Anthology of Modern Christian Views of History* (New York, 1977), 23. See also James M. Connolly, *Human History and the Word of God: The Christian Meaning of History in Contemporary Thought* (New York, 1965); Van Austin Harvey, *The Historian and the Believer: The Morality of Historical Knowledge and Christian Belief* (New York, 1966); and Carl E. Braaten, *History and Hermeneutics,* vol. II of *New Directions in Theology Today* (Philadelphia, 1966). A book filled with illuminating insights, and written (by a historian) from a perspective different from most of the works discussed in this chapter, is John Lukacs, *Historical Consciousness: Or the Remembered Past,* rev. ed. (New York, 1985).

2. Joan Wolski Conn, "From Certitude to Understanding: Historical Consciousness in the American Catholic Theological Community in the 1960s" (Ph.D. diss., Columbia University, 1974); Bernard J. F. Lonergan, "The Transition from a Classical World View to Historical Mindedness," in James E. Biechler, ed., *Law for Liberty; The Role of Law in the Church Today* (Baltimore, 1967), 126–33; John Courtney Murray, "The Declaration on Religious Freedom," *Concilium* 15: *War, Poverty, Freedom: The Christian Response* (New York, 1966), 11–16. Accord-

ing to David Tracy, "It would seem a fair generalization on the central problematic of contemporary theology that the phenomenon of historical consciousness is the primary factor behind both the central achievements and the crucial difficulties for Christian theology from Troeltsch through Bultmann and . . . Bernard Lonergan." Tracy, *Blessed Rage for Order* (New York, 1975), 73.

3. Emil L. Fackenheim, *Metaphysics and Historicity* (Milwaukee, 1961), 13. Hans-Georg Gadamer says substantially the same thing: "The concept of historicity expresses nothing about the relationship of events—that it really was so—but rather states something about the mode of being of man who is in history and whose existence can be understood fundamentally only through the concept of historicity." Gadamer, "The Continuity of History and the Existential Moment," *Philosophy Today* 16 (1972), 232.

4. Canon Albert Dondeyne, "The Historicity of Man According to Modern Philosophy," *Lumen Vitae* 17 (1962), 73–84, quotation 74. All italics in original.

5. Ibid., 76–82, italics in original.

6. John W. O'Malley, "Reform, Historical Consciousness, and Vatican II's Aggiornamento," *Theological Studies* 32 (December 1971), 573–601. For notice, see Wolski, "From Certitude to Understanding," 7–9; Avery Dulles, *The Resilient Church: The Necessity and Limits of Adaptation* (Garden City, N.Y., 1977), 200; James Hitchcock, *Catholicism and Modernity: Confrontation or Capitulation?* (New York, 1979), 20, 234. Hitchcock is critical of O'Malley's position. In a more recent article, O'Malley refers to, presupposes, and builds upon the 1971 essay discussed here. See O'Malley, "Developments, Reforms, and Two Great Reformations: Towards a Historical Assessment of Vatican II," *Theological Studies* 44 (1983), 373–406.

7. O'Malley, "Reform," 573, 575–76, 589–90.

8. Ibid., 590–95.

9. Ibid., 595–96.

10. Ibid., 596.

11. A qualifying phrase of the "for-the-historian" type recurs four times in the three paragraphs on which my summary is based. Ibid., 596.

12. Ibid., 596–97.

13. Ibid., 597–98.

14. Ibid., 601, 575–76.

15. David J. O'Brien, *The Renewal of American Catholicism* (New York, 1972), 26–50.

16. Ibid., 27–28, 37–40, 28–31, quotation from 38.

17. Ibid., 30, for allusion to Beard's call for written history as an act of faith. Beard himself stated: "Contemporary criticism shows that the apostle of relativity is destined to be destroyed by his own brain. If all historical conceptions are merely relative to passing events, to transitory phases of ideas and interests, then the conception of relativity is itself relative. When absolutes in history are rejected the absolutism of relativity is also rejected." Charles A. Beard, "Written History as an Act of Faith," as reprinted in Hans Meyerhoff, ed., *The Philosophy of History in Our Time* (Anchor paperback, 1959), 147.

18. O'Brien, *Renewal,* 37–38.

19. Ibid., 32, 36–37.

20. Ibid., 28–29, 40. O'Brien "suggests that scholarship requires an activist stance," commends the activism of the radical historians of the late 1960s who strove to "unify their politics, the scholarship and their lives," and endorses their view that "The rigid segregation that traditional leaders of academic life make between their profession, their politics and their lives is wholly abhorrent." (28) What O'Brien characterizes as a "rigid segregation" of different realms is what I am calling the traditional goal of maintaining scholarly objectivity.

21. Ibid., 39–40. In a later chapter, O'Brien writes: "The object of historical study is the making of history. 'The past is ransacked,' [Staughton] Lynd writes, 'not for its own sake, but as a source of alternative models of what the future might become'" (189).

22. Eric Cochrane, "What Is Catholic Historiography?" *Catholic Historical Review* 61 (April 1975), 169–90, esp. 169–76.

23. This is the first chapter of Enrique Dussel's *History and the Theology of Liberation* (Maryknoll, N.Y., 1976), 1–35.

24. Ibid., 2, xvi, 5, 28. Dussel is called "liberation theology's principal historian and ethicist" by Alan Neely, translator of Dussel's *A History of the Church in Latin America: Colonialism to Liberation (1492–1979)* (Grand Rapids, Mich., 1981), xiii.

25. Dussel, *History and Theology of Liberation,* 2, 19 ff., 27–28.

26. Ibid., 5, 28, 9–10, 139. The interweaving of existentialist and Marxian ideas about history is apparent in Gustavo Gutierrez, *A Theology of Liberation* (Maryknoll, N.Y., 1973). In his Introduction, Gutierrez states that he gives special attention to the critical function of theology with respect to "the presence and activity of man in history" (x). The word "liberation," he goes on, "emphasizes that man transforms himself by conquering his liberty throughout his existence and his history" (x). It is largely "due to Marxism's influence that theological thought, searching for its own sources, has begun to reflect on the meaning of the transformation of this world and the action of man in history" (9). The confrontation with Marxism "helps theology to perceive what its efforts at understanding the faith receive from the historical praxis of man in history . . ."(10). It is, according to Gutierrez, the rediscovery of the eschatological dimension in theology that leads to consideration of the "central role of historical praxis. Indeed, if human history is above all else an opening to the future, then it is a task, a political occupation, through which man orients and opens himself to the gift which gives history its transcendent; the full and definitive encounter with the Lord and with other men" (10). From this Gutierrez derives the concept of orthopraxis, or action in conformity with faith (10). Theology, he continues, fulfills its prophetic function "insofar as it interprets historical events with the intention of revealing and proclaiming their profound meaning" (13). And in carrying out this prophetic function, the theologian becomes what Gramsci called an "organic intellectual"—one who is "personally and vitally engaged in historical realities with specific times and places." This kind of engagement on the part of the theologian is demanded, for "in the last analysis, the true interpretation of the meaning revealed by theology is achieved only in historical praxis" (13). For more on history, Hegel, Marx, Freud, Marcuse,

and "freedom as a historical conquest" and "the continuous creation . . . of a new way to be a man, a *permanent cultural revolution,*" see 27–33.

See also, Jose Miguez Bonino, "Historical Praxis and Christian Identity," in *Frontiers of Theology in Latin America,* edited by Rosino Gibellini (Maryknoll, N.Y., 1979), on Gutierrez's emphasis that there is "only one history," and for Bonino's own view, stated in italics, that *"The unity of God's work and human history constitutes the inescapable starting point for any theological reflection"* (270, 271). The similarity between these views and those of O'Brien is obvious.

27. Juan Luis Segundo, "Capitalism Versus Socialism: Crux Theologica," in Gibellini, *Frontiers of Theology,* 258, 254. Segundo states that a "left" orientation "must be the form of any reflection in which historical sensitivity has become the key" (257). He likewise makes clear that liberation theology is not just one kind of theology among a "pluralism" of approaches; rather it is the one and only theology possible for a true Christian. Specifically he writes: "What is designated as 'liberation theology' does not purport to be merely one sector of theology, like the 'theology of work' or the 'theology of death.' Liberation [theology] is meant to designate and cover theology as a whole. What is more, it does not purport to view theology from *one* [sic] of many possible standpoints. Instead it claims to view theology from *the* [sic] standpoint which the Christian fonts [sources?] point up as the only authentic and privileged standpoint for arriving at a full and complete understanding of God's revelation in Jesus Christ" (241). For "nonhistorical orthodoxy," see Michael Novak, *The Open Church: Vatican II, Act II* (New York, 1964), 56–70.

28. Jacques Barzun and Henry F. Graff, *The Modern Researcher,* 3rd ed. (New York, 1977), 206.

29. On ransacking the past, see O'Brien, *Renewal,* 189.

30. James Hitchcock, *Catholicism and Modernity: Confrontation or Capitulation* (New York, 1979), 21, and chap. 2 passim.

31. Bernard J. F. Lonergan, *Method in Theology* (New York, 1972), 214–24, 235 ff.

32. Ibid., 178–79, 185, 232, 185. For an extreme formulation of the view that historical understanding must be completely separated from any living concern, see Michael Oakeshott, *On History and Other Essays* (Totowa, N.J., 1983). See also Steven B. Smith's critical review of this book in *Review of Politics,* 47 (January 1985), 150–53.

33. Lonergan, *Method in Theology,* 178.

34. Responding to criticism of views he had expressed in a book review, Gordon Wood recently reaffirmed that historians must adhere to the belief "that the past 'out there' really existed," and that historical study can bring us closer to "knowing the truth about that past 'as it really was,'" even if the full and complete truth about the past will always remain beyond their grasp." This faith, he adds, "may be philosophically naive, may even be philosophically absurd in this skeptical and relativist-minded age; nevertheless, it is what makes history writing possible." *New York Review of Books,* December 16, 1982, p. 59. A reading of Lonergan convinces me that this position is neither naive or absurd, and that Wood need

not have acquiesced in its being equated with "nineteenth-century positivism." For the statement of a somewhat similar position, see Christopher Dawson's critical review of E. H. Carr's *What is History?* in *Catholic Historical Review* 58 (October 1962), 406–8. See also G. R. Elton, *The Practice of History* (London, 1967), and Arnaldo Momigliano, "History in an Age of Ideologies," *American Scholar* 51 (Autumn 1982), esp. 506–7.

35. See Henri-Irenee Marrou, *The Meaning of History* (Baltimore, 1966), esp. 89–92. I can no longer recall whence I derived, or what first suggested to me, the threefold differentiation of levels of historical inquiry developed here, but I suspect that Marrou's book (which is the English translation of his *De la connaissance historique* [1959]) had more to do with it than any other work on historical theory and method.

36. Jacques Barzun, *Clio and the Doctors: Psycho-History, Quanto-History & History* (Chicago, 1974), 89, 90; George C. Homans, *Sentiments & Activities: Essays in Social Science* (New York, 1962), 6–7. See also Lukacs, *Historical Consciousness* (note 1 above), 37, and J. H. Hexter, *The History Primer* (London, 1972), esp. 359–62. Contrasting the intuitive and the mathematical minds, Pascal says that in the former case, "the principles [on which the mind operates] are in ordinary usage and there for all to see," but "are so intricate and numerous that it is almost impossible not to miss some." They are, he continues, "perceived instinctively rather than seen, and it is with endless difficulty that they can be communicated to those who do not perceive them for themselves. These things are so delicate and numerous that it takes a sense of great delicacy and precision to perceive them and judge correctly and accurately from this perception." Blaise Pascal, *Pensees* (Penguin paperback ed., 1966), 210–11.

37. Lonergan, *Method in Theology*, 230, 216. Barbara Tuchman quotes G. M. Trevelyan to somewhat the same effect: "Trevelyan wrote that the best historian was he who combined knowledge of the evidence with 'the largest intellect, the warmest human sympathy and the highest imaginative powers.'" Tuchman, *Practicing History* (Ballantine paperback ed., 1982), 47. See Marrou, *Meaning of History*, 89, 247, for passages on which Lonergan draws. Marrou also (70, 83) calls attention to the pertinence of Pascal's observation: "The more intelligent one is, the more men of originality one finds. Ordinary people find no difference between men." Pascal, *Pensees*, 209.

38. Barzun and Graff, *Modern Researcher* (note 28 above), 152.

39. Carl Becker said that he was led to the writing of his famous essay "Everyman His Own Historian" (*American Historical Review* 37 [Jan., 1932] 221–36), "by the necessity . . . of finding some answer to the frequent question: 'What is the good of history?'" Although usually regarded as manifesto of historical relativism, Becker assured a colleague that his paper "was intended to find a natural and necessary basis in the nature of the human animal for the study and writing of history, to prove that history is a fundamental and most important branch of knowledge; to show that Mr. Everyman has and will have history, true or false, and that one function of the historian is to keep Mr. Everyman's history, so far as possible, in reasonable harmony with what actually happened." Becker to Wil-

liam E. Dodd, January 27, 1932, in *"What Is the Good of History?" Selected Letters of Carl L. Becker, 1900–1945,* edited by Michael Kammen (Ithaca, N.Y., 1973), 156–57.

40. John Henry Newman, *The Idea of a University,* edited by Martin J. Svaglic (Rinehart paperback ed., 1960), 77–78.

41. Richard Hofstadter, *Anti-intellectualism in American Life* (New York, 1963), 27, 25.

42. Staughton Lynd quoted in O'Brien, *Renewal,* 189.

43. "The mind," Burckhardt wrote, "must transmute into a possession the remembrance of its passage through the ages of the world. What was once joy and sorrow must now become knowledge, as it must in the life of the individual. Therewith the saying *Historia vitae magistra* (History is the guide of life) takes on a higher yet a humbler sense. We wish experience to make us, not shrewder (for the next time), but wiser (forever)." *Force and Freedom: An Interpretation of History,* edited by James Hastings Nichols (Meridian paperback, 1955), 77–78.

44. Quoted from Faulkner's *Intruder in the Dust* in C. Vann Woodward, "The Future of the Past," *American Historical Review* 75 (February 1970), 722n.

45. See Edward Shils, *Tradition* (Chicago, 1981), and Jaroslav Pelikan, *The Vindication of Tradition* (New Haven, Conn., 1984).

INDEX

Abbott, Walter, 188
Abolitionism, parallel to civil rights, 94
Abortion, 71, 196–97
Abramson, Harold, 194
Academic freedom, 190–91
Accademia, New York priests form, 162
Acton, Lord, 15, 160
Adam, Karl, 182
Adams, John, 40
Adams, John Quincy, 99
Adams, Henry, 26, 29, 34, 151
Adler, Mortimer J., 27
Aeterni Patris (Leo XIII), 23, 166–67
Aggiornamento, 14, 32, 34, 60, 85, 188; and school question, 116–17
Agnosticism, danger of, 119–20
Alemany, Bishop Joseph S., 131
Alexander, Calvert, 24
Alienation, 30
America, 110
American Catholic Historical Association, 136, 139
American Catholic Philosophical Association, 23, 141ff.; identity crisis of, 70–71
American Catholic Psychological Association, 67
American Catholic Quarterly Review, 101
American Catholic Sociological Review, 60, 87
American Catholic Sociological Society, 68–70
American Catholics, assimilation of, chap. 2 passim, 87. *See also* Americanization

American Catholics, social mobility of, 64–65, 87
American celebration, 31, 184
American Ecclesiastical Review, 165
American Jewish Committee, 37
American Protective Association, 133
Americanism, 35; controversy over, 41–43, 133–34, 160ff.; P. Guilday ignores controversy, 107, 109–10; and school question, 133–34; as subject of study, 185–86. *See also* Americanization
Americanization: ambiguities of, 78–81; of Catholic Church in U.S., 40–43; on group level, 66–71; immigrant model of, 60–63; on individual level, 63–66; and intellectual life debate, 71–78; and language issue, 50; and national parish, 48–49; theoretical analysis of, 60ff.
Anti-Americanism, 56, 71
Anticlericalism, in Europe, 127–28
Anti-ghettoism, as theme in 1940s–50s, 184ff.
Anti-historical outlook, 26–27, 213
Anti-intellectualism. *See* Intellectual life, American Catholic
Apologetics, 18–19; in Catholic intellectual life debate, 73ff.; in commemorative writings, chap. 5 passim; and defense of faith, 157ff.; new approach in Modernist era, 165–66
Apostolate, as term in 1930s, 182
Aquinas, St. Thomas, 17, 24. *See also* Neoscholasticism